# *Ten Crucial Days*

## Washington's Vision for Victory Unfolds

Other Books by William L. Kidder

*The Pleasant Valley School Story: A Story of Education and Community in Rural New Jersey* (2012)
(Winner of the 2013 Scholarship and Artistry Award presented by the Country School Association of America)

*A People Harassed and Exhausted: The Story of a New Jersey Militia Regiment in the American Revolution* (2013)

*Farming Pleasant Valley: 250 Years of Life in Rural Hopewell Township, New Jersey* (2014)

*Crossroads of the Revolution: Trenton, 1774-1783* (2017)

Edited by William L. Kidder

*Meet Your Revolutionary Neighbors* (2015)

# *Ten Crucial Days*

## Washington's Vision for Victory Unfolds

*by*

**William L. Kidder**

KNOX PRESS

A KNOX PRESS BOOK
An Imprint of Permuted Press
ISBN: 978-1-68261-961-2
ISBN (eBook): 978-1-68261-962-9

Ten Crucial Days:
Washington's Vision for Victory Unfolds


Cover image is *General George Washington at the Battle of Princeton, New Jersey in 1777* 2007 (oil on canvas), Troiani, Don (b.1949) / Private Collection / Bridgeman Images



PERMUTED PRESS
KNOX PRESS

Permuted Press, LLC
New York • Nashville
permutedpress.com

Published in the United States of America

*Dedicated to*

*Professors Dr. Jay Luvaas, Dr. Paul Knights, and Dr. Paul Cares of Allegheny College in the 1960s who encouraged me to research and write about history.*

# Acknowledgements

This work expands on the research associated with my two earlier works on New Jersey in the Revolution, so everyone acknowledged in those works was also part of this project.

I need to acknowledge the audiences for the many talks I have given over the past several years about subjects related to New Jersey in the Revolution. Audience members have asked a wide variety of questions that have made me think and look at things in different ways. The continuous thinking stimulated by those questions played an important role in the development of this story.

Friends in the local historical community in Mercer and surrounding counties have provided inspiration and support in many ways through their many inquiries and offers of help. I would especially note Richard Patterson, Executive Director of the Old Barracks Museum, and members of his staff. Members of the Princeton Battlefield Society and the Historical Society of Princeton were very enthusiastic about this project and always offered support. The Newtown, Pennsylvania Historical Society library provided important resources for understanding Washington's time spent in Bucks County before and after the battle of Trenton. Washington Crossing State Park (NJ) provided several important documents and artifacts and I greatly appreciate the help and conversations with Clay Craighead, Mark Sirak, and Nancy Ceperley, who also read parts of the manuscript and offered valuable suggestions. My friend and fellow author and interpreter, David Price, provided encouragement and discussion on several topics that was most helpful and kept me thinking.

Tom Gilmour and Amanda Donald of the Trenton Downtown Association, as well as other members of the committee planning the annual Patriot's Week events in Trenton, that highlight the Ten Crucial Days, have also been very supportive and inspirational in thinking of ways that history can be presented to the general public of all ages in ways that create an enjoyment of and interest in history.

Librarian Kathie Ludwig, and her husband David, again provided not only help with the resources of the David Library of the American Revolution, but also many conversations that kept me thinking about how to present the story.

Once again, the New Jersey State Archives provided a vast array of important documents and the staff always made visits there productive and pleasant.

During my research I communicated with a number of historical researchers who shared ideas and resources with me. I would especially acknowledge Jerry Hurwitz, Bob Selig, Bill Welsch, and Glenn Williams who read the entire manuscript and provided many valuable suggestions for improvements and made sure I was consistent and appropriate with terminology as well as information.

While the work of previous writers on the subject of the Ten Crucial Days (including William Stryker, Thomas Fleming, William Dwyer, Samuel Stelle Smith, and David Hackett Fischer) needs to be acknowledged for introducing me to the topic and developing my deep interest in it, I want to especially acknowledge the work of Kevin Bradley, Wade P. Catts, Matthew Harris, and Robert A. Selig for the extensive recent research they have done on the Battle of Princeton and their reports prepared for the Princeton Battlefield Society. I would also like to thank Robert Reid for sharing with them his meticulous research shedding light onto the previously obscured activities of Colonel Hausegger and the German Battalion during the Battle of Princeton. Their reports were part of what inspired me to write on this topic and look at parts of it in new ways.

I am greatly indebted to my publisher, Roger S. Williams, for his enthusiasm and support for this project. As always, it has been a joy to work with him.

As always, I must thank my wife, Jane, for putting up with my concentration on this project that must have seemed an all-consuming obsession at times. And, I cannot omit acknowledging the continuing contributions of my cat, Izzy, who so enjoys being with me when I work that she literally told me to get to work each day. As usual, she is with me as I write this.

While all these people, and no doubt others I have failed to mention, helped me improve this work, any errors are my responsibility and I welcome having them pointed out to me.

# Contents

# Maps

# Tables



The information for these tables has been gathered from several sources, including:
Fischer, *Washington's Crossing*, 390-396, 408-411,
Smith, *Battle of Trenton*, 28-30
Smith, *Battle of Princeton*, 36-37
Selig, Harris, and Catts, *Battle of Princeton Mapping Project*, 38-42
Stryker, *Battles of Trenton and Princeton*, 344-347, 351-358, 430-431

When troop quantities ae given, they should be considered as estimates and sources may differ on them. In many cases, contemporry documentation is missing.

Names given in italics are people mentioned or quoted in the text. These military units were not "things", but consisted of individual men with personal experiences.

# Introduction

*"Ambuscade, surprise and stratagem are said to constitute the sublime part of the art of war, and that he who possesses the greatest resource in these will eventually pluck the laurel from the brow of his opponent. The stratagems of war are almost infinite, but all have the same object, namely, to deceive – to hold up an appearance of something which is not intended, while under this mask some important object is secured; and be a General never so brave, if he be unskilled in the arts and stratagems of war, he is really to be pitied; for his bravery will but serve to lead him into those wily snares which are laid for him."*

- Major General William Heath[1]

What we know as The Ten Crucial Days, December 25, 1776 through January 3, 1777, were vital in restoring confidence for a favorable outcome of the War for Independence and solidifying the military reputation of General George Washington. Major General William Heath, commander of a portion of Washington's troops on the Hudson River during those ten days, wrote the words quoted above in his memoirs while evaluating the events of January 2 and 3, 1777, that capped them off. Heath was praising Washington for demonstrating these abilities with decisiveness and persistence, some would say for the first time, during those ten days and by contrast the lack of those abilities demonstrated by his opponents. Before the Ten Crucial Days, Washington's bravery in combat was unquestioned, but his possession of the qualities expressed by Heath was suspect. Then, just when the war for independence seemed on the verge of collapse, Washington revealed the complexity and depth of his audacious and decisive character while restoring confidence and spirit in the American cause that ultimately led to victory.

The word "Revolution" has a number of definitions and historians have looked at the American Revolution through the lenses of several in their efforts to understand it. This story focuses on the definition that a revolution is the replacement of an established government by the people it governs, or at least a portion of them. The story of this revolution began as a movement to resist change and then to remove local governments from control by the British Parliament. Finally, the desire to completely remove the colonies from British government control, and declare independence, grew out of a complex mixture of ideological and practical forces. Various geographical, religious, political, and economic forces shaped the development patterns of the thirteen individual colonies over time and made independence seem inevitable to some, while anathema to others.

Several towns, beginning with Worcester, Massachusetts on October 4, 1774, and colonies, including South Carolina, North Carolina, Rhode Island, and Virginia, had declared their independence before the adoption of the 13 colony Declaration of Independence declaring, "That these United Colonies are, and of Right ought to be Free and Independent States." The series of sometimes violent protests against the actions of the British Parliament, notably levying taxes without the consent of local legislative bodies, had become a war of protest for some and independence for others on April 19, 1775 at Lexington. The Declaration of Independence in July 1776 was a statement justifying the independence already declared by local entities made the war's goal the independence of all thirteen colonies.

Although many good people disagreed about particulars, leaders on both sides engaged in fiery political rhetoric to promote ideological ideas, creating an "us" and "them" divide. Neither in England nor her American colonies were all the people convinced that their leaders were doing the right, and honorable, thing. British leaders had to navigate between those who felt the provincials should be punished for their actions and those who wanted an amicable reestablishment of their loyalty.[2] The Americans had to decide whether it was better to remain under the British government they knew, and in general respected highly, or abandon it with only an optimistic hope that a new government would be more to their liking.

Dr. Benjamin Rush, a signer of the Declaration of Independence and an active participant in the ten days of this story, reflecting on the War for Independence in 1788 discussed why it was so intense. He noted that the events were of deep interest to everyone and "an indifferent, or neutral spectator of the controversy, was scarcely to be found in any of the states." This was at least partly because "the scenes of war and government which it introduced, were new to the greatest part of the inhabitants of the United States, and operated with all the force of novelty upon the human mind." He also believed that, "the controversy was conceived to be the most important of any that had ever engaged the attention of mankind. It was generally believed by the friends of the Revolution, that the very existence of freedom upon our globe, was involved in the issue of the contest in favor of the United States." Thirdly, because "the revolution was conducted by men who had been born free" their "sense of the blessings of liberty was of course more exquisite than if they had just emerged from a state of slavery." The Americans separated from a nation to whom they were historically tied by consanguinity, laws, religion, commerce, language, interest, and a mutual sense of national glory; and shattering those ties increased the resentment they felt.

Because of the intensity of the struggle Rush believed, "the friends and enemies of the American Revolution must have been more or less than men, if they could have sustained the magnitude and rapidity of the events that characterized it, without discovering some marks of human weakness, both in body and mind."[3] Everyone on both sides was severely tested.

The Americans had spent over a decade protesting multiple actions of the British Parliament between 1763, the close of the French and Indian War, and July 2, 1776 when the Continental Congress declared the thirteen colonies to be independent states. During those 13 years of protest, many provincials began to accept, and then promote, the idea that they must be independent of Great Britain in order to maintain their liberties. While taxes were the focus of protests, taxes in general were not the issue. The provincials accepted that they had an obligation to help pay for their defense, and the taxes actually placed a relatively low burden on them compared with taxes paid by citizens in England. But, they insisted that only their colonial assemblies could levy taxes on them, because only the general assembly of each colony contained representatives voted into office by provincials eligible to vote. In spite of British efforts to convince them that each Member of Parliament represented all Englishmen, the colonists did not accept that they had representatives in Parliament, because they did not vote for them.

Parliament refused to renounce its right to tax the provincials, believing it fundamental to its supreme authority, and put down the resulting protests with measures that the provincials judged to be tyrannical and evidence that Britain considered them to be second class citizens not entitled to the full rights of Englishmen. However, throughout these years of protest, Americans continued to believe that the British government was the finest in the world and they just wanted to possess and maintain the same rights and respect as its citizens living in the mother country. The Declaration of Independence was not a plan to institute a new form of government, it was simply a declaration of independence, justified by a long list of grievances, necessitating the creation of a new government, modeled on Great Britain's or something entirely new. It wasn't even clear whether there would ultimately be thirteen new countries or one nation combining the former thirteen colonies in some manner, and it would take years to finalize a structure. By December 25, creating articles of confederation to define the new government had been loosely discussed, but a final document would not take effect until March 1, 1781.

Many months before the Declaration of Independence, the protest leaders began establishing extralegal government bodies that operated in parallel with, and ultimately replaced, the imperial governments. Organized violence led to the creation of independent militia companies that became the New England Army of Observation that laid siege to the British army in Boston after the actions on April 19, 1775 and was superseded by the creation of the Continental Army which ultimately forced the British to leave, while other Continental forces invaded Canada seeking to defeat British forces there and bring Canada into the struggle as the 14th colony. On the same day that independence passed in Congress, the largest military force ever assembled by Britain up to that time was arriving in New York harbor to begin a campaign to establish New York as British headquarters.

Those provincials who had been working to seek redress of grievances, even to the point of violence, now had to decide whether or not they wanted to take the ultimate step and become traitors. Not everyone wanted to, and a number of men in the Continental Army and the local militias left their units and joined with those who had been "friends of government" during the protests, declaring themselves to be Loyalist supporters of the mother country. This split meant that the subsequent military activity was not only a war for independence from Great Britain, but also a civil war between those fighting to stay with Britain, and continue trying to work out their differences, and those fighting for independence. Both wars would be bloody and tear asunder communities and families.

As 1776 was drawing to a close, British leaders were concerned that the rebellion had not been crushed with the ease they had anticipated. While British armies had experienced a number of victories, they had not decisively destroyed the rebel Continental Army or Congress. British leaders still expected ultimate victory and were planning for a decisive campaign to take place in 1777. For Americans, though, by December 24, 1776 the war for independence had lost its early optimism and glamour and was feared to be failing. For people caught in the swirl of events, the outcome was very unclear and individuals did not know that the ten days beginning December 25 would be crucial in preventing the collapse of the war effort and provide renewed momentum that ultimately led to victory and independence for the thirteen states.

This story is told as it unfolded day by day and follows the events through the experiences of military men of all ranks and civilians living among or serving in the variety of military forces in central New Jersey and eastern Pennsylvania. We also look at what was happening with the Continental Congress, having fled Philadelphia for Baltimore, and the British high command in New York, as well as the government in London. People directly involved in the events are seen in the context of the daily situations they faced and the decisions they confronted. Each of the ten days was uniquely crucial to the larger significance of that long week. While Washington pursued an overall goal, he demonstrated his talents as a skilled improviser and planner when reacting to changing situations, rather than as a dogmatic theoretician. No participant knew exactly what was coming the next day or that the outcome of the ten days would be so significant in the winning of American independence.

To tell this story we draw on various documents, created by imperfect human beings reflecting personal thoughts at a given moment in time or recalling a memory of events; such as in a diary entry made the same day or the reminiscences of a grandparent expressed many years later. Details included in quoted passages written by participants represent what the person thought or remembered, not necessarily what actually happened. In these personal accounts it is often difficult to know precisely where and when during an event the described actions took place. This account of the Ten Crucial Days aims at developing an understanding of the human elements – the decisions made, the reactions to events, the hopes, fears, etc. – rather than attempting to report precise details of events in a definitive manner. Hopefully, it will encourage the reader to visit the various locations described and try to mentally strip away the many years of changes to gain a deeper understanding of these events.

This story illustrates that, like everything in human history, the American Revolution, the War for Independence, and the humans participating in them were extremely complex. We see how participants on both sides dealt with constantly changing situations while trying to keep focused on their important overall objective.s They had to work through elements beyond their control, such as weather, changing information, decisions by their opponents, mistaken preconceived ideas, and actions of subordinates.

The real benefit of studying history is to better understand what it means to be a human being. People often justify learning history by using the phrase that those who don't know history are bound to repeat it. While it is true that progress results from knowing both the present and the past about something, especially for scientific discoveries and inventions, it is also true that for complex interpersonal and cultural issues, like war and peace, humans seem to continually find new ways to repeat old mistakes, often by misusing history to justify preconceived ideas, rather than using it to learn and grow from. In common with our forebearers, we live in an increasingly complex world that we must negotiate using as much skill as possible. We especially need to appreciate that we are not alone in experiencing a dangerous and seemingly uncontrollable human and natural environment. Our forbearers who experienced the Revolution could compare stories with us about problems they encountered in life that are similar to ours.

**Join us now** as we begin our look at the human events of the Ten Crucial Days beginning December 25, 1776 that played such an important role in the success of our American Revolution and creation of our country. How did people in various locations, with access to variable amounts of current and correct information, experience that Christmas Day? What were their hopes and fears? What problems did they face?

First, we look at the British government leaders, far from the events that would go far towards either fulfilling their goal to restore the loyalty of their rebel provincials, or dashing it.

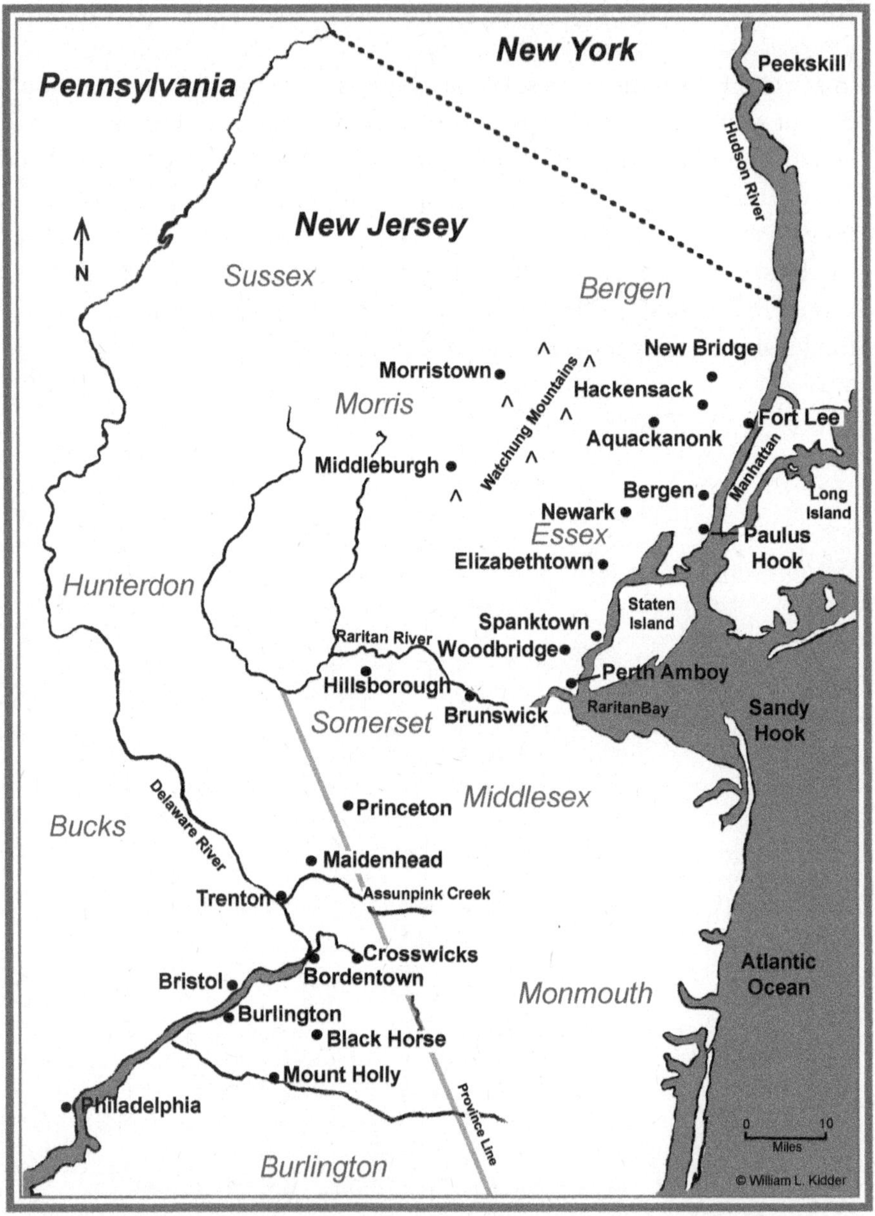


**Map 1: Central and Northern New Jersey - December 25, 1776**

Two proprietary colonies, East Jersey and West Jersey, were united in 1704 into the one royal colony of New Jersey. The line dividing them was drawn several times and one is still evident today as part of civic boundaries and roads. During the War for Independence, New Jersey had two capitals, Burlington, and Perth Amboy.

# Chapter 1

## England, Wednesday, December 25, 1776

By Christmas 1776, Great Britain's leaders had been struggling for more than a decade to settle on a consistent strategy for subduing their rebellious, recently turned traitorous, American colonists. Their choices lay between employing overpowering military force to break the rebellion and force the colonists who survived into complete submission, or working with rebel leaders to modify their colonial relationship with the mother country, creating a structure agreeable to both parties, even though the rebels had replaced the local British colonial government structure and its officials, taken control of colonial militias, and collectively declared independence in a Continental Congress. When considering what actions to take, British leaders consistently worked from the belief that the rebels were only an influential minority and the majority of provincials remained loyal to Britain. The British leaders had no intention of submitting to the demands of the provincials and persisted in pursuing their ultimate goal to convince the rebellious colonies that they could not resist the overwhelming power of the British Empire and should quickly reach a settlement restoring their peaceful pre-war status.[1]

WHAT BEGAN AROUND BOSTON in 1775 as actions to put down local internal rebellion, using minimal military force, had developed in 1776 into a much wider war, complicated by fighting against and among fellow British subjects. The rebels controlled local governments and until they were overthrown the British could only control scattered areas they occupied with military force, and spreading troops in small units throughout the thirteen colonies would be militarily and economically unsustainable. The British aimed to win control of key economic and political locations, destroy the rebel army through intimidation and battle, capture rebel leaders, and restore to power those provincials who remained loyal to the British government. British Major General Henry Clinton used an expression that became familiar to Americans during another war 200 years later when he wrote of the necessity "to gain the hearts and subdue the minds of America."[2] However, British leaders decided to augment the army, an alienating force by its very presence, and in mid-1776 landed the largest armed expeditionary force in British history at New York to reestablish within one year a peaceful and mutually beneficial imperial relationship with the 13 colonies. This force would secure New York as a base of operations for troops to be used in combination with an army coming south from Canada through Lake Champlain and the Hudson River valley to cut off New England from the other colonies.

From the beginning of military activity, British officials interacting with the rebels avoided statements or actions that could be interpreted as giving legitimacy to rebel leaders and their illegal government structures. This made issues such as dealing with prisoners of war very complex. Many officials felt provincial loyalty could only be renewed by confronting rebels with an insurmountable force to compel their surrender or create internal divisions splitting the rebels apart.[3] But, others saw a war against the colonies in America as unwinnable.

A pamphlet published prior to the New York campaign began that, "indeed the ministers have already thrown out in parliament, that forty thousand men will be requisite. A less number would be an army of inability and irritation. Nor have I indeed an idea that such a force, though formidable, will be effectual. It may check, but it cannot conquer America." This was because the war was being fought "at more than three thousand miles distance, against an enemy we now find united, active, able and, resolute; where every foot of ground is to be won by inches, and at the same fatal expence with Bunker's hill[4]; in a country where fastness grows upon fastness, and labyrinth on labyrinth; where a check is a defeat, and a defeat is ruin – it is a war of absurdity and madness. We shall sooner pluck the moon from her sphere, than conquer such country."[5] While this argument overestimates the colonists' unity in opposing England, it gives a realistic picture of the problems the British government faced. Additionally, the American problem was just one of many contributing to the costs of empire, making its speedy resolution important. While Britain was expanding its use of resources to subdue the American rebellion, it was dealing with other imperial needs while also maintaining military resources to defend the homeland from potential wars with other European countries, such as France and Spain.

**About a week before Christmas,** King George III learned that the rebels had been forced to leave "the Province of New York except Fort Washington which Gen. Howe was preparing to attack." This "very good news" was over a month old due to the slow passage of ships across the Atlantic and left open the question whether the rebellion would definitely be crushed within the one year goal.[6] London businessman Robert Grant kept his longtime friend Major General James Grant, then commander of the British forces in the colony of New Jersey, informed of the London news in their frequent correspondence. General Grant had believed the rebellion would be crushed quickly and expected to serve in America for only a year. However, Grant wrote him on December 20 that "as from the situation of affairs you may be detained in America longer than you expected I have sent you your [London] news papers up to this time." Prospects were still promising and the most recent news from America encouraged Grant's belief that "if the rebel army is in such a dispersed situation as we imagine, they will never be able to collect them again." However, he had also heard the disappointing news that Major General Sir Guy Carleton had returned his victorious army from southern Lake Champlain back north to Canada for the winter, rather than capture Fort Ticonderoga, and this retrograde action would delay beginning the 1777 campaign, if it was needed.

There was concern the American war would spread and Robert Grant had seen a letter the previous night from a man who had spoken with Benjamin Franklin, representing the American States at the Paris Court, reporting that the French had dispatched a fleet supposedly to St. Domingo, but actually headed for America with 120 officers, including a general and several engineers given four years leave of absence to work with the Americans. Grant also mentioned the rumor that Americans were offering France, in return for assistance or alliance, exclusive trade for a number of years, the restoration of Canada,

Mississippi, Nova Scotia, Cape Breton and the Newfoundland fishery, "and any number of troops the French may want for the protection of their West India settlements." France's unofficial support for the rebels concerned British leaders who knew that American negotiators, including Franklin, were in France seeking a more open and extensive relationship, even a military alliance.[7] Ending the rebellion quickly would eliminate the potentially wider conflict.

Several generals returned home from America for the winter with dated news. Major General John Burgoyne celebrated Christmas Day at the Brooks's Club in London with Charles James Fox, leader of the opposition to the war in Parliament. Burgoyne had arrived home on leave on December 9 after serving in the 1776 campaign in Canada and New York State, mistakenly believing that General Carleton was wintering his troops at Crown Point at the southern end of Lake Champlain. The optimistic Burgoyne bet Fox 50 guineas that he would "be home victorious from America by Christmas Day, 1777." As a Member of Parliament, Burgoyne had supported the actions taken against the colonies for their protests, although he preferred persuasion rather than force to settle their problems. He was aware that he was fighting British subjects in arms rather than a professional foreign army and appreciated the psychological differences encountered in a war to maintain the British Empire and its constitution from those in a fight to gain possession of additional land. Burgoyne brought with him Carleton's draft proposal for a 1777 campaign that he had edited and expanded, adding his own commentary.

Burgoyne's plan was in tune with his King's wishes to execute bold strokes rather than hold anything back and was a modification of the previous plan to cut off New England from the other colonies by bringing the army in Canada south through the Lake Champlain/Hudson River valley to unite at Albany with part of Howe's army marching north from New York. His modification was to send a third force from the west taking the Lake Ontario, Lake Oswego, and Mohawk River route to join those armies at Albany. That force would also demonstrate government support for the many Loyalists in the Mohawk Valley. He was also considering an additional force that would attack Connecticut. This plan was still developing in his mind on December 25 and would not be presented to Lord George

Germain, Secretary of State for America, until the end of February.[8] The 1776 campaign had only been partially successful, but this proposed 1777 campaign would bring victory.

**British political and military** leaders have often been caricatured as tyrannical buffoons, but in reality they were capable professionals who took their work seriously in dealing with a very difficult and complex situation. They were not at all opposed to liberty and representative government. Like the Americans who opposed them, they believed in freedom and the need for a balanced government to prevent tyranny. The real story of the Revolution does not pit stereotypical buffoonish tyrants against demi-god fighters for liberty, and the outcome of the war in favor of the Americans was not an inevitable step in the evolution of human freedom. Leaders on both sides suffered from human foibles and cultural influences, such as defending their perceived private honor at times when public service badly needed to take precedence. Several leading generals commanding troops in America were members of Parliament who had opposed the policies that angered the colonists.

Ironically, during the 1776 military campaign both sides justified their actions as defending the guarantees of the British Constitution. Although castigated by the Revolutionaries as tyrannical, British leaders believed they were defending liberty and the rule of law, both of which they believed could only be maintained if Parliament held supreme authority. British leaders and the colonists who remained loyal to them often believed the rebels were the ones establishing a tyranny, by suppressing dissent and using coercion to enforce compliance with their views and new governments.[9]

Leaders on both sides in the conflict made critical decisions while holding erroneous beliefs about their opponents. American revolutionaries believed the king and his government were conspiring to destroy American liberties, while leaders in the British government believed the American rebellion was engineered by a small group of provincials who wanted to seize power for themselves by declaring independence from Britain and then ruling over their lower ranking provincial neighbors. However, some insightful members of Parliament believed as early as January 1775 that government leaders were deluded in their perception that the majority of Americans fully supported the

British government and that the Revolution was confined to Boston and a few men in each colony.

Other members simply looked down on the rebels and considered Americans to be so undisciplined, lazy, unclean, and of such weak character that they could not stand up to the British army. General James Grant, for example, believed that 5,000 British regulars could march from one end of the North American colonies to the other without serious opposition. Having served previously in America, he proclaimed in 1775 that he "knew the Americans very well, was certain they would not fight; they would never dare to face an English army, and that they did not possess any of the qualifications necessary to make a good soldier." In an oration to Parliament, "he repeated many of their common place expressions, ridiculed their enthusiasm in religion, and drew a disagreeable picture of their manners and ways of living."[10]

**Both houses of Parliament** had recessed on December 13 and were not scheduled to meet again until January 23, but work on the war continued. Thirty-eight-year-old King George III was fully aware that many of his American subjects considered him to be a tyrant and no longer their legitimate leader. George had been crowned King in 1760 at the age of 22 and, like many of the provincial leaders, was a man of the Enlightenment who exhibited its positive intellectual traits. Due to the long history of efforts to limit the power of England's monarch, he had much less power than his fellow monarchs in Europe and had initially tried to use those limited powers to restrain his ministers from pursuing even more extreme measures affecting the colonies. However, when war broke out he became a strong advocate for crushing the rebellion, because he believed Parliament's authority was essential for maintaining order throughout the empire. As monarch, he saw himself as an important component in a system of checks and balances guarding against any aristocratic excesses of the House of Lords or overly democratic ideas of the House of Commons.[11]

George immersed himself in the details of his empire. He had a deep knowledge of army and navy officers, ships, and regiments, bishops and parishes, university faculties, harbor soundings of European countries, strengths and weaknesses of fortified towns, and a wide variety of other information. He was quite possibly neurotic, or obsessive compulsive, about his duties as King, but fortunately, was usually quite energetic, allowing him to indulge his passion for work. George saw himself as the royal father of wicked children, the rebellious colonists, and long after Parliament and the British people tired of the war, he would continue to insist on pursuing it. His outward appearance of positive strength camouflaged a basic insecurity. He continually played the role of a strong and resolute King, forcing himself to be the man he felt he needed to be in order to gain respect as King. Once he decided that war was the best method to subdue the rebels, he wanted it pursued vigorously to a successful conclusion and was always confident of the outcome.[12]

The written protest statements by colonists against specific acts of Parliament were accompanied by pleas to their trusted and beloved King to step in and defend them. The provincials were happy to be subjects of the King, but wanted to be subject to actions of their local governments rather than those of Parliament. However, George did not support this concept and, consequently, by 1776 he was condemned as a tyrant, leading to disfigurement and destruction of his images and logos in the colonies. George was erroneously accused of taking complete control of Parliament to become a tyrant, over both Britain and America. The Declaration of Independence greatly exaggerated his role when the leaders of the Revolution sought greater support for their cause by focusing people's hate on an easily identified individual, rather than a faceless institution. When the colonial conflict became a war for independence, King George saw it as a watershed event and he no longer simply acted to defend the authority of Parliament and the British Constitution, but expanded his concern to the larger issue of preserving Britain's place as a great power among the nations of Europe. Hence his rejection of the Olive Branch Petition in August that established him as an enemy of a peaceful settlement to the colonial grievances.

In consultation with his cabinet and military advisors, George personally selected the top generals to conduct the war in America. While he favored the aggressive, high-risk military strategies of Major General John Burgoyne and Major General Lord Charles Cornwallis, he also selected William Howe and Henry Clinton who advocated more cautious strategies. He believed in taking risks to prevent the war from becoming stagnant and he would rather make it a short, spirited war or go down in glorious defeat. While in contrast, he also wanted to leave the door open for a negotiated settlement following a complete surrender.[13]

This Christmas Day, George only knew that the historically large expeditionary force sent to take and occupy New York had won a series of battlefield victories that forced Washington's army to abandon New York, retreat across New Jersey and then flee across the Delaware River into Bucks County, Pennsylvania. His General Howe did not always "think in terms of annihilation" accomplished by one large battlefield victory, but rather focused on accumulating a series of small victories, making the British seem invincible and demoralizing the provincials. Howe also did not want to absorb high casualties, similar to those at Bunker Hill, because he would be losing well-trained men who could not be replaced quickly. Although knowing that the goal was to end the war in one year, shortly after the battle of Long Island at the end of August 1776 Howe concluded another campaign would be necessary in 1777 and his objective shifted to wearing down the Continental Army from his base at New York.[14]

As 1776 drew to a close, while pleased to know the British army had secured New York and controlled its environs, along with much of New Jersey, George might have been less pleased to know that Howe occupied New Jersey in a string of winter cantonments, playing dangerously by dividing his forces over a wide area that made them vulnerable to harassing attacks by the enemy.[15] He may have agreed with Howe that Washington's demoralized army was so reduced in numbers that it would probably dissolve during the rigorous winter conditions, and with many British leaders who believed the rebel provincial governments would soon collapse due to the inflated rebel paper money that added to the ravages of war. However, Washington's army was still intact and state governments, with their militias, continued to operate in a confederation under the Continental Congress. Member of Parliament John Yorke sensed what perhaps others were feeling, that "there is something which supports and keeps them together which the Ministers have not yet discovered."[16] George probably did not understand it either.

**The Royal Navy played** important roles in the expanded war to put down the American rebellion. Fifty-eight-year-old John Montagu, the Earl of Sandwich, began sitting on the Admiralty Board in his mid-twenties and became First Lord of the Admiralty in January 1771, after serving 37 years in Parliament. Montagu had many interests, from linguistics and art to reputedly being the best cricket player of his day. However, he loved his Navy and his devoted concentration on it impressed everyone who met him. One acquaintance described him as "a tall stout man," with "looks as furrowed and weather-proof as any sailor in the Navy; and like most of the old set of that brave tribe, he has good nature and joviality marked in every feature." He endured long hours of work at his Admiralty desk and is said to have invented the sandwich in order to keep up his energy.[17] Without enough ships to both support the army and enforce a blockade to prevent the importation of military supplies from France and other locations, he had also been trying throughout 1776 to protect British merchant ships from rebel privateers. Things were better now in December and he was able to add ships to the American coastal blockade. General William Howe's brother, Admiral Lord Richard Howe, commanding the British fleet in America, informed Montagu about the poor condition of many ships in his fleet, with some rapidly becoming unfit to go to sea. Sandwich, along with Howe, did what he could to keep the fleet at sea fully manned and increase the number of ships, but his opponents in the cabinet kept challenging all requests for more ships.[18]

Sandwich was faced with finding ways to prevent the navy from becoming merely the system for transporting men and supplies while essentially forfeiting its ability to defend England and win offensive victories at sea. Obtaining provisions and forage in America was essential and by the end of 1776 he expected to obtain produce from New Jersey's farmers and reduce the need to transport across the Atlantic the huge quantities of food required by the troops. Still, the war in America badly stretched Royal Navy resources and Sandwich feared that France and Spain would become allies of the American rebels, expanding the war to the rest of the British Empire.

France was eager for revenge after the French and Indian War and began rebuilding its navy and encouraging Spain to build up its fleet. Sandwich decided to keep much of the British fleet at home, thus allowing American rebel privateers to become a serious and growing problem at the end of 1776.[19] He refused on three occasions to provide Howe with additional warships and when ships were sent home to England for repairs, he kept them there.[20] Sandwich also tried to convince government leaders that any ships sent to the North American colonies must be replaced by new construction to guard home waters. However, increasing the fleet would also spur other countries to enlarge their fleets.[21] Both France and Spain rebuilt their navies with heavier ships than Britain's and by 1776 their combined navies outweighed the British fleet in total tonnage, although the British still had more ships.

Self-interest led the French to support the Americans. The French considered Britain to be an aggressive nation that might strike them at any moment and saw the American war of independence as beneficially keeping the British army and navy occupied. Furthermore, if America succeeded in gaining its independence, Britain's power would be reduced and American markets would be open to the French and Spanish.[22]

Adding to Sandwich's concerns, in December a petty criminal turned incendiary terrorist, James Aitken, alias John the Painter, tried unsuccessfully to burn the ships and docks at Portsmouth and other English seaports. Aitken believed that by doing this he was contributing to the American cause by disabling British navy support for the military in America.[23]

**Another man faced with** making decisions on the war effort was England's leader in Parliament. However, King George's 44-year-old Prime Minister, Lord Frederick North, had broken his arm in September and, while recovering at his country home, suffered from a persistent fever that kept him from meeting with the cabinet to plan a 1777 campaign.[24]

North became Prime Minister in 1770, inheriting the rising tide of protest and making his first speech to Parliament the same day as the Boston Massacre. He was awkward and ungainly in appearance, which made him ripe for satire, but was popular even with opponents due to his "self-deprecating humor and urbane manner." North was a highly skilled public speaker who maintained a majority of support in the

House of Commons. Originally a strong advocate and supporter of the actions which led to the protests, including the right of Parliament to tax the colonies, he became more conciliatory towards the colonists after becoming Prime Minister and removed all the Townshend Duties, except the tea tax, because he believed the duties made no economic sense. He also loosened the restrictions on western expansion associated with the Proclamation Line of 1763. But, along with many British leaders who wanted to maintain the loyalty of the colonies, while ensuring Parliament's authority to govern them, he was conflicted over whether to be firm or lenient with the demands of the provincials.

North became less sympathetic and, in his outrage over the Boston Tea Party, introduced the Coercive Acts to punish Massachusetts and avoid making concessions, but those strictures only led to widespread protests. He had been working to establish a peace commission since the outbreak of armed conflict in 1775 and in May 1776 he appointed two peace commissioners, brothers General William and Admiral Lord Richard Howe. Both men opposed the policies that had precipitated the war. While serving as peace commissioners, they were simultaneously commanders of the massive land and sea forces committed to taking New York City. This exemplified the indecisive government policy and by December 1776 North was more skeptical than the King and his colleagues in the cabinet about the ultimate success of military intervention. Although North had expressed his concern from the beginning that the 1776 New York campaign would not go well, he was now viewed by some as the reason Washington's army still existed in spite of the massive military force he had been given.[25]

**Another leader in the war** effort was 60-year-old Lord George Germain who brought 34 years of experience in Parliament when he became Secretary of State for the Colonies in November 1775. He was six feet tall with a muscular physique and commanding presence, an impressive figure who was a bit reticent in public, but more relaxed in private with his family. He was known as an engaging conversationalist who adapted well to his audience, spoke clearly, and was easily understood, making him highly regarded in Parliament where he earned praise for his speeches and debates. He had served in the army and was known for his courage, although he had been court martialed for disobeying orders and pronounced unfit for service after the battle of Minden in 1759. This incident caused more than a little difficulty when he was dealing with officers who had served in that battle.

While others happily believed things were going well in America, Germain was angry because the 1776 campaign had failed to isolate New England. Germain considered General Guy Carleton, the commander in Canada, responsible for the lack of complete success in his theater, because of his delay during the campaign leading to the Battle of Valcour Island on Lake Champlain and then removing his troops back to Canada rather than keeping them at Crown Point in readiness for the 1777 campaign.[26] He was also displeased that General Howe had not finished things off with Washington's army.

Germain believed coercion was necessary and that any conciliation could only come after Americans submitted unconditionally to British authority. There would be no negotiations between "equals" and before any talks took place the rebels must acknowledge the authority of Parliament. Thomas Walpole, was one member of Parliament who believed this would not work and argued that Germain knew very little about human nature, "if he thinks the motives which have induced them to associate, arm and fight in the defense of their supposed rights will not for ever prevent the return of peace, unless more adequate and just provision be made for obtaining it." There was continual debate about what process to use to achieve reconciliation and whether a formal inquiry into colonial grievances would be part of it. Germain's biographer believes his "misconception of the whole revolutionary movement made it utterly impossible that this aspect of his policy should meet with any substantial measure of success." After employing both coercion and conciliation in the 1776 campaign, coercion had attained only limited success and conciliation no success at all.[27]

**These British leaders** far from the scene of action felt confident they would win back their colonists' loyalty to the king and Parliament, but were unhappy that it was taking longer than expected. How did their generals and troops stationed in America experience this Christmas Day and understand the progress they had made in the 1776 campaign? Did their hopes and fears coincide with those of their leaders back in England? How long would they need to be away from their homes in

Europe? Would a military campaign in 1777 be necessary and, if so, how would it unfold? Whatever their belief about the past, what were their expectations for the next ten days?

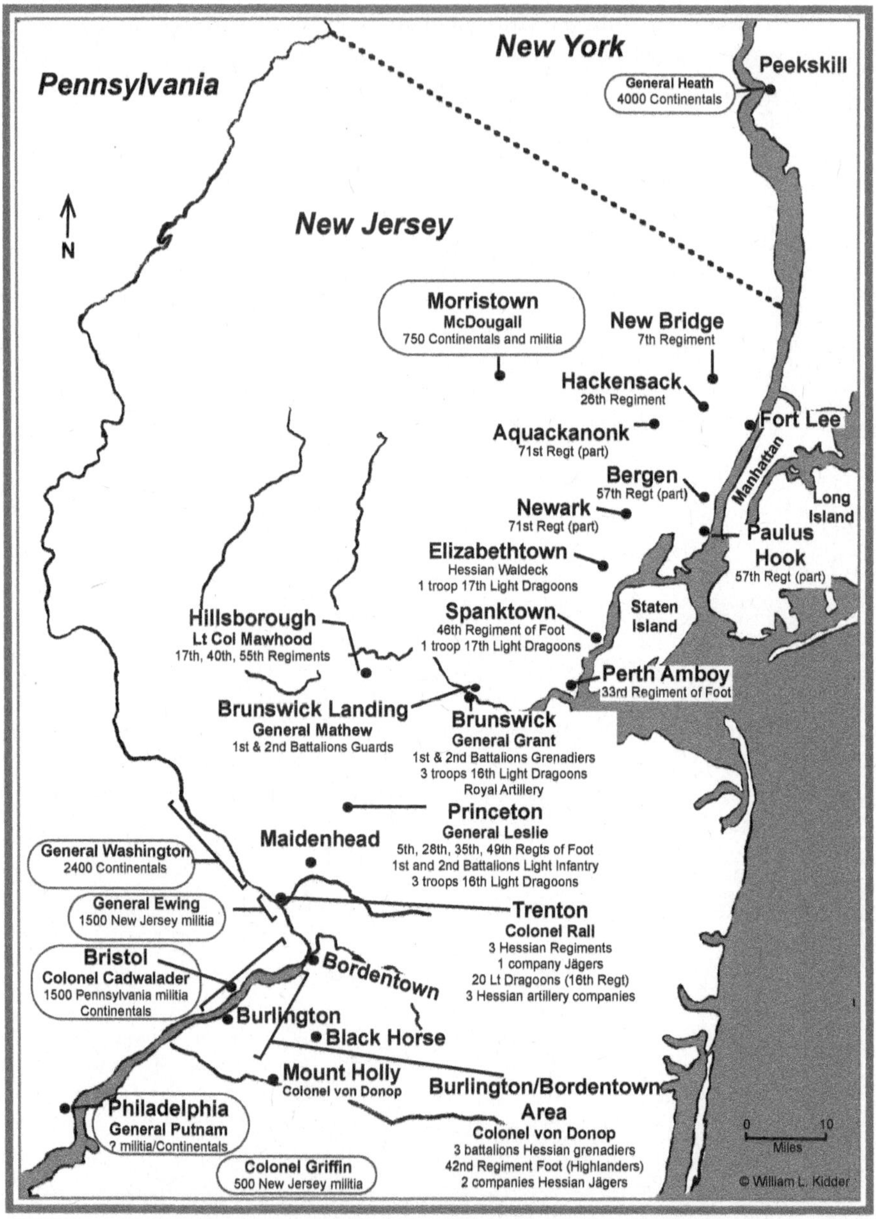


**Map 2: British Occupation of New Jersey - December 25, 1776**

The British winter contonments established by General Howe controlled a broad swath of central New Jersey focusing on the primary transportation route between New York City and Philadelphia. This military occupation caused the state government to disperse and positioned the British for an attack on Philadelphia, which was greatly feared in December 1776.

# Chapter 2

## British America, Wednesday, December 25, 1776

After a hard frost on December 24, temperatures in New York moderated on Christmas Day.[1] General William Howe and his brother Admiral Richard Howe, the British commanders at New York, were physically imposing men with a strong military bearing. They were close, mutually supportive, and had strong military reputations. Both had previous experience in North America and had been innovators who modified the military for operations there.[2] Newly knighted William Howe had greatly enjoyed his French and Indian War service in North America and had warm feelings for the Americans, who had paid for a memorial to his brother George who had been killed in the war.[3]

THE HOWE BROTHERS HAD TAKEN and occupied New York with their huge army and naval forces as part of the overall strategy to separate New England, the perceived heart of the rebellion, from the other colonies. Between August and December they had defeated, reduced in numbers, but not destroyed, the American army in a series of battles around New York City. General Howe's increasingly obvious hesitation to press the American army to its death derived in part from both Howe brothers considering their duties as peace commissioners to be an integral part of their military command function, requiring them to confront the rebellion with their large military force while also extending an olive branch. As early as August, Ambrose Serle, Admiral Howe's secretary, had reflected the views of both Howes when he wrote to the Earl of Dartmouth that the American army was "the most motley, ragged, filthy crew that can be represented" and consisted of "old men, boys, people of every color, size and condition, [that] are jumbled together." If the winter proved to be severe they would suffer more damage than from two or three battles. He believed the rebel strategy was to prolong the war until Britain tired of it, when "neither the wealth nor the will of the nation will molest them" any further. However, Serle was convinced "the perseverance of Great Britain, followed by its justice, in another year, may settle all things upon a permanent foundation" and prevent any rebel alliance with France or Spain.[4]

On December 23, the Loyalist mouthpiece *New York Gazette, and Weekly Mercury* had reinforced Howe's view of the rebel weakness and described the rebels as "every where mouldering away like a rope of sand" and lacking the spirit to make a stand. The rebel State governments were "nearly drained of their resources" and, therefore, ruin and "destruction must be the consequence to them of continuing the war any longer." The rebels "have suffered much already by continuing the campaign so far into winter, which, by the thinness of their cloathing and their wants in other respects, they are but ill qualified to bear."[5]

General Howe's men, along with their uniforms and shoes, were also worn out from the six-month campaign, about half the buildings in British occupied New York had burned down, and the nearby farms could not support his entire army. Necessary food and military supplies had to cross 3,000 miles of ocean in ships, many of which were also worn out. General Howe had planned to occupy eastern New Jersey only as far west as Brunswick. Reports of strong loyalist support in New Jersey encouraged Howe to attempt to gain their support and obtain resources by occupying territory.

When so many New Jersey people came in with their arms in response to an amnesty proclamation of November 30, Howe decided to extend the occupation to three Delaware River towns roughly six miles apart, Trenton, Burlington, and Bordentown. The cantonment garrisons spread across New Jersey could then support Loyalists, suppress the rebels, and obtain provisions for the New York based army, if they acted quickly before the rebels could destroy them.[6] Twelve miles northeast of Trenton troops were stationed at Princeton while the main cantonment was at Brunswick, 35 miles from the Delaware River.[7] Howe reflected, "the chain [of cantonments], I own, is rather too extensive but I was induced to occupy Burlington to cover the county of Monmouth in which there are many loyal inhabitants, and trusting to the almost general submission of the country to the southward of this chain and to the strength of the corps placed in the advanced posts, I conclude the troops will be in perfect security."[8] General Clinton advised against this dispersal of forces, noting that the enemy had demonstrated skill in attacking isolated outposts.[9]

Howe's main objective for the winter was to get his troops rested and conditioned for the 1777 campaign, but he also looked forward to spending more time with stunning blonde Elizabeth Loring, his mistress and wife of Joshua Loring whom Howe had given the lucrative position of prison commissary in New York.[10] For winter entertaining, Howe maintained a luxurious floating palace at New York, the converted East Indiaman *Britannia* sporting state rooms, enlarged port holes for better views, white lacquered walls, and gold skirting boards. Two decks had been knocked through to make large halls.[11]

On Christmas Day, General Howe could look back on the previous year with some satisfaction, even though he had not totally defeated the American rebels. He had taken command of British forces at the same time rebel committees and congresses were taking power away from royal governors throughout the colonies. In late June, he had led the expeditionary force into New York and in a series of battles from August through November had successfully secured New York City and its surroundings as headquarters for British military activity in the colonies.[12] In November and early December he had forced Washington's rebel army to retreat across New Jersey and the Delaware River into Bucks County, Pennsylvania, while leaving British troops in control of central New Jersey and forcing many people to conclude that the British military was invincible and it was time to make peace. He had essentially conquered one of the rebellious colonies and dispersed its rebel government.

However, Howe had not helped himself in the struggle for hearts and minds when as military commander, in an attempt to reduce harassing warfare by small groups of local militia, on December 12 he issued orders to his men to summarily execute provincials not in military uniform, such as most militiamen, when caught in violent acts of rebellion.[13] In contrast, as peace commissioners, the Howe brothers had issued a proclamation on November 30 inviting rebels, within 60 days, to pledge loyalty to the King in return for pardon and protection from harm by British military forces. Thousands of people, especially in New Jersey, accepted the offer and reaffirmed their loyalty to the British government. However, as British Sergeant Thomas Sullivan of the 49th Regiment of Foot believed, while many people legitimately swore loyalty and got protections, others "more attached to their delusive leaders, used it only as a means to conceal their knavery, and deceive if possible both sides; as many of them that got Protections were afterwards taken [prisoner] under arms."[14]

Amnesty seekers came from all walks of life and included several members of Congress. The British erroneously thought the large numbers represented victory, while the Americans feared it meant defeat. As Sergeant Sullivan and others suspected, the protection seekers misrepresented the true number of people returning to British loyalty. Lord Germain, along with many other British leaders, believed offering amnesty would not help and some members of Parliament saw the proclamation as an example of mixed objectives and actions in prosecuting the war, reflecting the mixed views among government leaders, as well as the general population in England, concerning the nature of the conflict.[15] Loyalists in America angrily felt the proclamation allowed rebels who had persecuted them to escape punishment.

**Lieutenant Stephen Olney,** in Colonel Daniel Hitchcock's 1st Rhode Island Regiment, saw that Loyalists had been greatly encouraged by the British occupation and "an insurrection appeared ready to explode in this very province of New Jersey" against the Whig government. Then, when the Howes issued their proclamation, "to the disgrace of the country and of human nature, great numbers flocked to confess their political sins to the representative of Majesty, and to obtain pardon. It was observed, that these consisted of the very rich and the very poor, while the middling class held their constancy."[16] The large number swearing loyalty led Howe to expect an increasing level of Loyalist support and he especially believed the area around Trenton was heavily

Loyalist, so any troops cantoned at Trenton should be well received by local Loyalists who would encourage additional people to return to British loyalty. However, many people accepting protection were simply employing "passive obedience" by making peace with whatever army controlled their area, and enduring a tyrant or conqueror as a judgment of God on sinners.[17] The extensive swearing of loyalty, combined with the extreme difficulty in getting militia to turn out in November and early December, increased fear of the revolution's imminent failure.[18]

On December 22, the Howe brothers wrote to Lord George Germain reporting on the success of their amnesty proclamation, stating, "The whole of the Jerseys, except a very inconsiderable part which we think must of course follow, has submitted." While they had not yet received all the returns, they could say "from the successful circulation of the proclamation … and from the avidity with which the terms of it have been hitherto embraced, we have reason to conclude that very material good consequences will accrue from it before the sixty days shall be expired."[19]

The Loyalist *New York Gazette* reported on December 23 that some leading citizens of Philadelphia had claimed the protection of the British army and "great numbers in the Jersies have likewise come in" and "most of them express the deepest sorrow for their late delusion, and freely acknowledge that when they lost British protection, they fell into real slavery, and into slavery of the worst kind – the slavery of weak and wicked men." Toasts being raised in England included: "Liberty and Britain, with confusion to all Congressional slavery," and "Britain and America united in one Constitution for ever!"[20] However, British officers found that "while in our power they [the provincials] conceal their arms, and secret whatever would be of use to us, appear friends and pretend to be good subjects but the moment we move [they] harass and annoy us." The Americans, it seemed, fully understood that, "if Great Britain cannot conquer us, she cannot govern us."[21]

On Christmas Eve, Loyalist New York Governor William Tryon reported to Germain that he had reviewed Long Island Loyalist troops and explained to the inhabitants how the rebels had seduced and mislead them. He gave about 300 protection certificates, adding to the large number already given out so that Lord Howe's secretary Ambrose Serle, "was much employed for the most part of the day" in issuing pardons, just as he had been the previous day.[22] Tryon believed, "the late successes of His Majesty's arms in the Jerseys and Rhode Island will assuredly open considerable resources of provisions and forage for the army, which with the plentiful and abundant supplies from the mother country will enable this high-spirited and victorious army to take the field early next spring."[23]

**While modestly pursuing the** disintegrating American army across New Jersey, Howe was already planning the 1777 campaign to secure New England, Philadelphia, and the Hudson River. As part of his plan, he sent General Clinton with a combined army and naval force to take control of Rhode Island and secure Newport as an ice free anchorage for the Royal Navy.[24] Clinton took possession of Rhode Island on December 8 and established Newport on Narragansett Bay as a fine base for a war-ending campaign against New England.[25] Obtaining food for men and horses required a gigantic effort, and occupying New Jersey went far towards solving the provisions and forage problem, while the Rhode Island campaign allowed the army to stockpile hay and grain for the next campaign.[26]

Holding New Jersey put Howe closer to Philadelphia and if the Delaware River froze he wanted to attack it before the spring campaign. Howe firmly believed his "principal object in so great an extension of the cantonments was to afford protection to the inhabitants, that they might experience the difference between his majesty's government, and that to which they were subject by the rebel leaders."[27] He planned to make every effort to keep his troops under control and not aggravate the population by refusing to honor the protection papers of the amnesty proclamation, but claimed the need for additional officers in order to prevent plundering by his troops.[28]

The Howe brothers wanted to help Loyalists regain control of local government, while conducting military operations only when necessary. In spite of those goals, Howe found himself at war with the local population of New Jersey and ordered his men to travel in groups and confine their movements to a few days each week. When Howe ordered New Jersey garrisons to supply themselves with food and fuel, the need to forcibly obtain local supplies clashed with the pacification policy. Hessian Colonel Carl von Donop, in command at

Bordentown, was ordered to take a census of cattle, grain and hay on local farms, collect what he needed, and pay with a paper receipt. Any food withheld by a farmer in excess of his family's needs was "to be considered as a rebel store, be seized for the Crown and issued to the troops as a saving for the public." Troops were given the tools they needed to supply themselves with firewood taken from the local inhabitants. If rum could be found it was to be taken in order to encourage the men in their work. Soldiers were sent out to confiscate any supplies not offered in sufficient quantity and the list of items to be taken was expanded to include personal items such as shoes, stockings, and blankets.[29]

Both Howe brothers failed to completely understand that the war had radically changed over time from a protest pressing for the redress of grievances to a war for securing the complete independence of a new country. Throughout the 1776 campaign they had seemed to lack spirit in bringing the war to a complete conclusion with a decisive battle, partly the result of their conflicting roles as military commanders and peace commissioners. Viewing their military actions as suppressing an internal rebellion rather than fighting a foreign country, although to the Americans it was a foreign invasion, they did not want to cause excessive death and destruction, recognizing that they needed to reconstruct the civil government.[30] In addition, knowing that it would be very difficult to replace large numbers of troops, they wanted to avoid high casualties.

Out of a long-standing distrust of large standing armies that could be used to tyrannize its own people, Britain maintained a relatively small, volunteer, professional army that competed for men with plentiful civilian job opportunities. This necessitated the need for supplementing the army with subsidized auxiliaries from other countries in times of war, although there was some opposition in Parliament to using foreign troops in this war, a purely domestic quarrel rather than a war between nations. Some members of Parliament expected little benefit from the Hessians and believed "that if Britain could not win the war using her own sons, she would not win the war."[31]

The Hessians were not the only German speaking men with the British army. Unable to recruit enough men from the British Isles to fill its regiments, which had been increased in size by almost 50% for the war, Britain had recruited men from other European states. The 17th Regiment of Foot had recently received some 40 German-speaking recruits and other regiments received anywhere from five to over 100. While other regiments spread their German recruits throughout their companies, the 17th Regiment placed them all in Lieutenant Colonel Charles Mawhood's company, possibly because one of the company officers spoke German.[32]

The Howes worked from their belief that the majority of Americans remained loyal and the revolution was essentially a coup d'etat carried out by rebel committee leaders who had started and spread revolutionary ideas to promote an experiment in government that Loyalists believed would likely lead to anarchy and tyrannical oppression of its citizens. The British army was in America to rescue people already suffering from that developing oppression. While destruction of the Continental Army was certainly a goal, rather than killing everyone in battle, it could be achieved by demoralizing individuals enough that they would desert in the face of insurmountable odds. Continually pressing and fighting moderate battles would do the trick without resulting in large numbers of British casualties.[33]

Howe no longer believed that he could destroy the rebel army during the current campaign and had sent a report to Germain on November 30 proposing a plan to finish the war the next year, if the rebellion and its army did not dissolve over the winter. Believing that it would take General Carleton until September to get south from Canada to Albany, Howe planned to focus on subduing New England, because it had been a cradle of the Revolutionary movement. To carry out his plan he needed an additional ten ships of the line and 15,000 troops hired from Russia or the German states, to give him an army of 35,000 to oppose the estimated 50,000 troops he understood the Continental Congress had authorized to be raised for the 1777 campaign.[34] Howe believed this plan would eliminate any possibility of French aid, cause the rebellion to evaporate, and allow his troops to recover territory that had fallen into the hands of the rebel state governments. Wherever the British army controlled territory, Loyalists would reveal themselves and actively assist British forces to reestablish British governmental authority.[35]

By December 20, things had changed in the Middle States, especially in New Jersey, when Howe sent Germain a radically revised campaign plan for 1777. Howe's latest intelligence estimated there were about 8,000 American troops on the Pennsylvania side of the Delaware, with an additional 500 militiamen in Morris County, and about 3,000 troops at Peekskill and other posts in New York. With Philadelphia vulnerable and the revolution on the verge of collapsing, Howe's 1777 campaign focus was shifting away from New England and towards Philadelphia, the third largest city in the empire, a major seaport, a cosmopolitan center of culture, and the functioning capital for the 13 recently declared independent states. The middle colonies in general had been less in favor of independence, with many people very happy being subjects of Great Britain. Recent British successes that summer and fall had increased opposition to the rebellion and taking Philadelphia would increase it further.

Howe now proposed postponing the advance into New England so he could first send a force against Philadelphia before supporting Carleton in the fall. The British had committed a very large amount of military resources to the war in America, largely to discourage the French from intervening to seek revenge for its defeat in the Seven Years' War. British victories in the summer and fall had held France back from declaring open support for the colonies, but Britain still needed a major victory to prevent greater French involvement. Capturing the rebel capital of Philadelphia would now be the primary objective to end the War for Independence.[36]

Regardless of their reputation for plundering, Howe decided to post Hessians at Trenton and Bordentown because they were normally posted on the left of his line as a badge of honor and those cantonments were on the left of the long chain. Deference to rank and positions of honor were critical to morale and Howe felt, "had I changed it upon this occasion it must have been considered as a disgrace ... and it probably would have created jealousies between the Hessian and British troops, which it was my duty carefully to prevent." Additionally, the Hessians he assigned had demonstrated formidable abilities in combat, including at the capture of Fort Washington.[37]

**Lord Cornwallis, who had led** the forces in New Jersey, was in New York this Christmas Day waiting to board the 64-gun ship of the line *HMS Bristol*, set to depart on December 27. He had been granted leave by Howe to return to England for the winter to spend time with his ailing wife and two-year-old son. Cornwallis was the most aristocratic of the British generals in America and, unusual for his class, he had married for love. He had joined the army at 18, becoming a lieutenant colonel by age 23, and he was now 38 years old and an enthusiastic student of warfare who worked hard at developing his military skills. His physique tended to be heavy, he described himself as "rather corpulent," and he had an eye with a whitish iris, the result of a hockey injury at Eton. He was not pretentious as a soldier and had no patience with pomp, fanfare, and the vanity of titles; instead valuing his reputation for valiant actions in battle and taking care of his men, suffering in the same ways that they did. This made him popular with both officers and enlisted men.

After serving in Europe during the Seven Years' War, Cornwallis entered Parliament where he disapproved of the policies that the colonies protested against. In 1765 he voted against the Stamp Act and then opposed the Declaratory Act that confirmed the absolute authority of Parliament over America. He did not approve of the war, believing the American rebels were free Englishmen standing up for their rights, but volunteered to serve in it anyway from his sense of duty and was promoted to Major General before he left for America. After arriving in America he became less sympathetic, believing the rebels were led by tyrannical and wicked men. He believed the only way to win back the the loyalty of the rebels was to convince them that it was in their best interest to do so. He hoped that the rebellion would end while he was on leave and he would not need to return. General Howe had chosen Cornwallis, for his first independent command, to lead the pursuit of Washington's army across New Jersey, ordering him to keep the rebels retreating but to avoid engaging in a major battle while pursuing Washington as far as Brunswick, just 60 miles from Philadelphia.[38]

However, after determining the advantages of continuing to push Washington, Howe joined Cornwallis with Major General James Grant's brigade and the combined force proceeded to push Washington through Princeton and Trenton to the Pennsylvania side of the Delaware. When Howe discovered that Washington had rendered pursuit impossible by removing all boats from the river, he gave Cornwallis permission to return home on leave and placed the 56-year-old General Grant in command in New Jersey at Brunswick. Howe praised Cornwallis for his leadership during the 80-mile march across New Jersey that prevented the rebels from destroying or removing stores his army needed, all the while dealing with felled trees, destroyed bridges, and enemy ambushes.[39] As a peace commissioner, though, Howe should have been more forceful in curtailing the plundering and abuse of civilians by his British and Hessian troops during the American retreat. Severe plundering of both rebels and Loyalists occurred and General Clinton, second in command to Howe, believed they had no business expecting loyalty from local people while in winter quarters established in areas where plundering and physical abuse occurred.[40]

**Admiral Howe's secretary, Ambrose Serle,** had entered into his diary on December 24 that, "The Declaration or Address of the Congress, dated Decr. 10th, was put into my hands this morning, and … It is full of falsehood, bravado, and despair." He believed that, "it contradicts the knowledge & experience of every man of sense throughout the colonies. I cannot help calling it, one of the dying groans of rebellion." The document he described had been passed in Congress "not only to promote unanimity and vigour through the whole States, but to excite the inhabitants of Pennsylvania, New Jersey, and the adjacent States, to an immediate and spirited exertion in opposition to the army that now threatens to take possession of" Philadelphia. While losing Philadelphia would be fatal to the cause, "yet while it can be saved, let us not, in the close of the campaign, afford them such ground of triumph; but give a check to their progress, and convince our friends in the distant parts that one spirit animates the whole." This document reiterated grievances expressed in the Declaration of Independence and, referring to Howe's November 30 amnesty proclamation, complained that even now "the boasted Commissioners for giving peace to America have not offered, and do not now offer, any terms but pardon on absolute submission." In other words, unconditional surrender.[41]

General Howe's aide Captain Friedrich von Muenchhausen, a 23-year-old Hessian aristocrat known as Fritz to his friends, had arrived in New York on the afternoon of December 24 after completing a three day assignment taking charge of the Koehler Hessian grenadier battalion and a train of English artillery, containing large 18- and 24-pounders, and transported them in seven ships to Amboy. Howe planned to send this force to western New Jersey to reinforce Colonel Donop in the Burlington area to defend against the galleys of the Pennsylvania navy.[42]

**Howe held prisoner in New York** a large number of men captured during the 1776 campaign and most were suffering greatly, considered rebel traitors who did not deserve humane treatment. Connecticut militiaman Oliver Woodruff had been captured with 815 others at the surrender of Fort Washington on November 16 and was imprisoned in New York at New Bridewell, "then unfinished with loose floors, and no windows." Having no fires contributed to the prisoners "suffering more than has ever been written or told."[43] York, Pennsylvania militiaman John Adlum, also captured at Fort Washington and imprisoned at Bridewell, was fortunately paroled to act as a servant to family friend Colonel Robert Magaw, who had surrendered the fort, and a group of paroled American officers quartered with him in a private house belonging to a Mrs. Carroll, who was a favorite of British General Robertson, commandant of the town. To Alexander Graydon, one of Mrs. Carroll's prisoner boarders, "she played her cards with much address, and bent her politics, if she had any, to her interest. She was, no doubt, tory or whig, as best suited the company she happened to be in." She was always willing, for a monetary tip, to provide the prisoners with news or anecdotes she had heard. Her house was not large, but General Robertson had taken possession of the building adjoining which the officers furnished with their own mattresses and blankets. They pooled their weekly coal allowance to supply Mrs. Carroll with a fire for her parlor and kitchen.[44]

Adlum noted that the prisoners "confined in the sugar house and churches began to die very fast" in December due to diseases contracted in the winter cold with lack of adequate food and clothing. In Bridewell there were fireplaces in each room and some wood scattered about which the prisoners took in small amounts when permitted by the guards, but they had to ration it carefully.[45] Colonel Magaw petitioned for better treatment of the men, but burial details were unable to keep up with the deaths by Christmas. About this time, the Commissary of Prisoners, Joshua Loring, husband of Howe's mistress, began releasing large numbers of men, apparently the most sickly and least likely to survive the winter. On December 24, Loring had crowded about 225 New England men aboard the ship *HMS Glasgow* and it sailed for Connecticut.[46]

**General Henry Clinton was at** Newport, Rhode Island, where he had been sent by Howe with an invasion force of more than 6,000 men. Sending Clinton to Rhode Island had distanced him from Howe, and that may have been part of Howe's plan. Clinton was a 48-year-old widower (his 25-year-old wife, Harriet, had died in 1772) with two sons and two daughters who lived with relatives in England. He had joined the army at age 15 and served in the Seven Years War in Germany where he suffered a serious wound in 1762 that caused him pain the rest of his life. He read about and discussed tactics and military matters, reading both ancient and modern writers and especially enjoyed French authors, whom he thought were the best authorities on warfare. He took extensive notes on his reading and believed officers needed to understand the broad political, economic, and geographical contexts of battles.

As a commander, Clinton focused on raids, sieges, and pacification; saving battle for situations where his army was clearly in the advantage. He was a Member of Parliament from 1772 and, while supporting the government of Lord North, was not hawkish on the war and hoped for peace. Unlike the Howes and Cornwallis, he had not opposed the government policies that had led to the colonial protests. He was against the use of the Hessian auxiliaries and would have preferred to settle things without bloodshed, and as noted previously, rather "gain the hearts and subdue the minds of America."[47]

Clinton opposed conciliation, arguing that the objective should be to destroy the rebel army and capture rebel leaders in order to end the rebellion. When ordered to take Rhode Island, he unsuccessfully argued to take troops instead into New Jersey to cut off the rebel retreat, or be sent by sea to Philadelphia so he could take it and the Continental Congress.[48] He believed the war was in its final stages and Howe could crush it quickly.[49] As for Howe's winter quarter cantonments in New Jersey, Clinton had futilely warned him that they were too widely spread apart and vulnerable to attack.[50]

Serving under Clinton, British grenadier Lieutenant John Peebles of the 42nd Regiment of Foot was a veteran of the New York campaign. Born in Scotland, Peebles was 37 years old, well-educated and a veteran of service in America during the French and Indian War. He was about eight or nine years older and had served about three years longer than the average infantry lieutenant. Peebles' company occupied a house at the south end of Newport, while he lived at a tavern. His men carried out their usual daily duties and exercises, with lack of firewood being their greatest concern. The weather was "fine, clear cold" but the streets were so slippery that his battalion received 200 ice creepers to attach to their shoes to give them traction.

This Christmas Day, Peebles was furious about the atrocities committed by some of his fellow soldiers and noted that a man condemned to death for rape was pardoned "at the intercession of the injured party," but that other instances of similar abuses had not yet come "to public notice."[51] Also serving under Clinton, Lieutenant Frederick Mackenzie of the Royal Welsh Fusiliers was interested in the retaking of a British ship that had been taken by the American privateer *Alfred* and sent into Newport not knowing the British had taken control of it.[52]

**Commanding Howe's forces** in New Jersey while Lord Cornwallis was on leave, General James Grant was quartered at Brunswick. Grant was a very bright Scottish clan leader who had studied law at the University of Edinburgh before entering the army. Although he was highly regarded by his superiors, he was hated and despised by those who served under him who often felt he only lived for himself and focused on promoting his own interests. He publicly liked the good things in life, including good food and entertainment. However, his biographer believes Grant was as "passionately devoted to promoting the interests of the British Empire in the last half of the eighteenth century as he was to promoting his own advancement. Indeed, like many public men in that age, he saw no contradiction between the two." He served the crown for over 60 years as soldier, governor, and Member of Parliament and gained much praise from contemporaries and historians, but of course he also had his detractors. In spite of repeated failures, Grant was supported by his superiors and just the day before he had written to Colonel von Donop, commanding at Bordentown, that "We are all in a great favour at home. His majesty has ordered spruce beer to be issued to the Troops," without deducting the cost from their pay, as they celebrated their recent victories.

Grant held both the American rebels and his Hessian soldiers in contempt. To continue the work of pacifying the population, he had sent out Lieutenant Colonel Charles Mawhood and General Alexander Leslie into upper Hunterdon County and Essex County and began to discover just what a vast area of land the British were trying to control and that they were stretching their resources to the limit. Only expecting to serve for a year in America, Grant was greatly disappointed when he had to assume Cornwallis's command. He was pleased, though, that Howe recommended him for the post with the statement that he was an officer "in who's approved good conduct I place the greatest confidence." He believed the war was just about over because the rebels did not have the spirit needed to succeed and even though they might hold out over the winter, they would certainly surrender in the spring. He only agreed to stay in America out of a sense of duty, and in hope of future rewards for his sacrifice.[53]

In the days before Christmas, Grant had received requests from General Howe concerning detachments of men to be sent to Bound Brook, Springfield, New Bridge, Hackensack, Fort Lee, Aquaqanock, Newark, and Morristown, needed to counter attacks from bands of rebels, but he did not want to deplete the forces he had at Princeton. He also was kept constantly busy with details of supplies and wagons to carry them, hospitals, security, intelligence, and wood-cutting tools.[54] Grant also began signing protection papers, strengthening his confidence that the rebellion was collapsing.

On December 22, Grant had recommended to Howe that two regiments be sent to Morristown either to raid that area or to set up a permanent garrison to prevent rebels coming out to ambush British patrols. Howe approved an expedition to Morristown and told Grant that similar "little invasions" would help keep the enemy off balance during the winter, but, with Christmas approaching, Grant temporarily set aside the Morristown plans while he prepared to celebrate the Christmas holiday.[55]

Grant's troops occupying the Jerseys wasted their opportunity to build good will with the people. For example, Princeton had been occupied by British troops under General Alexander Leslie since December 7 and had suffered greatly. Many people had left town and the nearby area abandoning their property and possessions. Those who stayed in their homes could not protect them. British officers took over houses for their use and British soldiers stationed about Princeton burned up firewood residents had collected for the winter, in addition to stripping wood from houses and shops, fences, wood supplies of carpenters and joiners, and cutting down fruit trees. Both tanned and untanned leather was taken for apparently no other reason than to make it scarce. Some buildings, such as a gristmill with its wheat and flour, a fulling mill with its cloth, and the recently built large house of delegate to Congress Jonathan D. Sergeant, were burned down either by accident or design.[56]

Leslie's troops were paid on December 23 and routine matters in the day's orders included ordering that an officer strictly examin the "necessaries" every Saturday. Some of the soldiers had apparently sold government property to civilians for extra income, so the sergeant majors of the two regiments in Princeton notified residents not to buy anything from the soldiers, or face a 40 shilling fine. To help win hearts and minds, troops were ordered not to mistreat or impose on "the country people bringing in provisions to market." Additionally, sentries were "to let the country people pass into town on the market day without stopping them." The brigade wagons and the quartermaster sergeant of each regiment or battalion, escorted by a sergeant and 12 men, had been sent to Brunswick on December 24 to obtain a four day supply of flour and rum. Work parties had been organized to cut and deliver fire wood and build a guard house. Empty flour barrels were ordered delivered to the commissary, because new ones could not be provided. Because the local civilians were in "great want of sheep skins" and "bullocks hydes," the army butchers were permitted to "dispose of them for their own profit."[57]

**The British 17th Regiment of Foot** was quartered at Hillsborough just north of Princeton and concerned with proper forage distribution. Its commander, Lieutenant Colonel Charles Mawhood, was a 24-year veteran of the army who was highly respected by his men. He was a bit eccentric and routinely rode into battle on a brown pony accompanied by a pair of spaniels. He boarded with a Dutch doctor who noted he often spoke freely about politics, was opposed to the American war, and called Lord North "a villain for being the cause of it." On the evening of Christmas Day, Mawhood "was blaming the English generals for dispersing the army so much in Jersey and said if he was in General Washington's place he would make an attack on several of the principal posts at the same time, that they were all so weak that he might certainly cut them off and be in possession of Jersey in a few days." He prophetically mentioned specifically Trenton, Burlington and Mount Holly as possible American targets.[58]

Among the officers in the 17th Regiment of Foot was General Leslie's 25-year-old nephew, Captain William Leslie, known to family and friends as "Willie." On Christmas Day, Captain Leslie wrote his mother a letter from Hillsborough giving her news about an old family friend, Dr. Benjamin Rush, who had become acquainted with the family while a medical student in Edinburgh, and had he remained in Scotland might well have married one of the Leslie girls.

Willie told his mother, "I'm afraid Rush has not only joined the American Cause, but likewise denied Allegiance to his King – Mr. Witherspoon who was President of the College at Princetown is obliged to fly for the same crime." He noted that the "famous College is now turned into a barrack." Altogether, "the desolation that this unhappy country has suffered must distress every feeling heart, altho the inhabitants deserve it as much as any sort of people who ever rebelled against their Sovereign." They had brought this on themselves because they had "lived in plenty even to luxury, every man was equal to his neighbor & not one beggar in the whole country; but now too late they feel [page torn] the ravages of war, every day pres[ents] objects of distress." He had observed "great numbers" of people responding to the Howe's proclamation. He then reported his own good health, in spite of the "severe campaign" and his hopes for the health of those at home.[59] Captain Leslie carried with him a letter from Dr. Rush that he could give to any American officer if he was captured. The letter could be forwarded to General Washington or General Lee, with the request that Leslie be given parole and Rush offered his house in Philadelphia to be Leslie's home until exchanged.[60]

THE ARTICLES OF WAR WERE read to the British troops this Christmas Day, in addition to the regular daily orders. Howe gave his commanding officers permission to grant each company captain and subaltern, in turn, ten days leave to go to New York City. The December 25 general orders rather routinely stated there would be a brigade court martial the next morning at 11:00am and the men assigned to a patrol the next day were to cook one day's provisions that evening. Rum for the patrol was to be put in canteens, but not delivered to the men until they paraded. The daily orders were amended at 3:00pm to emphasize the importance of properly manning guard posts, sending out frequent patrols during the night, and preventing "depredations & disorders," because "the security of the garrison entirely depends upon their doing their duty properly as soldiers."[61]

Basically, the British felt things were under control and routine, but they still needed to be alert. But, did they really have everything under control? Aside from the military men, how much did the widely separated people in the American states know about the current situation and how did they feel about it? Were they really as ready to give up their struggle as the British leaders believed?

# Chapter 3

## America, Wednesday, December 25, 1776

Three days before Christmas, Scottish born New York Brigadier General Alexander McDougall was at Morristown in northern New Jersey where the new Continental Army for 1777 was slowly being assembled. McDougall notified Washington that New Jersey was "totally deranged, without government, or officers civil or military in it that will act with any spirit. Many of them have gone to the enemy for protection, others are out of the state, and the few that remain are mostly indecisive in their conduct. The militia are without leaders and many of them are dispirited. Besides they have numerous and active enemies and false friends among them." He anticipated even worse conditions now that the State was under British control.[1] New Jersey Assembly Speaker John Hart found his Hopewell house plundered, his wife deceased, and his children hiding out on Sourland Mountain. Hart joined them and hid out among the rocks for several weeks.[2] Even beyond the British controlled areas, Loyalists were helping to administer oaths of allegiance in exchange for protection papers and in Monmouth County, Loyalists posted notices at taverns that all able-bodied men of militia age, 16-50, should gather with their arms at the Freehold court house on December 30 to take the oath and the county militia, formed by the new State government, should assemble to support the British government.[3]

**Although the British** felt things looked positive for the next campaign, some Americans believed the British had made fatal mistakes in 1776. Ashbel Green, a New Jersey teenager who would serve as a militia sergeant and after the war become a Presbyterian minister declared, "Never was war conducted with less wisdom than the war of our revolution, on the part of the mother country." He believed British leaders should have known that the Americans were "a people brought up under free institutions [who] can never be governed by mere force and compulsion, unless the force be absolutely overwhelming, and be constantly applied" and they could not "be subdued except by kindness, and a treatment marked by a strict regard to equity and humanity." He recalled people saying that during the devastating December occupation of the Jerseys that "the whole population could have been bought for eighteen pence a head," but when the Howe's offer of pardon and protection proved hollow, "the Jerseymen became some of the most obstinate and inveterate enemies to British domination in the whole country."[4]

Harsh British actions produced a hard core of people determined to carry on, even when things looked very bleak, and the spirit of the Revolution remained so strong among some of Washington's troops that if the army ceased to exist, remnants of it would likely withdraw to remote areas while local militias could be strengthened to keep the Revolution going in populated areas.[5] Many supporters of the War for Independence believed they could pass that test, but were eager to avoid it.

While some Americans on Christmas Day saw reasons to hope for success, many others feared that the story of their nearly six-month old confederation of independent American states would be recorded in history books as a small event in the story of the British empire and end with words to the effect that "a fickle people, impatient of the restraints of regular government, had in a fit of passion abolished that of Great Britain, and established in its room free constitutions of their own, but these new establishments, from want of wisdom in their rulers, or of spirit in their people, were no sooner formed than annihilated," and surviving political and military leaders executed.[6] Those Americans convinced that only independence from Great Britain would guarantee their traditional freedoms and see them passed on to succeeding generations, feared their struggle was on the brink of failure, while those desiring to remain British citizens welcomed what appeared to be the final days of the rebellion. The many people who simply wanted to conduct their lives as best they could and cared little for politics just hoped that peace might soon be restored. In spite of General Howe's failure to end the rebellion using a combination of superior military force and offers of amnesty, the people of New Jersey had been cowed as much as if Howe had destroyed the Continental Army in a devastating battle.[7]

Between 1774 and 1776 rebel leaders had taken over legislative, judicial, and executive functions from the colonial governments, including control of the militias that they now used in combat against the British army and to enforce compliance with their new governments. The Continental Congress created a Continental Army and put George Washington in command. This army forced the British military to evacuate Boston, but the subsequent New York campaign had cost it hundreds of casualties and over 4,000 men taken prisoner, shrinking the army from about 20,000 to only about 3,500 men, along with the loss of over 200 cannon, thousands of cannonballs, and almost 3,000 muskets. This had led Thomas Paine to write *The American Crisis* and famously proclaim, "These are the times that try men's souls."[8]

Most of the men remaining in the army were inadequately clothed, retreating, short-timers whose one-year enlistments ended on or about December 31. In September, the Continental Congress had authorized raising a new, longer term, army, hopefully including veterans from 1776, but the ability to create this new army "was both distant and uncertain." According to contemporary historian David Ramsay, the December 13 capture of General Charles Lee "caused a depression of spirits among the Americans, far exceeding any real injury done to their essential interests." There was even speculation that Lee "chose to fall into the hands of the British," and although there was no foundation to those suspicions, "they produced the same extensive mischief, as if they had been realities." At a time when the British army seemed invincible and many people were seeking pardons, the loss of an officer many people considered him the best American general, "was to many an extinguishment of every hope."[9]

Many people distrusted the remaining Continental Army general officers whom they saw as "heaven-taught and book-taught" and advanced by seniority rather than ability.[10] Even some of Washington's closest colleagues doubted his abilities to successfully prosecute the war. As early as the fall of Fort Washington in November, Major

General Charles Lee and Washington's Adjutant General, Joseph Reed, had privately expressed doubts to each other about Washington's "fatal indecision of mind which in war is a much greater disqualification than stupidity or even want of personal courage—accident may put a decisive Blunderer in the right—but eternal defeat and miscarriage must attend the man of the best parts if curs'd with indecision."[11]

Some people saw a glimmer of hope. One of Washington's aides, 23-year-old Samuel B. Webb of Connecticut, believed the American situation "has been the Devil, but is to appearance better." The reduced and battered Continental Army had "been obliged to run damn'd hard before abt 10,000 of the enemy," but "never was finer lads at a retreat than we are." He believed any additional British troop movements would result in "no fun for us that I can see; however, I cannot but think we shall drub the dogs" and "all will come right one of these days."[12]

Lieutenant Colonel William Tudor, Washington's 26-year-old Judge Advocate General, in a letter to his future wife, Delia Jarvis, on December 24, reflected the steadfast loyalty many people felt towards Washington. He told her that he had lost all hope of returning home anytime soon, but declared he could not "desert" Washington, a man who had "deserted every thing to defend his country" even though a large part of that country lacked the "spirit to defend itself." Tudor loved his country and was sure that Delia's "friendship would revolt at the idea of my quitting it's service disreputably … at a crisis important as the present," even though she came from the Loyalist Jarvis family of Boston. However, he was concerned about the apparent lack of spirit for the cause in Boston and closed with, "I often blush for my native town."[13]

Several days before Christmas, Virginia Brigadier General Adam Stephen, who had known Washington since they served together in the French and Indian War, wrote to Thomas Jefferson that, "The enemy like locusts sweep the Jerseys with the besom of destruction. They to the disgrace of a civilisd nation ravish the fair sex, from the age of ten to seventy. The Tories are baneful in pointing out the friends to the American Cause, and giving notice of every motion we make." Stephen mistakenly felt that, "owing to the weakness of our counsels and our attempt to maintain the Forts Washington and Lee" the British had made even greater progress in the campaign than they anticipated. He knew that America's only salvation lay in raising the new army as quickly as possible and he was encouraged by the overly optimistic news reports, from October, that France was "on the eve of a war with England." But, he feared that the anticipated loss of Philadelphia "will go near to ruin us. They will open the port, give great prices for wheat and flour and seduce the body of the people."[14] Washington wrote to Robert Morris in Philadelphia declaring, "I hope the next Christmas will prove happier than the present to you." But, his intelligence reports still indicated that the British intended to move on Philadelphia "as soon as the ice is sufficiently strong" and that the British winter quarters were only a feint. An intercepted letter written by a Loyalist with the British to a friend in Philadelphia confirmed the British planned to take possession of Philadelphia by December 26, or as soon as the river ice allowed it.[15]

Many Americans agreed with Stephen that the new Continental Army was necessary and should be the primary force defending the independence of the thirteen states, while the militia played a lesser role. When fighting had first broken out, leaders believed that the "virtue" and defiance of patriotic citizens acting collectively and serving in local militias would win the war handily. However, since declaring independence, Americans had come to realize that participating in protests against the acts of Parliament, or turning out during the *rage militaire* that grew from the initial successes around Boston, was completely different than facing the British army in continuous combat over many months. Dr. Benjamin Rush lamented that there were so many "furious Whigs who considered the tarring and feathering of a Tory as a greater duty and exploit than the extermination of a British army. … These men were generally cowards, and shrunk from danger when called into the field by pretending sickness or some family disaster."[16]

Suspicious of hierarchical elites and standing armies, while strongly believing that independence was inevitable, many Americans dismissed altogether the need for an army. However, once the revolutionary leaders reluctantly agreed that the Continental Army was an absolute necessity, they subjected its operations to exaggerated praise or criticism. Other people, feeling tied to the ultimate success of the army, often sought to downplay its potential evil.[17] Enlistment terms had previously been set at one year, to prevent the creation of a professional army, but now, with the prospect of a long war, Congress had authorized raising a new army enlisted for three years, or the duration of the war. The new army would dissolve if the war ended in less than three years, but if hostilities continued beyond three years it would stay intact until the war ended.[18] The enlistment terms were not always clear to potential recruits, many of whom were looking for short enlistments. This partly accounts for why recruiting was already difficult and it would continue to be weak if the 1776 campaign produced only military defeat and retreat.

Upon exiting New York, Washington had not retreated to a defensible position at Morristown, where he had small numbers of militia and troops being raised for the new army, because that would leave the way open for the British to advance on Philadelphia. However, by retreating into Pennsylvania he had essentially left the British in control of New Jersey, thereby giving encouragement to anyone leaning towards the Loyalists and discouraging those who supported the war for independence to any degree. General Howe then reinforced Loyalist support by establishing his cantonments across the State, even though they seemed to be stretched a little thin. Washington had put together his own spy network to keep him informed about the enemy and, acting on the advice of General Lee, began to place more trust in his own judgement rather than always making decisions in a council of war, but he still consulted with his officers separately before a council so that "he alone knew what all had recommended."[19]

**Believing that the British** were intent on attacking Philadelphia before ending the 1776 campaign, and at the strong urging of Major General Israel Putnam and Brigadier General Thomas Mifflin, the Continental Congress left town on December 12 to convene at Baltimore on December 20. The last resolution of Congress before adjourning and leaving Philadelphia stated "that, until the Congress shall otherwise order, General Washington be possessed of full power to order and direct all things relative to the department, and the operations of war."[20] In many ways Washington was on his own and almost a military dictator.

Some New England delegates opposed the relocation of Congress as being unnecessary and because it took them further from the scene of action and their own states. Looking for a benefit, Elbridge Gerry felt there were fewer Loyalists at Baltimore to "diffuse their poisonous & destructive principles to the weak & wavering."[21] But, the enemy was within striking distance of Philadelphia, adding to the fear that "the people of Pennsylvania, influenced by fear, folly or treachery, would have surrendered their capital to appease the anger of the two [Howe] Brothers, and atone for their crime in suffering it to remain so long the seat of rebellion." On the positive side, Sam Adams was hearing exaggerated reports that the people had risen to defend themselves and "that hundreds are flocking daily" to join Washington. This optimistically raised his hope that Washington would successfully strike back and "if our Army are as expeditious in pursuing as they have been in retreating, we may hope they will take the enemy all prisoners before they will be able to reach the borders of Hudsons River."[22]

A major concern of the Congress since declaring independence had been writing Articles of Confederation to formalize the new government of independent states. It had now been six months and, while articles had been proposed, nothing had been finalized. Discussions had been delayed by delegate absences and by hesitation to initiate debates that would bring out antagonisms between the new states on a number of issues. Although it was one of the areas of disagreement, the Congress had agreed to restructure the Continental Army, putting control of the army more firmly in the hands of Congress and the commander-in-chief, rather than the 13 states with their various ideas and jealousies. The new plan did not completely eliminate these issues, so top officer assignments and basic necessities, such as provisioning the army, continued to trouble Congress and hurt the army.[23]

Rather than go to Baltimore, delegate to Congress Dr. Benjamin Rush sent his family to a relative's house in Cecil County, Maryland and some of his furniture and all of his books to the house of a patient near Darby, Pennsylvania. He joined the volunteer Philadelphia Associator militia forming under Colonel John Cadwalader. Rush later stated, "I was then resolved to stand or fall with my country. I accompanied my fellow citizens to Bristol [Pennsylvania] ... superintending their health, and encouraging them to firmness and perseverance in defense of our liberties and independance."[24]

Delegate Robert Morris sent away his family, books, papers and many valuables, but at Washington's request remained in Philadelphia to carry on Congressional work until forced to leave.[25] Washington expected the British to attack the city when the Delaware iced over and after army enlistments expired at the end of the year, in the belief that "you might as well attempt to stop the winds from blowing or the sun in its diurnal as stop" soldiers from leaving when their time was up. Morris did all he could to get the various Continental warships out to sea and prepare for removal of all Continental stores from the city, while continually dealing with the declining value of Continental currency and the many people refusing to accept it. He warned John Hancock that, "Some effectual remedy shou'd be speedily applyed to this evil or the game will be up." Already, grist mills refused to grind grain for the army commissary "either from disaffection or dislike to the money."[26] To find a way to stabilize or reverse these inflated prices throughout the new states, a multi-state convention began meeting at Providence, Rhode Island on December 25, with delegates from Massachusetts, Rhode Island, Connecticut, and New Hampshire.[27]

One urgent need was to provide the troops with clothing and Morris promised to do what he could to expedite making clothing, but most of the local tailors were serving with the Pennsylvania militia. Morris listed the items captured at sea by the *Andrew Doria* and brought to Philadelphia; including stockings, jackets, coats, blankets, muskets, and many other necessary items. These items had been earmarked for the Continental regiments being raised, but the current need was dire and he asked Washington to let him know which items were needed for his troops.[28] Another issue was completing construction of the Continental warships and Morris needed tradesmen to finish the frigate *Delaware* but, again, the needed tradesmen were out in the militia and could not be released.[29] Other items were also badly needed and when Captain Morris of the Light Horse of Philadelphia was asked by the Commissary General on this Christmas Day to excuse Corporal James Hunter to return to Philadelphia to make needed quantities of soap and candles, Captain Morris refused because he judged Hunter to be too important to the troop.[30]

Morris wished he would hear that the desperately needed new army regiments had been filled with recruits and expected Congress would soon ask for even more troops to be raised.[31] Army recruitment in New England was going very slowly, partly "owing to that excessive rage for privateering" that infected them. Many Continental soldiers were just waiting for their enlistments to expire so "that they may partake of the spoils of the West Indies."[32] His concern was shared by New Hampshire delegate William Whipple in Baltimore who was aware of the pillage and rape in New Jersey and predicted that if the British should invade New England "we are to expect, if possible, greater cruelties than New Jersey has experienced." Whipple had not heard from New Hampshire for more than a month, but hoped to hear that the new regiments were nearly completed. Like Morris, he anticipated another regiment would be required from New Hampshire because the army needed to be even larger than currently planned.[33]

Samuel Adams was also concerned about the slow progress being made to raise the new troops in New England. He knew these troops would be needed to counter a British campaign there in the spring because, "the British Tyrant will not quit his darling object of subduing" New England, believing the rest of the colonies would then surrender. He noted the troops under Clinton in Rhode Island and, not knowing of Carleton's retreat back to Canada, expected he would take Ticonderoga when Lake Champlain froze. He expected that "the infamous behavior of the people of Jersey & Pennsylvania will give fresh spirit to the British Court," and encourage them to seek up to 20,000 additional troops from "every power in Europe where they can have any prospect of success." Rumor had it that Russia had already been approached. It was now necessary for all Americans "to strain every nerve to defeat their design. The time is short. Let this be the only subject of our thought and consultation." The one positive situation he saw was that Howe's troops had penetrated Jersey further than intended and, thus weakened, Adams felt they could be driven back to New York for winter quarters.[34]

For those still in Philadelphia, the December 24 issue of the *Philadelphia Evening Post* consisted of only two pages, rather than the normal four, and contained news from other states dating from October through early December, along with more recent news from the city. Thomas Paine's *The American Crisis*, first published as a pamphlet on December 19, was advertised as "printed and sold by Styner and Cist, six doors above Arch Street, in Second Street." The Loyalist *New York Gazette* announced the previous day the publication of a pamphlet entitled *The True Interest of America Impartially Stated* that had been written to counter Paine's arguments.[35] There was also information on the encounters between British troops and American forces under Virginia Colonel Samuel Griffin in the area of Mount Holly, New Jersey several days earlier. Philadelphians were apprehensive that the British would very soon advance on their city.[36]

**Moving to Baltimore had not** been easy for the Congressional delegates. John Hancock described his move as "really distressing," because his wife had given birth just nine days previously and he had a large family and a number of possessions. He found "such a number of passengers on the road" that it was difficult to find shelter among strangers. His family bore the journey well and although no residence had been arranged in advance, he was accommodated for ten days by important Baltimore patriot Samuel Purviance and his wife. Hancock expressed his gratitude for their "utmost civility" and actions "free from ceremony, & desirous of making our stay agreeable." When he was finally able to rent a house, it meant moving from the comfort of the Purviance's house in a good part of town to living "in a remote place, among whores & thieves." Hancock told friends that "I had not been forty eight hours at my house before it was Rob'd. The thieves took out a trunk with linen books, papers, some hard money &c. but the money was recover'd & part of the things." To secure his home, he was "oblig'd to keep a good watch lest they should take every thing out of the house."[37]

Other delegates were also not entirely pleased with their accommodations. William Ellery of Rhode Island wrote on Christmas Eve, "I should like the place well enough if it was less distant from the Army, less dirty and less expensive. It is long since I have heard from my constituents." He felt he had no more knowledge of how matters stood in Rhode Island than "an inhabitant of the moon." He hoped that his family had been able to escape when the British army came on December 8 and that Congress would provide a salary raise because living costs kept rising.[38] Connecticut's Oliver Wolcott also found Baltimore "too dirty and too dear," as well as too distant from "my friends."[39] Benjamin Harrison of Virginia wrote to Robert Morris that, "If you wish to please your friends come soon to us, but if you desire to keep out of the damdest hole in the world come not here."[40] On a more positive note, New Hampshire's William Whipple felt that Congress was "now doing business with more spirit then they have for some time past." He hoped the air in Baltimore, which he found much purer than Philadelphia's, "will brace up the weak nerves. I think it already has that affect."[41]

More than good air was needed, because, as William Ellery noted, recent events had been attended by "a fatality strange;" the loss of Fort Washington and 2,600 men, the loss of Fort Lee and a large quantity of stores, and the capture of General Charles Lee.[42] Elbridge Gerry noted there was concern that even some high ranking leaders were rumored to be giving up. However, Gerry also thought there was "a prospect of checking the progress of the enemy in the Jersies very soon, as the militia are in motion in the middle Colonies & will very generally turn out." Given the turnout of the Pennsylvania militia and the arrival of Lee's troops under General Sullivan, if they were employed in spirited operations they could make the British "retreat to their kennel in New York."[43] Dr. Rush wrote to Richard Henry Lee the same day that, "Col: Griffin with only 800 men keeps How's whole army under constant alarms in [southern] New Jersey. He has had several successful skirmishes with them. Our militia who croud in daily call aloud for action!"[44]

Some men were discouraged and reluctant to turn out, but he explained "their backwardness does not proceed from want of spirit, but from a dissatisfaction … with the Constitutions formed for their future governments, with many of the people now in power, with the scarcity & high price of salt and many other articles." If supporters of independence did not like how things were developing, those opposed to the revolution "take advantage of the present confusion, work on the fears of the timid, incite the jealousies of the suspicious and in short one way or other prevent the force of the Country from being exerted in this day of Tryal."[45]

Contemporary historian David Ramsay was impressed that while Congress was "devising plans to save the states from sinking under the heavy calamities which were bearing them down," it was "remarkable" that Congress never entertained "the most distant idea of purchasing peace, by returning to the condition of British subjects." Congress also recommended that each State "appoint a day of solemn fasting and humiliation, to implore of Almighty God the forgiveness of their many sins, and to beg the countenance and assistance of his providence, in the prosecution of the present just and necessary war."[46]

Dr. Rush, now with the army, saw that, "the sufferings of our brave Continental troops from the want of cloaths exceed all description." He asked Congress to do nothing for at least three weeks except work on clothing and officering the army. He speculated, "Suppose an application is made to every man in America for one or two of his own shirts for the benefit of the Army? The application I am sure will be successful." He had been told that even distributing second hand clothing three months ago would have resulted in the reenlistment of "three fourths of the poor ragged fellows whose times are now expired."[47] New Hampshire delegate Matthew Thornton considered the inadequate support thus far provided to Continental soldiers to be life threatening. He wrote, "An inexcuseable neglect in the offi[ce]rs, want of fidelity, honour, & humanity, in the D[octo]rs, & averice in the suttlers, has slain ten soldiers to the enemies one, & will soon prevent everyman of common sense from putting his life, & fortune in the power of such as destroy both without pity, or mercy." He recommended each state regulate the sutlers (camp following merchants) since each state took care of its own men.[48]

Contemporary historian David Ramsey wrote shortly after the war that for many delegates to Congress the only path to success required assistance from European countries jealous of Britain's power. Some delegates proposed to offer France "the same monopoly of their trade, which Great Britain had hitherto enjoyed." However, critics noted this would "destroy the force of many arguments heretofore used in favour of independence, and probably disunite their citizens." When the proposal was modified to "offer a monopoly of certain enumerated articles of produce" the conflicting interests of the states produced so much opposition that the idea was scrapped. Congress also rejected the proposal to offer France "a league offensive and defensive."

Delegates conversant with international politics believed that France would aid them only when it was convinced that the Americans were determined to win, and were capable of maintaining, their independence, thereby reducing Britain's power. Congress, therefore, resolved to continue fighting for independence and offer "freedom of trade to every foreign nation." Copies of the resolutions were sent to "the principal courts of Europe, and proper persons were appointed to solicit their friendship to the new formed states." These resolutions fell into British hands and were published, exactly what Congress hoped would happen to help convince other countries of Britain's valid fears, show that the conflict was more than just "a domestic quarrel," demonstrate the colonists' determination to succeed, and see that assisting the Americans would be sound policy for countries who "wished for the dismemberment of the British empire."[49] However, the delegates also knew that the British Court was "trying every art in their power" to dissuade every Court in Europe from helping.[50] Even without public support from France, the American struggle for independence was already part of a multi-state power struggle. John Adams later wrote, "A compleat History of the American war . . . is nearly the History of Mankind for the whole Epocha of it. The History of France, Spain, Holland, England, and the Neutral Powers, as well as America are at least comprised in it."[51]

The Congressional delegates read in the December 24 shortened issue of *Dunlap's Maryland Gazette* that as of December 19, "the main body of the enemy's forces are yet at Trenton, from which place they send out parties of infantry and cavalry to harass the country, and procure provisions." To counter them, Washington had sent detachments across the Delaware River into "the Jersies to harass the enemy and intercept their supplies of provisions, which it was expected might soon oblige them to retreat." The Maryland militia was urged to "comply with the recommendation of the Continental Congress, by marching without delay to reinforce General Washington's army, that a stop may be put to the progress of these cruel Foreign Spoilers." The Hessians were reported to have sent troops to Burlington, but the Pennsylvania row galleys had made them abandon it and the American troops positioned in Bucks County for more than forty miles along the river, joined by Philadelphia city and Pennsylvania county volunteer militia companies, left "no doubt but the enemy will be repulsed with great slaughter, if they should attempt to cross the river."

To encourage more enlistments in the expanding Continental Army, there was the report that Congress now allowed the option of enlisting for three years, unless discharged earlier, rather than only for the duration of the war. There was also a notice that unpatriotic people were not accepting Continental money in payment for goods. A December 19 report from the Council of Safety at Annapolis stated that some people had taken it into their hands to order the unjust banishment of suspected – but not proven – loyalists. Everyone should "discourage such extrajudicial and disorderly proceedings, tending in their consequences to prejudice the common cause, and to the destruction of order and regular government." With the city in danger of attack, information was given on troops in Philadelphia and the need for people to assist in erecting fortifications "in and about the city." To prevent panic, stores and shops were told to conduct business as usual. The people of Philadelphia were reported to be in good spirits and there were the usual announcements of runaway indentured servants, apprentices, horses, etc. and sales of property and other items.[52]

The Continental Congress conducted normal business on Christmas Eve dealing with various letters and a number of issues concerning money, supplies – especially artillery and ammunition - and the threat to Fort Ticonderoga from the British troops in Canada under Sir Guy Carleton. Then Congress adjourned and took Christmas Day off.[53]

**Throughout the American states,** people not involved with the army or the new government were dealing with their immediate, individual situations produced at least partly by the disruptive, still inconclusive war. Twenty-six-year-old Englishman Nicholas Cresswell found himself on Christmas Eve at Pennyroyal Hill in Frederick County, Virginia, staying with William Gibbs and directing workmen constructing a pump for Gibbs's "still house." Cresswell had come to America from Derbyshire, England in 1774 hoping to find a successful business venture. Instead, he had become involved in the colonial controversies and war for independence. He felt no commitment to either side and, after failing in enterprises in the west, just wanted to return to England. He noted in his diary that Christmas was "but very little observed in this country except it is amongst the Dutch." He had spent a long time in Virginia avoiding the pitfalls of the war while suffering from illness and finding that he was drinking alcohol more heavily and more often. He was convinced that the Revolution was very tragically leading to social decline and loss of liberty. Although leaders promised people impracticable freedoms, they were instead subject to "all the dreadful horrors of war, poverty and wretchedness" and he saw Virginia "turn'd Topsy Turvy changed from an earthly paradice, to a Hell, upon Terra Firma."

Only two months previously he had lamented that "religion is almost forgot, or most basely neglected" and religious leaders, especially the Presbyterian clergy, were focusing on delivering political messages from the pulpit. However, he also had little use for British government actions and believed that in "the short space of three years, the villainous arts of a few and the obstinacy of the many, on this side of the water added to the complicated blunders, cowardice, and knavery of some of our blind guides in England has totally ruined this country." The Americans had chosen leaders "from the most violent part of the people" who were "in general very fond of using their usurped authority without mercy" and were comfortable using force to compel loyalty to their side of the conflict with the result that "under the fallacious pretence of nursing the tender plant, Liberty, which was said to thrive so well in American soil, [the Revolution leaders] have actually tore it up by the very root."

The only hope he saw for the Americans was to "awake from their delirium and refuse further to submit to the new tyranny."[54] For Cresswell, it would be a blessing if the Revolution was indeed nearing failure.

Travelers often provided eyewitness war reports and on a December evening in Plymouth, Massachusetts, Elkanah Watson joined with a group of "devoted Whigs" talking with a Continental officer who had recently left the army during its retreat across New Jersey. The officer vividly described the widespread deep discouragement so that

Watson and his friends "looked upon the contest as near its close," and the Americans as "a vanquished people." They discussed their probable imminent need to emigrate to "some spot where liberty dwelt, and where the arm of British tyranny" did not reach. On a positive note, the officer told them that "Washington was not dismayed, but evinced the same serenity and confidence as ever." Everyone agreed that all their hopes rested on Washington.[55]

Newspapers provided limited and often quite out of date information. Readers of the December 24 issue of the *Freeman's Journal or New Hampshire Gazette* found Howe's November 30 proclamation inviting pardon printed in full and an item dated December 14 reported, "that general Howe, and about 9000 of his troops, are at Brunswick and Elizabeth Town; that general Washington, with part of the American army, are in the enemy's front, at Princeton and Trenton, and the generals Lee, Gates and Sullivan, in their rear; so that we may daily expect important intelligence from that quarter." The most recent news was that Washington had retreated to Trenton on December 3rd and the army was considerably reduced in size, but was being reinforced by New Jersey and Pennsylvania militia, with additional reinforcements expected from General Charles Lee and Major General Horatio Gates. While the paper gave a very positive spin to things, there was still the fearful belief that the British were preparing to attack Philadelphia.[56] Fearing the loss of New Jersey, Washington had ordered Lee to join him to attack the British so that the people of New Jersey, especially the militia, would not feel they were being abandoned. If New Jersey fell, Pennsylvania might fall next and that would be a fatal blow. Lee, who was seeking to replace Washington and spreading the idea that Washington was not up to the task, delayed obeying Washington's order and New Jersey came under British control.[57]

**In southern New Jersey,** Swedish citizen and Lutheran minister Nicholas Collin served churches at Penn's Neck and Swedesboro and, while not enthusiastic about the Revolution, did his best to deal with the violence around him. Collin recorded "there was constant alarm" as the British spread over New Jersey in November and December. People were afraid to visit his church, because authorities might show up to impress both horses and men. He noted that before the Continental

Army retreated through the State, nearly everyone had "been eager" to participate in the war, but "now as the fire came closer, many drew away, and there was much dissension among the people." He "saw the roads full of naked, half dead soldiers; several thousands of them died from dysentery and army fever." People became scared and "many concealed themselves in the woods, or within their houses." Some men were forced into the militia while others resisted or refused to turn out and about Christmas he was at his Penn's Neck church when a young man was shot at while trying to escape from going out on militia duty. Collin recorded that the young man "hurried up on his horse and away; [and] the bullet which barely missed him, penetrated deeply into an oak tree." This action led to "dreadful quarreling" between supporters of both sides that threatened to develop into bloodshed until Collin stepped in and lectured the quarrelers on their mad, un-Christian behavior and told them he would not conduct further church services until their behavior improved.[58]

**Colonel Anthony Wayne of Pennsylvania** commanded the roughly 1700 American troops still stationed at Fort Ticonderoga, many of whose enlistments expired on January 5.[59] While Wayne did not have to deal with any imminent British attack, he was dealing with a number of war related problems. His men did not have proper clothing, many items needed for survival were in very short supply, many men were sick or weak from hunger, and all were discouraged. Wayne was furious that his superior, General Philip Schuyler, only sent mundane orders to keep the men and quarters clean, and sweep out chimneys every two weeks, but did not mention important items such as sending supplies and arranging to improve the fort's defenses. Wayne was also deeply concerned by reports that several junior colonels were about to be promoted over him. This was a common complaint among the Continental officers and, if it was true, he planned to retire from the army and return home. However, while other officers in similar situations left the army, Wayne did not.[60]

Massachusetts Colonel Asa Whitcomb had two sons in his regiment at Ticonderoga whom he designated as his waiters. One was a trained shoemaker and set up a workbench in his father's quarters to help keep the soldiers' worn shoes in repair. Some of the "gentlemen" officers from other states, especially Pennsylvania, found this arrangement demeaning to Whitcomb's rank. This Christmas Day, Lieutenant Colonel Craig of Wayne's Pennsylvania regiment, probably inebriated, vowing to teach Whitcomb proper respect for his rank, broke into his quarters, smashed the cobbler's bench, and attacked the elderly colonel, bruising him badly. When Massachusetts soldiers came to their colonel's defense, Pennsylvania troops rushed to the scene where they fired 30 or 40 rounds while driving the Massachusetts men from their huts and barracks, severely wounding several. Craig calmed things by sending several Pennsylvania soldiers into the woods where they shot a fat bear and Craig invited Colonel Whitcomb and his officers to share in making a meal of it. Whitcomb forgave Craig and everything returned to normal, although it took several weeks for some of the wounds received by Massachusetts men to heal. Doctor James Thacher of the Massachusetts troops explained Whitcomb's faux pas by commenting that, "our Colonel is a serious, good man, but is more conversant with the economy of domestic life than the [military] etiquette practiced in camp."[61]

**At the Bethlehem, Pennsylvania** military hospital all the doctors not on duty had celebrated "the vigils of Christmas Eve," but during Christmas Day a courier interrupted them to deliver orders to Dr. William Shippen and his principal surgeons "to report at once to the army of Washington, who was moving to the surprise of the Hessians at Trenton." Dr. Shippen had just arrived after riding through a heavy snow storm from the Oxford Furnace in northwestern New Jersey.[62] He was now one of very few people outside Washington's inner circle who knew that he was going to go on the offensive and attack Trenton. The vast majority of Americans believed both Armies were settled in winter quarters and Washington was going to spend the winter rebuilding his army in Pennsylvania after losing the city and environs of New York and leave New Jersey occupied by the British.

**If most Americans** believed that the British were settled into winter quarters to rest, resupply, recoup their energy, and prepare for the next campaign, while the Continental Army was simply struggling to survive the winter, was their perception accurate? Although communication was irritatingly slow for everyone, the Hessians at Trenton were close enough to have daily contact with their enemy and obtain current information from any local inhabitants they lived among who wanted to help them. They should be completely aware of their particular situation.

Those Hessians are often described as enjoying the more relaxed duties of winter quarters and celebrating the holiday season, including heavy rum consumption, while feeling completely safe from the dispirited, ragged Americans just across the Delaware River from them. But, does that description reflect reality? Were the Hessians enjoying the holiday in high spirits? Just like their counterparts across the Delaware River with Washington, they had been through a debilitating campaign between July and November so they felt they deserved one.

**Table 1: American Troops in South Jersey – December 25, 1776**

**Griffin's Brigade, New Jersey Militia** (*Colonel Samuel Griffin*, Virginia) - 497

- 1st Cumberland County Regiment (Colonel Silas Newcomb)
- 2nd Cumberland County Regiment (Colonel David Potter)
- 1st Gloucester County Regiment (Colonel Enos Seeley)
- 2nd Gloucester County Regiment (Colonel Joseph Ellis)
- 3rd Gloucester County Regiment (Colonel Richard Somers)
- 1st Salem County Regiment (Colonel Samuel Dick)
- 2nd Salem County Regiment (Colonel John Holme)
- Virginia Artillery (2 companies)

**All New Jersey militia regiments** were in disarray in December 1776 due to structural changes made during the months of the New York campaign and the formation of the Five-Month Levies whose enlistments expired at the end of November. All regiments listed should be considered as partial and commanding officers may not have been present.

## Table 2: British Troops at Trenton and in the Bordentown area on December 25, 1776

### Trenton

**Rall's Hessian Brigade** (*Colonel Johann Rall*) –1382

Grenadier Regiment Rall (*Lieutenant Colonel Balthasar Brethauer*) – 512 effective

*Major Johann Matthaeus, Captain Henrich Bocking, Captain Johann Brubach, Lieutenant Johann Sternickle*

Fusilier Regiment von Knyphausen (*Major Friedrich Ludwig von Dechow*) – 429 effective

*Captain Friedrich von Biesenrodt, Lieutenant Andreas Wiederholdt, Henrich Kothe, Corporal Kustner*

Fusilier Regiment von Lossberg (*Lieutenant Colonel Francis Scheffer*) – 345

*Major Ludwig von Hanstein, Captain Ernst Altenbockum, Staff Captain Friedrich Wilhelm von Benning, Captain Emanuel von Wilmousky, Lieutenant George Christian Kimm, Lieutenant Jacob Piel, Lieutenant Ernst Schwabe, Second Lieutenant Georg Hermann Zoll, Ensign Friedrich Grabe, Ensign Christian von Hobe, Friedrich Hartmann, Kurt Mensing, Philip Obenhausen, Friedrich Wilhelm Oliva*

Jägers, 1 company (*Lieutenant Friedrich von Grothausen*) - 50

*Corporal Franz Bauer*

16th Light Dragoon Regiment (Lieutenant Colonel William Harcourt) - 20

Artillery – six 3-pounder guns (*Lieutenant Friedrich Fischer* and *Lieutenant Johann Engelhardt*)

2 guns with each regiment

### Burlington, Bordentown, and vicinity

**Donop's Hessian Brigade** (*Colonel Carl von Donop*) - 1500

Grenadier Battalion von Bloch (Lieutenant Colonel Justus von Bloch)

Grenadier Battalion von Minnegerode (Lieutenant Colonel Friedrich von Minnegerode)

Grenadier Battalion von Linsing (Lieutenant Colonel Otto von Linsing)

Field Jäger Corps (*Colonel Carl von Donop*)

*Captain Johann Ewald*

42nd Regiment of Foot (Royal Highland ) (*Lieutenant Colonel Thomas Stirling*)

Artillery - 7 or 8 guns

# Chapter 4

## British along the Delaware, December 25, 1776

The British forces at the western end of Howe's chain of cantonments were not enjoying their winter quarters on Christmas Day. Both the officers and soldiers felt as if they were still on an active campaign and were suffering accordingly. Hessian Colonel Carl von Donop was in charge at Trenton, Bordentown, and Burlington, under the command of General Grant, and ordered to maintain communication with Brigadier General Leslie at Princeton. Aristocrat Donop was a 45-year-old career officer who hoped the war would be short and a good opportunity for advancement.[1] At Trenton, Colonel Johann Rall, under Donop's command, led a brigade of about 1500 troops and six field pieces. South of Trenton in the Bordentown and Burlington areas, Donop personally commanded about 2,000 men, including the Linsing, Block, and Minnegerode Hessian grenadier battalions, Captain Johann Ewald's company of Jägers[2], and the British 42nd (Royal Highland) Regiment of Foot and seven or eight field pieces.[3]

Donop's men were expected to be as self-sufficient as possible, so axes, wedges, and cross cut saws were sent for his troops to cut up firewood secured from the local landscape and population. To save on forage[4] he was ordered to reduce the number of officers' horses and dismiss as many regimental wagons as possible. Any wagons he needed were to be hired from local farmers.[5] Burlington civic leaders negotiated with him to make their town neutral to avoid continual military action with the armed galleys of the Pennsylvania State Navy. Donop quickly found that attacks by the row-galleys made Burlington too dangerous to quarter some of his troops and came to rely on Bordentown as his headquarters, while expecting heavy artillery to be sent to use against the galleys.[6]

**Civilians in the area** occupied by Donop's troops had numerous interactions both with them and the American troops that harassed the Hessians and local Loyalists. Margaret Morris was a 39-year-old widow with two sons, 14 and 17 years old, and two daughters, 10 and 16, living in Burlington at Green Bank, the former home of Royal Governor William Franklin. She was a Quaker who tried to remain neutral but supported her Loyalist neighbors and recorded in her diary the various interactions between the British and the Pennsylvania State Navy galleys on the Delaware River and the alternate search parties looking for rebels and Loyalists.

On the 25th, Morris heard that an officer was sent to Bristol from Donop "with a flag, and offers of letting our town remain a neutral post." She heard that Continental Army Adjutant General Joseph Reed was at Philadelphia and was to meet with Donop the next day. At one point, Continental Marine Captain William Shippen, whom Morris described as a "smart little fellow," threatened to shoot her son as a Loyalist spy when he was caught looking at the Americans through a spy glass after they landed and were looking for Loyalists hiding in houses.[7]

Donop's troops were tired on Christmas Day after engaging in a series of skirmishes during the previous week. At Moorestown, 30-year-old Virginia Colonel Samuel Griffin had a small group of Virginia artillery along with some Pennsylvania Continentals, together with about 500 New Jersey militiamen from Cumberland, Salem, and Gloucester counties. Loyalist Barzella Haines had reported to Donop that the Americans were unimpressive troops because almost half were mere boys and most were militia. Colonel Thomas Stirling, commanding the 42nd Regiment of Foot, learned from a source on December 21 that the Americans were at Mount Holly and believed they intended to attack, so he began calling in his foraging parties and suggested that Donop should attack the Americans first. Donop agreed and set out for Black Horse.[8]

Colonel Griffin had arrived at Mount Holly on December 20 about 3:00pm and found the enemy had abandoned it, apparently in great confusion, leaving supplies behind and fires burning. Griffin set out after the British, but local Loyalists kept the British informed of their progress. The British were now at Black Horse with about 700 men and three cannon, while Griffin only had about 600, although expecting a reinforcement of 200 men. Hoping to attack the British the next day, Griffin informed General Putnam in Philadelphia that Mount Holly was "a very dangerous post, & cant be held without a large reinforcement."[9] On December 22, an ill Colonel Griffin led his men in a skirmish at Petticoat Bridge near Mount Holly, killing several Hessians and forcing them to retreat rapidly while abandoning their knapsacks and other gear. One item found was a hat that had been shot through the crown.

Reinforced British troops advanced the next morning with seven or eight cannon and the Americans retreated in good order. That evening there was another firefight at Mount Holly on Iron Works Hill where the Americans lost two killed and seven or eight wounded. John Gibbon was captured retreating from Mount Holly and sent to the prison ship *Jersey*, where he died on June 23, 1777. The American forces were now mostly at Moorestown while the British were at the largely abandoned and plundered Mount Holly, where Colonel Donop made his quarters on December 23.[10] Margaret Morris heard that all the women had removed from Mount Holly "except one widow of our acquaintance."[11] A large quantity of wine was discovered and drunkenness was rampant by evening. Captain Ewald's Jägers were in a section of town "poorly stocked" with wine so his men remained sober, until some grenadiers brought in "so much wine that the majority of the Jägers became merry toward midnight, and I had great trouble to keep them together."

Early on Christmas Eve morning, Ewald took 20 Jägers and 50 Scottish soldiers of the 42nd Regiment to investigate the condition of the Long Bridge on the road to Moorestown. He got there about 10:00am and found it destroyed. Shots were exchanged with Americans hidden in several houses and one British soldier was killed. Ewald withdrew and returned to Mount Holly where he was immediately ordered to take 10 Jägers and 50 Hessian grenadiers to

Burlington to ascertain whether any American vessels covered it from the river. He did not get back to Mount Holly until about midnight, because the snow that day was so deep that he "could hardly get through."

During the day "a trumpeter arrived in Mount Holly from General Washington, who presented a proposal to Colonel Donop concerning the exchange of some of his officers who had been captured at Mount Holly." Ewald believed that this was "a ruse to find out whether the colonel was still in Mount Holly or was already marching back to Bordentown, which every reasonable man desired, since Trenton as well as Mount Holly were without any further support."[12] This may be connected to a message from John Cadwalader, or Joseph Reed, sent to Colonel Donop dated December 25 referring to some "business he purposed mentioning to you at the interview he requested." Reed was expected to return the following morning and "he will then request you to name another time & place which may be convenient to you." This message may have been calculated to remove from Donop's mind any suspicion of an imminent attack on Trenton.[13]

About 2:00am on the 25th, Captain Ewald learned that Lieutenant Colonel Thomas Reynolds of the 2nd Burlington County militia regiment had come to New Mills with two captains who were now lodging at his house awaiting their wives. After reporting this to Donop, Ewald took eight of his Jägers and 20 Scots and just before daybreak arrived at the house which he surrounded with his Jägers and positioned the Scots to defend the area, knowing the enemy was only an hour away. Ewald took two of the Scots, entered the unlocked house, heard people talking loudly in a room, and knocked on the door. When someone called out "Come in!" he stepped into the room where three officers and four ladies were drinking tea. He bid them good morning and they offered him a chair and cup of tea, which he accepted. When one of the ladies got up to exit the room, she was "somewhat rudely pushed back" by one of the Scots and, now recognizing who these strangers were, uttered "Oh! Lord!" Ewald identified himself and "announced the agreeable news" that they were now his prisoners.

After initially reaching for their swords, the Americans surrendered to prevent bloodshed and were taken to Mount Holly, reaching it about noon.[14] Ewald was one of those officers who "wanted to spare the King's subjects and hoped to terminate the war amicably."[15] He was 32-years-old and had been a soldier since the age of 16. His left eye was glass, the result of a 1770 duel. He was courageous, strict with his troops, and sometimes considered too aggressive by his commanders, but he always expressed the best manners.[16]

The militia actions against Donop's troops fatigued them, but also gave them confidence that the Americans could be defeated and led Donop to focus his forces on Mount Holly rather than Bordentown which put them further from Trenton and increased the dispersal of British troops in New Jersey. Although apparently not part of the larger plan, Griffin's actions greatly supported Washington's plan to attack Trenton.[17]

Mary Field, living at White Hill, near Bordentown, had experienced both harrowing and very cordial interactions with the Hessian occupation forces. Captain Ewald diplomatically arranged to quarter at her house for over two weeks and she said he gave her no trouble because he supplied his own food and brought his cook, footman, waiting man, butler, and a hostler to keep track of his eight horses. She described Ewald as "the sweetest little Dutchman you ever see, the politest obliging creature in the world." She also quartered a Hessian doctor who took tender care of her sick daughter, Molly. Mary also became acquainted with quartermaster Captain Gamble and Commissary McCullough whom she described as "two very clever fellows, and the only English officers in Bordentown."

Mary also had very good things to say about Colonel Donop and described the pageantry of his arrival on a visit to her home. His party was led by "a flying Mercury" elegantly dressed "beyond your conception." Next came four grenadiers, the colonel and his two aides-de-camp, his nephews, Captain Donop and Captain Heister, son of Major General Heister commander of the Hessians in America, then four more grenadiers. Donop confirmed Mary's belief that "many thousands came every day" to seek protections and provided her with protection from his soldiers. Several Loyalists who stayed close to Donop, including John Lawrence of Burlington, Joseph Galloway, Mr. Hicks and Jonathan Odell came almost every day to visit and have tea and did so this Christmas day with several British and Hessian officers. Mary got the distinct feeling from her Hessian guests that they expected to continue on and take Philadelphia.[18]

**Trenton residents who** stayed in town after the British and Hessian troops arrived on December 8 had attempted to protect their families and, often with less success, the safety of their property. Just days before Christmas, Loyalist leaning Isaac Pearson of Nottingham fell victim to plundering and his wife "saw a quantity of hay, oats, & sheep taken from the house & farm" by Hessian troops and "a team with two horses & two oxen was impressed by the Hessians and kept in their service a considerable time." When she submitted claims to the British government after the war, she identified Assistant Commissary Thomas Watson as the man responsible for taking 11 quarters of beef on December 20 and five quarters on December 24. She also enumerated 21 days that her four-horse team and driver were used to carry a total of 60 bushels of oats, six tons of hay, and 14 "fatt sheep" to the Hessians at Trenton.[19] Howe had reported to Germain on December 20 that his Hessian troops were in need of clothing, tents, and all sorts of camp equipage and on December 21 the quarter masters from each of Rall's and Donop's regiments had gathered together at Trenton with a convoy of wagons to go to New York for supplies and pay for their regiments. They set off escorted by eighty men and had not yet returned.[20]

Although it is impossible to know the exact number, it appears that many people who remained in town had taken advantage of the Howes' offer of amnesty and protection, but not always because they had given up on the American cause. Samuel Tucker, one of the State Treasurers, chose not to cross over to Pennsylvania with the American army before the British arrived the first week of December and instead took important personal property and government papers, including a large amount of unsigned public money, and hid them at the house of John Abbott in nearby Nottingham Township.[21] Some of the papers related to fines levied on "friends of government" and their paroles.[22] Tucker hid outside of Trenton while his family stayed at their home in town, where Howe made his headquarters while in Trenton in early December.

Why Tucker did not cross to Pennsylvania, or at least make sure the unsigned public money he was responsible for got across, is not clear. Like everyone else, he was faced with how to secure his family, property, and person and each individual did what seemed appropriate at the time, amid all the fears, rumors, and confusion. The British, with the help of local Loyalists, quickly discovered Tucker's property and took possession of it.[23] Tucker remained in hiding, fearing what might happen to him and his family. However, when he heard that his family was suffering, he came out of hiding and was violently accosted by a group of Loyalists who had come to Trenton to assist the Hessians and they took him to Robert Pearson's house.

These Loyalists were among those who felt empowered by the British occupation of New Jersey and were anxious to get revenge on Whigs like Tucker. When Tucker returned to Trenton under military escort he asked about his confiscated property and was told it would not be returned until he proved his loyalty to the Crown. The British had taken not only government papers and money but also papers and money relating to several estates that Tucker was settling. Because Mrs. Tucker had accommodated Howe for his headquarters, he consented to return her watch and some trinkets, but would not return other private property that he judged belonged to her husband. Still loyal to the Whig cause, Tucker was in the tough situation of needing his papers back, worried about his sick wife, fearing for the safety of his family, aware that many other Whig supporters had sought protections, and knowing that the Whig cause was in desperate straits. Needing to act quickly, Tucker applied for protection and it was granted by Colonel Rall on December 17. Like others though, he still lost four cows and a number of other items to the occupation troops who did not honor the protection papers. Tucker paid a high price among his fellow Whigs and was denied holding public office for several years before he was able to recover at least part of his reputation and be elected to the assembly.[24]

Wealthy merchant Abraham Hunt had a long Whig pedigree and currently served as lieutenant colonel of the 1st Hunterdon County Regiment of militia. He had stayed in Trenton when the army crossed to Pennsylvania and had received protection papers, somehow quickly convincing General Howe that he was once again devoted to King and Parliament. Possibly, as some historians have suggested, he was ingratiating himself with the side he now expected to win the war

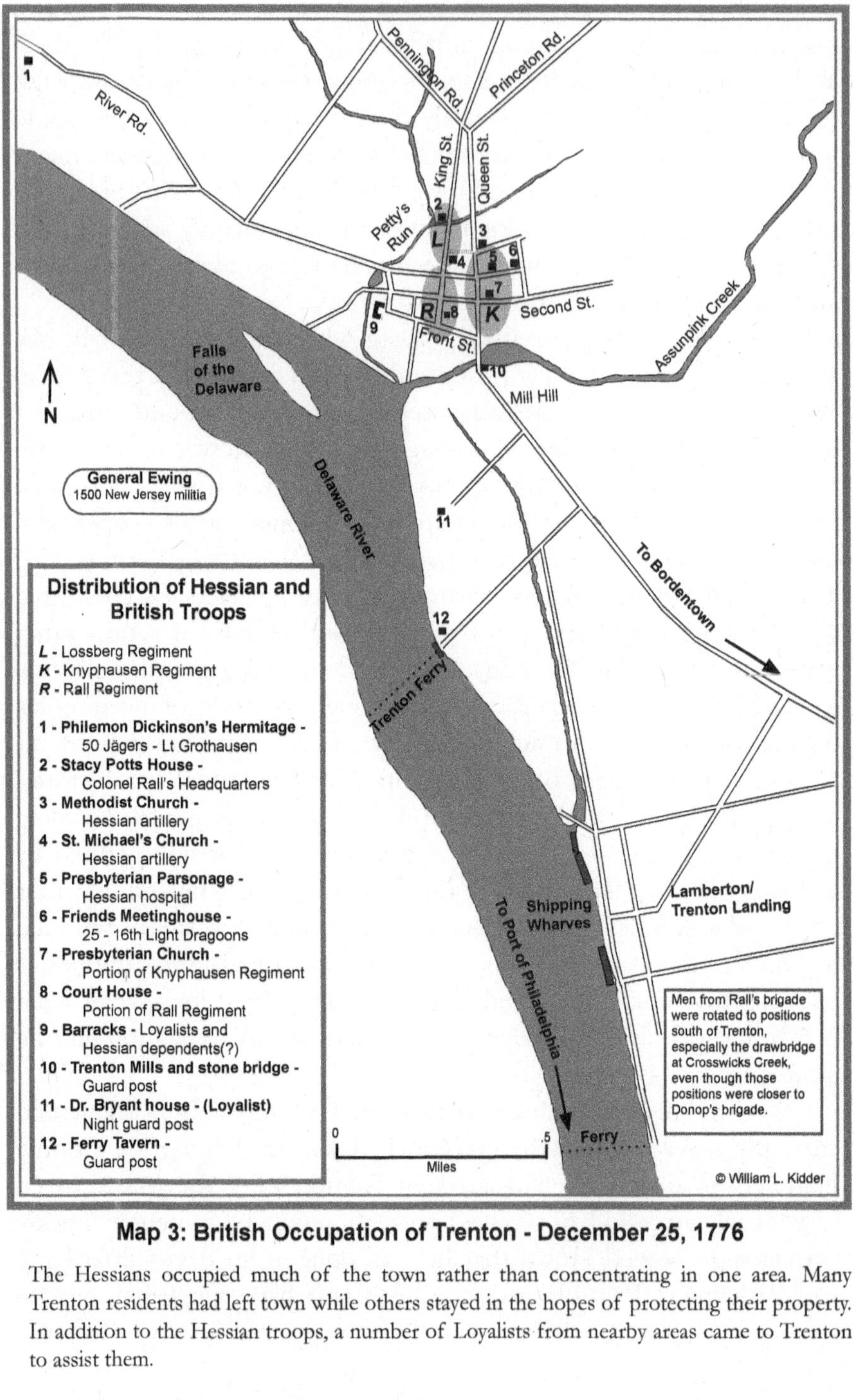


**Map 3: British Occupation of Trenton - December 25, 1776**

The Hessians occupied much of the town rather than concentrating in one area. Many Trenton residents had left town while others stayed in the hopes of protecting their property. In addition to the Hessian troops, a number of Loyalists from nearby areas came to Trenton to assist them.

and he was a clever, opportunistic, self-serving individual who looked out for himself whatever was happening, always going with the flow and managing to stay afloat. But, as suspected by some Hessian officers, another intriguing possibility is that he went undercover to be in position to help the Whig cause at some point during the British occupation. Whatever his motive, he spent the Hessian occupation living comfortably in his Trenton home, cooperating with and entertaining the enemy, while other officers and men of his regiment were suffering in their camps across the river at Yardley's Ferry; while their homes, families, farms, and businesses were subject to British depredations.[25]

**Colonel Johann Rall was pleased** that Howe put him in command of the troops assigned to winter quarters at Trenton on December 14, but was not pleased to be under the command of Donop. The two officers despised each other. For his part, Donop was not happy that Howe gave Rall about 1500 troops, believing that his own force should be larger and that Trenton should only be an outpost with about 150 men regularly rotated from among Donop's troops. Rall knew he was being rewarded for his bravery and skill demonstrated in the New York campaign, especially at the taking of Fort Washington. However, he realized that he was in charge of a post vulnerable to attack and closest to the main American force just across the Delaware from him. He and most of his men did not speak English. Still, Rall was naively reassured by so many people in Trenton and nearby taking advantage of Howe's amnesty offer and signing oaths of loyalty to the British government, giving him the perception that the rebellion was near defeat.

To many people it seemed odd that Howe would assign Hessians to the posts closest to the American army among people who spoke a different language. Rall spoke only a Hessian dialect of German while Donop also knew French which he used to communicate with English officers.[26] Some of the Hessian officers were quite young while others had many years of experience. Eighteen-year-old Hessian Lieutenant Johann von Bardeleben wrote in his diary for December 25-26 reflecting on his age for the position he held and the problems of understanding the situation he was in. He recognized that "due to my fortunate situation, I find more opportunities to experience things than would otherwise have been possible. However, only the wisest of the wisest Germans can fully understand the peculiar attitude of the English toward the Americans. And therefore, the average uninitiated person of my age and experience understands even less."[27]

Rall only quartered his troops in occupied houses when empty houses were not available. He kept regiments and companies in close proximity; his Rall Regiment on and about lower King Street, the Lossberg Regiment on and about upper King Street (with several detachments quartered on the northern and southern edge of town), and the Knyphausen Regiment on and about southern Queen Street. Twenty troopers of the British 16th Light Dragoons occupied the Friends meeting house and the artillery companies Anglican St. Michael's and the Methodist churches. His 50 Jägers were posted at the Hermitage, the estate home of New Jersey militia Brigadier General Philemon Dickinson just outside Trenton near the Delaware River. Rall took over the vacated Presbyterian parsonage for use as his hospital. In general, Rall wanted to keep his troops quartered far enough away from the river that they would not attract artillery fire from the Americans on the opposite bank. The French and Indian War era stone barracks was close enough to the river that he did not want troops quartered there, but it is probable that the Hessian dependents and some of the Loyalist civilians who came to Trenton to help the British and Hessians were quartered there, in the belief that the Americans would not cannonade women and children.

With his men spread throughout town, Rall needed to designate places for companies to muster and regiments to parade, and also where the troops would form up quickly if the town came under attack. From the later testimony of his officers it appears he did not thoroughly develop such a plan. He also did not order any defensive earthworks to be constructed, such as redoubts at the head of King and Queen Streets and south of town across the Assunpink Creek. It was Hessian standard practice to build redoubts in situations such as Rall found himself and there is also evidence that his superiors recommended this, perhaps even ordered it, and supplied an engineer officer to help him, whom Rall ignored. Rall had six brass 3-pounder cannon and could have mounted several in each redoubt to engage attacking forces. Instead, he kept the cannon in town, including the two guns assigned to his regiment near his headquarters on King Street at the house of merchant and town clerk Stacy Potts. The conclusion of many that Rall was culpable for not providing routine defensive positions and orders for his troops on how to react to attacks on the town seems appropriate. He and his superiors were convinced that the American army was too weak, and the revolution too dispirited, to fear a serious attack. Small harassing attacks were frequently occurring, but the Hessian troops could handle those relatively easily, although they were taking casualties and getting worn out.

By Christmas Day, the Hessians occupying Trenton had endured almost two weeks of constant military activity and periodic skirmishes with small detachments of the American army, especially militia. While Colonel Rall had failed to prepare defensive earthwork redoubts, he did keep his troops on alert, patrolling out from Trenton and manning guard posts in and outside the town. Reacting to frequent early morning enemy forays south of town, after December 19 two cannon and 70 men were marched over the Assunpink bridge each daybreak with orders to take position behind Mill Hill in order to surprise any enemy raids across the Delaware in the vicinity of Trenton Ferry. At the northern end of town the country was very open and the town could be attacked from almost any angle over fields or through light woods. Two cannon, with an effective range of about 300 yards, posted in a redoubt there would have only limited use and could be easily skirted by attacking forces. Rall was aware of this vulnerability and defensively told Donop on the December 21 that "I have not made redoubts or any kind of fortifications because I have the enemy in all directions."[28] When the Hessians had to patrol outside of Trenton they noted, it was "almost impossible to attack the enemy at any time by surprise because each house which we pass is more or less a lookout. The farmer, his son, or the farmhand either fire a rifle or run along a footpath to inform the enemy."[29]

In spite of the general feeling among British and Hessian officers that the American forces were very weak, Rall still felt the need for more troops or closer support. Several days before Christmas, Rall had refused a request from Donop to send a regiment to reinforce the troops at Bordentown. Donop stated, "he was in momentary expectation of being attacked by the enemy [Griffin]" whose troops were "on his right flank as well as on his rear" in large numbers. However, Rall believed that giving up any troops would make it impossible to defend Trenton and he would be forced to evacuate the town "and go into bivouac with the other two battalions and remain so."[30] Rall's requests to Grant for troops to be stationed at Maidenhead, where they could more easily support him, had been denied.[31] But, General Leslie at Princeton did send the 1st Light Infantry Battalion to Donop by way of Trenton. However, they learned at Trenton that Donop had been given false intelligence. With the threat removed, the battalion returned to Princeton.[32]

While not fearing an attack in force, Rall expected that his troops were in for a long winter of harassment attacks and turning out on false alarms. Intelligence on December 23 indicated many rebels were sick and many near the end of their enlistments and determined not to extend their time. The only sizeable force in New Jersey was part of the 3rd Hunterdon Regiment of militia under Colonel David Chambers with about 80 men near Howell's Ferry.[33]

Loyalists in and about Trenton provided Rall with intelligence and warnings of American attacks. On December 23, the known, but tolerated, Loyalist Dr. William Bryant had come from his Kingsbury estate to pass on intelligence from one of his slaves, who had returned from a trip across the river, that the American army had been issued rations for several days in anticipation of an attack on Trenton. Colonel Rall dismissed the report as "old woman's talk."[34] The next day at 11:00pm, General Grant wrote to Rall that, "Washington has been informed that our troops have marched into winter quarters, and has been told that we are weak at Trenton and Princeton, and Lord Sterling expressed a wish to make an attack upon these two places. I don't believe he will attempt it but be assured that my information is undoubtedly true, so I need not advise you, to be on your guard against an unexpected attack at Trenton."[35]

A number of Loyalists from Monmouth County had come to Trenton to help the British and Hessians in any way they could. They were glad to see the British and sought their protection from people such as militia Colonel David Forman who had been sent into Monmouth to suppress a Loyalist uprising on November 24.[36] John Leonard and

Anthony Woodward, led a group of Monmouth Loyalists to Trenton but, even working diligently, they had not been able to collect all the supplies requested by the Hessians. On Christmas Eve, Acting Deputy Quartermaster General Gamble had issued a circular to the people of Hunterdon and Burlington counties, stating that the residents had not brought in enough forage and stores for the British troops at Trenton and Bordentown, as well as the forces at Brunswick, and listed prices the British would pay for hay, oats, Indian corn, wheat, flour, bran, pork, and beef. Higher prices were listed for products delivered by farmers or mill owners, and lower ones if the army had to come get them. The circular also carried the blatant threat that if not enough supplies were brought in, there was the "disagreeable alternative of having them seized by foraging parties." Bordentown was able to collect a good sized magazine of supplies through the willingness of local farmers to sell their products to the British.[37]

General Grant reinforced the idea that Rall and Donop should not overly fear the American forces. He told Donop on December 17 that, "I am sure there is no rebel force on this side of the Delaware, which will attempt to stand before Hessian grenadiers." He was sure Washington would remain in Pennsylvania, writing, "I can hardly believe that Washington would venture at this season of the year to pass the Delaware … as the repassing it may on account of the ice become difficult." In the winter, river conditions could change quickly with temperature fluctuations. On December 21 Grant tried to calm Rall by picturing the over-estimated 8,000 or so American soldiers as being no threat because they had "neither shoes nor stockings, are in fact all most naked, starving for cold, without blankets, and very ill supplied with provisions." The rebels on the New Jersey side of the river were simply scattered militia parties only interested in ambushing light dragoons.[38] This poor opinion of the Americans filtered down to the Hessian soldiers.[39]

When General Grant learned that Rall had responded to attacks on mounted couriers between Trenton and Princeton by increasing the size of their escort to a hundred men and a piece of artillery, Grant told him instead to vary the times messages were sent and under no circumstances send cannon, because it gave the appearance of weakness. When Rall requested 45,000 musket cartridges for his brigade, and indicated he would need more in the future, Grant advised him to use caution to prevent waste.[40]

By Christmas, Colonel Rall was very concerned about his brigade's worsening fatigue from the continuous hit-and-run harassment by the enemy in the cold weather and their efforts to prevent these attacks. Just the previous day he had sent a two pronged heavy patrol to the little village of Pennytown (Pennington). One group took the direct road and the other went up the river to Johnson's Ferry, opposite McConkey's Ferry, and then turned east to Pennington. The group coming up the river found thirty Americans at Johnson's Ferry. When the Americans saw Jägers approaching, they immediately got to their boats and rowed hard to get out of range of the Jägers rifles. The Jägers believed they wounded one officer and two privates and their fire was returned by four volleys from American artillery on the Pennsylvania side of the river. On the return to Trenton, one of Ralls' officers recommended sending daily patrols to Johnson's Ferry to prevent any surprises, but Rall rejected the idea.[41] Fatigue from over two weeks of constant activity had led to illness, and Rall had only two officers in his regiment that he considered fit for duty. While all three regiments had similar complaints, the Lossberg Regiment was in especially bad shape, having suffered more than any other regiment in the recent campaign.[42]

Major Friedrich von Dechow reported to Colonel Rall that the baggage and supplies of the brigade were vulnerable if the town should be suddenly attacked and urged him to have them removed to safer locations. However, Rall had become very irritated by the frequent concerns expressed by his subordinates and simply told Dechow that if the rebels came and were successful, which he sincerely doubted, they could "have all the stores and the baggage to my very last wagon." In his opinion, the best the rebels could hope for if they attacked Trenton was to retreat successfully.

Temperatures on Christmas Day were in the 20s, but the weather was fair with sunshine and some clouds. On Christmas morning, Colonel Rall received a message from General Grant that an American detachment under General Stirling was near Trenton and might make some kind of attack that day. Rall dismissed this, and it was in fact erroneous information, but he did ride around the outskirts of town with some troops, visiting guard posts and pickets. He returned to his quarters late in the afternoon after finding everything quiet and struck up a game of checkers at his quarters with his host, Stacy Potts. During the game, at about 7:30pm, musket fire was heard from the northwest part of town - a single volley followed by a few scattered shots. Not knowing the size of the American force and whether the attack would continue, the Hessians prepared for action. It turned out the attackers fired on a 16-man picket post at the Howell cooper shop on the Pennington Road just outside of town. The attackers withdrew quickly and disappeared into the woods after six Hessian soldiers had been wounded and several muskets and some ammunition captured by the Americans.

In response, the Lossberg Regiment gathered under arms at their company quarters. The Rall Regiment formed up in front of St.Michael's Church and marched to the head of King and Queen Streets. The Knyphausen Regiment on southern Queen Street and a company of the Lossberg Regiment south of the bridge gathered by their quarters. Picket posts were reinforced. Patrols were sent out, but "returned without having seen or discovered anything of the enemy and the regiments therefore marched back to quarters." Lieutenant Andreas Wiederholdt of the Knyphausen Regiment was sent with ten men to reinforce the picket post at the Howell cooper shop.

Captain Altenbockum's company of the Lossberg Regiment quartered for the night in the houses of John Chambers and Warrell Cottnam near their captain's quarters closer to town on the Penningthon Road. The regimental officers assembled to report their situations and Rall decided that this attack had been the one General Grant had warned him about, or had been some local farmers(i.e., militiamen) who had gotten together just to annoy him. Some felt it had been a rebel probing attack to determine the location of picket posts. Meeting at the head of King Street, Major von Dechow urged Rall to send out a heavy patrol to all the ferries and up the roads, but Rall thought it could wait until morning. Dechow, extremely angered by Rall's lack of concern, took care to put sentinels at each of the houses occupied by soldiers of his regiment and ordered his men to remain in their quarters and be prepared for an alarm.[43] Wiederholdt later criticized Rall for not sending out patrols as far as the ferries, while defending his own actions that night, detailing seven pickets and sending out continuous patrols.[44]

**RALL APPARENTLY FOUND THE CHECKERS GAME** with Stacy Potts to be a less enjoyable way to spend what was left of a tumultuous Christmas Day than a more lively party at the home of, apparent Loyalist Abraham Hunt down the street. There, Rall relaxed in his belief that all was well. A storm developing in the night contributed to putting his mind at ease about any further attack, and he enjoyed his card games while eating and drinking in Abraham Hunt's comfortable home.[45] His soldiers were not so indulged and were kept on alert rather than relax and celebrate. The men in Mr. Hunt's rebel militia regiment in the area of Yardley's Ferry, Pennsylvania on the river also did not have a relaxing night.

# Chapter 5

## Americans on the Delaware, Wednesday, December 25, 1776

While Colonels Rall and Donop coped in December with American harassment attacks and the developing winter weather, George Washington had been struggling with the need to do something to save the war. While organizing his troops in Bucks County, Pennsylvania on Christmas Day, Washington did not have time to worry that his reputation was suffering among members of Congress unhappy about the loss of New York City and some of his officers who had decried his "fatal indecision."[1] Although battle casualties, illness, prisoners, and desertions had greatly reduced the size of his army, Pennsylvania militiamen were joining him in significant numbers and those Continentals still with him had been through some serious combat, had tolerated the lack of proper food and supplies, had not deserted, and seemed very loyal to him. They were survivors.

After nearly losing his army in the traditional, European style battles of the New York campaign, Washington contemplated adopting a Fabian strategy involving smaller actions, retreating when outnumbered, and using superior forces to attack smaller enemy units and outposts without risking the survival of his army. Keeping his army in the field and his focus on the overarching goal of independence was more important than sacrificing it in a vain attempt to prevent the capture of any post, no matter its value. Still, Washington would have preferred to have "a regular, eighteenth-century army that could defend the capital, meet the enemy on the plain, or take New York back by siege and assault."[2] During the five months of the New York

### Table 3: Troops with Washington – December 25, 1776

**Light Horse of Philadelphia** (*Captain Samuel Morris*)
*Cornet John Dunlap, Corporal James Hunter*

**Brigadier William Alexander, Lord Stirling's Brigade – 673**
1st Virginia Regiment(*Colonel Isaac Read*, Capt. John Fleming) – 185
*Captain Graham, Lieutenant Abraham Kirkpatrick, Lieutenant Bartholomew Yates, Jonathan Grant*
3rd Virginia Regiment(*Colonel George Weedon*) – 181
*Captain John Chilton, Captain John Thornton, Captain William Washington, Lieutenant James Monroe, Sergeant Thomas McCarty*
Delaware Regiment (*Colonel John Haslet*) – 108
*Captain Thomas Holland*
Miles' Pennsylvania Rifle Regiment (*Major Ennion Williams*) – 199
*Captain John Marshall, Sergeant James McMichael, Cary McClelland*

**Brigadier General Adam Stephen's Brigade – 549**
4th Virginia Regiment (Colonel Thomas Elliott) – 229
*Major Charles Fleming, Captain George Wallis, Ensign James Buxton, Ensign William Dennis Kelley*
5th Virginia Regiment (*Colonel Charles Scott*) – 129
*Major George Johnston, Major Thompson, Captain Henry Fauntleroy, Ensign Robert Beale*
6th Virginia Regiment (Col. Mordecai Buckner) – 191
*Colonel Lawson, Major Richard Parker, Ensign James Barnett, George Blakey, William Montgomery*

**Brigadier General Hugh Mercer's Brigade – 838**
*Major John Armstrong, aide to Gen. Mercer*
20th Continental Regiment (Connecticut) (Colonel John Durkee) – 313
*Sergeant Nathaniel Root*
27th Continental Regiment (Massachusetts) (Col. Israel Hutchinson) – 115
Colonel Philip Burr Bradley's Battalion, Connecticut State Troops – 142
*Philemon Baldwin*
Smallwood's Maryland Regiment (Lt. Col. John Stone) – 163
*Captain Maynard, Cornelius Wells*
Maryland & Virginia Rifle Battalion Volunteers (Capt. David Harris) – 105
2nd Maryland Regiment (Col. Stewart)
*John Boudy*

**Brigadier General Matthias Alexis Roche de Fermoy's Brigade – 638**
1st Pennsylvania Rifle Regiment (*Colonel Edward Hand*) – 254
*Captain Henry Miller, Jacob Bottomer, George Tilson*
German Battalion (4 Maryland and 4 Pennsylvania companies) (*Colonel Nicholas Hausegger*) – 374
*Major Ludowick Weltner, Conrad Beam*

**Colonel John Glover's Brigade – 977**
3rd Continental Regiment (Massachusetts) (Colonel Ebenezer Learned) - 217
*John Dewey*
14th Continental Regiment (Massachusetts) (Marbleheaders) – (*Colonel John Glover*) - 177
*Captain William Blackler, Captain Theophilus Munson*
19th Continental Regiment (Connecticut) (*Colonel Charles Webb*) - 216
*Captain William Hull, Lieutenant Elisha Bostwick*
23rd Continental Regiment (Massachusetts) (Colonel John Bailey) - 146
26th Continental Regiment (Massachusetts) (*Colonel Loammi Baldwin*) - 221
*Moses Smith*

**Colonel Paul Dudley Sargent's Brigade – 827**

13th Continental Regiment (Massachusetts) (Col. Joseph Read) - 122

*Captain Oliver Pond, Christopher Burlingame*

16th Continental Regiment (Massachusetts) (*Colonel Paul Dudley Sargent*) - 152

*Oliver Corey, Jacob Francis, David How, Ebenezer White*

Colonel Andrew Ward's Continental Regiment (Connecticut) - 157

6th Battalion, Connecticut State Troops (Colonel John Chester) - 260

1st New York Continental Regiment (Captain John Johnston) - 56

3rd New York Continental Regiment (Lieutenant Colonel Baron Friedrich von Weisenfels) - 80

**Brigadier General Arthur St. Clair's Brigade – 500**

5th Continental Regiment (formerly 1st New Hampshire) (*Colonel John Stark*)

*William Chamberlin*

8th Continental Regiment (formerly 2nd New Hampshire) (*Colonel Enoch Poor*)

2nd Continental Regiment (formerly 3rd New Hampshire) (Lieutenant Colonel Israel Gilman)

15th Continental Regiment (Massachusetts) (all field officers absent)

*Rev. David Avery, Sergeant Madden, John Greenwood*

**Colonel Henry Knox's Regiment of Continental Artillery – 418**

New York Company of Continental Artillery (*Captain Sebastian Baumann*)

3 guns - 85

Massachusetts Company of Continental Artillery (Captain Lieutenant Winthrop Sargent)

2 guns – 55

*Lieutenant Samuel Shaw*

New York State Company of Artillery (*Captain Alexander Hamilton*)

2 guns – 36

*Captain Lieutenant James Moore*

Eastern Company, New Jersey State Artillery (*Captain Daniel Neil*)

2 guns – 63

Western Company, New Jersey State Artillery (*Captain Samuel Hugg*)

2 guns – 55

*Hosea Husted*

2nd Company, Pennsylvania State Artillery (*Captain Thomas Forrest*)

2 brass mounted 6-pounders – 52

*Lieutenant Patrick Duffey, Sergeant Joseph White*

2nd Company of Artillery, Philadelphia Associators (*Captain Joseph Moulder*)

3 guns – 85

*Second Lieutenant Anthony Cuthbert, Sergeant Godfrey, Zebulon Applegate*

**Additional troops:**

**1st New Jersey Regiment** (1777) (*Captain John Flahaven*'s recruiting company) - 40

**1st Hunterdon County Militia Regiment** - ferrymen and guides for the night march to Trenton - 25

*Captain John Mott, David Lanning, Joab Mershon*

**Individuals from disbanded Continental regiments from Fort Ticonderoga - ?**

*Captain John Polhemus, Captain John Lacey, William Chamberlin*

**Individual local Pennsylvania and New Jersey militiamen** caught in the confusion of the time and not connected with their regiments. - ?

*John Burrowes*

campaign, Washington strove to preserve his army while making the British pay heavily when engaged. The British maintained constant pressure on the Americans to make their power seem invincible, while Washington strove to keep the Revolution alive by keeping an army in the field and hoping for a decisive blow. However, while doing this Washington lost large numbers of men and supplies and always showed retreat. Although preventing outright British victory, he had not convinced Americans that the British would ultimately be defeated or would grant them independence. Several days after the loss of Fort Washington on November 16, Washington told his brother, John Augustine Washington, that, "I am wearied almost to death with the retrograde motions of things, and I solemnly protest that a pecuniary reward of 20,000£ a year would not induce me to undergo what I do," especially because it was not only the enemy, but also reputed friends, that created obstacles to his success. He was continually trying to figure out how to keep from always being in retreat.[3] A month later, Washington was very caught up in the obstacles he faced and in another letter to John Augustine he wrote, "However under a full persuasion of the justice of our cause I cannot … entertain an idea that it will finally sink[,] tho' it may remain for some time under a cloud."[4]

Adopting a Fabian strategy was questioned by those who "judged the war by visible standards of ground held, strong points won and lost." If the British army came into an area and stayed, people wondered whether Whigs who accepted Howe's offer of protection would only "pretend" to be loyal British subjects or would they gradually return to real loyalty? However, a Fabian strategy made sense to many of Washington's generals because the army was essential for continuing the war. For some civilians, the mere existence of the Continental Army kept alive their hopes for ultimate victory, measured by the amount of ground the army controlled. However, the mixed perception of the importance of the army allowed the states to rely on it more than they wanted to while providing it less support than it required. After victories, people could claim the army was less necessary than "its officers claimed."[5]

As the campaign drew to a close, Washington believed that even just one victory would do more than anything else "to eradicate the stain of his recent mistakes." That belief focused his thoughts as he had retreated across New Jersey constantly contemplating turning around to attack his pursuers, but not doing so because he never had enough men and General Lee made no effort to reinforce him.

To prevent British pursuit after the retreat across New Jersey, Washington had issued similar orders to several units to gather up all boats on the Jersey side of the Delaware River north and south of Trenton for many miles and remove them to the Pennsylvania side after all his men and supplies got across at the two Trenton ferries. All boats were to be secured where they would not be seen by British patrols along the New Jersey side, but where they would be available to carry groups of men back across to New Jersey on harassing attacks.[6]

While in the middle of transporting his army's supplies across the Delaware at Trenton, Washington wrote to John Hancock on December 5 expressing his frustration with retreating out of New Jersey. He wrote, "I conceive it to be my duty, and it corresponds with my inclination, to make head against them, so soon as there shall be the least probability of doing it with propriety." Once in Pennsylvania, Washington established a string of camps between Coryell's Ferry (modern New Hope, Pennsylvania) and Bristol ordering each to guard the crossing points and observe British movements, especially watching for any evidence of assembling boats. Howe made no effort to obtain boats from the rivers to the east or the Royal Navy at New York and by December 14 had decided to take up winter quarters and put off advancing on Philadelphia until spring.

Skeptical of Howe's intentions, and not content to end the campaign with a retreat, Washington wanted to "attempt a stroke upon the forces of the enemy, who lay a good deal scattered," understood to be about 4,000 at Brunswick, 3,000 at Princeton, 1,500 at Trenton, and 1,500 at Bordentown.[7] Encouraged that the British cantonments were vulnerable, his urge to attack them was only tempered by the reality that he badly needed reinforcements in order to undertake anything significant and the enlistments of a large portion of his troops ended on December 31.[8] He did not expect these men to reenlist and their departure would leave him with only "a few southern regiments, almost reduced to nothing by sickness and fatigue." He continued to believe that General Howe's troops "close upon my front" were merely waiting for his army to dissolve when they could easily conquer

Pennsylvania, just as they had New Jersey.[9] Nineteen-year-old Major James Wilkinson noted in his memoirs that he saw Washington "in that gloomy period, dined with him and attentively marked his aspect; always grave and thoughtful, he appeared at that time pensive and solemn in the extreme."[10]

Washington and at least some of his generals were already thinking about ways to redeem the 1776 campaign by retaking at least part of New Jersey. Two or three days after the army crossed to Pennsylvania, Major John Armstrong, an 18-year-old aide-de-camp to Brigadier General Hugh Mercer, overheard several conversations between Mercer and Adjutant General Joseph Reed discussing whether it would be possible, or advisable, to attack and destroy some or all of the enemy cantonments. They agreed action should be pursued and each took responsibility for bringing up the subject with Washington and those officers likely to be part of any council of war.[11] Washington welcomed their conversations and by December 14 was working through various options when he wrote to General William Heath that, "I should hope we may effect something of importance, or at least give such a turn to our affairs as to make them assume a more pleasing aspect than they now have."[12] To Governor Trumbull of Connecticut he suggested that, "A lucky blow in this quarter, would be fatal to them, and would most certainly raise the spirits of the people, which are quite sunk by our late misfortunes."[13] To General Gates, believed to be bringing him reinforcements from Ticonderoga, he wrote, "If we can draw our forces together, I trust, under the smiles of providence, we may yet effect an important stroke, or at least prevent Genl. Howe from executing his plans" regarding Philadelphia.[14]

The many conversations no doubt included multiple scenarios for possible actions and while Washington may have hoped for secrecy, by December 18, Philadelphian Christopher Marshall had heard "news that our army intended to cross at Trenton into the Jerseys."[15] On December 19, General Nathanael Greene sent a note to General James Ewing from "Bougarts Tavern" in Buckingham Township relaying Washington's request for 16 Durham boats and four "flats," i.e. ferry boats, to be sent down to McConkey's Ferry "as soon as possible" under the "care and direction of some good faithful officer."[16] This indicates that Washington was planning a major re-crossing of the Delaware by his army, not just another harassing raid.

Two days later Major General Nathanael Greene wrote to Governor Nicholas Cooke of Rhode Island from Coryell's Ferry that they would "give the enemy a stroke in a few days. Should fortune favor the attack perhaps it may put a stop to General Howes progress."[17] Robert Morris in Philadelphia wrote to Washington the same day that, "I have been told to-day that you are preparing to cross into the Jerseys. I hope it may be true."[18]

Between December 8 and 25, Washington gathered intelligence on the British and Hessian troops and cantonments and pondered how he could attack and defeat some portion of them with his small army. Howe had established his cantonments across New Jersey to support and encourage the Loyalists and Washington believed he must now force the enemy troops out of New Jersey in order to revitalize the Whigs. Washington's plan for the December 26 attack, to launch a short campaign to drive the British from as much of New Jersey as possible, developed over time from conversations with various officers and analyzing multiple intelligence reports. He might capture Trenton in a day with a surprise attack, but that would only be a symbolic victory if he could not follow it up with additional actions and retreated back to Pennsylvania. But, unless he could convince his troops to extend their enlistments, he would only have one short week to accomplish anything larger before his army became even more a shadow of its former strength. He was running out of time and resources.

Washington's Adjutant General, Colonel Joseph Reed, born to a Trenton family and well acquainted with the town and vicinity, gathered intelligence while serving with the Pennsylvania militia under Colonel Cadwalader at Bristol. Apparently not knowing that Washington had already come to the same conclusion, Reed was very direct with Washington on December 22 that the officers at Bristol "are all of opinion, my dear General, that something must be attempted to revive our expiring credit, give our cause some degree of reputation, and prevent a total depreciation of the Continental money, which is coming on very fast." In this time of crisis, Reed believed doing nothing was worse than failing at doing something, and "in short, some enterprise must be undertaken in our present circumstances, or we must give up the cause." The Howe's amnesty offer extended through January and, unless some favorable action took place, Reed expected large additional numbers of militia and civilians would take up their offer.

Reed believed "our cause is desperate and hopeless, if we do not take the opportunity of the collection of troops at present, to strike some stroke." The troops needed inspiration if they were to continue, so he asked, "Will it not be possible, my dear General, for your troops, or such part of them as can act with advantage, to make a diversion, or something more, at or about Trenton?" Reed believed that if even only part of New Jersey could be retaken, "the effects would be greater than if we had never left it." He apologized for being so blunt, but believed it was his duty to do so, as well as his concern for his family and the potential "ruin and poverty that must attend me, and thousands of others" if the cause failed. His letter served to strongly reinforce Washington's thinking.[19]

Washington called a Council of War at Brigadier General Lord Stirling's headquarters on December 22 to begin finalizing a plan of attack now that he had more men than were garrisoned in any one of the Hessian cantonments near the Delaware River. He and his officers discussed how many of the four closest cantonments to attack, if any. The Council adjourned after several hours without deciding on a definite course of action. Always worried about spies, Washington had warned his officers since crossing to Bucks County that "we are in a neighbourhood of very disaffected people. Equal care therefore should be taken that one of these persons does not undertake the business in order to betray us."[20] However, a spy somehow learned of the council and alerted the British that an attack was being planned.

That evening a smaller, more secure, group of officers developed a general plan of attack for December 26. Washington notified Reed and Cadwalader on December 23 that the attack was scheduled for the 26th and begged them "for Heaven's sake keep this to yourself, as the discovery of it may prove fatal to us, our numbrs, sorry am I to say, being less than I had any conception of: but necessity, dire necessity, will, nay must, justify an attempt." Another council met at General Greene's headquarters at Samuel Merrick's house on Christmas Eve to finalize the attack details.[21] By the time Washington was putting the final touches on his plan, he was not just interested in a quick

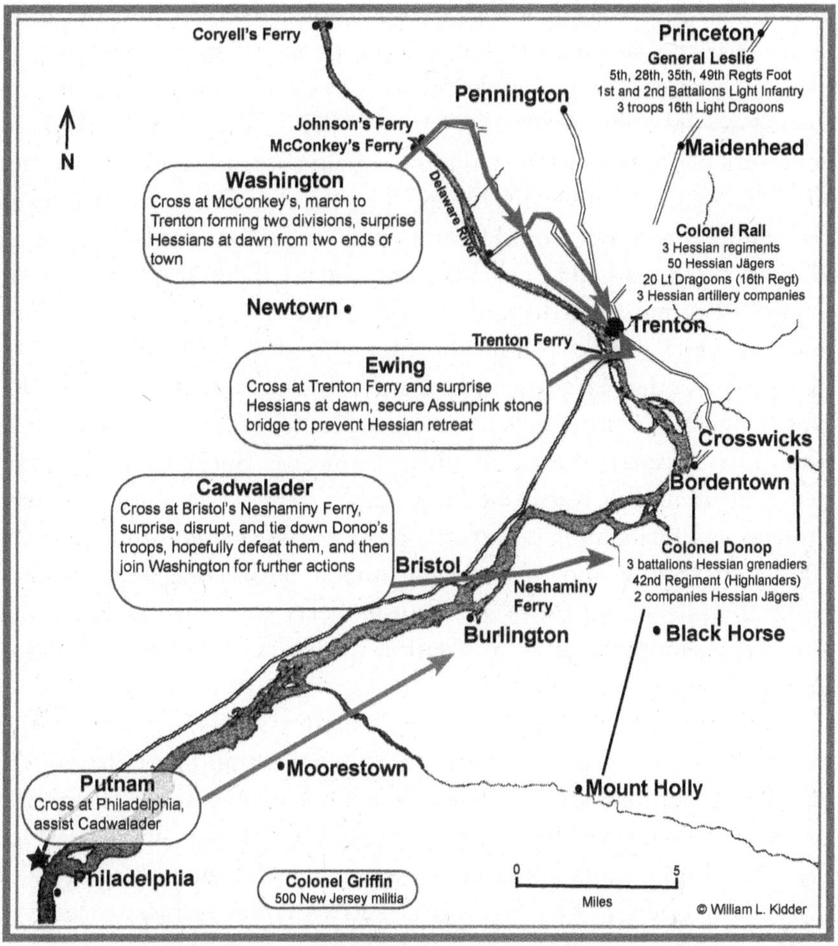


**Map 4: Washington's plan for the attack on Trenton**

symbolic victory at Trenton, but saw Trenton as a first step in driving the British out of New Jersey. Leaving New Jersey occupied over the winter would not be acceptable to his officers, the Congress, and many ordinary supporters of the fight for independence. Beginning with Trenton, he would take advantage of having a greater force than any of the individual British cantonments and find a way to attack them in sequence while preventing them from supporting one another.

Washington knew an attack on Trenton must be quick and decisive in order to succeed. He could not lay siege to the town or become involved in a lengthy, drawn out battle because the British troops at Bordentown and Princeton could quickly reinforce Rall and pin the Americans against the river. The objective was to capture the entire garrison at Trenton, remove the prisoners across the river to Pennsylvania, and then to make further attacks on British cantonments to restore the ability of the Whigs to operate the New Jersey State government. To do this, Washington's main force of about 2,400 men would cross the river at McConkey's Ferry and march to the hamlet of Birmingham where it would form two divisions, one led by Nathanael Greene, accompanied by Washington, which would approach Trenton on the Pennington Road and the other led by Major General John Sullivan which would follow the River Road to Trenton. The 1500 militiamen under 34-year-old Colonel John Cadwalader and the 900 New England Continentals of Colonel Daniel Hitchcock's Brigade at Bristol would cross there and advance towards Burlington to distract that cantonment. It was hoped that militia being collected by General Putnam at Philadelphia could also cross to assist them. Finally, some 700 Pennsylvania and New Jersey militia under Brigadier General James Ewing would cross at Trenton Ferry and secure the bridge over the Assunpink Creek in Trenton to prevent a Hessian retreat to Donop's forces.

This complex, some would say overly complex, plan assumed fair, though cold weather. The army would surround and prevent the Hessians from forming defensive formations or escaping to Princeton or Bordentown. Greene's division would attack the upper part of town at the same time Sullivan's division attacked the lower part. The brigades of Greene's division were tasked with three primary objectives. First, Stephen's brigade, leading the division on the march, would go a bit north and east of town to secure the road to Maidenhead and Princeton and deploy to prevent escape on the east side of town. Second, Stirling's brigade would attack at the head of town and engage the Hessian troops that turned out on King and Queen Streets and, third, Mercer's brigade would peel off as the division got to town and attack the Hessians on their flank from behind the house lots on King Street. On the lower edge of town, Sullivan's division would attack the Hessian Jäger outpost at Philemon Dickinson's Hermitage and push the retreating Jägers into town, trapping the Hessians quartered in town between themselves and Greene's division. They would also cooperate with General Ewing's men to seal off the escape route across the Assunpink Creek bridge. This very complex plan required careful coordination (with communications limited to the speed of a horse), energetic movements by the troops, overwhelming firepower at each point of attack, disabling the Hessian ability to respond with coordinated force, and preventing British assistance from, or Hessian escape to, Bordentown or Princeton.

As Washington's plan took shape in his mind, he conversed with various deeply trusted officers, including 26-year-old Boston bookseller Colonel Henry Knox. Knox not only had made a study of artillery, but had created an artillery force that was both very capable and steady in combat. He had earlier worked successfully on designing lighter weight and more maneuverable gun carriages to make it easier for artillery to keep up with the infantry on the march, although an unexpected side-effect was an increased number of disabled carriages with broken axles and wheels.[22] Just a week before Christmas, Knox had drawn up and submitted to Washington and Congress a plan outlining the structure for a Continental artillery corps, complete with magazines and laboratories to support it. He stressed that in "modern" warfare "there is nothing which contributes more to make an army victorious than a well regulated and well disciplined artillery provided with a sufficiency of cannon and stores."[23] Knox boldly offered to command this artillery corps, but stated that he would resign if not promoted to general for that command. Washington supported Knox's plan and recommended his appointment to command the artillery corps with the rank of brigadier general.[24] While Knox was thinking and writing about the uses and organization of artillery, Washington's developing plan for his attack on Trenton clearly reflected Knox's influence.

Before the Revolution, it was unusual for armies in America to travel with artillery in any quantity. By one estimation, when artillery did accompany an army the usual ratio was two or three cannon per 1000 infantrymen, so one would expect Washington, with about 2400 men, to bring along perhaps six to eight cannon at the most; instead of the 18 artillery pieces, of several types, that he distributed among his brigades. The variety of cannon firing 3-, 4-, and 6-pound cannon balls and howitzers firing 5 1/2-inch shells created normal supply complexities including the need for horses to pull the cannon and wagons carrying ammunition and powder along the challenging icy dirt roads. To cross the Delaware River, everything connected with the artillery required transportation by the flat ferry boats built to take wagons and horses, as well as people, across the river. The decision to bring so much, or even any, artillery seemed to fly in the face of the need for speed and coordinated timing. However, Washington was planning on surprise as a key element of the attack and the artillery would add an element of shock to the enemy's surprise, while also providing a huge psychological benefit for his own men.[25] Washington was convinced the artillery was important enough that he committed to overcoming the obvious difficulties it created.

Washington's Continentals were scattered in the vicinity of Newtown in Bucks County with officers generally quartered at farm houses near the camps of their men. Farmers found their woodlots cut down by soldiers seeking firewood. A Pennsylvania soldier wrote that they were forced to "Ly ought in the woods night and day" because the British were on the other side of the river and the two sides exchanged artillery fire regularly until December 25.[26] Washington came up from his headquarters at Thomas Barclay's house at Trenton Falls to William Keith's house at Newtown about December 14. Keith had built his two story stone house with an attached kitchen in 1763 on his 240 acre property on the south side of Jericho Hill (modern Bowman's Hill) and from its peak lookouts could see for miles up and down the river. Troops quartered on the south side of the hill were protected from northwest winds. Washington felt Keith "talked too much and asked too many questions" and frequently interrupting him with annoying complaints about the soldiers. Washington moved around a lot and seems to have gone back and forth between Barclay's and Keith's.

General Nathanael Greene occupied Samuel Merrick's two-story square stone house with attached kitchen on the road from Newtown to Neely's mill. The house had been constructed in 1773 and was not yet completely finished. Greene had the walls of one room painted with a pastoral scene of flower gardens, houses, and trees, and over the fireplace the rising sun. The officers and servants lived and cooked "exclusive in the new end of the house." Samuel Merrick "was an even-tempered, amiable man, always disposed to make the best of everything and got along with the officers and men in a harmonious manner." On one occasion, while in conference with several officers in his room,

General Greene observed children playing in the yard. Greene was amused by the children and tried talking to them, but they were afraid. He finally was able to offer young Hannah Merrick a shiny tea canister that she accepted after finding him to be a very pleasant, kind man and she kept it until her death. When Washington had dinner with Greene on Christmas Eve, Hannah waited on them and kept the plate Washington used as a memento. Knox, Stirling, and Sullivan were no doubt present also and after supper the family was sent to a neighbor's for the night to avoid hearing the evening council of war. Opposed to war, Quakers in the area generally did not give aid or comfort to the enemy, including providing useful information on army movements, and "were trusted by Washington."[27] Still, Washington wanted them away while he talked with his officers.

Colonel Henry Knox and Captain Alexander Hamilton quartered at Doctor Chapman's, with Knox occupying the east end of the first floor while Hamilton lay sick in the back room. It was about a mile from Keith's on the other side of the mountain on the road which crosses Jericho Hill. General Sullivan was at John Hayhurst's next to the farm of William Keith, and Brigadier General Roche de Fermoy was quartered at Oliver Paxon's house.[28]

Major Ennion Williams, commanding Miles' Pennsylvania Rifle Regiment stationed at Neely's Mill and house several miles below Coryell's Ferry, kept losing men to desertion because many were barefoot, thinly clothed, and had not been paid for three months. His request to quartermaster Owen Biddle for shoes and stockings was turned down, because any available supplies were earmarked for the troops being raised for the new regiments.[29] Williams's men were quartered in huts "made of boards in a rough manner" while Colonel Edward Hand's and other regiments were quartered in farm houses. Lieutenant James Monroe was quartered at the Neely house and suffered greatly from the "itch." The 6th Virginia Regiment had marched up after crossing at Trenton to what they called the "Cold Camp."[30]

**Washington wanted to make** the lives of enemy soldiers in New Jersey miserable, while also giving encouragement to Whigs. In a letter to the New York Legislature on December 16 he ordered that if Major General William Heath whom he had left on the Hudson after the battle of White Plains "finds any of the enemy's posts at Hackensack or elsewhere weakly guarded he is to endeavor to beat them up." Even a small victory would help with recruiting the new regiments.[31] Washington firmly believed that the British had spread their cantonments over so wide an area in order to "strike a damp into the spirits of the people, which will effectually put a stop to the new inlistment of the army, on which all our hopes depend, and which they will most vigorously strive to effect." Washington recognized that the British occupation of New Jersey empowered the Loyalists, so two days later he encouraged General Heath, "As soon as you find yourself in a situation to send a force into the upper parts of Jersey, I would have you immediately communicate your intentions to the people, with assurances that you will be ready to back and support them in any movements which they may make in your favor." He was certain that the increase in Loyalist activity in southern New Jersey was "as much owing to the want of an Army to look the enemy in the face, as to any other cause."[32] On December 20, Washington told John Hancock that "the enemy are daily gathering strength from the disaffected; this strength like a snow ball by rolling, will increase, unless some means can be devised to check, effectually, the progress of the enemy's arms."[33]

Each day between December 14 and 25, the Americans harassed Hessian guard posts, patrols, forage parties, and messengers. Perhaps Washington's intent was to make garrison life so difficult that Howe would recall his Hessians closer to New York. Whatever the intent, these harassments created a perception among the British and Hessians that the weaknesses of Washington's army limited him to making small raids. The badly stressed British and Hessian soldiers who suffered from these harassing attacks and ambushes retaliated with depredations against civilians that motivated local militiamen to make even more harassing attacks. Howe had increased suspicion and fear among the populace with his offer of amnesty leading loyalists and patriots to become increasingly angry with each other. Washington needed to make a dramatic strike to demonstrate his support for the people of New Jersey. Howe believed that the large number of people responding to his amnesty offer were sincerely returning to the fold, but, many were simply acting to preserve life and property and essentially feeling forced at gunpoint to sign the loyalty oaths. Washington believed he could win them back if he could make the British army evacuate the state.[34]

WASHINGTON'S ARMY CONTINUED TO decline in numbers as enlistments expired. Philemon Baldwin of Colonel Bradley's regiment of Connecticut State Troops completed a six-month enlistment on December 25. General Mercer asked him and others in the same situation to extend their enlistments for 15 days, promising each man three dollars and a pair of shoes. Only Baldwin and one other man agreed while about 60 men in their company were discharged and headed home.[35] However, other Connecticut State Troops in Colonel John Chester's regiment whose enlistments expired on January first agreed to extend in larger numbers several days later.[36]

Washington received reinforcements in December, but not the numbers he really wanted. The two New Jersey regiments at Ticonderoga had been ordered by Congress to march south and join him, but their enlistments expired and they disbanded.[37] Captain John Lacey, from a Quaker family in Buckingham, Bucks County, had served in Colonel Anthony Wayne's 4th Pennsylvania Regiment in northern New York, but had returned home by early December threatening to resign his commission in response to the "tyrannical and haughty treatment" he had received from Wayne. Lacey was troubled to find that loyalties had shifted in Bucks County since his departure. He found "a sullen, vindictive and malignant spirit seemed to have taken hold of a large portion of the people in this County, whose hostility to the Revolution was too apparent not to be noticed, and seemed only waiting a good opportunity to brake forth openly in favour of England, and against their own country." When he had departed in February "all was peace and harmony among the people in the neighbourhood," but now "they appeared all hostile to each other," and the Loyalists "were secretly doing the Whigs all the harm they could possibly do … committing hidden acts to weaken the Americans cause, and applauding the British, representing the power of Great Britton to be omnipotent, and that it was the height of madness and folly to oppose her." Lacey was particularly disappointed when his friends and relatives encouraged him to go over to the British side. He refused to do so, but responding to their fear of being found out he promised to keep their Loyalism secret and not betray them. He did resign his commission, but only temporarily.[38]

Private William Chamberlin, 21 years old and serving in Colonel John Stark's 1st New Hampshire Regiment, arrived at Newtown with Major General Horatio Gates on December 20 or 21 after an exceedingly unpleasant journey from Fort Ticonderoga during which "our shoes [were] scarcely sufficient to keep our feet from the frozen ground without wraping them in rags, the allowance of provision being poor, fresh beef without salt to season it." The few members of his company still with the army were himself, his friend Sergeant Seth Spring and only four or five other privates. They paraded in the morning "and kept the field until sunset."[39]

Rev. David Avery with Colonel John Paterson's 15th Continental Regiment arrived at Newtown on December 22 where he met his brother Jabez, a sutler with Colonel John Durkee's 20th Continental Regiment. He found the people around Newtown to be "cold & indisposed to show kindness to the army. The Quaker conscience will not allow of their treating those well who are engaged in war." The rest of the regiment came in the next day and General Gates set off for Philadelphia. The General Orders that day required troops to be equipped for battle so Avery left his horse with Mr. Christian Van Horn "as we expect to be gone upon an expedition some time." He also left "a shirt & tenting irons in a white Holland handkerchief" with Mr. William Ashburn in Newtown.[40]

John Davis of Solebury Township had spent some time during his youth at the house of William Neely and his mill, and had served as a substitute for his father in a militia company assigned to the Flying Camp from August to December in the New York campaign. He was only 16 years old when the Continentals came to Bucks County and some encamped at Jericho Hill in Upper Makefield very near his home. When Washington crossed the Delaware on Christmas night to attack the Hessians at Trenton, there are indications that some local militiamen accompanied him. For example, John Davis frequently related the incidents of that memorable night to his children and may have gone as a volunteer to help strengthen the Continental forces.[41]

Some discharged men returning from Fort Ticonderoga to their homes near Trenton chose to join with Washington's army as individual volunteers while others connected with local militia units. Captain John Polhemus of the 1st New Jersey Regiment found his wife had fled to nearby mountains for safety from the British troops, so he joined Washington as a volunteer officer not yet mustered into the new version of the 1st New Jersey Regiment then being recruited.[42] Private John Cheston of Polhemus' company apparently joined also. Cheston was from Maidenhead and enlisted in December 1775, possibly while intoxicated, and went to Canada, leaving behind a wife and several children who would not see him again until the afternoon of January 3, 1777.[43]

Joseph Brearley of Maidenhead returned after serving in Canada as a captain in the 2nd New Jersey Regiment in 1776 and "dressed in the garb of peace and friendship as a Quaker" took on the identity of "an humble huckster selling eggs & apples, butter and potatoes, etc. to the officers and soldiers of his 'Loyal King and Master'" and reported any important information he discovered to Washington.[44]

**Collecting boats to carry** the men and gear across to New Jersey was only the first part of the actual crossing plan. There was also the need for properly skilled men to operate the boats. Some of Philemon Dickinson's militiamen had operated ferry boats at several of the crossing points on the river and could help with those. For the Durham boats, Washington had the mariners of Colonel Israel Hutchinson's 27th Continental Regiment that contained many sailors and fishermen from Salem, Lynn, and Danvers and Colonel John Glover's 14th Continental Regiment from Marblehead, Massachusetts. Short, stocky, 44-year-old Glover had been a ship owning merchant and his men were mostly sailors and fishermen who continued to wear their seafaring garb in the army. Glover's and Hutchinson's men had proven themselves in several amphibious actions in the New York campaign, including the tricky overnight retreat from Long Island across the East River to Manhattan.

Philadelphia Associator Alexander Graydon generalized most of the New England troops as "miserably constituted," but in Glover's regiment he found "an appearance of discipline" and "the officers seemed to have mixed with the world, and to understand what belonged to their stations. Though deficient, perhaps, in polish, it possessed an apparent aptitude for the purpose of its institution, and gave a confidence that myriads of its meek and lowly brethren were incompetent to inspire." Expressing the common prejudices of his time, the only drawback he saw was that "there were a number of negroes, which, to persons unaccustomed to such associations, had a disagreeable, degrading effect."[45]

Romantic tradition says that Washington asked Glover just prior to the crossing if his men could get the boats across the river and Glover enthusiastically responded that they could. However, it is more likely that Washington, or Knox who would be in charge of the crossing, discussed the developing plans with Glover, and Glover knew that his Marbleheaders would man the boats well before they formed up for the crossing.[46] Another group called upon to help with the boats was Joseph Moulder's Pennsylvania militia artillery company. Moulder was a 62-year-old Philadelphia shipbuilder who commanded a Pennsylvania artillery company consisting of 82 young men aged 17 to 23 possessing skills such as ship carpenter, mast, block and sail-maker, and rigger.[47]

After crossing the river from McConkey's to Johnson's Ferry, Washington would need guidance from local people who knew the roads to get his army to Trenton in the middle of the night. The guides chosen for this duty came from Philemon Dickinson's militiamen stationed at Yardley's Ferry. On December 24, at the request of General Greene, Dickinson sent Captain John Mott with 25 militiamen of the 1st Hunterdon County Regiment from Hopewell, Maidenhead, and Trenton townships to General Adam Stephen's quarters, and then to General Stirling's quarters to provide information on local roads. These militiamen provided each Continental brigade with "two good guides."[48] It is likely that militiamen with ferrying skills were also pulled out from their companies about this time.

The temperature was in the mid-20s on Christmas Eve when a man General Dickinson described as a "proper person" had been in and about Trenton doing his best to determine the location of Hessian guard posts on the various roads leading into Trenton, the number of guards on the Assunpink Creek bridge, the location and number of Hessian cannon, the number of Hessians in Trenton and whether any reinforcements had recently arrived or if any had marched out. His report of about 2,000 enemy troops was somewhat overestimated. Dickinson had also just learned from a person returned from the Jersey side of the river that a British commissary at Pennytown was giving out "large quantities of Continental pork" to poor people, but refusing to give it to anyone who had not taken a protection. This was part of the plan to encourage the loyalty of the people through kindness, but it paled next to the plundering that people endured, whether they took protections or not. In a post script, Dickinson added that a Hessian patrol had come up as far as Johnson's Ferry that morning and overnight they "heard wagons going all night, & tis imagined the enemy have had notice of the boats being brought down to McConkey's, & conjecture how wagons or carriages carried up field pieces."[49]

**Units began to move towards** McConkey's Ferry early in the afternoon. Roche de Fermoy's and Stirling's troops came down from near Coryell's Ferry and Mercer's troops came up to McConkey's. General Stephen's brigade was already in the area. All units were expected to parade on the Wrights Town Road a mile back from the ferry at precisely 4:00pm when the drums beat half an hour before sunset. Washington gave orders for officers to synchronize their watches with his.[50] His plan was to be across the river with his roughly 2400 men by midnight, so they would be able to launch the attack on Trenton at 4:00am, well before dawn.[51]

Major James Wilkinson had set out on horseback from Philadelphia early that morning to rejoin the American army at Newtown after accompanying General Horatio Gates that far on his way to Baltimore to meet with Congress. Wilkinson had found Gates "much depressed in mind" and convinced that while Washington was wasting his time watching from across the river, the Hessians would construct boats to take them across and "take possession of Philadelphia before he was aware of the movement." Gates believed Washington should instead be forming his army south of the Susquehanna River. Gates had encouraged Wilkinson to accompany him all the way to Baltimore, but Wilkinson felt his "duty forbade the thought" and departed from him at Philadelphia to return to camp. He arrived back at Newtown about 2:00pm and discovered that the army was assembling nearby.

**Table 4: American Troops near Trenton Ferry and Yardley's Ferry – December 25, 1776**

**Ewing's Brigade, Pennsylvania Militia (Brig. Gen. James Ewing) – 826**

Cumberland County Regiment (Colonel Frederick Watts)
Lancaster County Regiment (Colonel Jacob Klotz)
Cumberland County Regiment (Colonel William Montgomery)
York County Regiment (Colonel Richard McCallister)
Chester County Regiment (Colonel James Moore)
Bucks County Regiment (Colonel Joseph Hart)

(Colonels Watts, Montgomery, and McCallister were captured at Fort Washington and were prisoners in New York.

*Captain Jehu Eyre*'s Pennsylvania militia artillery company - 67

**Dickinson's Brigade, New Jersey Militia (Brig. Gen. Philemon Dickson) – 500**

1st Burlington County Regiment (Colonel Joseph Borden)
2nd Burlington County Regiment (Lieutenant Colonel Thomas Reynolds)
1st Hunterdon County Regiment (Colonel Isaac Smith)
*Lieutenant Colonel Abraham Hunt, Joseph Brearley, Benjamin van Cleve, John Mott, David Lanning,*
2nd Hunterdon County Regiment (Colonel Nathaniel Hunt)
3rd Hunterdon County Regiment (*Colonel David Chambers*)
4th Hunterdon County Regiment (Colonel John Mehelm)
Small units of militia from other counties

ALL NEW JERSEY MILITIA REGIMENTS were in disarray in December 1776 due to structural changes made during the months of the New York campaign and the formation of the Five-Month Levies whose enlistments expired at the end of November. All these regiments should be considered as partial and commanding officers may not have been present. (See: Kidder, *A People Harassed and Exhausted*, chapters 4-9 passim.)

He received directions for catching up with the troops and found their "route was easily traced, as there was a little snow on the ground, which was tinged here and there with blood from the feet of the men who wore broken shoes."[52]

Before marching to McConkey's, Washington sent his baggage to Newtown for security and his aide Robert Harrison took possession of the Harris house there. On Christmas afternoon local people saw the army marching toward McConkey's Ferry. Blacksmith James Linton saw them, but had no idea of their objective. The Knowles family heard soldiers marching by their house and next morning saw their bloody tracks in the snow. [53] A number of Washington's soldiers were ill and unfit for action and men were dying daily. While the army was assembling and marching to McConkey's Ferry, 24-year-old Captain

Lieutenant James Moore, "a promising officer" in Captain Alexander Hamilton's New York Artillery company, died at the Neely house "after a short but excruciating fit of illness."[54]

**Washington also had troops** stationed at ferries to the south of McConkey's. Guarding the crossing at Yardley's Ferry were New Jersey militiamen under the command of General Philemon Dickinson, who lived about a mile outside of Trenton where the Hessian Jägers were stationed. He divided responsibility for the area along the river between Trenton Falls and Yardley's Ferry with Brigadier General James Ewing and established guard posts and sent out patrols to watch enemy movements. Washington urged him to "spare no pains or expense to obtain intelligence" and Dickinson for many days had been sending groups of men across the river to both harass the enemy and scout the area around Trenton to identify Hessian positions and patrol patterns. He found it difficult to convince individual men to go into Trenton as spies, because many were afraid they would be recognized and betrayed by inhabitants, such as Trenton Loyalists who had returned to town when the British occupied it, the Monmouth and Burlington County Loyalists who had come into Trenton to help the British, or perhaps by men who had taken protections.[55]

One local militiaman who apparently crossed to Trenton for Dickinson was David Lanning of Trenton Township who worked as a cooper at Captain Mott's grist mill. Several days before Christmas, Lanning was taken into custody near the Delaware River, marched to Trenton, and confined in a house at Tucker's Corner. The resourceful Lanning took advantage of a commotion distracting his guards, slipped out the back door of the house, and after negotiating a high board fence in the back yard made his way to the house of merchant Stacy Potts, Colonel Rall's headquarters. Potts was a Quaker who risked condemnation by both sides in the conflict by refusing, on religious grounds, to swear allegiance to either government. But, on this occasion he concealed Lanning who the next morning covered himself with an old ragged coat and floppy hat, put an axe under his arm, and headed out assuming a limp and bowed head. Appearing to be an elderly wood cutter, he passed safely through the Hessian sentries and was not called out by any Loyalists. At the Pennington and Scotch

**Table 5: American Troops at Bristol – December 25, 1776**

**Cadwalader's Brigade, Pennsylvania Associators (Colonel John Cadwalader) – 1500**

Morgan's Regiment, Philadelphia Associators (Colonel Jacob Morgan)
Bayard's Regiment, Philadelphia Associators (Colonel John Bayard)
Cadwalader's Regiment, Philadelphia Associators (Lieutenant Colonel John Nixon)
Matlack's Rifle Battalion Philadelphia Associators (Colonel Timothy Matlack)
Kent County Delaware Militia Company (*Captain Thomas Rodney*)
Artillery Company, Philadelphia Associators (*Captain Jehu Eyre*)
Artillery Company, Philadelphia Associators (*Captain Joseph Moulder*)
*Zebulon Applegate*

The Associators were volunteer militiamen. Pennsylvania did not have a mandatory militia system like New Jersey.

**Colonel Daniel Hitchcock's Brigade – 822**

4th Continental Regiment (Massachusetts) (*Colonel John Nixon*)
9th Continental Regiment (Rhode Island) (Colonel James Varnum)
11th Continental Regiment (Rhode Island) (*Colonel Daniel Hitchcock, Major Israel Angell*)
12th Continental Regiment (Massachusetts) (*Colonel Moses Little*)
Rhode Island State Regiment (*Colonel Christopher Lippitt*)
*John Howland*

**Continental Marines**, recruited at the Tun Tavern, Philadelphia, 1776 (Capt. Robert Mullen) - 50
*Lieutenant William Shippen*

Road intersection he felt safe, threw down the axe, entered Dickinson's swamp and escaped back across the river to rejoin his militia company and report his findings to General Dickinson.[56]

General Ewing commanded some 800 Pennsylvania militia on the Pennsylvania side of the river at Trenton Ferry guarding possible river crossings.[57] He sent men across the river daily during the week before Christmas to attack the Hessian guard posts and patrols near the river bank, causing the Hessians to conduct a daily early morning heavy patrol towards Trenton Ferry. One of Ewing's officers, Captain Jehu Eyre, a 38-year-old veteran of the French and Indian War, commanded a company of Pennsylvania militia artillery. He was a shipwright and shipbuilder from Philadelphia at Northern Liberties and his company was composed of men with shipbuilding and rigging skills. On December 23 he had detailed seven of his men to repair defective craft located at the Trenton Ferry, in anticipation of needing them two days later.[58]

**At Bristol, Colonel John** Cadwalader had about 1,200 Philadelphia Associators, well provided for duty, and about 500-600 New England Continentals under Colonel Daniel Hitchcock who were without stores or blankets and in general "very badly equipped for winter service." Cadwalader's primary duty was to guard the Bristol ferries, Dunks' and Neshaminy.[59]

Among his men at Bristol was Joseph Hodgkins, a lieutenant in Captain Nathaniel Wade's company of Colonel Moses Little's Massachusetts regiment, who had marched to Bristol on December 22 "and camped in the woods near the town." He was a 31-year-old shoemaker from Ipswich, Massachusetts, and a veteran of Bunker Hill and the New York campaign. Nearing the main army on December 20 he wrote to his wife that he was fatigued from the long march they had endured since November 29. Now within 10 or 12 miles of Washington's army, "we expect to be there to night but how long we shall stay there I cant tell." The close proximity of the enemy troops and Loyalists had made their march dangerous. He hoped to survive and eventually get home, but he could not predict when that would be because traveling was so difficult at that time of the year. He hoped to leave soon, since his enlistment was about up, and reported the weather had been "extraordinary pleasant" although there was now a snow storm.[60]

Sergeant John Smith of Colonel Christopher Lippitt's Rhode Island Regiment had fought through the New York campaign and arrived with Sullivan at Buckingham on December 20. On December 21 they marched four miles to Makefield Township and then to Newtown and finally Bristol where they arrived before nightfall on December 22 and "drew provisions & pitched tents in a grove by ye town," because the Pennsylvania militia had taken up all the houses. They had come 19 miles that day and "we drew provisions & serv'd it out to the companys & rested here." On the 23rd he got a pair of stockings and shoes from his colonel for 19s and 6d. On the 24th they had orders to "draw two days provisions & to cook it which we did in order to march if cald upon." Now, on the 25th they paraded in the afternoon and all the men able to go on duty were ordered to prepare to march.[61]

Thirty-one-year-old Dr. Benjamin Rush had offered his services to the army after Congress left Philadelphia. Rush has been described as "generous and idealistic to a fault, [but] he was also impulsive, opinionated, and filled with an amount of zeal and self-righteousness that taxed friends and family alike. His public and professional life was punctuated by quarrels, jousts and battles." Just about a year earlier, Rush had passed through Trenton on his way to marry 16-year-old Julia Stockton at Morven, the Stockton family home in Princeton. Rush had attended and graduated from the college at Princeton before he was 15 years old and had known Julia since she was four years old. His knowledge of the area would prove useful. He and Dr. John Cochran, a man Rush found possessed of "humanity as well as skill, and is dear to all who know him,"were now with the Philadelphia militia at Bristol.[62]

On December 23, Rush and Joseph Reed had visited Washington at his quarters and spent more than an hour with him the next morning. Rush found him "much depressed, and lamented the ragged and dissolving state of his army in affecting terms." Rush reassured him that he had the full support of Congress and while they talked noticed Washington writing on "several small pieces of paper." One piece fell on the floor near Rush's feet and he "was struck with thc inscription upon it. It was 'Victory or Death.'"[63]

Another officer with Cadwalader was 31-year-old Captain Thomas Rodney of the Delaware militia. Rodney observed that "a general dismay seemed spread over the Country" and felt his "mind anxious and uneasy," while his brother Caesar, who had signed the Declaration, "was very apprehensive for the safety of our cause."[64] Rodney managed to gather and arm 35 men willing to go with him to join Washington's army on the Delaware River and they marched from Dover, Delaware on December 14.[65]

On the road they encountered many people fleeing Philadelphia, as well as other militia companies heading for the army. The general gloom and doubt was only tempered by the hope that General Lee, whom they did not yet know had been captured, would do something to prevent the British from crossing the Delaware. If that didn't happen, then "Congress would be obliged to authorize the Commander in Chief to obtain the best terms that could be had from the enemy." Rodney urged the gloomy people he met not to despair and "not say anything on their way that would discourage the people," but instead to do all they could to encourage people and point to the militia turnout as a positive development.

Rodney's militia company arrived in Philadelphia on December 18 with the men in good health and spirits, but some with blistered feet. What he found in the city was extremely disquieting, because "more than half the houses appeared deserted, and the families that remained were shut up in their houses, and nobody appeared in the streets." There were no troops in the city, but General Putnam was there to give orders to militia units passing through. Rodney detailed a man as sentinel at Putnam's residence and put his other men in guard positions in the city. As Rodney lingered in Philadelphia, people tried to convince him to give up the cause, promising to do all they could to help him become reestablished as a loyal British citizen. He replied, "by pointing out those circumstances that were still favorable to America, and concluded by assuring them that I should not change my determination, that I knew my business and should not return until the British were beaten, but they treated this as levity and concluded that I was an obstinate man, and must be left to take my own way."

Rodney left Philadelphia on December 21 and got to Bristol on December 22 where his company took quarters in two houses. Rodney and half the company quartered at Mrs. Andrew Allen's. Sarah Allen had three children and her husband and two brothers were prominent Loyalists who were with Howe. Lieutenant McCall and the other half of Rodney's company quartered about 200 yards away at the house of Sarah Allen's father, William Coxe. Sarah was concerned that the soldiers would harass her because her husband was a Loyalist. Rodney assured her that he would not let that happen, because "our cause is a just one and should be maintained with justice."[66] Private Nehemiah Tilton noted that both families were "exceeding kind" and that "Mrs. Coxe gave a turkey & goose to the company at her house & Mrs. Allen has done the same for Christmas dinner tomorrow."[67]

Cadwalader told Rodney that evening that he had about 800 men left of the 1,200 he had at one point, because "many had gone off one way or another." He thought Washington had about 1,500 men but expected more from General Lee's force. Cadwalader felt the capture of General Lee "had damped the spirit of the army very much, and everything looked very gloomy," but Rodney countered that it would free up Washington "to exert his own talents" and not rely on Lee.[68]

On December 23, Rodney was with Colonel Cadwalader about 9:00am when he received an express from Washington announcing the plan to attack the British posts about an hour before daybreak on the 26th. Cadwalader was told to cease harassing Donop's troops and prepare for that battle, whose details he would receive in a day or two.[69] Rodney "rejoiced" and assured Cadwalader that they "should certainly be successful."[70] Washington implored them, "for Heaven's sake, keep this to yourself, as the discovery of it may prove fatal to us; our numbers, sorry am I to say, being less than I had any conception of; but necessity, dire necessity will, nay must, justify my attack." On the 26th, Washington wanted Cadwalader to attack as many enemy "posts as you possibly can, with a prospect of success; the more we can attack at the same instant, the more confusion we shall spread and greater good will result from it." He explained the attack had not been feasible sooner because things had been so unsettled in terms of troop numbers and the troops that arrived under General Sullivan had been "in want of everything."[71]

On the 24th, Washington told Cadwalader to work out points of attack with Colonel Griffin "but let the hour of attack be the 26th, and one hour before day (of that morning)." Hitchcock's brigade was ordered to join Cadwalader's and "if you should be successful (of which I have the highest hopes) move forward if possible, so as to form a junction with me, if the like good fortune should attend our enterprize, either at Trenton or Princeton." Anticipating several days of action, he told Cadwalader to provide his men with blankets and three days of cooked rations.[72] These communications demonstrate that Washington planned to do much more than just attack Trenton and retreat back to Pennsylvania.

Washington was not completely despondent and was hopeful the war would continue the next year and on December 24 wrote to Colonel Griffin about recruiting men for one of the 88 regiments authorized by Congress. While he was very critical of the way Congress appointed officers, he laid out what would be required for Griffin to earn Washington's appointment to command a regiment he would raise "as far as possible in the Jerseys."[73]

On the night of December 24, Joseph Reed went to Philadelphia to urge General Putnam to reinforce Colonel Griffin and divert the enemy's attention on the 25th. However, Griffin was very ill and two of his companies had returned, leaving behind two small cannon and a few militia at Moorestown and Haddonfield. General Putnam could not use the militia then in Philadelphia to support an action due to its current condition, the confusion in the city, the fear of insurrection in the city if he left it, and other circumstances. This was just the first glitch to Washington's plan. Reed returned to Bristol where Cadwalader was determined to attack Donop at Mount Holly on the morning of December 26 as a diversion from the planned action at Trenton.[74] On December 25, Rodney joined Cadwalader's brigade and was ordered to be ready to march that night.[75]

**As sunset approached**, all the units of Washington's army were making ready to cross the Delaware River to the Jerseys and many of the men were no doubt unaware of exactly what they were about to engage in, and probably did not really care. Doing something was better that nothing and would at least be a change. What they could not anticipate was that the weather this night and the action the next morning would become two of the most vivid memories of the war that they would keep for the rest of their lives. As the soldiers marched to the river crossing points, the people on both sides of this war wondered just how much longer it would continue. Major changes in a war seldom took place in the winter.

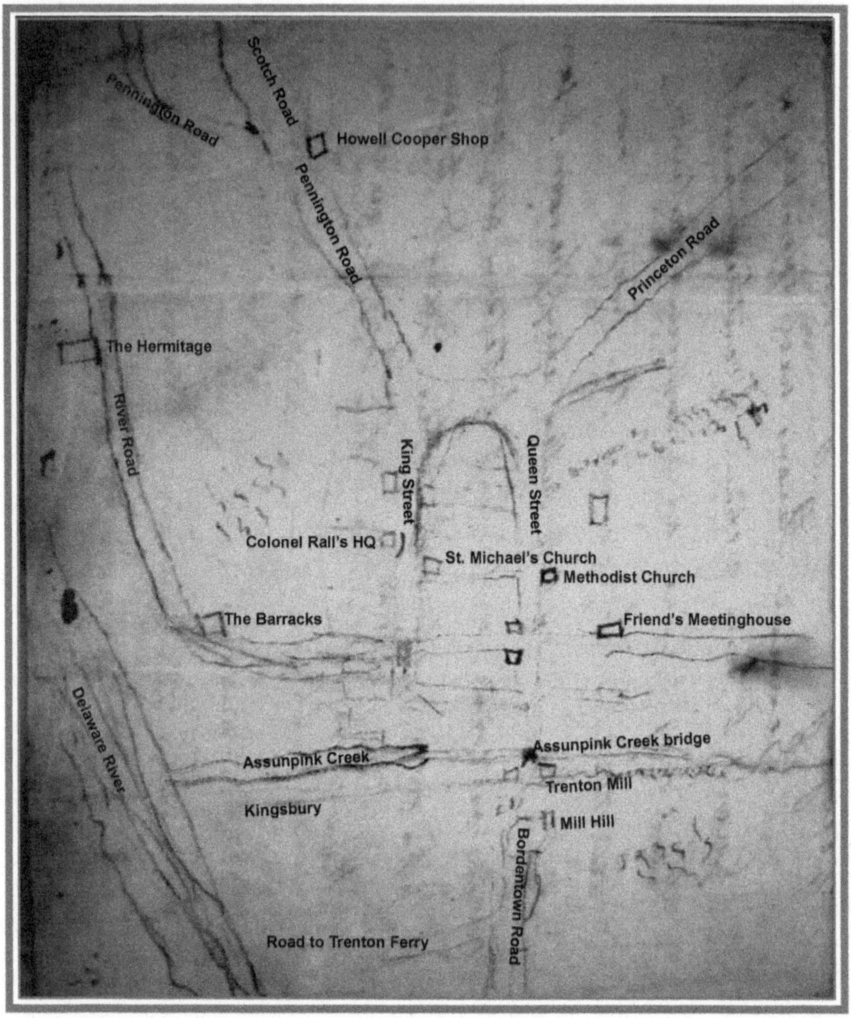


**Map 5: General Henry Knox's Map of the Trenton Battle Plan**

This sketch of the town of Trenton was included with Knox's copy of Washington's order of battle dated December 25, 1776. While it is not to scale and does not show how the attack would proceed, it does give an overview of some of the key spots in town and the important roads, which have been labeled by the author. (Source: *The Papers of Henry Knox, 1719-1825)*

# Chapter 6

## Delaware River Night Crossings, Wednesday - Thursday, December 25-26, 1776

Washington chose to cross his army over to New Jersey at McConkey's Ferry, about nine miles north of Trenton, because it was distant enough from Trenton not to draw attention and it provided ferry boats for the cannon, wagons, and horses. Across from McConkey's was Johnson's Ferry in the typical Delaware River ferry pattern of separately owned ferries on each shore across from each other. Both were well-established and had been operating for many decades, and both operators were ardent Scoth-Irish Presbyterian supporters of the war for independence. Samuel McConkey had owned and operated his ferry since purchasing it on December 5, 1774, when it was known as Baker's Ferry. Abraham Harvey had purchased the New Jersey ferry in 1770 from Robert and Rut Johnson and leased its operation to James Slack throughout the War for Independence. Ferries were often known by multiple customary names, rather than a legal name, usually associated with an owner, an operator, or a location. Johnson's Ferry had been known by several names, including Eight Mile Ferry, but the name Johnson's persisted and was the name most familiar to people. Crossing at this location must have been one of Washington's earliest decisions as his plan of attack developed because Washington arranged for Durham boats and flats to be brought there as early as December 19.[1]

The famous Durham boats were used to transport the troops, being completely unsuited for transporting artillery, horses, and wagons. Designed to carry heavy loads, the sturdily constructed Durham boats were between about 40 and 60 feet long, three and a half feet deep, about eight feet wide, flat bottomed, and pointed at both ends like a canoe. The draft varied from about four inches up to 28 inches depending on load weight. The bow and stern were decked over for about 12 feet from each end. There were narrow walking boards on each side between the decked areas, allowing crewmen to walk the length of the boat. The crew leader took position at the stern and steered the craft with a sweep thirty-three-feet long and ending in a blade one foot wide. The crew used setting poles to drive the boat against a current or fend off rocks and 18-foot-long sweeps for rowing.[2] In icy conditions the setting poles could be used to break up or fend off floating ice and the hull of the boat itself was strong enough and well-shaped, to act as an ice breaker against sheet ice. Just how many Durham boats were actually used for the crossing is not known, but it is estimated that between 16 and 25 were brought down from behind Malta Island upriver from McConkey's Ferry.[3]

As part of their commercial operation, ferries had to safely transport horses and wagons, as well as human passengers. The ferry boats, often called "flats," were shallow, wide, rectangular wooden boxes about 40 feet long with flat floors consisting of two layers of planks. They had a very shallow draft and were very stable. The floor sloped up towards each end and had narrow battens fastened across it to provide footing for any animals the ferry carried. At each end was a hinged gangplank the full width of the boat that could be lowered, to make loading or unloading easy, and then raised during the passage across the river to keep it out of the water. The ferries did not require docks, but could simply run up against the river bank and lower the gangplank. If desired, simple structures to accommodate the gangplank could be provided where roads leading to a ferry came to the river bank. Delaware River ferry boats were often attached to a rope stretching across the river. Two pulleys on the rope had lines that attached to cleats on the ferry toward each end. When starting across the river, the forward line was shortened and the after line lengthened to put the ferry at an angle in the current. This way the current helped push the boat across the river, not unlike how wind acts with a sail. Crewmen also used long poles to push against the river bottom to get the boat moving or to modify its course.

Just how many crossing ropes were set up at McConkey's/Johnson's to facilitate Washington's artillery, horses, and wagons is not known, but some flats must have crossed between the normal docking points while others simply went up against the unmodified shore. We do know that at least four flats were brought to McConkey's Ferry after December 19.[4] Local militiamen, including David Lanning and William Green, who knew how to operate ferries were pulled out of their companies, just as they had been the first week of December when Washington crossed the army to Pennsylvania at the Trenton ferries.[5] James Slack, 20-years-old, who lived a mile above Yardley's Ferry and knew the river and its ferries also assisted with the ferry boats.[6] Marbleheaders, Moulder's men, and local militiamen finished preparing the boats for the crossing during the morning and afternoon while the troops collected about a mile back from the river and ferry.

Sergeant Thomas McCarty of Colonel George Weedon's 3rd Virginia Regiment in Stirling's brigade marched off with his company "in order of battle" during the afternoon to McConkey's Ferry after receiving money to settle ration accounts that morning. The day before, he had heard talk of marching, but no details, and drew provisions for his troops.[7] Eighteen-year-old David How of Colonel Paul Sargent's regiment marched at 12:00pm for McConkey's Ferry. He had spent Christmas Eve "drawing cateridges and provisions" needed for an unspecified "scout."[8] The soldiers around William Keith's "were very busy the day before the battle scouring up their guns; were sure something was to be done, but knew nothing about the character of it."[9] As the troops collected, all officers were ordered to "have a white paper in their hats to be distinguished by."[10]

Major James Wilkinson caught up with his brigade near the ferry about dusk where he found Washington "alone with his whip in his hand, prepared to mount his horse." Wilkinson handed him a letter from General Gates and Washington solemnly commented, "What a time is this to hand me letters!" He asked Wilkinson where Gates was and when told he was on his way to Congress, Washington exclaimed "On his way to Congress!" and broke the seal. Wilkinson wisely departed and joined St. Clair at the assembly point.[11] Washington was no doubt angered because two days before he had told Gates that he had no objection to his going to Philadelphia on account of a health issue, but asked him to go by way of Bristol "in order to have conducted matters there in cooperation with what I hinted to you as

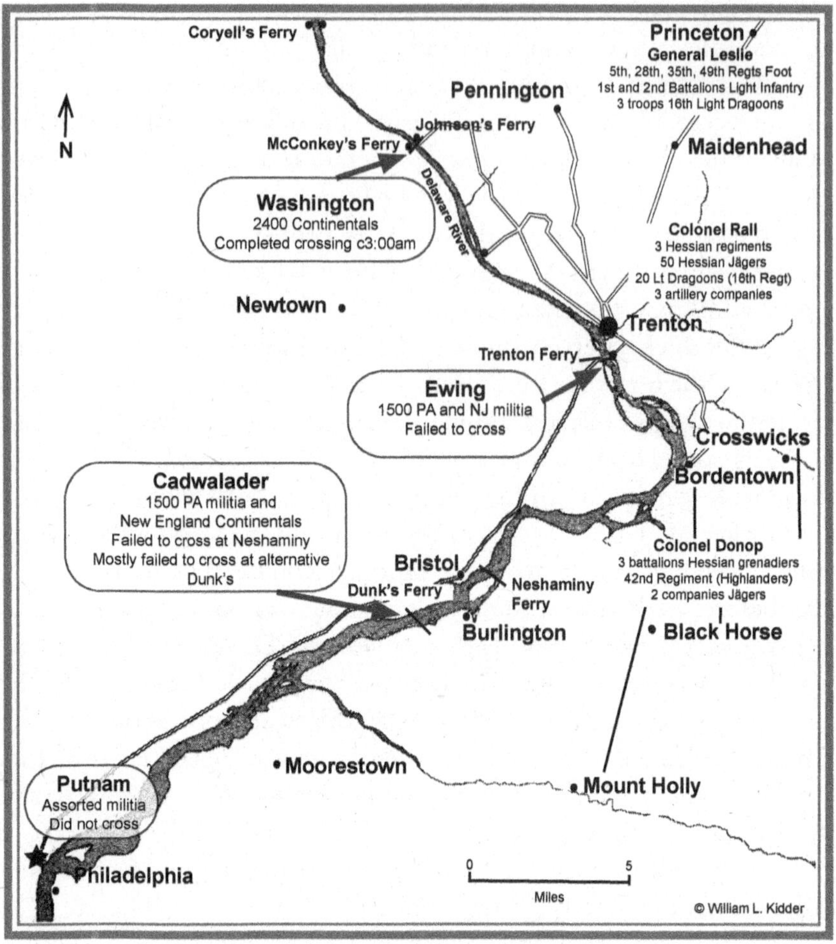


**Map 6: Night Crossings of the Delaware River, December 25-26, 1776**

having in view here." It would help if General Gates could stay just two or three days "to concert with Colonels Read & Cadwalader a plan & direct in what manner it is to be conducted."[12] In other words, he hoped Gates could briefly, and appropriately, take command over the colonels at Bristol for the crossing there.

John Greenwood, a 16-year-old fifer in Colonel John Paterson's 15th Continental Regiment of General St. Clair's Brigade, was one of about 170 veterans of the Canadian campaign who had arrived from Albany a few days earlier without tents and some men without shoes. Their chaplain was 30-year-old Rev. David Avery. They paraded about 4:00pm, about half an hour before sunset with the sun shining brightly. On their march to the ferry they stopped at William Keith's where they were issued ammunition and flints before marching on to the ferry where they halted, kindled fires and left their packs. Each man in Greenwoods's regiment was issued 60 cartridges and even though he was a fifer, Greenwood carried a musket. He put some of the cartridges in his pockets and "some in my little cartridge-box." At sunset it began to drizzle and by the time they got to the river it was raining. He crossed "in a flat-bottomed scow" and was among the first men to cross in St. Clair's brigade.[13]

Getting the boats safely across the river would be difficult due to "the force of the current, the sharpness of the frost, the darkness of the night, the ice which made during the operation, and a high wind."[14] They had to struggle with various sized pieces of sheet ice (floes) floating with the current that had broken off from the banks of the upper branches of the Delaware where the river had frozen on December 20. There was a delay in getting started because of the river and weather conditions and the fact that not all the troops had arrived. Colonel Henry Knox was in charge of the embarkation and initially remained on the Pennsylvania side of the river getting the men started across.[15] As the crossing developed and problems arose, Knox may well have made several round trips to assess changing situations personally. Knox was a large man later described as having "bland and dignified manners" while at the same time being "sprightly, very playful, yet of sensible conversation," altogether "a very distinguished as well as very amiable man." He was beloved by everyone and known for his "deep bass" voice that "resounded through the camp, when exercising the artillery." During the crossing "his stentorian voice was heard above the crash of ice which filled the river with floating cakes, and very much embarrassed the boats that were conveying the army."[16] Those "stentorian lungs and extraordinary exertions of Colonel Knox" proved essential to the successful crossing.[17]

The first to cross and immediately begin their march, no doubt led by 1st Hunterdon County Regiment militia guides, were two, 40-man advance parties under Captains William Washington and John Flahaven with orders to check the roads and set up roadblocks at intersections about three miles outside Trenton where they would "make prisoners of all going in or coming out of town" so that word of the attack could not be spread. Their guides would get them to the proper intersections and identify the people they detained. Captain William Washington, of Colonel Weedon's 3rd Virginia Regiment, was a second cousin of the commander-in-chief and still suffered from a wound received at the Battle of Long Island. Lieutenant James Monroe, 19-years-old, had been a second year student at the College of William and Mary the previous year and was now a combat veteran serving in Captain Thornton's company of Weedon's regiment. When he heard about Captain Washington's mission, Monroe volunteered to accompany it and was accepted. The Virginians set off on the route that General Greene and Washington would follow to Trenton. Highly regarded Continental veteran Captain John Flahaven, now part of the 1st New Jersey Regiment, led the other party, consisting of recruits for his regiment, and took the road General Sullivan's division would follow.[18]

Virginia Brigadier General Adam Stephen's brigade followed sometime later, with a group of artillerymen, and upon landing spread out designated units to form a chain of sentries around the assembly area where the army would form up and ordered them not to let anyone pass, in either direction. Stephen's artillerymen crossed without cannons, but carried spikes, hammers and drag ropes for use in capturing or disabling enemy artillery. Next came the other brigades marching with Nathanael Greene's division, Mercer's, Stirling's, and Roche de Fermoy's, followed by the brigades of John Sullivan's division, Sargent's, Glover's and St. Clair's.[19] Sometime after Stephen's brigade crossed, Washington dismounted and crossed to New Jersey with his staff.[20]

There are several stories about men who reputedly commanded or crewed the boat that took Washington across the river. One concerned Captain John Blunt, a sea captain and merchant who knew the Delaware River and upon being pointed out to Washington, was told by him "to please take the helm." This story is unlikely, because the Delaware River at McConkey's Ferry was nothing like the tidal and much wider river below the falls at Trenton. Blunt did not know the portion of the river where Washington was crossing.[21] Captain William Blackler of Glover's regiment said after the war that he had commanded the boat that carried Washington across and his account was supported by private John Roads Russell who claimed to be one of the oarsmen. Second Lieutenant Anthony Cuthbert of Captain Moulder's artillery company is another man claimed to have been in charge of the boat that carried Washington across. Moulder's men were very familiar with boats and ships and were known to have helped, so this could be accurate. None of these stories can be corroborated with documentary evidence.[22]

Between about 10:00 and 11:00pm a severe storm with high winds developed, making it even more difficult to safely ferry over the horses, artillery and wagons.[23] While the conditions made the ferry boat crossings very difficult, getting the Durham boats across safely was perhaps even more difficult. These boats were designed to travel up and down the river, not across it. Once out in the river's current the crew needed to find a way to counteract the current pushing them downstream against the side of the boat. This required some strenuous rowing, directed partly upstream against the current and partly across the river, and perhaps also using the long poles to push against the river bottom to propel the boat against the current as well as across. To these issues were added the problems caused by the ice. It was exhausting work for the boat crews. But, if Washington now considered proceeding without the artillery, or reducing its numbers, he dismissed those thoughts knowing that artillery was considered a foul weather weapon that could be used successfully when wet conditions reduced the reliability of muskets. The artillery was now more important than ever.

According to tradition, but no concrete evidence, once across, Washington sat down on a box which may have once been used as a beehive, where he could be undisturbed and fight any anxious thoughts challenging his determination to achieve "victory or death."[24] He demonstrated the characteristic admired by men such as Major Wilkinson who described him as "born with iron nerves, and an unbending dignity of port, which distinguished all his actions, and struck the most presumptuous with awe." Even "amidst those scenes which 'tried men's souls,' [Washington was] serene, tranquil, and self-possessed, excited the admiration of his followers, and exhibited the heroic example of a chief determined to brave danger and dare death in support of a just cause, and the defence of the most precious rights and interests of mankind." Washington later wrote that, "as I was certain there was no making a retreat without being discovered, and harassed on repassing the River, I determined to push on at all events."[25]

Private William Chamberlin of Stark's regiment in St. Clair's Brigade recalled that they marched about sunset to the ferry, where "the anchor ice in the river so obstructed the boats that we were a long time in crossing."[26] The troops were still not over by midnight, as had been planned, and the crossing was about three hours behind schedule.[27]

**While Washington's troops assembled** back of McConkey's Ferry, Cadwalader's troops began their march from Bristol to Neshaminy Ferry with Colonel Timothy Matlack's regiment in the advance. Joseph Hodgkins of Moses Little's regiment marched to a ferry about seven miles from his camp where he expected to cross the river and attack an enemy force then at Mount Holly.[28] Sergeant William Young's company received orders to hold themselves ready to move with two days of provisions and meet on the grand parade at 7:00pm.[29] Thomas Rodney and his company marched off without even telling their hosts, the Allen and Coxe families, that they were leaving.[30]

At Neshaminy Ferry, Cadwalader found the river so full of ice that crossing it was impossible. He could not wait long for conditions to improve and soon ordered all the boats he could gather down to Dunk's Ferry and sent his troops off to Dunk's on an almost six mile roundabout march passing through woody and uninhabited land to prevent detection by the enemy.[31] Rodney, with the light infantry and militia, marched to Dunks Ferry where the brigade met up with Colonel Hitchcock's New England brigade of Continentals. In order not to alert the enemy, the troops were discouraged from building any fires near the shore while they waited to embark. However, the cold made it impossible to eliminate all fires.[32] Perhaps Washington was even more disappointed about Gates going to Baltimore when, early in the evening, he learned from Joseph Reed about the river ice conditions at Neshaminy Ferry and Cadwalader's decision to march his troops to Dunk's Ferry and try to cross there. At 6:00pm Washington wrote a short note to Cadwalader letting him know that he was determined to make his crossing and attack Trenton in the morning. Recognizing that Cadwalader might not be able to successfully get across, Washington ordered him to do everything he could "as far as you see consistent with propriety" and "at least create as great a diversion as possible."[33]

Ensign Philip Hagner of the 2nd Battalion of the Philadelphia Associators set off for Dunk's from Bristol in cloudy weather about 9:00pm. A violent storm of snow, hail and rain driven by high wind began between 10:00 and 11:00pm. Hagner did not know "the object of the march, but it was generally understood that the whole plan was suggested by Gen. Reed, whose activity was very conspicuous." It is typical for ice to build up along the New Jersey bank where the river is tidal, as at Bristol. Ferries and other craft had to land passengers and cargo at the edge of this ice. Men and sometimes even horses could often walk across the ice, but wagons or artillery could not traverse it.[34] While some light infantry troops got across the river, Hagner said, "the piling of the ice on the Jersey shore prevented the rest of the troops among whom I was one."[35]

About 600 men of the light infantry battalion, consisting of Rodney's company and four companies of Philadelphia militia under Captain George Henry, got over and marched about 200 yards where they formed up in four columns of double files to guard the landing area and prevent anyone from alerting the enemy. Once the light infantry had secured the shore, men from Colonel Jacob Morgan's and Lieutenant Colonel John Nixon's regiments entered the boats and pushed off. They almost got across, but the strong wind picked up and the ice extended out a greater distance from the shore preventing them from landing safely. Joseph Reed and two or three militia field officers crossed over to direct the landing, but found "to their great surprise & mortification" that the ice "had drifted in such great quantities upon the Jersey shore that it was absolutely impossible to land the artillery." An attempt to land their horses proved so difficult that all hope was lost for the cannon.[36] Boats carrying two artillery pieces found the ice extended out about 150 yards from shore and while the men could walk on the ice, it would not support the weight of artillery. Rodney found "the river was also very full of floating ice, and the wind was blowing very hard, and the night was very dark and cold, and we had great difficulty in crossing."[37]

After three hours on the New Jersey shore, about midnight, Rodney was informed that Cadwalader and Hitchcock "had given up the expedition, and that the troops that were over were ordered back." Cadwalader had consulted with his field officers who believed it would be improper to advance without artillery. Ensign Hagner of the Associators did not cross and says, "We remained at the ferry until about 3 o'clock [am], when we marched on our return to Bristol where we arrived at daylight."[38]

The withdrawal took until almost 4:00am, about the time Washington was beginning his march to Trenton. As his troops marched back to Bristol, Cadwalader could only "imagine [that] the badness of the night" must have also prevented Washington from crossing – but he could not be sure.[39] Greatly irritated, some of the officers that got across wanted to make an attack without Cadwalader or Hitchcock, or the artillery, but others opposed this because, "if Gen. Washington should be unsuccessful and we also, the cause would be lost, but if our force remained intact it would still keep up the spirit of America; therefor this course was abandoned." Rodney had to "wait about three hours more to cover the retreat, by which time, the wind blew very hard and there was much rain and sleet, and there was so much floating ice in the River that we had the greatest difficulty to get over again, and some of our men did not get over that night. As soon as I reached the Pennsylvania shore I received orders to march to our quarters, where I arrived a little before daylight very wet and cold."[40]

**Trying to cross** at Trenton, Ewing contended with even worse conditions than Cadwalader. When ice coming down the Delaware meets an incoming tide it piles up below the rapids known as Trenton Falls. In about four hours it can accumulate up to five feet thick and extend for about half a mile downstream. This packed ice may have three or four narrow open channels of rushing water, but it is impossible to cross the river in a boat. The ice pack can change rapidly, growing or breaking up, over a day or two, or longer, depending on temperature, precipitation, and tidal schedule.[41]

Although some have judged so, Ewing and Cadwalader did not fail to cross to support Washington because they lacked determination or courage. The river ice conditions, boat types, and troop skills were different at each of the three crossing sites. If the Marbleheaders were indeed significant to Washington's crossing, then their absence at the other two crossings is also significant. Cadwalader and Ewing either didn't have Durham boats that could cut through the ice or the ice was too thick even for them. They may not have had enough experienced river men, or the river ice conditions were too severe even for them.

Cadwalader received three boats about 1:00am and kept the two most valuable that had carried down "the twelve-pounders." These were ferry boats from Dunks's. Even so, "if the wind blows we cannot transport our cannon." The next day, Cadwalader wrote to the Pennsylvania Council of Safety, "We have got our boats up from Dunks's, and shall embark in the morning, before day. We are greatly at a loss for the boats you promised to send up to transport our cannon. I ordered the three horse-boats that arrived last night (which were very useful) to remain till further orders; but they went off last night. If the gundolas were to come up again, they would be of great use." PS. "Pray let the gundolas make the attempt, and return if impracticable to get up."[42]

WHILE THE AMERICAN forces were crossing, or attempting to cross, the Delaware River that night, Colonel Rall continued to enjoy Abraham Hunt's hospitality feeling secure that the evening alarm had been the expected attack and the foul weather would discourage any further enemy movements. According to unsubstantiated tradition, at some point a Loyalist from Bucks County delivered a note to Rall at Mr Hunt's warning of Washington's attack and Rall put it in his pocket unread. Even if Rall had received such a note, he would have discounted it as old news. He continued his relaxing evening well into early morning before returning to his quarters at Stacy Potts's house, expecting to sleep late the next morning, as was his usual habit.[43] His soldiers maintained their normal alertness with an added edge resulting from the evening harassing attack, but also feeling some security because of the raging storm. The main problem with the rebel forces across the river was that they kept harassing them so they felt they were on campaign rather than in winter quarters. They had already been harassed once this evening and may well be harassed again the next day so they had to stay prepared for battle as usual throughout the night.

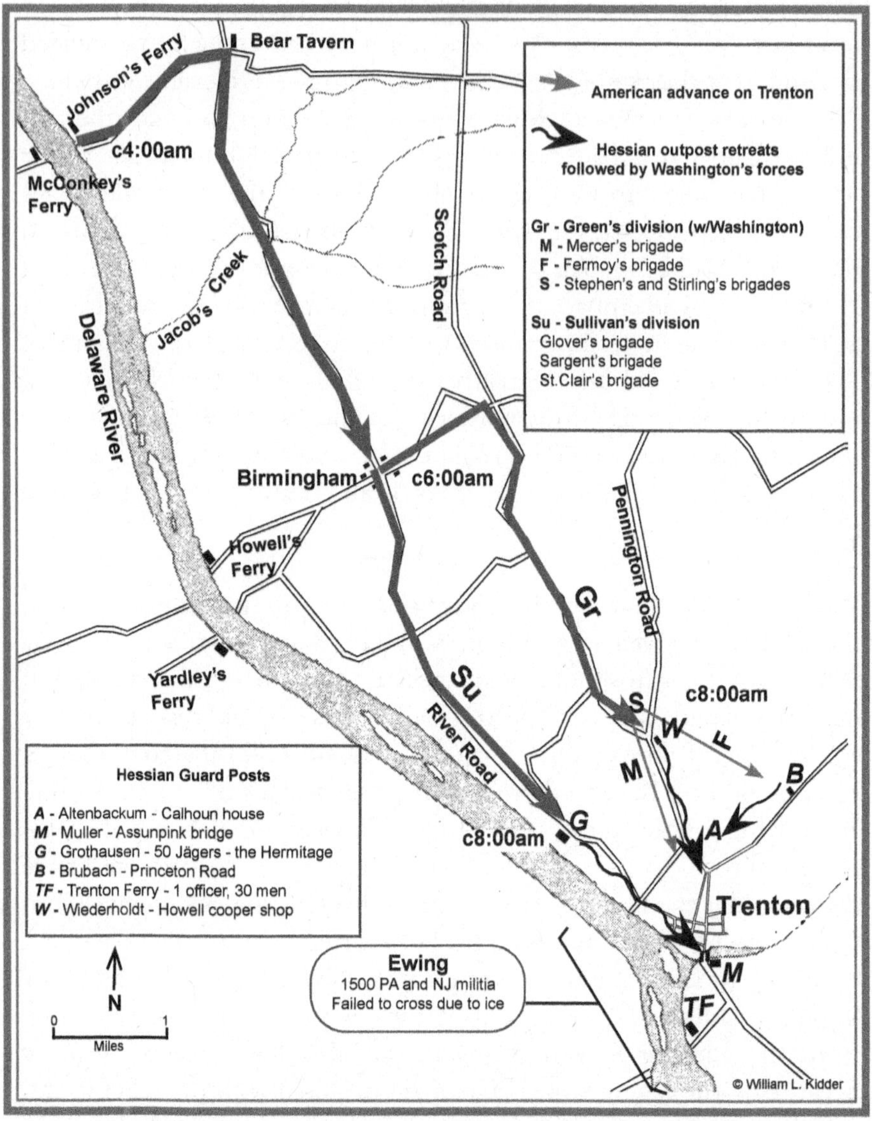


**Map 7: The Night March to Trenton and First Encounters, c4:00am -c8:00am**

The army crossed at McConkey's Ferry and Johnson's Ferry before beginning, very much behind schedule, the march to Trenton. The army split at the crossroads settlement of Birmingham, not at the Bear Tavern as some early accounts mistakenly say, and marched on to attack Trenton from both its north and south sides. The initial contacts were made outside the town at Hessian guard posts commanded by Lieutenants Wiedgerholdt and Grothausen and the Hessian troops were forced to retreat under heavy pressure to town. Although establishing well-manned guard posts, Colonel Rall had refused to build any defensive works for protection from an overwhelming force, such as the Americans had for this attack.

# Chapter 7

## Night March to Trenton, December 26, 1776

As Washington's soldiers disembarked on the Jersey side of the Delaware, they built fires to help keep warm during the seemingly interminable hours they suffered through the storm awaiting orders to march. Soldiers and equipment continued to come across while units gathered together behind the screen formed by the Virginia Continentals from Adam Stephen's brigade. Fifer John Greenwood joined others in pulling down fences to make warming fires because the storm was increasing in strength and "it rained, hailed, snowed, and froze, and at the same time blew a perfect hurricane" causing the wind and fire to cut the rails in two "in a moment." To keep warm, he had to keep turning around "before the large bonfire." For Greenwood, "the noise of the soldiers coming over and clearing away the ice, the rattling of the cannon wheels on the frozen ground, and the cheerfulness of my fellow-comrades encouraged me beyond expression, and, big coward as I acknowledge myself to be, I felt great pleasure, more than I now do in writing about it."[1]

It was not until about 2:00am that the infantrymen all got across while the artillery was not all over until 3:00am. Henry Knox found that "the floating ice in the river made the labor almost incredible. However, perseverance accomplished what first seemed impossible." Given the importance that Washington placed on surprise and the critical need for victory, it took great persistence and faith in the value of the artillery to allow it to dictate the pace of the crossing and then the march. But, the wet weather conditions increased the importance of the artillery, the foul weather weapon.

The army was finally formed up and ready to march about 4:00am, now four hours behind schedule.

Although no evidence has been found to prove it, undoubtedly Washington left troops at the ferry as a rear guard to protect the boats as well as soldiers who had been unable to cross due to illness or injury, and any supplies, wagons, and artillery left behind. It is known that the 6th Battalion of Connecticut State troops under Colonel John Chester, with about 19 officers and 241 enlisted men, did not cross and they may have been at least part of such a rear guard.[2]

**About that same time in Trenton,** Hessian artillery Lieutenant Friedrich Fischer began his normal routine and ordered horses hitched to the two brass 3-pounder cannon stationed in front of the guard post on King Street. He then sent men to report that all was ready for the morning patrol to the "Doctor House," Dr. Bryant's Kingsbury home near Trenton Ferry. This patrol had become routine because of the frequent early morning harassment attacks by Ewing's troops from across the river that focused on the ferry area. The men returned, though, reporting that Major Dechow decided to cancel the patrol for that day, so the horses were unhitched, but not unharnessed because they were always kept harnessed, and returned to their stables. The weather and impassable river conditions made this patrol cancellation seem reasonable.

At 5:00am, three Hessian Jägers set out on an early morning patrol from the guard post at Philemon Dickinson's house. Normally, there would have been more men and they would have patrolled out further from Trenton. But, they only went up the river as far as the home of grist miller and militia Captain John Mott before returning to report no sign of the enemy. The Jägers did not know that at the very moment they reached Mott's mill, Captain Mott was one of the guides directing Washington's army to Trenton on that very road in the storm that seemed to preclude an attack that day.[3]

**Adam Stephen's brigade of Virginia Regiments** retrieved it's perimeter guards and with local 1st Hunterdon County Regiment militiaman Joab Mershon serving as one of his guides led off the American army, marching eight men abreast. Washington and Knox hoped that the surprise, swift attack would make at least some Hessian cannon vulnerable to capture and had prepared accordingly. The artillerymen without cannon carried drag ropes to help maneuver any of the six Hessian cannon they could capture. Horsepower was required to move cannon any distance, but artillerymen could use the ropes to move them short distances and position them for firing. For any captured cannon they could not take with them, they carried hammers and spikes to pound into the vents where the primer was inserted to fire the guns, thus disabling them.[4] The rest of Nathanael Greene's second division followed Stephen's advance brigade led by Mercer's brigade with four cannon at its head, followed by Stirling's brigade with three, and then Roche de Fermoy's with two. General Sullivan's first division came next, led by Sargent's brigade with four cannon, then Glover's with three, and finally St. Clair's as the reserve with two. Each division had nine cannon and the total army stretched for about a mile along the road.[5]

Still suffering from the constant snow, rain, and hail, the troops finally began to march and fifer Greenwood remembered, "we began an apparently circuitous march, not advancing faster than a child ten years old could walk, and stopping frequently, though for what purpose I know not."[6] Lieutenant Elisha Bostwick noted that the march through the storm was lighted by torches secured to the artillery carriages and they "sparkled & blazed in the storm all night."[7] They marched the first mile and a half up a hill rising about 200 feet on a rough and icy road with the storm blowing in their faces.[8] When they reached the crossroads near the Bear Tavern[9], the guides directed them to turn right and march more comfortably towards the southeast with the storm at their back, although the road was still slippery and difficult to follow.

**THEY MARCHED THROUGH A COMBINATION** of open fields and forested wood lots. Every farm required quantities of wood for building, repairing, cooking, and heating, so patches of forest were maintained in areas less suitable for field crops. Early roads in America tended to follow farm and lot boundaries rather than cross properties, so they were often winding. Roads often had rotting stumps from trees cut when creating the road and the roads were usually ungraded and were subject to poor drainage. Road conditions varied even in good weather because each stretch was maintained by a local man, chosen each year at town meeting who drafted men to perform road maintenance where he saw fit and each resident was only responsible for three days of road labor a year. For drainage, when it was attempted at all, the men often just plowed a gutter on the side of the road and threw the plowed soil back into the middle of the path. When called out for roadwork, the local men did what they could to make the day's labor with their shovels and hoes as short as possible. How much care was given to a stretch of road was determined by the local men. Road supervisors were only required to inspect the roads every two months and call out men as needed.

One thing supervisors were required to watch for was encroachment on the roads by owners of the land bordering them. The roads were uneven and strewn with rocks, stumps, and ruts and holes that filled with water in wet weather. Having been built for local convenience, with some exceptions, travelers were pretty much on their own without sign posts, mile markers, or other conveniences. For variable distances the army marched on dirt road bordered by fields, alternating with stretches flanked by trees and no stretch was easily passed by large groups of men marching eight abreast with their officers on horseback, with flanking guard parties, horse drawn cannon, and horse drawn ammunition wagons. The dirt roads were not only difficult for wheeled vehicles, such as cannon and supply wagons, but the narrow wheels of these heavy conveyances created significant ruts. All stretches of road were more difficult for the troops bringing up the rear to navigate than they had been for the leading troops.[10]

After about a mile and a quarter, the army's van came to a deep ravine containing Jacob's Creek. The guides had no doubt warned Washington about this obstacle so preparations could be made to get the artillery through it. Bostwick remembered that the "horses were unharness'd [more likely he meant unhitched] & the artillery prepared." The road angled as it descended in order to reduce its steepness. Still, the cannon had to be slowly lowered down the ravine attached to long ropes that could be wrapped around trees as mooring posts and wheels locked in place by tree branches run between them to jam the wheel spokes and prevent wheel rotation and a runaway object. At the creek, the ice cold water was fordable, but it was churned by the storm and the passage of the army. After crossing the creek, each cannon and wagon had to be hauled up the other side, taking up a lot of time and greatly contributing to fatigue of man and horse.[11]

While Washington was riding along the column, Lieutenant Bostwick saw the back feet of Washington's horse slip from under him on the road ice and begin to fall. In a colorful demonstration of his superb horsemanship, Washington seized the horse's mane and pulled its head up while shifting his own position to enable the horse to regain its balance and footing.[12] This was one of many instances that put Washington's soldiers in awe of him and Bostwick remembered the scene for the rest of his life.

**After clearing the Jacob's Creek** ravine the road leveled out with only a gradual rise. However, the storm increased in fury with alternating rain, snow, and hail driven by varying and often intense winds. John Greenwood recalled vividly "that at one time, when we halted on the road, I sat down on the stump of a tree and was so benumbed with cold that I wanted to go to sleep; had I been passed unnoticed I should have frozen to death without knowing it; but as good luck always attended me, Sergeant Madden came and, rousing me up, made me walk about." Several other soldiers were not so lucky and did freeze to death on the march. The men had to watch out for each other because so many were ill or had trouble keeping up due to fatigue.

Greenwood later wrote that "none but the first officers new where we were going or what we were going about, for it was a secret expedition, and we, the bulk of the men coming from Canada, knew not the disposition of the army we were then in, nor anything about the country." However, this was pretty normal for Greenwood because he had "never heard soldiers say anything, nor ever saw them trouble themselves, as to where they were or where they were led. It was enough for them to know that wherever the officers commanded they must go, be it through fire and water, for it was all the same owing to the impossibility of being in a worse condition than their present one, and therefore the men always liked to be kept moving in expectation of bettering themselves."[13]

After crossing a plateau, the road began to gently descend again for about a mile to the crossroads hamlet of Birmingham, about three and a half miles from Bear Tavern, where the road intersected the road leading west to Howell's Ferry and east to the Scotch Road.[14] They reached Birmingham, about half way to Trenton, just about 6:00am, a little before daylight. During the march Bostwick had heard Washington encouraging his soldiers and when he passed by Bostwick during the pause at Birmingham, Washington ordered "in a deep & solemn voice" for the soldiers to "keep by your officers for Gods sake keep by your officers." He did not want anyone to stray away or drop off to sleep and perish.[15] The noise of the passing army aroused the family of Benjamin Moore at Birmingham. Moore was the father of 1st Hunterdon County Regiment militiaman Israel Moore, who served in Captain Mott's company, and the uncle of two other militiamen. The Moore's brought out food and drink which Washington accepted with thanks and consumed on horseback while gathering his senior officers for consultation.[16]

As preplanned in consultation with the militia guides who knew the roads, Washington split his army to attack Trenton from two directions. The original time schedule was in tatters by this point, but Washington ordered each officer to again set his watch by his and they fixed a new time for the simultaneous attack to begin.[17]

Greene's division left Birmingham first, turning left onto the Howell's Ferry Road and marching away from the river towards the Scotch Road which they would follow to the Pennington Road and take it just outside the northern edge of Trenton. They had the more difficult and slightly longer route, so Sullivan delayed a bit before heading straight through Birmingham to take the River Road aiming to attack Trenton from the south.[18] It is interesting to speculate why Washington sent Greene on the route closest to British troops at Princeton that might have patrols out and why he accompanied Greene rather than Sullivan. Certainly he knew Greene's troops better because Sullivan had only joined him recently with the troops that had been under General Lee. He may have viewed the attack on the upper part of Trenton as the more complex and crucial, so wanted to be there personally with troops he knew. He did not leave any explanation, so we can only speculate.

Conrad Beam of Hausegger's German Battalion later commented that as they had marched "thru hail, rain & sleet[,] our cloaths [were] now frozen to our back."[19] On the march to Birmingham the soldiers had made every effort, mostly in vain, to protect their gunpowder from getting wet. Stories were told afterwards that when Washington learned of this he told his officers they still had to carry on and simply "advance and charge," with bayonets if necessary. However, while most regiments were armed with muskets designed to carry bayonets, lack of supplies meant many soldiers did not have them. For example, in fifer Greenwood's regiment "there was not more than one bayonet to five men." Additionally, several regiments were armed with rifles which were not designed to mount bayonets. While Washington probably did not dramatically command his men to use something many didn't have, he no doubt did tell them to persevere with whatever they did have and continue their efforts to keep powder and flash pans dry by using the blankets they had recently been issued.[20]

General Adam Stephen's Virginians led General Greene's column under orders to "attack and force the enemy's guards [on Pennington Road] and seize such posts as may prevent them from forming in the streets, and in case they are annoyed from the houses to set them on fire." Stephen's brigade was followed by General Hugh Mercer's and Lord Stirling's, designated the reserve brigade, with orders to support him. General Fermoy's brigade was to march behind Greene's troops and upon approaching Trenton, "file off from the Pennington road in such direction that he can with the greatest ease and safety secure the passes between Princeton and Trenton." Their exact disposition to prevent the British from escaping Trenton and heading to Princeton would be determined by the militia guides who "will be the best judges of this." They could also intercept any troops that might be coming from Princeton to support Rall. General Sullivan's division consisted of Glover's and Sargent's brigades with St. Clair's brigade forming the reserve. In each column, each brigadier was to send out flanking parties and the reserve brigades were to "appoint the rear-guards of the columns."[21]

THE TWO ADVANCE PARTIES under Captains Washington and Flahaven established their roadblocks and detained people who were out and about during the night. Flahaven's men were on the River Road ahead of Sullivan and Captain Washington's were on the Scotch Road ahead of Generals Greene and Washington. Future President James Monroe long remembered one man encountered by Captain Washington's party. He came out of his house awakened by his dogs barking and thinking the troops he saw were British he violently and profanely ordered them off. Lieutenant Monroe threatened to take him prisoner unless he went back in his house. The man, John Riker, now realized the troops were American and because he was a strong Whig he brought them food and offered to join them. He was a doctor from Long Island who had studied in Princeton, begun his practice in New Jersey, and was in the process of seeking appointment as a medical officer in one of the New Jersey Continental regiments then forming for 1777. To strengthen his offer to go to Trenton with them, he argued that as a doctor, "I may be of help to some poor fellow." Captain Washington accepted his offer.[22]

Just after sunrise, about 7:30am, Greene's column came up to this advance party. They were then surprised to run into a group of about fifty American soldiers coming towards them out of the storm from the direction of Trenton. These men turned out to be a company under Captain George Wallis of the 4th Virginia Regiment, part of General Adam Stephen's brigade. Several days earlier one of their men had been killed by Hessian Jägers while in a boat on the river. Before the timing of the secret Trenton attack was known, General Stephen had sent Wallis across the river on a raid to avenge this loss. This was the group that had attacked the Hessian outpost earlier that Christmas night and interrupted Colonel Rall's evening at Stacy Potts's house and caused him to form up troops to counterattack. Wallis's group had escaped in the darkness and the Hessians had returned to their posts in and near town.

Adam Stephen and Washington did not have a particularly friendly relationship due to many past conflicts in Virginia, and Washington was furious when he heard Wallis's story and demanded of Stephen if it was true. When Stephen confessed that it was, Washington angrily exploded exclaiming, "You, Sir! You, Sir, may have ruined all my plans by having put them on their guard." Witnesses said they had never seen Washington so angry and given all that he had been through while planning for and then persevering for this attack one can understand it. Washington, however, was able to keep his mind focused on the situation at hand, got control of his anger, turned away from Stephen, and spoke more kindly to Captain Wallis and his soldiers, personally inviting them to join the column.[23] Wallis's Christmas night fire-fight had been one of the factors that led Colonel Rall to feel safe from attack, because he considered it to be the attack he had been warned about – so it was over and done. It actually helped set up the surprise rather than ruining it.

**As the army came upon** the outskirts of Trenton, Greene's division was positioned to make first contact with Hessian pickets stationed at Richard Howell's cooper shop on the Pennington Road about a mile from the center of town.[24] When about 800 yards from the Hessian guard house the Americans formed three columns, with Mercer's brigade on the right, Stephen's brigade in the center, and Fermoy's brigade on the left. As the attack began, Major George Johnston of the 5th Virginia Regiment recalled that "our noble countryman, the Gen'l, at the head of the Virginia Brigades, exposed to the utmost danger, bid us follow. We cheerfully did so in a long trot."[25]

At virtually the same moment, about 8:00am, the advance of Sullivan's division was approaching the Jäger pickets at Philemon Dickinson's estate on the River Road, also about a mile from the center of Trenton. Everything was about four hours behind schedule but the element of surprise was maintained by the ferocity of the storm. Not yet knowing the weather was bad luck by preventing his forces at Trenton and Bristol from crossing to carry out their supporting missions, Washington must have appreciated how the good luck of the weather had maintained that advantage of surprise. Both divisions had arrived simultaneously in spite of the weather, now would his advantage in numbers of artillery pieces provide the edge for victory in the foul weather?

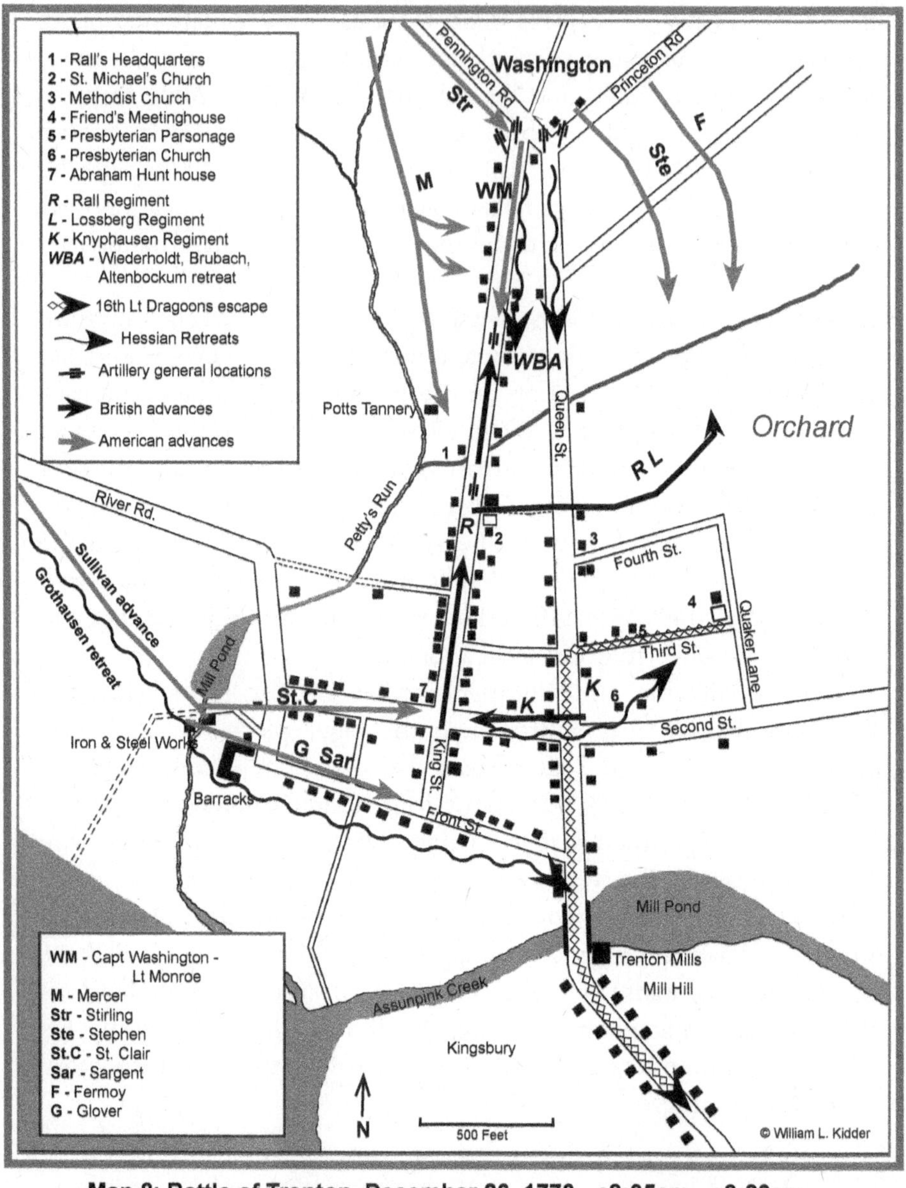


**Map 8: Battle of Trenton, December 26, 1776 - c8:05am - c8:20am**

Lieutenant Wiederholdt's fusiliers retreated into town and Lieutenant Grothausen's jägers retreated across the Assunpink Creek bridge. The light dragoons at the Friends Meeting House also retreated out of town across the bridge. Perhaps they expected the other troops to join them on Mill Hill. The Rall and Lossberg regiments engaged Greene's division and moved out to an orchard on the edge of town, while the Knyphausen Regiment engaged troops from Sullivan's division in the southern part of town.

# Chapter 8

## Battle of Trenton, Thursday, December 26, 1776

After the previous evening's raid had been repulsed, Lieutenant Andreas Wiederholdt took command of the strengthened guard post of 24 Knyphausen Regiment fusiliers at Howell's cooper shop, established a line of seven sentry posts connecting with other outposts like his, and sent out continuous patrols during the night. The latest went out about dawn and, although they may not have gone very far out into the storm, returned between 7:30 and 8:00am reporting everything was quiet. The severe storm limited visibility in the early morning daylight and Wiederholdt's sentries let down their guard a bit, partly because of the harsh weather and partly because previous early morning raids had occurred in the area of the ferry crossing at the other end of town.[1] In addition, a routine morning patrol sent by the Inspector of the Guards, Captain Brubach, from the picket on the Princeton-Trenton Road, was expected.

**About 8:00am, after a morning cup** of coffee, Wiederholdt stepped out of the Howell house to take a look around and noted the withdrawal of the Jägers from their night sentry posts between his post and the river. Suddenly, Wiederholdt saw armed men coming toward him out of the storm and immediately realized that, "if I had not just stepped out of my little guard-house and seen the enemy, they might have been upon me before I had time to reach for my rifle." He quickly got his men "under arms and awaited the approach of the enemy with fortitude, thinking that it was merely a skirmishing party," part of the pattern that was keeping them so exhausted. Wiederholdt's men, tired from the night and morning patrols, quickly took up their muskets and exited the cooper shop. Peering into the storm, Wiederholdt first estimated there were only about 60 attackers, perhaps a return of the harassing party of the previous evening, and experience told him that after a few volleys they would retreat. After receiving three long range musket volleys from the Americans, no doubt including a number of weather-induced misfires, Wiederholdt ordered his men to return fire and they engaged the attackers until quickly finding themselves "almost surrounded by several battalions," making it clear this was not just another harassing probe.[2]

He could also see Mercer's brigade moving southwest toward Stacy Potts's tannery and the lots behind houses on upper King Street. Moving off to the east, Fermoy's brigade advanced to attack the Hessian outposts on the road to Maidenhead and Princeton and block access to that road. To prevent being surrounded, Wiederholdt led his men in an orderly, fighting retreat attempting to at least slow down the attackers.

**Within minutes of Greene's** division opening fire on the Pennington Road, General Sullivan's division engaged the Jäger picket posts near Philemon Dickinson's home, The Hermitage, on the River Road. Major George Johnston was impressed that Greene and Sullivan, in spite of the long night full of obstacles and delays, "exhibited the greatest proof of generalship by getting to their respective posts within 5 minutes of each other, tho' they had parted 4 miles from the Town, and took different routes."[3] Also believing this was just another harassing attack, Jäger Lieutenant Friedrich von Grothausen exited The Hermitage with 12 Jägers, ordering the rest of his men to take defensive positions behind trees or fences up on the road just north of the house.

At his post on the road, Jäger Corporal Franz Bauer could see his lieutenant on his right and when he saw Grothausen begin retreating towards town, pressed by a large American force, he and the other Jägers also began to retreat. Captain John Flahaven's 40 New Jersey recruits led that attack followed by Colonel John Stark's New Hampshire regiment, with at least some men using bayonets. Winthrop Sargent's

Massachusetts Continental artillery company with two 6-pounder guns along with a New Jersey State company with two 3-pounder guns were also at the front of the division.[4]

Leaving their knapsacks at The Hermitage, the Jäger's retreated hastily toward town while receiving ten rounds of relatively ineffective artillery fire from General Dickinson's militia troops across the river.[5] When they got near the stone barracks they formed up and delivered just one volley before the Americans were upon them and they resumed their retreat.[6] The Jägers hurried along Front Street heading for the bridge over the Assunpink Creek, still held by their picket, and escaped over it. The twenty British dragoons at the Friends Meeting House also quickly left town by way of the bridge.[7]

While many at the time attributed these two retreats to cowardice, their actions may more likely reflect the lack of planning by their superiors. Their standing orders had been to report to Rall's headquarters to receive orders if the town was attacked. Unable to go there, and receiving no orders from him, they were forced to improvise. The officers were probably aware of the advantages to be gained by retreating to Mill Hill, and may have felt that other units would join them there. However, finding no officer organizing a defensive position on Mill Hill they continued to retreat to Bordentown or Princeton and one observer on the Pennsylvania shore reported, "the Light Horse & Hessians were seen flying in great confusion towards Bordentown but without cannon or wagons."[8]

**Fifer John Greenwood** in St. Clair's Brigade, the reserve of Sullivan's Division, recalled that "as we were marching near the town, the first intimation I received of our going to fight was the firing of a 6-pound cannon at us, the ball from which struck the fore horse that was dragging our only piece of artillery, a 3-pounder. The animal, which was near me as I was in the second division on the left, was struck in its belly and knocked over on its back. While it lay there kicking the cannon was stopped and I did not see it again after we had passed on."[9]

Private Jacob Francis, a young black man in Sargent's 16th Continental Regiment marched into town on the River Road and advanced to the corner of King Street where he could see Greene's troops attacking the Hessians further up the street.[10] Colonel John Stark's

New Hampshire regiment, accompanied by an artillery detachment, turned at Alexander Chambers' house at the corner of Second Street and River Road and marched toward the Knyphausen Regiment coming at them from the Bull Head Tavern. In the advance, a captain, sergeant, and 16 men of Stark's regiment captured 60 Hessians. The rest of the division headed to Front Street to take possession of the barracks and then cut off access to the bridge over the Assunpink.[11] Rev. David Avery says the battle was so short that Paterson's regiment got to Trenton "just before the action was over."[12]

AT THE NORTHWEST corner of town, Lieutenant Wiederholdt's soldiers sought sheltered firing positions wherever they could, including house lot gardens, but they could not stem the pressure from the advancing Americans.[13] They retreated until reaching Captain Altenbockum's company of the Lossberg Regiment, which Wiederholdt said, "had rallied during my engagement and had taken up a position straight across the street in front of the Captain's quarters" at the Alexander Calhoun house. "I posted myself at their right wing and together we charged the enemy, but we were again forced to retreat in the same manner as before, so as not to be cut off from the garrison."

Loyalist Major John Barnes, a Trenton brewer who had left town to fight for the British, was back in Trenton and apparently staying at the house where Altenbockum's squad was posted. He witnessed this attack and later testified that Altenbockum "behaved well, and made a retreat which redounds to his honour."[14] The two detachments even impressed Washington with their professional behavior in "keeping up a constant retreating fire from behind houses" while fighting a delaying action that gained time for the main garrison to form up.[15] The main picket on the Maidenhead/Princeton road commanded by Ensign Grabe of the Lossberg Regiment, with Captain Brubach of the Rall Regiment, came across the fields to assist Altenbockum, but found him in retreat with Wiederholdt.

While retreating on the Pennington Road, Captain Altenbockum lost several men killed, including 18-year-old Lieutenant Georg Christian Kimm, who fell "only about six or eight yards from" Lieutenant Wiederholdt. Captain Samuel Morris of the Light Horse of the City of Philadelphia, fighting in his first battle, took pity on the mortally wounded Kimm and wanted to assist him, but obeyed General Greene's orders to continue advancing.[16] When the retreating Hessians got to town, some went down Queen and the others King Street to find their regiments and many sought shelter between the two main streets in gardens just north of the alley at St. Michael's Church.

Wiederholdt headed for Rall's headquarters to report.[17] He was angry that "nobody came to see what was going on, no one came to our assistance with reinforcements," not even the duty regiment of the day, Rall's. Still, he "took up [his] position in front of one of the first houses of the town and fired at the enemy who was just forming in battle order on the upper side of the town."[18]

Colonel Rall's adjutant, Lieutenant Jacob Piel of the Lossberg Regiment, had been up since 5:00am at his quarters in the house of Miss Rebecca Coxe, next door to his Colonel's quarters on King Street. When Piel heard the firing at the edge of town he ran across the street to the main guard post where men were turning out in some confusion. Then, Piel knocked loudly on Colonel Rall's door and a sleepy Rall in his night-clothes opened an upper window and shouted down, demanding to know what the problem was. When told of, and then hearing, the firing, Rall yelled that he would be out in a minute, and appeared in a very short time.[19]

AWAKENING AFTER THE STORMY Christmas night, Martha Reed recalled, "in the grey dawn, came the beating of drums, and the sound of firing. The [Hessian] soldiers quartered in our house, hastily decamped, all was uproar, and confusion." Martha's mother herded her children to the cellar, but Martha later became aware that "our next door neighbor was killed on his doorstep, a bullet struck the blacksmith as he was getting into his cellar, and many other townspeople were injured by chance shots."[20] One of Stacy Potts's daughters, while running home from a neighbor's house, was slightly wounded when a musket ball hit, and sent flying, the comb in her hair.[21]

When the first units of Stephen's brigade reached the point where King and Queen Streets met at the northern end of town, an intersection known as "the gateway,"[22] Captain Thomas Forrest's cannon and howitzers were moved into the intersection, unlimbered, and wrestled into position by men using drag ropes. When Captain

Alexander Hamilton's company arrived shortly after, Forrest positioned his four guns at the head of Queen Street and Hamilton's two guns were positioned to fire down King Street.[23] Captain Sebastian Baumann's New York artillery company contributed three more guns.

Stephen's and Fermoy's brigades formed in a double line stretching across to the Assunpink Creek to prevent any Hessian flight to the north. Stirling's brigade formed at the head of the two streets and Washington took position above the intersection of King and Queen Streets on high ground along the farm lane leading north out of town to Nathan Beakes' plantation where he could oversee the town and observe enemy movements.[24]

**After arousing Colonel** Rall at Stacy Potts's house, Lieutenant Piel told his friend, Second Lieutenant Georg Zoll, who quartered with him at the Coxe house, to cross the street to the English Church and get the artillerymen, Lieutenant Colonel Francis Scheffer's company, and the regimental flags out into the street. Scheffer had been very sick for five days, but left his sick bed to go on duty.[25]

Coming into town, Wiederholdt saw "Colonel Rall and his regiment leave his quarters and move along the street and pass the church [St. Michael's] in the upper city. As I saw him first here, and not outside the city, and initially assumed that he not only did not know the strength nor the movements of the enemy, I considered it my responsibility to report as much as I knew to him and said: 'Herr Colonell, I am the officer from the picket which had been posted on the Pennington Road. The enemy are not only here about the city, but are circling the city and already are actually on your flanks and are stronger than they might seem.'" When Rall ordered his troops forward the men "had not entirely moved into the street from behind the houses."[26]

Rall was mistakenly convinced that he was surrounded, but the Americans were not yet on the east side of town. Importantly, his Hessians still held the Assunpink Creek bridge that provided an escape route to defensible Mill Hill or to friendly troops in the Bordentown area or at Princeton. Had Rall known this, he might have given different orders, although his contempt for the fighting qualities of the American troops made him confident that a quick, strong, counter-attack would succeed. When Rall asked Wiederholdt about enemy strength, he could only report, "I could not possibly tell that with accuracy as I had had to look after my men, however I had seen about 4 or 5 battalions advancing from the woods and from three of these I had withstood the firing before I had abandoned my post." Wiederholdt later commented that while Rall shouted to his regiment to advance, "he tottered back and forth without knowing what he was doing."[27] Washington also noted from his observation post that from their motions, the Hessians "seemed undetermined how to act."[28]

Rall ordered the Lossberg Regiment to form up on Church Alley behind a row of poplar trees, essentially in the cemetery, and then rode down King Street to where his regiment was forming up under Lieutenant Colonel Balthasar Brethauer in front of Pinkerton's Alley. As the Hessians began to advance up King Street, artillery shots flying down the street broke their ranks. Simultaneously, they received musket fire on their left from Mercer's soldiers who had entered the rear of Stacy Potts's extensive tannery and moved among its buildings that provided them with protective cover.[29] Severely ill, Brethauer left the field when his horse was shot from under him, because he was too weak to walk. By this time, American artillery fire was scattering the troops trying to form to resist.[30]

Ordered by Major Johann Matthaus to advance the two brass 3-pounder cannon stationed on King Street in front of the main guardhouse, artillery Lieutenant Johann Engelhard sent for the always harnessed artillery horses. The artillerymen advanced, without infantry support, north and across the small bridge over Petty's Run, perhaps as far up as Charles Axford's tavern, while absorbing fire from Captain Forrest's artillery company at the head of the street and musket fire from Mercer's brigade. The Hessian artillery got off six rounds while suffering eight casualties. Then, with five horses killed and too few men left to move the guns, the Hessians fired one last round of canister[31] at the Americans across Stacy Potts' tan yard and, panic struck, took off running through town toward the Assunpink Creek bridge where, along with other individual panicked Hessians, they got across the bridge and headed for Bordentown.[32] Major Johnston saw the leading troops of Stephen's brigade, units he called the "forlorn hopes," pursue the retreating Hessians to "the very middle of the town, where the whole body of the enemy, drawn up in a solid column, kept up a heavy fire

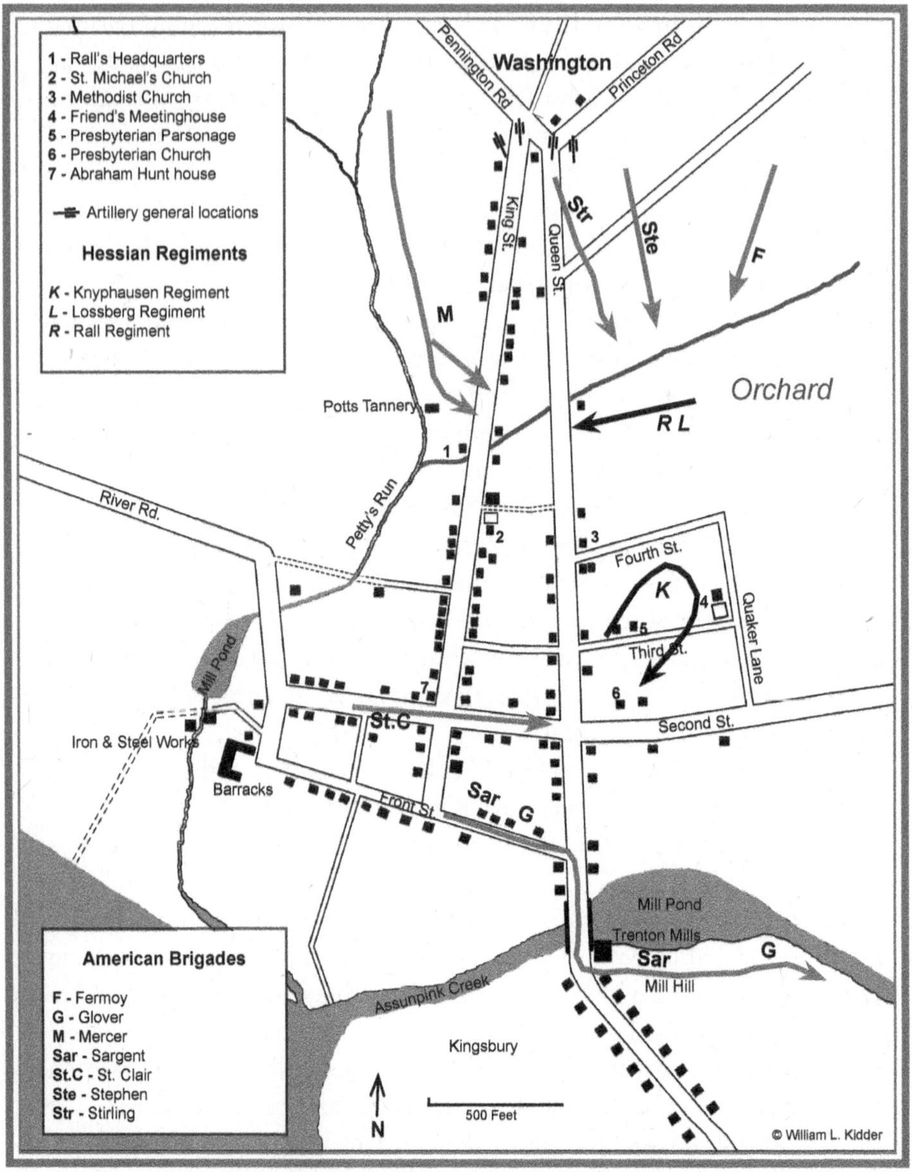


**Map 9: Battle of Trenton, December 26, 1776 - c8:20am - c8:40am**

Resistance from Greene's division led Rall to try to reenter the town while the Knyphausen Regiment trying to join with them experienced confusing orders and turned back against Sullivan's troops. Sargent's and Glover's brigades sealed off the Assunpink Bridge escape route and took control of the Mill Hill area.

with cannon and muskets, till our cannon dispersed and threw them in confusion."[33]

Peering through the sleet and smoke of battle, Washington saw the frenzied commotion of "men running here and there, officers swinging their swords, artillerymen harnessing their horses."[34] Nathanael Greene found that, "the storm of nature and the storm of the town exhibited a scene that fild the mind during the action with passions easier conceived than describd."[35] Washington's troops continued to suffer musket misfires and while Hessian firearms at first functioned properly, Hessian Lieutenant Colonel Scheffer later reported that, "The riflemen hid in the houses and fired continuously. It rained balls and grape shot, and sleet and hail beat steadily into our faces. Soon not another of our weapons could fire. The enemy closed in on our flanks and rear. Under these conditions it was impossible to maintain ranks and formations, and without an organized corps, it was impossible to use bayonets."[36] The wet, freezing weather conditions thus probably kept the number of casualties low on both sides.

Henry Knox's vivid memory was that, "we … entered the town with them pell-mell, and here succeeded a scene of war of which I had often conceived but never saw before. The hurry, fright, and confusion of the enemy was [not] unlike that which will be when the last trump shall sound. They endeavoured to form in the streets, the heads of which we had previously the possession of with cannon and howitzers. These, in the twinkling of an eye, cleared the streets. The backs of the houses were resorted to for shelter. These proved ineffectual: the musketry soon dislodged them." Knox was glad that although "the storm continued with great violence" it was at the backs of his artillerymen and "consequently in the faces of our enemy."[37]

Lieutenant Patrick Duffey of Captain Forrest's Pennsylvania artillery company was in the thick of the fighting on King Street "in front of the savages" and "sustained the fire of several guns from the houses on each side, without the least loss, must attribute my protection to the hand of Providence."[38] Men on both sides suffered from lack of suitable clothing. John Boudy of the 2nd Maryland Regiment in Greene's division stated he "was but thinly clad, and entirely barefoot all the while."[39] Private Cornelius Sullivan remembered that many of the Hessians turned out and "entered the action with nothing but their shirts on," while Captain Forrest, who referred to the Hessians as "the Brass Caps and Crous Coups" also noted the lack of shoes and watch coats among his men.[40]

Mechanical stress from the third shot fired from Sergeant Joseph White's howitzer in Forrest's Company broke the axle-tree of its carriage, disabling it. Shortly after, Colonel Knox rode up to the artillerymen, calling them "my brave lads," and ordered them to take the two Hessian cannon on King Street "sword in hand." White joined the attackers, led by Captain William Washington and Lieutenant James Monroe, and recalled, "I hallowed as loud as I could scream, to the men to run for their lives right up to the pieces. I was the first that reach them." The Hessian artillerymen had abandoned the cannon, "except one man tending vent – run you dog, cried I, holding my sword over his head, he looked up and saw it, then run[.] We put in a canister of shot, (they had put in the [powder] cartridge before they left it,) and fired. The battle ceased." General Stephen remembered a little differently that, "We had a Christmas frolick at Trenton, … You never saw so many good shot made in your life time – We drove the enemy from their cannon in our shooting." He saw how one "brave" German remained at his artillery piece and "was loading her by him self after the rest had left him – A Virginian as brave as he, would not let him but run up knockd him down wt the butt of his gun & took him prisoner."

Both Captain Washington and Lieutenant Monroe received wounds in this action, Washington took bullet wounds in both hands and Monroe took a bullet "through his breast and shoulder." They were carried to a house and attended by Dr. John Riker, the man who had joined the army during its march to Trenton just a few hours earlier, thinking he might be able to help some poor fellow. Dr. Riker saved future president Monroe's life by stopping the bleeding from a bullet severed artery in his shoulder.[41] During the cannon duel, the Lossberg and Knyphausen artillery companies hitched horses to their four cannon in front of the guard house and then moved them into the churchyard where the Lossberg and Rall regiments had formed.[42]

Hessian troops sent forward were forced back down King or Queen Street under heavy artillery and musket fire from advancing

American troops and from openings in board fences that sheltered other Americans. The Hessians also sought cover in buildings and during the fighting in town a group of Hessians sought protection in a barn from which they fired on the Americans. Several troopers of the Light Horse of Philadelphia under Cornet John Dunlap were ordered to take them and were able to approach the barn from the rear and then negotiate the surrender of the Hessians who believed they were significantly outnumbered.[43] Hessian artillery and infantrymen retreated rapidly down Queen Street heading for the creek while receiving fire from some of Colonel Glover's men stationed behind a red board fence standing between the Assunpink Creek and the house of Loyalist John Barnes on the west side of Queen Street. Like the Jägers and dragoons had earlier, some Hessians were able to escape by crossing the Assunpink bridge and heading to Bordentown.[44]

**The slowly retreating men of** Wiederholdt's, Altenbockum's, and Brubach's detachments felt unsupported and without clear orders decided to make the effort to rejoin their regiments, if they could find them. Without a detailed defensive plan, the Hessian officers and soldiers had to improvise as they reacted to developing and changing situations. Had Rall designated Mill Hill, which today is much reduced in height as a result of subsequent development, as the rallying point when attacked from the top or west side of town, the battle would have developed very differently. At one point Rall ordered Lieutenant Piel to see if the bridge was still available for a retreat, however, by that time it was too late. After wrongly perceiving that his troops were surrounded, Rall decided to counterattack and break through the enemy lines. Still believing in the inferiority of the Americans as soldiers, he did not hesitate to attack a strong point rather than look for a weak one.[45]

Having lost Lieutenant Engelhard's cannon and still receiving heavy fire from Mercer's troops in sheltered positions behind, between, and inside houses on King Street, Rall decided to move his two regiments and their artillery pieces to the east across Queen Street and beyond to an apple orchard on the edge of town. While Hessian units retreated toward the orchard, stragglers from all three regiments attempted to get to the Assunpink bridge, but were encircled and surrendered on

Queen Street between Second and Front streets. Colonel Stark led his troops on Second Street driving the Hessians into a field on the edge of the orchard just north of the Assunpink Creek.[46] While perhaps initially seeking to convert the battle from street fighting to a more traditional open field action by going to the orchard, Rall decided to strike north quickly from the orchard for the Princeton Road. However, this move was checked by the attack of General Roche de Fermoy, led by Colonel Hand's regiment and the German Battalion.[47]

Failing to reach the Princeton Road, Rall decided to retake the town. The brigade band began to play in an attempt to raise morale. Officers urged their men on and got back to Queen Street below Church Alley. The Knyphausen Regiment at this time was moving uptown to join with the other two regiments and Lieutenant Wiederholdt was able to rejoin it. They engaged St. Clair's Continentals on Second Street and an apparent miscommunication turned the Knyphausen Regiment back toward the Friends meeting house and away from the other two Hessian regiments.[48] Rall commanded his grenadiers to advance. He advanced without artillery support because the Lossberg cannon were now with the Knyphausen Regiment and disabled, having burned out vents. The advance of Stirling's brigade from the north on Rall's flank, combined with fire from Mercer's brigade in its front, prevented his retaking the town. The Hessian troops received fire from all sides and became demoralized, although some men made heroic efforts to counter the American onslaught. Captain von Lowenstein's company of the Lossberg Regiment marched along Second Street toward its intersection at King Street, and encountered heavy American fire. When he received a thigh wound, Lieutenant Ernst Schwabe of the Lossberg Regiment turned over command of his company to his ensign, and was carried to safety behind Isaac Yard's house.[49]

**In the heat of battle**, at least one American soldier, a sergeant, was heard singing one of his favorite songs that contained words something like: "Exert yourselves with power and might, See how American boys can fight, Drums are beating, colours flying, Cannon roaring, men lie dying, These are the known effects of war." He was totally unaware that he was singing and only learned of it later when told by comrades who had heard him.[50]

During the mayhem of street fighting, some Hessians believed that civilians shot at them from houses, and one reported seeing a woman mortally wound an officer.[51] Lieutenant Piel noted that they had barely had time "to take up our weapons before we lost many people in the city, due to the small arms and cannon fire of the enemy." During the battle, "our weapons, because of the rain and snow could no longer be fired; and the rebels fired on us from all the houses."[52]

One captured Hessian later commented to the son of Rev. Henry Muhlenberg that when the Hessians had "entered Trenton and occupied the region, the inhabitants swore their allegiance to the king of Great Britain" in response to General Howe's November 30 offer of amnesty and protection. But then, these same residents shot at them when the American army attacked. Rev. Muhlenberg felt that if this was true, "it corroborates the proverb which says that oaths obtained by force are an outrage to God. The submissiveness, obedience, and loyalty which are obtained by force do not have the permanence of the virtues which have their basis in love, righteousness, and justice."[53]

Everyone was now moving by various paths towards the bridge over the Assunpink and the smoke of battle, even though reduced by wet powder problems, combined with the storm precipitation made identifying friend or foe difficult.[54] At some point, the officer and 27 Hessian soldiers in the picket at Trenton Landing moved out on the road to Bordentown and reported to the picket at the Crosswicks Creek drawbridge.[55] Some Hessian units fragmented and recombined in new formations, forcing officers and privates to adapt to unfamiliar, makeshift squads while fighting for their lives. Ensign Christian von Hobe of the Lossberg Regiment was disabled by a wound to his leg from a spent bullet and hobbled to the Methodist Church on the corner of Queen and Fourth streets for shelter. Lieutenant Piel's friend, Second Lieutenant Zoll, took a bullet in the spine and lay bleeding in the street.[56]

When Colonel Rall was finally ready to order his troops to retreat to the Assunpink Creek bridge, the Americans controlled it and two cannon manned by General Sullivan's division had begun firing on Queen Street from the corner of Second Street. Rall ordered a retreat toward the apple orchard and then almost immediately fell from his horse, having received two severe wounds in his side. He fell in front

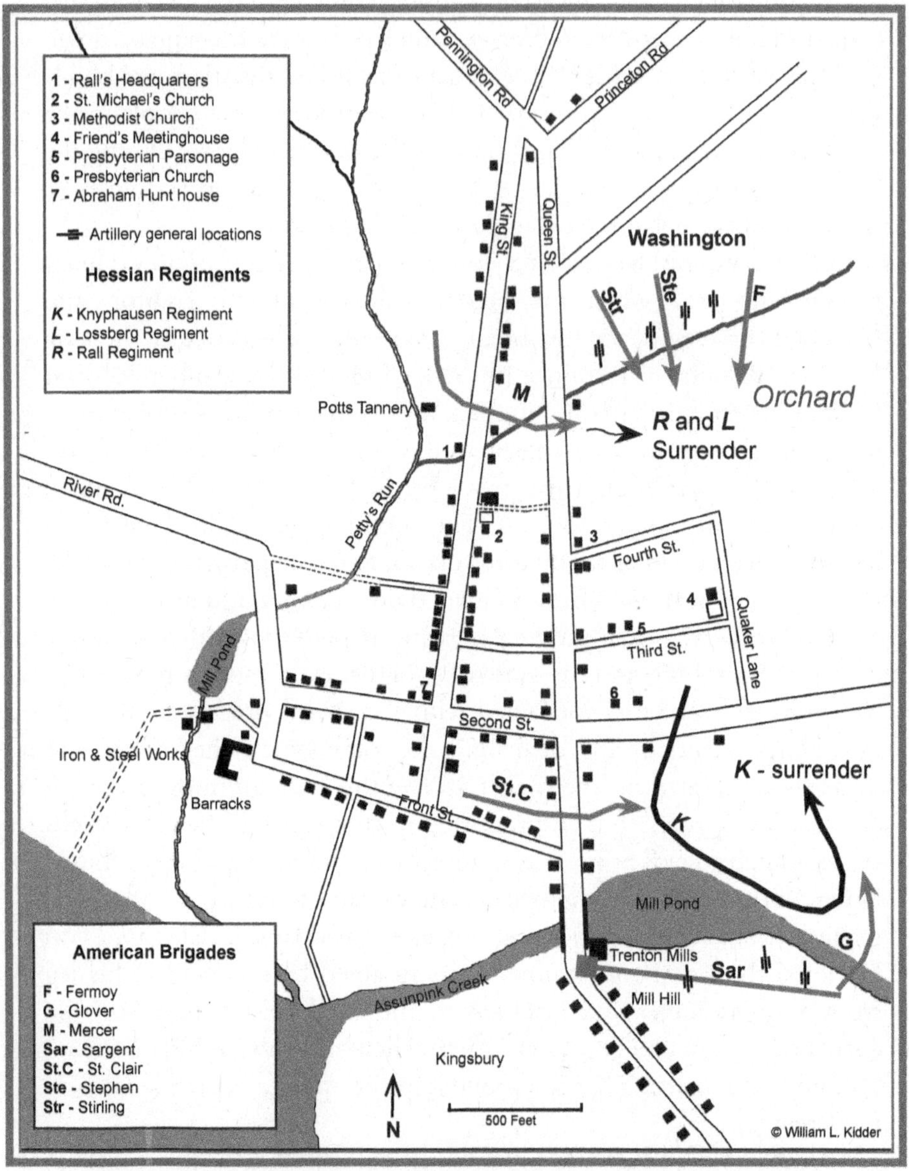


**Map 10: Battle of Trenton, December 26, 1776 - c8:40am - c9:00am**

Pressed in several directions by the troops of Greene's division, Colonel Rall was mortally wounded and the Rall and Lossberg regiments were forced to surrender. The Knyphausen Regiment continued trying to deal with Sullivan's division, but was also forced to surrender a short time later. Throughout these actions, the American artillery was active while the Hessian artillery became inactive, giving the Americans a distinct advantage.

of Isaac Yard's house on the west side of Queen Street about 200 feet north of Pinkerton's alley. Two soldiers lifted Rall and helped him painfully walk to the Methodist Church, passing the seriously wounded Lieutenant Zoll.[57]

Major von Hanstein notified the ill Lieutenant Colonel Scheffer, the next senior officer in the brigade, of Rall's wound and Scheffer conferred hurriedly with him and Major Johann Matthaeus and they decided to again try to break through to the Princeton Road. However, Greene's division basically surrounded the two Hessian regiments. Hamilton's artillery company came south and faced them from the west, while Forrest's and Bauman's advanced on the north and east. While Mercer's and Stirling's brigades were fighting in the street and from houses, Washington ordered Roche deFermoy and Stephen to form a line to the east to cut off any retreat route to Princeton. Bauman's artillery company was probably placed where they joined.[58]

Major Thompson of the 5th Virginia Regiment was with the left wing and when the Hessians tried to move toward the Princeton Road found that his brigade, "being on the left wing and nearest the course the enemy took, were ordered to pursue them with all expedition. We stepped off with alacrity, in full cry, and fortunately got into the thickest of them while they were fording a small creek [the Assunpink]. L'd Stirling's brigade soon came to our assistance."[59] Captain Henry Miller, 26 years old, of Colonel Hand's 1st Pennsylvania Regiment in General Stephen's brigade later recalled they "advanced within sixty yards" of the Hessians "without firing a gun, but with such rapidity and determination as to strike terror into them."[60]

**Captain Altenbockum was** struck in the head by a bullet, but was able to mount Colonel Rall's horse and retreat toward the orchard. Lieutenant Colonel Scheffer found the two regiments had mixed together in their retreat. They came under fire from Roche de Fermoy's brigade advancing on them from the northeast and could hear the Americans shout at them in both English and German to ground their arms and surrender. Amid the shouts to surrender, an American officer galloped from town and offered terms that Scheffer accepted. The American officer then took Captain Altenbockum back to town for medical treatment. He was carried to the quarters of the very ill

Lieutenant Colonel Brethauer and ironically found a Hessian medical officer bleeding Brethauer to cure him, while throughout the town many other Hessians were bleeding from wounds.[61]

The officer reported that Scheffer had agreed to the surrender terms and several American officers came out to accept the surrender of the Rall and Lossberg regiments.[62] The Hessians lowered their standards and grounded their muskets, while the officers put their hats on the points of their swords to hold up as a sign of submission. Some of the soldiers, seeing the surrender as an indignity, broke the stocks of their muskets by striking them against the ground, cut their cartridge pouch straps, or threw their muskets as far as they could into the woods. By military custom, they should have simply placed their muskets on the ground in front of them.

**Separated from the other two** regiments, the Knyphausen troops could see that both were close to surrendering about a quarter mile away. They could also see American troops down by the Assunpink Creek bridge, but they decided to attack there and try to get over the bridge and make their way to Bordentown. As they moved along the creek, their cannon became stuck in the mud and the delay, while they tried to free them, allowed the Americans to secure the bridge and the Mill Hill beyond it. Sargent's and Glover's brigades crossed and occupied ground along the Assunpink Creek while St. Clair's forces secured the bridge.[63] Some troops used the stone mill as a fortress while fighting any Hessians trying to cross the bridge.[64]

After about half an hour at the foot of King Street, Private Jacob Francis saw some officers ride up to Colonel Sargent and talk with him. Then Sargent marched them through town toward the Assunpink Creek, then across the bridge and along the creek.[65] Once across the bridge, Colonel Sargent's artillery began firing across the Assunpink at the Knyphausen Regiment. Major Dechow, who commanded the regiment, was mortally wounded and with no possibility of escape decided to surrender. Some of his officers wanted to continue the fight but he told them, "My dear sirs, do as you like, I am wounded." Dechow hobbled along toward Queen Street aided by Corporal Kustner who tied a white handkerchief to a spontoon and held it up as they walked toward Joshua Newbold's house to give themselves up. Dechow apparently surrendered to General Sullivan when he reached Queen Street.[66]

After Dechow left, the Knyphausen Regiment marched up the Assunpink to look for a ford they could escape across and ran into Colonel Glover's brigade which had crossed back toward town at a ford they could have used. One group attempted to ford the ice-cold water in the creek and some men found themselves up to their necks in the frigid water, negotiating a muddy bottom. At least one officer did get across, while several men drowned and others found it too deep and turned back. The panic of the troops increased from hearing the frantic noises made by the regiments' servants, women, and musicians who were gathered by the creek with much of the brigade's baggage. A detachment of skirmishers from the Knyphausen Regiment was sent to high ground towards the back of William Roscoe's house and the Presbyterian Church to see if it was possible to escape across the creek. While some of the Knyphausen men were trying to swim across the mill pond, Stirling's brigade came marching up and came within 40 steps where they formed into two columns with two cannon in front.

The Knyphausen Regiment was now surrounded by Stephen's and Fermoy's brigades on the north, Glover's brigade on the east, Sargent's brigade to the south, and St. Clair's brigade guarding the bridge. Mercer's and Stirling's brigades held the rest of the town. An officer from Stirling's brigade rode toward Captain Friedrich von Biesenrodt, now the senior Knyphausen officer. Biesenrodt did not speak English, so he sent Wiederholdt to talk with the American officer. When Wiederholdt returned, he told Biesenrodt that General Stirling wanted to talk with him and they went to the American lines. Soon the Knyphausen Regiment surrendered to Stirling, and Private Francis, with Sargent's regiment that was formed up in line across the creek from the Knyphausen men, saw them ground their arms.[67] St. Clair agreed to allow the officers to keep their swords and baggage and the noncommissioned officers their swords and knapsacks. However, about an hour after the surrender, their swords and knapsacks were taken from them.[68] After the surrender, some of the American soldiers ran among the prisoners "and after satisfying their curiosity a little, they began to converse familiarly in broken English and German."[69]

Sergeant Thomas McCarty of the 3rd Virginia Regiment expressed his pleasure that they "beat the damn Hessians" on what was "the worst day of sleet rain that could be."[70] No doubt as the Hessians surrendered many of the officers felt as Lieutenant Piel did that, "we had only Colonel Rall to thank for our complete misfortune. It never struck him that the rebels might attack us, and therefore he had made no preparations against an attack. I must concede that on the whole we had a very poor opinion of the rebels, who previously had never successfully opposed us. Our brigadier was too proud to retreat one step from such an enemy as from the start, there was no other choice for us but to retreat."

Piel judged that when Howe put Rall in charge at Trenton he, "judged the man from an incorrect historical view. Otherwise, he would hardly have entrusted to him such an important post as Trenton." Piel also understood Rall's good qualities and noted, "Colonel Rall was truly born to be a soldier, but not a general. This man, who by capturing Fort Washington, earned the greatest honor because he was under the leadership of a great general, lost his entire reputation at Trenton, where he was himself the general. He had courage enough to undertake the most audacious task. However, he lacked the presence of mind which it is necessary to have in an engagement such as the attack on Trenton. … A thought came to him, then another, so that he could not settle on a firm decision." Piel understood Rall's weaknesses as a military leader, but this did not lower his respect for him as a human being. "Considered as a private individual, he merited the highest respect. He was generous, magnanimous, hospitable, and polite to everyone; never groveling before his superiors, but indulgent to his subordinates. To his servants he was more friend than master. He was an exceptional friend of music and a pleasant companion."[71]

The heaviest fighting had lasted only between half and three-quarters of an hour. General Greene wrote to his wife that it was forty-five minutes long while others on each side gave varying estimates up to an hour and a half. Typically, several oficers claim to have informed Washington of the final Knyphausen surrender and he was undoubtedly elated.[72]

**Back in Bucks County**, a crippled soldier on crutches who had not been able to go with the army, came outside by the Merrick house the next morning and, enduring the intense cold, listened to the gunfire from Trenton and when it stopped he cried out "Victory! The day is ours," and gave three cheers for "Our Boys." Merrick asked him how he knew it was a victory for the Americans and he answered, "I know our men would never give up that quick."[73]

**Judging by General William Heath's** statement describing the qualities of a great commander, expressed in the quotation at the beginning of the this book, Rall was a brave soldier, but "unskilled in the arts and stratagems of war," who was to be pittied because that blind bravery led Rall into the snare Washington laid for him.

Washington had made a good first step, but still needed to force the British out of New Jersey. When word of his victory slowly spread throughout the 13 states and eventually to Europe, each person receiving the news would be anxious to know what happened next. Would Washington take the offensive against other cantonments in New Jersey, even in winter time, or would he continue the pattern of retreat by staying in Pennsylvania? By now he knew that Ewing had not been able to cross to assist him at Trenton, but what about Cadwalader?

What could he do next to keep the momentum of victory going?

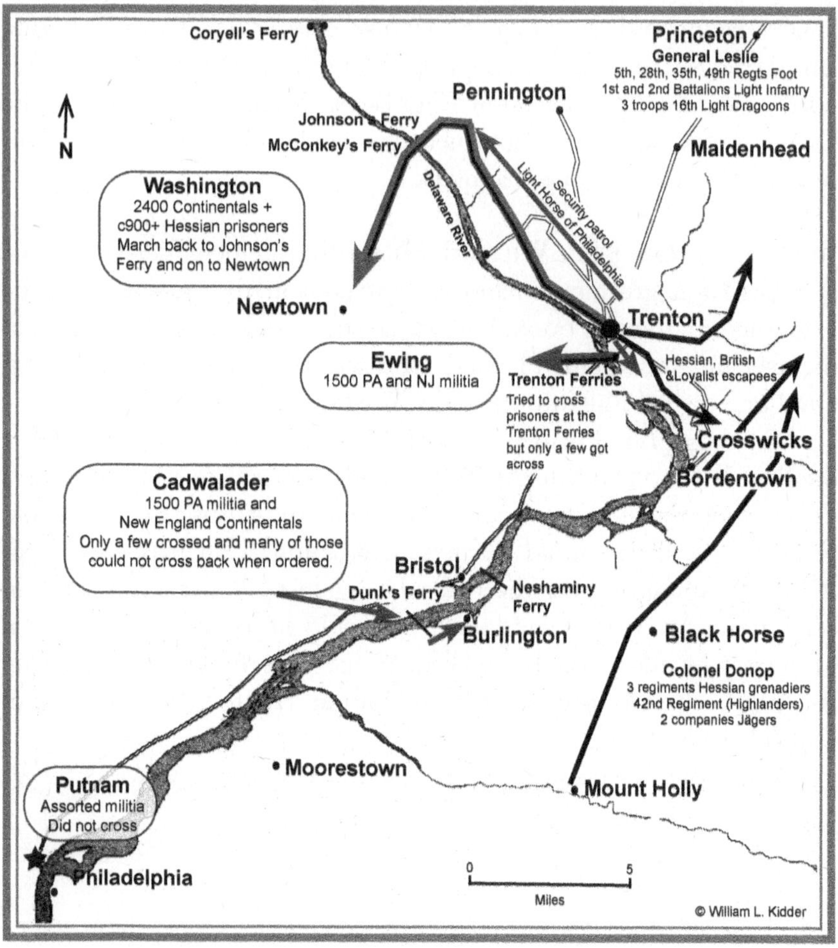


**Map 11: Afternoon and Overnight, December 26-27, 1776**

In addition to the units that escaped over the Assunpink Creek bridge at the beginning of the battle, some Hessians escaped by fording the creek. Other Hessians were at outposts across the Assunpink from the town and they were able to escape towards Bordentown unopposed. Altogether, about 400 Hessians and British light dragoons escaped capture. When Colonel Donop at Mount Holly heard of the fighting from fugitives, he began to retreat his forces towards Princeton, taking with him those men that had escaped capture at Trenton. The 900 plus Hessians captured at Trenton were taken to the Newtown area during that afternoon and overnight.

# Chapter 9

## Aftermath of Battle, Thursday, December 26, 1776

As combat ceased, Colonel Rall was carried on a bench from the Methodist Church through Church Alley to his quarters at the Stacy Potts house where he was visited by Generals Washington and Greene who promised to treat his men well. The house had been in the midst of some of the heaviest fighting and was badly damaged by musket and cannon fire. One glass window pane with a bullet hole through it was kept as a relic of the battle.[1]

Loyalists in town with the Hessians had escaped as fast as they could to join elements of the British army.[2] Trenton lawyer Joseph Taylor sought safety in New York.[3] However, 18-year-old Edward (Neddy) Shippen, son of Chief Justice Shippen of Philadelphia, had been sent to New Jersey on business where two Loyalist friends, John and William Allen, persuaded him to go with them to seek protection within the British lines, but he dallied in Trenton and was taken prisoner. However, when Washington learned of the circumstances he ordered young Neddy to be released.[4]

Private Chamberlin of Stark's Regiment was near General Washington "when he took possession of the standard of the enemy," and then was immediately sent with a party in pursuit of the Hessians that had escaped down the river, so that Chamberlin "neither went into a house nor took any refreshment."[5] Lieutenant Elisha Bostwick's company of the 19th Continental Regiment was also ordered to pursue any Hessians who had crossed the Assunpink bridge and headed toward Bordentown. Bostwick said that after about a half-mile march, they were in sight of the Delaware River when they suddenly received fire from American artillery on the Pennsylvania side that mistook them for the enemy. Bostwick's Colonel, Charles Webb, "swang his hat & gave a shout & instantly every hat on both sides of the river was swinging & every voice rais'd with a shout."[6]

**When the noise of battle ceased,** Martha Reed heard "the voices of neighbors calling for us, reassured us, to venture out" and with the Hessian occupiers gone, "my mother went all through the house, and found it had been ransacked and pillaged from garret to cellar. Her stores of household linen, mostly of her own spinning and her feather beds were gone – every article of silver had vanished – tables, and chairs were broken, furniture defaced, china and glass utterly ruined, while not a crumb remained of our winter stores." The family's sense of loss was tempered only a little by knowing that most of the Hessians had become prisoners. Along with other families, Martha's began the slow process of restoring their home "to its usual orderly comfort." They all hoped that their town would never again be occupied by British and Hessian soldiers.[7]

Jane Richardson was about 10 years old at the time of the battle and recalled for the rest of her life that after the battle she saw several soldiers "indifferently clad" and "with but parts of shoes to their feet, leaving bloody footprints on the frozen snow and on the floor." Two tired and cold soldiers came to her house, stacked their muskets around the clock in a corner of the sitting room, and warmed themselves at the recently used bake oven.[8]

**Artillery Sergeant Joseph White** walked through town and ever after remembered "my blood chill'd to see such horror and distress, blood mingling together – the dying groans, and 'garments rolled in blood.' The sight was too much to bear; I left it soon, and in returning I saw a field officer laying dead on the ground and his sword by him, I took it up and pulling the sheathe out of the belt, I carried it off. It was an elegant sword, and I wore it all the time I staid in the army."[9]

Captain Oliver Pond of Colonel Joseph Read's 13th Continental Regiment picked up a Knyphausen Regiment fusilier cap as a souvenir.[10]

On its way through town, John Greenwood's company passed two Hessian brass cannon next to which lay seven dead Hessians and a brass drum. Fifer Greenwood eyed the drum as a possible souvenir, but one of the drummers in his company quickly claimed it and threw away his own drum. However, Greenwood remembered, "I obtained a sword from one of the bodies, and we then ran on to join the regiment, which was marching down the main street toward the market." Just before reaching the market house, they encountered General Washington who ordered Greenwood's colonel to "March on, my brave fellows, after me!" as he rode forward.[11]

Private Moses Smith of the 26th Continental Regiment, together with one of his friends, captured 20 British cavalry horses that they found grazing in a field and delivered them into the American service.[12]

Ensign Beale from Virginia recorded that when the battle ended, "our men fell into the utmost confusion, every man shifting for himself." Beale very nearly engaged in some looting after the battle and wrote, "after I had gotten pretty well refreshed with good old Jamaica and excellent beef and biscuits, I asked Captain Fauntleroy and our adjutant, by name, Kelly, to go to the stable and get us a horse apiece. We did so and all mounted, but it was much colder on horseback than on foot, so seeing Colonel Lawson of the Sixth Regiment in the street, asked him what would become of the property taken here. He told us it was for the general good and not individual advantage, upon which I dismounted and set my horse loose."[13]

**WASHINGTON COULD NOT** take time to enjoy his victory. His original plan had been to get his prisoners across to Pennsylvania and then use his troops, combined with Ewing's and Cadwalader's, to continue attacking British cantonments. But, he knew Ewing had not crossed and no doubt suspected Cadwalader had also failed to cross. He consulted with his officers and some argued that even without Ewing and Cadwalader the success should be followed up to enhance the effects of the victory and take advantage of the enemy's "pannick." Others did not want to risk the chance of ruining the advantages they had already achieved by the victory or risk disaster should the British mount a counterattack from Bordentown or Princeton. The weather remained foul and would only begin to clear in the evening.[14]

One reason some officers wanted the army to get back across the river quickly was that "there were great quantities of spirituous liquours at Trenton of which the soldiers drank too freely to admit of discipline or defence in case of attack." One officer reported that "we stove about forty hogsheads of rum we could not carry off."[15] It should not be assumed that this was all Hessian rum or that Hessian soldiers had been consuming rum liberally in the holiday season. Merchant Jacob Benjamin later submitted a claim for items taken by the American army, and the list included large quantities of rum, brandy, claret, porter, and gin, as well as large quantities of food for humans and horses, and personal items.[16] The troops were not just celebrating their victory with liquor, but were no doubt genuinely craving food and drink after the ordeal of marching all night and then fighting for their lives. However, inebriation was still a problem that could intensify if not curtailed. Washington decided to take his army, and its prisoners, back across the river and plan follow-up actions.

River conditions must have improved somewhat during the morning and Washington at first ordered the prisoners to be taken across at the two ferries just below Trenton, where Ewing had failed to cross overnight, but this proved quite difficult and dangerous. The nature of the craft available on the Pennsylvania side and the lack of Durham boats in any quantity, limited their ability. Private Francis was one of several men from Sargent's regiment that were "detached to go down & ferry the Hessians across to Pennsylvania." He recalled, "about noon it began to rain & rained very hard. We were engaged all the afternoon ferrying them across til it was quite dark when we quit." He "slept that night in an old mill house above the ferry on [the] Pennsylvania side."[17] A man who had been at Trenton Ferry that morning, reported to Cadwalader that after the battle ended a wagon loaded with Hessian arms was brought to the ferry at Trenton and safely brought across along with six Hessians.[18]

Because of the difficult river conditions at Trenton, Washington revised his plan and decided to re-cross back to Pennsylvania at Johnson's and McConkey's ferries. The army and its prisoners would retrace the route Sullivan had taken that morning, because it was a little shorter and put a little more distance between them and any British forces that might come looking for them. For security, the Light Horse of Philadelphia was ordered to patrol the River and Pennington Roads until dark and then cross at Johnson's Ferry during the night, with or without their horses depending on river conditions.[19]

Most of the army and Hessian prisoners, including the wives and children, left Trenton about noon and marched back to Johnson's Ferry, although both victors and prisoners were exhausted, wet, cold, and in many cases sick or injured.[20] Private Chamberlin and the squad sent towards Bordentown after the escaped Hessians, returned to Trenton just as the rear guard was leaving. Because of the snow and rain Chamberlin says, "I had got thoroughly wet before we began our retrograde march, and the rain and half-melted snow and water was almost over shoes – our feet was drenched in water at every step."[21]

Some things got left behind because of the orders to depart Trenton quickly. General Lord Stirling, "in order to facilitate the passage of the troops," left behind two of his very fine horses, complete with their saddles and bridles, and they were stolen during the night.[22] Washington's horse had been slightly injured during the battle by a musket shot and he had to find another horse at Trenton for the return to McConkey's Ferry that afternoon.[23]

As many as 48 Hessian officers and men too sick or badly wounded to move, including Colonel Rall, were left in Trenton and paroled under the care of Lossberg Regiment Assistant Medical Officers Friedrich Wilhelm Oliva and Philip Obenhausen, who were also paroled.[24] Several men died before the end of the day, including Staff Captain Friedrich Wilhelm von Benning of the Lossberg Regiment and Private Henrich Kothe of the Knyphausen Regiment. Twenty-nine-year-old, and twelve-year veteran, Lieutenant Zoll, who had been shot in the spine and left lying in the street, amazingly survived and stayed in Trenton for several months recuperating.[25] Although the number of casualties varies in different accounts, at least five Hessian officers and 17 men were killed and six officers and 78 men wounded, some mortally. By tradition, the dead were buried in a common grave near the Presbyterian Church.[26]

The wounded Hessians were left with the few civilian residents remaining in the bleak and torn town, already marked by houses "stripped and torn to pieces" by the occupying troops and then further devastated by the morning battle that involved much cannon fire and street fighting. Some people had remained in town with their property and many had taken protections, which had been ignored by the Hessians. Tench Tilghman, Washington's aide, learned that some people had sent their property to Philadelphia, believing that if Howe took that city his British troops would better honor the protections. They felt the problem in Trenton had been that Howe "did not pretend to restrain the foreigners."[27] One casualty in the town was the destruction of the "elegant public Library at Trenton" and perhaps only some of the books out in circulation survived.[28]

Damages to the Presbyterian Church included the loss of "303 feet of board fence three feet high, 45 round posts, and rails, which was round the burying-ground, 11 panel post and 4 rail fence, 140 panes glass, large gates, hooks, and hinges, a silk damask curtain and hangings, a silver can with two handles, and a large plate." Rev. Elihu Spencer had undertaken a mission on behalf of the Continental Congress to the southern colonies in 1775 that had made him, according to his daughter, "very obnoxious to the British." Damages to his parsonage, inflicted while it served as a Hessian hospital, included "1400 feet of boards stript off the stable, 310 feet board fence, five feet high, 40 posts and rails, round the parsonage garden, 2 large front gates, hooks, and hinges, 1 well-curb, bucket, and chain, 1 table cloth and about ten yards diaper." Another loss inventory included 524 fence panels, four rails with a post and 167 "good as new" red cedar post and rail fence panels, agricultural implements, wheat in the stalk and in the ground, cattle, furniture, maps, clothing, china, glass, three spinning wheels, provisions, and a "stable totally destroyed," possibly for firewood. Of particular grief to Dr. Spencer was the loss of his writings and library, which included school books, a large collection of Hebrew books, a French dictionary and several works in French, Pool's *English Annotations on the Holy Bible*, and many literary and theological works.[29]

Anglican Rev. George Panton, a Loyalist who had left Trenton, had more than 200 valuable books taken by the Americans during their attack on the Hessians, and a huge number of manuscript essays, sermons, criticism, and philosophical investigations either taken or destroyed. A number of people claimed they had fence boards torn down and burned, furniture broken up and burned, and clothing, household items, food, livestock, and various items taken away.[30] Just as Stacy Potts' house had suffered window damage, William Plaskett had 120 panes of glass in his house broken by cannon fire during the battle. Undoubtedly, other houses also experienced broken glass from the concussion of the cannon blasts, if not from musket or cannon ball strikes.[31]

**Sergeant White and** his gun crew wanted to take their damaged cannon back with them, but Colonel Knox told them "to leave that piece with the broken axle-tree." They considered the barrel of that particular cannon to be the best in the regiment, so White hired four men, including an experienced mate from a sailing vessel, who were able to rig it to move. They set off at reduced speed with their awkward cannon. The rearguard came up with them and the commanding officer told them to abandon the cannon, that he would not take charge of it. White said he would rather risk being captured than leave the cannon, now that they had come so far. The rearguard left White and his gun crew behind and on their own. Soon after, White's men thought they saw some enemy cavalry approaching, but thankfully discovered they were just "a party of old Quakers" who had tied handkerchiefs over their hats because of the snow storm. Later, Colonel Henry Knox himself rode up with a party of officers and asked White, "Sergeant what piece is that?" White told him it was the piece Knox had ordered left behind, but that he had wanted the victory to be complete. Knox told him, "You are a good fellow," said he would remember him, and then rode on.[32]

By the time he got near Johnson's Ferry, private Chamberlin experienced some sort of "ague fit" and "went into an house with my teeth chattering in my head, but though my kind host made a good fire and did everything to favor me, the fire failed to warm me for some time, and I expected to have been taken down with a violent fever." He did get warm after a while and then headed for the ferry where he says, "we had to stand by the river until the prisoners were first got over. The wind by this time had shifted, and blew a keen northwestern blast which chilled me to the heart." Seeking shelter, Chamberlin "went into an house at some distance from the ferry, where was a girl which was called Miss Chamberlin." He struck up a conversation with her about having the same last name, and she "got a bowl of warm, fresh meat broth, which was of great service to me." Once warmed he went down to the river to wait for the boats and found, "the ice was so thick near the shore as to bear for a rod or two. I went on the ice with a view to jump in [to a boat], but it broke and let me into the river up to my waste, and the boat was filled before I could recover myself. The next boat, however, that struck I waded into the river to meet it, threw my gun into it, made leap with all my strength. I got in, and got over [the river] to a fire, but almost dead with cold and fatigue."[33]

Private David How of Sargent's regiment noted in his diary that after the battle "we marchd back and got to the river at night and got over all the Hushing," but not themselves.[34] Due to the intense cold and floating ice forming into masses on the river it was after midnight before the Light Horse of Philadelphia could get across and the troopers did not get to their quarters until after daylight. At that point they had been two nights and one day without sleep and had consumed very little food. Now stationed at Newtown, the troop was used to carry dispatches and messages until December 30.[35]

When the Americans got back to Newtown they had to shift for themselves and the half dozen men left in Private Chamberlin's company "went back about a mile to a Dutch house, and hired a room for a week and our board until the last day of Decr." With their enlistments about up, they requested a discharge from General Stark, but he told them he did not have orders to discharge them yet and they would have to wait a day or two until he got them. Chamberlin and some others had purchased horses and were anxious to leave for home. While waiting for their discharges, they rode their horses to visit Philadelphia, "thinking we should never have another opportunity."[36]

**Among those detailed** to guard the Hessian prisoners that crossed at Johnson's Ferry and were taken to Newtown, Pennsylvania were twenty-three-year-old Hosea Husted of Captain Samuel Hugg's Western New Jersey Artillery Company and twenty-six-year-old Cornelius Wells in Captain Maynard's company of Colonel Smallwood's Maryland Regiment. Husted was quite sick and remained at Newtown until December 30, when he was discharged because of his health.[37] Re-crossing the river was difficult and Rev. David Avery, chaplain of Colonel John Paterson's 15th Continental Regiment, recalled, "I had the good fortune to cross the river before night, wh[ich] was exceedingly difficult to cross by reason of the abundance of ice. I was extremely chilled, and came near perishing before I could get to a fire."[38] Sergeant McMichael recorded that they crossed back across the Delaware at McConkey's Ferry and took the prisoners to Newtown and "after suffering much fatigue we reached our camp, and having obtained comfortable lodgings I found Morpheus had got possession of me."[39]

**Hessian Lieutenant Jacob Piel** recorded, "immediately after our capture, we were brought over the Delaware, by Johnson's Ferry, to Pennsylvania. The privates were brought to Newtown on the same day and we officers, 25 in number, remained in a house [the McConkey Ferry house] not far from the Delaware, in a small room, altogether, where we spent the night very miserably." Lieutenant Wiederholdt similarly recorded, "After being made captive we were immediately transferred across the Delaware in boats; the river being full of ice, we had to resign ourselves to the possibility of death. The wind was strong against us, and the ice prevented the boat I was in from reaching the shore, so we were driven almost two miles down the Delaware." Wiederholdt decided not to die slowly on the river, but to "jump into the river and either die quickly or to get on land." He jumped out, followed by the others in his boat, and says, "fortunately we reached land, but had to wade through water up to our chest for seventy yards, breaking through the ice in many places. It would be no surprise if this destroyed our health and instead of a promotion and good nest egg, returned home to an unhappy prince with a wasted body." Like Piel, Wiederholdt "spent the night in the ferry house, where 26 of us remained in a small room, where we could hardly stand, without food or drink. My own loss, although I saved some things, was nevertheless considerable. The honor gained and previously enjoyed, had made an honorable man grievous and painfully ill."[40]

Captain John Polhemus, who had served in the 1st New Jersey Regiment and returned as an individual to serve Washington, recalled driving the non-commissioned officers and privates to the Newtown Presbyterian church and "into the Newtown Jail & yard like a pack of sheep during a severe hail storm. We allowed the officers to wear their side arms, also the privilege of occupying part of the house with General Patterson and myself."[41]

Elisha Bostwick found the prisoners from the Rall Regiment to be "of a moderate stature [with] rather broad shoulders[,] their limbs not of equal proportion[,] light complexion with a b[l]uish tinge[,] hair cued as tight to the head as possible sticking straight back like the handle of an iron skillet. Their uniform blue with black facings[,] brass drums which made a timbling sound[,] their flag or standard of the richest black silk & the devices upon it & the lettering in gold leaf."[42]

SOMETIME AFTER THE battle, a farmer living about five miles from Princeton captured two armed Hessians when his "boy," his slave, discovered them in his stable among his horses and told his "master" who ran to the barn before daylight and forced them to yield using his pitchfork. One surrendered immediately and the other ran but was prevented from escaping by the farmer's dog who grabbed him by the coat until the farmer could take him. Both men explained they had fled from the Battle at Trenton.[43] Several hundred other Hessians had also successfully retreated from Trenton and were seeking refuge towards Burlington or Princeton. Would they find it?

They Hessians who escaped were not a cohesive unit such as a regiment or battalion and in many cases not even complete at the company level. They had fled in terror from a battle which had been a surprise and then an uncoordinated series of prods and retreats. There had been no central rallying point or a standing set of orders to keep units coordinated. They were skilled and brave soldiers, but they had been badly led by their commanding officer who had made the all too common error of underestimating his opponent.

While people living within the sound of canon and musket fire at Trenton knew something important was happening, people in more distant locations dealt with the normal routines of their daily lives, oblivious to Washington's bold, decisive move that had been aided by elements of luck and enemy errors. It would take some time for them to become aware of it and contemplate how Washington's boldness would affect their lives.

# Chapter 10

## Other Places, Thursday, December 26, 1776

While the fighting was taking place at Trenton, in Exeter, England, Samuel Curwen, a Salem, Massachusetts merchant with Loyalist leanings, was aware that some members of the government had doubts about the war and recorded in his journal that, "Mr. M. told me Lord [William] Barrington says in his private judgement he condemns the American war; thinks it impolitic, unjust, and will finally prove ineffectual, or successless, but votes with Government officially, or as a Minister of State being Secretary of War."[1]

**Most people in the** 13 new states were completely unaware of the action at Trenton. British Lieutenant John Peebles in Newport found the day after Christmas to be rather normal. Again the troops did not parade and the cloudy morning with a northeast wind brought drizzle and rain that turned to hard rain at noon, so that the snow was nearly gone by the end of the day. It cleared up in the evening and there was "no great frost."[2] Lieutenant Mackenzie noted that "the troops are now served with one days fresh, & six days salt provisions per week. Fresh provisions and loaf bread is issued to all the sick." He also noted that the troops had been ordered to be careful of the windmills on the island. These mills ground corn and were necessary because there were no streams on the island for water-powered mills.[3]

At Peekskill, General Heath was dealing with troops leaving for home and some New York militia coming in. He had parts of several regiments, including "naked, convaliscents, and sic" men, who were left there. Lack of pay for soldiers was a great concern and with enlistments running out, men needed money to get home. His artillerymen would all go home in a few days unless he could prevail on some to continue. He believed, "the Convention of this State for about a fortnight have been meditating a secret expedition, it is still a profound secret (but talked of everywhere)." He was concerned about a possible attack from some Hessians at Kingsbridge and had heard about Washington's orders concerning how to deal with enemy plunder and needed to know what was expected of him. He would make a return of all equipment and stores as soon as everything was collected and stored.[4]

**News of Washington's victory** arrived within hours at nearby locations. The 17th Regiment of Foot cantoned at Hillsborough, a bit north of Princeton, received morning orders that the officers "at the several farm houses do take care that the rolls be called every two hours in presence of an officer and that if any soldier be absent he be immediately reported to the major." This was because several soldiers of the 40th Regiment of Foot had been seen at some distance from the cantonment without passes. Most of the orders reflected normal camp concerns. For example, officers were reminded not to shoot "in the neighbourhood." During the "very bad weather the sentrys [were] to be relieved every hour by day & night. The sentrys to be posted single this night but the patrols to be sent out more frequently." Some confusion about the disposition of hides from butchered animals was clarified and the troops were notified that 400 bed ticks, six cross cut saws, 12 wedges, 12 axes and some nails would arrive that night for the use of the brigade. Army tailors were at work and a daily return of their work was to be made every morning at parade.[5] About 10:00am, Lieutenant Colonel Charles Mawhood's major, who had just received word from a light horse express rider, rushed into his quarters and, reflecting on Mawhood's outburst of the previous evening, said, "Well Colonel, General Washington has executed your last night's plan already for he has taken Trent Town."[6]

Early in the day, General Grant at Brunswick wrote a letter to General Harvey mentioning his new position as commander of the troops in New Jersey and that although this would keep him busy, he was looking forward to "a winter of ease and pleasure." His biggest problem was that his Hessians kept sending him reports of "an enemy, which, in fact, does not exist in the Jersies." Aside from militia, who were "still more despicable than the Continental troops," he believed there were not above 300 men scattered in small parties on the Jersey side of the Delaware. Ironically, by evening Grant was notified of Rall's defeat at Trenton that took place about the same time he had been writing words about the absence of significant American troops in New Jersey. Grant judged "this infamous business [is] the most unlucky affair which has happened to us in America."[7]

At Princeton, Pennsylvania Loyalist John Williams was summoned in the afternoon to meet with General Alexander Leslie. To prevent any further surprises from Washington, Leslie employed him as a spy to go out towards Trenton each night and report back his findings each morning.[8]

**Captain William Bamford** of the 40th Regiment of Foot at New York City, recorded in his diary, there had been some snow overnight and it was a very cold, wet and very windy morning. High winds in the afternoon drifted the snow.[9] Captain von Muenchhausen closed out his diary for the year because the 64-gun *Bristol* was setting sail the next day for England to be extensively repaired, and it would carry letters and General Cornwallis back to England. Cornwallis would return in the spring "if there is to be another campaign, which we doubt." He felt that the Congress and individual states were "keeping the common man under rebellious arms by making pleasing promises, such as the coming of a French auxiliary fleet and 50,000 auxiliary troops, partly French and partly Spanish. Were it not for these promises we would surely have peace now. The short but successful campaign and capture of their best general [Charles Lee] whom they counted on most, depresses the rebels considerably."

During the day, Captain Muenchhausen had taken a party of 20 dragoons to scout the area and reported that he "came upon five peasants with rifles who were lying behind a ditch. At that moment I had but one dragoon with me. They fired without hitting us, and then ran away. But we caught up with them. Two other dragoons, hearing the shots, rushed to our assistance. Two of the rebels were wounded, which must not be interpreted as cruelty, for a person is naturally hostile to anyone who has just endangered his life. Had I not intervened, all five of them would have been cut down by the dragoons."

Muenchhausen described life in New York City as one of "balls, concerts, and meetings, which I am already weary of. I do not like this frivolous life, and would much prefer that a campaign would begin again, or that there would be peace so that I could return to Brunswick and be a captain." He expected that "most of the English troops will probably stay here for some time after peace comes. A large volume of letters written to and by many prisoners must be read by us [aides] which keeps us busy many an annoying night."

He then detailed the disposition of the British forces in New Jersey, Rhode Island, New York, and Long Island. Lastly, he noted "the Delaware River does not freeze-up every year. If it should this year, I think we will push over it so as to have made the crossing before spring." In a P.S. he reported, "I have reopened this letter to report an unhappy affair. Colonel Rall, who was at Trenton with the Knyphausen, Lossberg, and Rall regiments and 50 Jägers, was compelled to surrender at dawn on the 26th, after a fight of one hour, owning partly to the suddenness of the enemy surprise, and partly to their superior power. Two officers and 17 men the only ones that saved themselves, brought the news to us. We know no further details at the moment." When Muenchhausen began his 1777 diary on January 1, he included additional information on the results of the battle at Trenton and noted it was fortunate that Rall had died from his wounds "because he would have lost his head if he had lived. This unhappy occurrence has caused us to leave the whole of Jersey except for posts at Brunswick and Amboy." This overstated the British removal of troops from the Jerseys because there were also still troops at Princeton.[10]

John Adlum's officers had guests who dined with them in their quarters. Among the guests was Colonel Ethan Allen who had been captured in Canada, taken to England, and was recently returned and on parole in New York City. According to Adlum, "Col. Allen was always a very welcome guest at our quarters. His manner of telling a story, his fund of anecdotes, his flashes of wit, and the force of his observations never failed of having an attentive and amused audience." On this occasion, Allen "gave a history &c of his voyage to England &c and back again mixed with his observations and interlarded with anecdotes that the company was so much amused that they sat at table until pretty late in the night."

As the night wore on, Adlum was asked to go out and purchase more wine. To do this he needed to know the countersign required to pass safely by British sentinels. He was able to get it from Mrs. Carroll, although reluctantly. When he went out he says that he, "knocked at the door of the house I usually got the groceries from. The owner came and opened the door and held a little lanthorn up to my face. When he saw who I was, he seized me by the hand and pulled me forcibly through a long entry into a little back room, when he kept shaking me by the hand and looking me in the face, unable to speak for some moments. I looked at him and thought him crazy or mad; but as soon as he could give utterance to his word he says to me, 'General Washington has defeated the Hessians at Trenton this morning and has taken 900 prisoners and six pieces of artillery!'" Adlum did not wait to hear more but ran back to Mrs. Carroll's, risking his life by not stopping to give the countersign at the sentinel posts he had passed earlier, and says, "by the time I got home I was quite out of breath and ran into the room where the officers were sitting around the table. Several of them asked what's the matter, and as soon as I could recover breath to speak I spoke with considerable emphasis" to convey what I had been told about Trenton.

The officers wanted to know where Adlum had gotten this information. When he told them, "some of the officers laughed and asked me various questions, while others did not say one word and looked very serious as if doubting the news, and others thought it too good to be true." One of the officers asked Adlum what the person looked like, so he described him "as a small slender [man] who wore a tailed wig with some wrinkles in his face and I supposed that he was between fifty and sixty years of age. One day that I called at his store I heard a gentleman call him colonel and I also described where he lived." At this point two of the officers "jumped up and said, 'Gentlemen, I congratulate you on the good news.... For as it came from the gentleman described you may rely on the truth of the information.'" The only question of doubt that remained was that it seemed almost impossible for the news to have travelled 60 miles from the time of the battle to between 9:00 and 10:00 pm.[11]

**Robert Morris in** Philadelphia received word of the victory at Trenton and wrote a congratulatory note to Washington that evening. In his enthusiasm, he speculated there would be additional moves and said that he had sent word to Congress in Baltimore and "almost promised them that you shou'd by following up this first blow, finish the campaigne of 1776 with that eclat that your numerous friends & admirers have long wished for."[12]

Morris had been informed that the attack had inspired the people of New Jersey and Pennsylvania and the militia were turning out in great numbers in spite of their previous reputation for indolence. He believed militiamen saw it was their duty to make the enemy pay "dearly for the barbarous outrages they have committed in the country, without regard to age or sex." Morris was confident that Cadwalader and Ewing would get across to New Jersey by that night, allowing Washington to join up with them to push the British away from being able to attack Philadelphia. Unsure how Washington planned to follow-up, Morris had heard that Washington had directed General Heath to keep harassing the British forces in northeast New Jersey. This would remove their attention from Washington and allow him to pursue the British troops toward Burlington and combine with Cadwalader to cut off British communication with any Hessian and British troops left in the Moorestown area. Morris felt that, "if this is the plan, I think it well laid & if the General is properly supported in the execution, why shall we not put a glorious end to the campaigne of 1776."[13]

Delegates to Congress were confident of obtaining help from France and Spain. Elbridge Gerry wrote, "The King of Spain has opened his ports to our commerce, privateers & prizes, & I have no doubt that France will engage in a war in the spring; this then is the time for America to exert herself, & to change the aspect of affairs in her favour." This could be achieved with "more of an interprizing spirit in the civil as well as military department."[14] Samuel Adams, still expecting a British foray into Massachusetts, was optimistically cautious, writing, "Our affairs in France & Spain wear a pleasing aspect, but human affairs are ever uncertain. I have strongly recommended to my friends in New England to spare no pains or cost in preparing to meet the enemy early in the spring. We have a righteous cause, and if we defend it as becomes us, we may expect the blessing of Heaven."[15]

Other delegates were working to obtain needed supplies such as flour, vegetables and vinegar to prevent illness, and casting brass and iron cannon.[16] Christopher Marshall in Philadelphia "waited upon General Putnam respecting some orders for sick soldiers; thence to [the] council of Safety, on account of the Commissary's refusing to grant rations to poor sick soldiers, coming to town without their officers."[17]

**Margaret Morris at** Burlington found the day very stormy and feared that Joseph Reed and Colonel von Donop would be unable to meet and negotiate the neutral status of Burlington. She also saw some flat-bottomed boats going up the river, but could not learn where they were headed for.[18]

Colonel Donop was at his quarters at Mount Holly where he was sharing quarters with "the exceedingly beautiful widow of a doctor," because as Jäger Captain Ewald noted, he "was extremely devoted to the fair sex." The "widow" was Mary Magdalene Bancroft whose husband had been arrested as a Loyalist earlier in the month and removed from Mount Holly. Donop's choice to quarter at Mount Holly with "widow" Bancroft destroyed his ability to respond with dispatch to any problem at Trenton.[19] In the early morning of December 26, Captain Ewald and Captain Lorey set out from Mount Holly with their men and "roamed over the different roads in the country to collect horses and slaughter cattle." Ewald noted both parties became "occupied with driving off several hundred oxen, cows, pigs, and sheep, amidst the fervent wailings of the inhabitants, who followed us constantly, when a messenger appeared who delivered us orders to come back immediately and leave all the animals behind." Both companies returned to Mount Holly in the afternoon and Donop gave them preliminary and partial information about the attack on Trenton. Ewald noted that, "at the same moment, the second messenger of doom arrived, confirming the report and adding that all had been taken prisoner."[20]

Word of the Trenton battle had reached the Hessians south of Trenton about 10:00am when four people from Trenton, possibly including John Barnes, galloped up to the picket guard at the drawbridge over Crosswicks Creek. Captain Henrich Bocking with 100 men of the Rall Regiment had been sent to this picket post on December 24. At first, Bocking felt, "I did not know if I should believe them as I had not heard any [artillery] gun fire much less small arms fire. But the weather was so stormy that it could have cut off the noise and around me was nothing but forests so it is possible that I could not hear the noise through the trees." The officer of the guard sent the information on to Donop at Mount Holly and about an hour later Hessian fugitives confirmed the information. Bocking then "expected the rebels every minute but they did not come." He set up his men in defensive positions and awaited the rebels. Lieutenant Colonel Minnegerode arrived with a company of grenadiers and they dismantled the bridge. Seven officers and about 500 men "with and without arms," the remnants of Rall's Trenton troops, were attached temporarily to the Minnegerode Battalion. Donop was short of ammunition and had erroneously heard that the Americans amounted to 10,000 or 12,000 so he decided to remove his troops immediately to safety. He ordered Minnegerode to march at midnight with all his troops and artillery to Reckless Town (today Chesterfield) to join with him. Due to a lack of wagons, he left behind a small number of sick and wounded.[21]

When Donop had come to Burlington on December 11, prominent Burlington lawyer John Lawrence and several other community leaders interceded with him to protect the town from pillage. Lawrence had Loyalist leanings and had been a member of the Colonial Assembly and mayor of Burlington before the war. He was well known in his neighborhood for helping to administer Howe's proclamation offering amnesty and protection.[22] Upon hearing of the defeat at Trenton, Donop expected that Washington would occupy the Crosswicks pass in his rear, "which had always been neglected," to cut off any retreat towards Princeton. Donop set out with his troops, along with Loyalists John Lawrence and Jonathan Odell, and expecting that Griffin would soon attack again, he left Ewald at Mount Holly with 150 Jägers, grenadiers, and Scots to guard his flank. Since the town was stretched out and Ewald did not trust the inhabitants, he took up station at the far end of town on a hill where he filled the houses with brush and straw. The wind blew toward town and he told the people that if they opposed him, or if the enemy attacked, he would set fire to the houses and this would result in the destruction of the town. He also sent out constant patrols.[23]

Chaplain David Avery heard the encouraging patriot belief that when Donop's troops heard about Trenton, "a general panic, immediately, ran through all the hosts of our enemies – and they, who a few hours before were triumphing in their inglorious deeds, spreading distress and terror all around, now fled by thousands from the river, in wild frantic disorder, like so many murderers before the avenger of blood! What a reverse of fortune! How wounding to tyrannic pride!"[24]

After dark, Donop's troops halted their march at the house of store owner John Pope near the Black Horse Tavern where Donop and his Loyalist companions asked for a candle and a room where they could meet in private. They called Pope into the room and asked him questions about the local roads leading towards Allentown, Reckless Town, Crosswicks, and Bordentown, including distances, road quality, and creeks they would encounter. Much of the conversation, spoken in French since Donop did not know English, involved a map showing the roads and discussed the locations of enemy troops. Lawrence recommended Pope to Donop as a guide for them as far as Reckless Town, but Pope tried without success to convince them that Lawrence knew as much as he did. At first they thought to go to Allentown by way of Waln's Mills, but obtained intelligence that the way to Crosswicks was clear, so they headed that way instead. Donop set off for Crosswicks, determined to cut through any enemy he encountered. At Reckless Town, Donop dismissed Pope, but warned him not to tell anyone, not even his best friend, about the Hessians and the routes they had taken, because, he later stated, "it might be fatal to the army and perhaps to myself also should it be discovered hereafter that any thing then communicated to me had passed my lips."[25]

That night, the soldiers and local men who had taken tea with Mary Field on Christmas Day at Bordentown took flight precipitately about 1:00am. The group included some Loyalists serving with the New Jersey Volunteers. Several were soon after captured by the Americans, but others, including Lieutenant Colonel John Barnes who had been in Trenton at the beginning of the battle, made their escape by keeping close to the retreating army.[26]

**Unaware of Washington's** successful crossing, Cadwalader's few troops that had crossed to New Jersey began to cross back just after midnight "with the greatest reluctance," because "by this time the ice began to drive with such force & in such quantities as threatened many boats with absolute destruction. To add to the difficulty about day break there came on a most violent storm of rain hail and snow intermixed in which the troops march'd back to Bristol except a part of the light infantry which remained [on the New Jersey side] till next day."[27] Colonel Reed found that, "It being impossible for us to cross [back] with our horses we went up to Burlington where we were concealed in the house of a friend – that part of Jersey being then considered as entirely in the enemys possession: - and the first objects that presented in the morning were two Hessian dragoons riding down to observe the river." When Reed heard firing from Trenton he "remained in great suspence & anxiety for the event of an enterprize on which the fate of America then seemed to depend."[28]

The troops that had not made it across the river for the morning attack spent much of the day in confusion while contemplating how best to support Washington as they gradually learned what he accomplished that day. On the morning of December 26, Cadwalader wrote to Washington and recounted his problems of the night before and asked if he should attempt to cross further down river and join forces with General Putnam. Putnam was expected to be crossing over from Philadelphia that day with 500 men to reinforce Colonel Griffin's 400 Jersey militiamen and divert British attention from whatever follow-up Washington may contemplate. At his present location he could not help Putnam and was concerned that continued inaction would lead to militia desertions. In addition, Colonel Hitchcock's Brigade was close to the end of its enlistment and to induce them to extend, he had gathered a good amount of shoes, stockings and breeches for them and noted "they are in good spirits & enlist very fast."[29]

Cadwalader wrote to Washington from Bristol at 9:00am that he was "perfectly prepared, & would cross immediately" and would proceed to Bordentown even though his troops had "lost their rest last night." He suggested that if Washington could use part of his army to "take possession of the other side of Crosswicks Bridge, which is a pass easily defended, and the main body march round by Crosswicks we might perfectly surround the troops at Bordenton so as to prevent one man from escaping." They could also take the 200 men posted at

Whitehill. Putnam was going to cross 1000 men from Philadelphia and 300 had crossed the day before. There were also 500 New Jersey militia there according to Colonel Griffin.[30]

Joseph Reed and Major Joseph Cowperthwaite crossed back to Bristol on the 26th and learned of Washington's success about 11:00am, but did not know what Washington's further plans might be. About 12:00pm the rest of Captain Thomas Rodney's company returned to Bristol and in the evening they "heard of General Washingtons success at Trenton and that he had captured 900 Hessians." Rodney thought the Ewing and Cadwalader crossings were only meant as "feints, for if our Generals had been in earnest, we could have taken Burlington with the light troops alone."[31]

Reed noted that, "such was the exhilaration" at the news of the victory, "that it was at once concluded that the Philadelphia troops should again attempt to cross into New Jersey, the point of embarkation being fixed at the [Neshaminy] ferry above Bristol. Orders were given for the troops to refresh, and be in readiness to march next morning at sunrise and proceed to Bordentown and then "endeavor to join Genl Washington then supposed to be at Trenton." Captain Rodney found that, "about dark[,] notwithstanding our fatigue[,] I received orders to appear at Bristol before Daybreak to-morrow morning."[32]

Sergeant John Smith recorded that soon after they crossed back to Pennsylvania, thundering cannon from the direction of Trenton added to the severe storm of rain, hail, and snow about 7:00 or 8:00am for a considerable length of time. While the storm increased, the cannon soon ceased and every man in his company made "himself [as] comfortable as he could with fires[,] for we had plenty of wood & soon after news came that General Washington had a Battle at Trenton with the Kings Troops or Hessians & this morning and had teaken 9 or 10 hundred of them prisoners & took their stores & baggage & intirly routed the whole nest of them." Smith's quartermaster went to find better quarters for the company and returned after finding a house about four miles from Bristol towards Philadelphia. Although they were ordered to go to that house, Colonel Lippitt, "thinking we should be as comfortable in our tents as we could be any wher[,] told us we may stay if we had a mind for to stay & goe in the morning early as possible & orderd us to turn out early & get our breakfast in order to march."[33]

**Although he had** achieved a significant victory at Trenton, at the end of the day Washington found himself retreating again to Pennsylvania instead of moving forward to attack other Hessian or British cantonments. Would he be able to make another reversal and resume the offensive before the enlistments of most of his Continental troops expired in just five days? Would Washington be able to drive even more enemy troops out of the state? He had expected to do more immediately after Trenton, but was now delayed and the enlistments of much of his army expired in just a few days. His victory at Trenton might speed up enlistments, but those recruits would not be available soldiers for several months and he needed men now. Perhaps militiamen from New Jersey and Pennsylvania would be encouraged to join him because of the victory and the possibility of retaking control of New Jersey. It was difficult to flesh out a plan when he did not know how many men he would have or how well armed and experienced they would be. He understood that enlistments for his Continentals had been for one year in order to prevent the creation of a standing army, but now he could see the folly of it and how it could prevent ultimate success.

# Chapter 11

## Friday, December 27, 1776

Most people in America were still ignorant of the victory at Trenton. In Virginia, Nicholas Cresswell at Pennyroyal Hill dined and spent an agreeable afternoon with several people whose pleasure was increased when they finally received word of the December 13 capture of General Charles Lee.[1] At Newport, Rhode Island, the British troops were going through their normal routines in the clear and moderate weather. Lieutenant Peebles had a good dinner with some guests, including his friend Willie, and they "completed the booze."[2] Lieutenant Mackenzie noted that the local rebels "have been tolerably quiet for some days past, and have not molested our advanced posts."[3]

Recruiting for the new version of the 1st New Jersey Regiment at Morristown, Major William DeHart was having the usual problems obtaining money to pay back wages to men reenlisting and current wages to new recruits. He told Washington that the British had troops at Elizabethtown and had withdrawn their outposts at Bound Brook to Brunswick. He knew the enemy had been discussing plans to attack Morristown, but "the spirit of our people begins much to revive[.] I have the greatest confidence that with care & attention we shall be able to maintain this part of the Province."[4]

**Word of the capture** of Trenton continued to spread in nearby areas together with increasing amounts of information and improving accuracy. In New York City, Friday morning was clear, but a hard frost made the streets a sheet of ice. The British forces began to

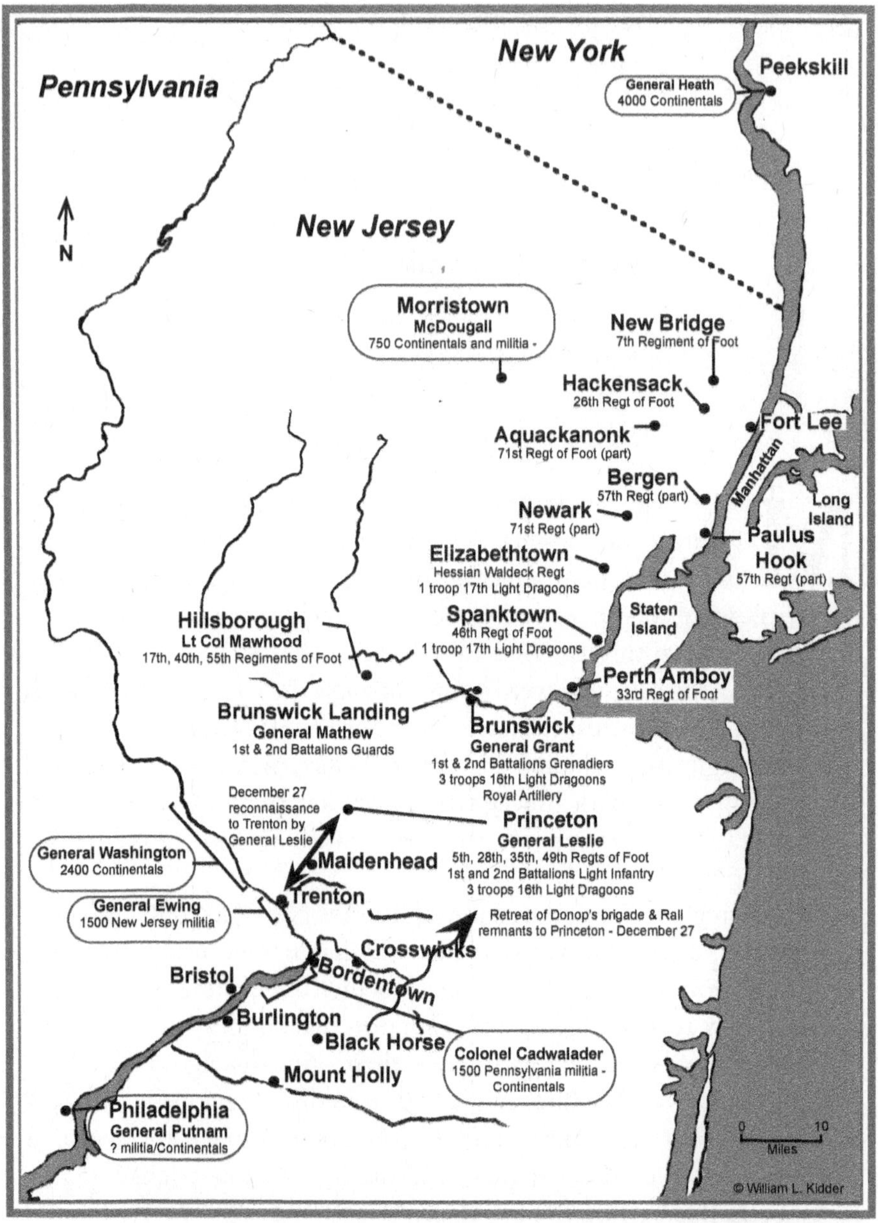


**Map 12: Aftermath of Battle of Trenton - December 27-28**

During the first days after the battle at Trenton the American army was primarily on the Pennsylvania side of the Delaware River while Colonel Donop's troops and those Hessians who escaped capture made their way to the Princeton area. The British did not attempt to re-occupy Trenton, but did reconnoiter the area while making Princeton the new western end of the cantonments chain.

hear sketchy information about Trenton and engineer Archibald Robertson was at Amboy when Sir William Erskine received an express from General Grant with the news. He forwarded an express to General Howe, who no doubt was hearing a variety of stories from multiple sources.[5] Captain William Bamford recorded in his diary that unofficial "accounts from the Jerseys" were "unfavourable, that a body of the Hessians are cut off by the rebels." When the accounts were later confirmed he jotted, "True."[6] British leaders were already worrying about their reputations. General Grant wrote to a fellow officer that while he was "quite miserable about" losing a post under his command, he could not "help the misbehavior of troops which are station'd thirty miles from me, where in fact I believed them to be as safe as you are at London." He refused to place any blame on General Howe or himself.[7]

A British officer later wrote that in spite of his defeats, Washington "was hardy enough to attempt repassing the Delaware, intending thereby to effect a surprise upon some of our cantonments that were the most adjacent." In contrast, "General Grant, who had fixed his head-quarters at Brunswick, notwithstanding good and faithful intelligence conveyed to him of the intentions and motions of the enemy – either depending on the arrangement already made, as sufficient to repel the attempt, or inattentive, from a supineness, to the information he received – suffered himself to be duped into a security, which proved afterwards the source of infinite misfortune, and national dishonor." In his judgement, "this negligence proved more fatal than all our preceding errors taken together, and finally gave the enemy such advantages as raised their hopes beyond all expectation."[8]

Major Stephen Kemble belonged to a socially prominent New Jersey family with ties to New York and was currently Deputy Adjutant General under Howe. He described in his journal learning about the capture of Rall and some of the confusion surrounding it. He believed that Donop had tried to assist Rall, but had arrived too late, and that General Stirling, rather than Washington, was in command of the American forces. Knowing he only had preliminary, partial information that could be wrong, he wrote, "we hope it is not so bad as represented and think it hardly possible, the whole should be taken away by surprise, only 6 or 8 people said to escape."[9]

General Howe justified his previous actions, while taking measures to prevent further problems. He told Grant that "no doubt Trentown was an abominably exposed post, but I could not believe the brigade could have been defeated in the manner reported." Not knowing Donop had already left Burlington, he ordered its abandonment, and therefore, Monmouth County's. The cannon ordered to Burlington would remain at Amboy for now. Howe suggested some troops at Princeton could be relocated to Pluckemin and Morristown, if Grant saw no objection, but he also took steps to strengthen Princeton. The 4th battalion of Hessian grenadiers could join Donop at Princeton and "the debris of Rall" (the several hundred men who had escaped Trenton) and the 42nd Regiment of Foot could be stationed at and near Bound Brook. Grant would send a battalion of grenadiers and one of Guards to Princeton and as soon as Donop arrived, General Leslie could march out to reconnoiter Trenton. One of Leslie's battalions should halt at Maidenhead while the others marched on to Trenton, and then all return to Princeton after reconnoitering.[10] Howe did not want any more surprises and was looking for an opportunity to get revenge for Trenton.

Lord Cornwallis, just hours away from setting sail for England on *Bristol*, wrote a final note to General Grant commenting that he had heard that the captured American General Charles Lee had requested a meeting with Grant and he "should like to have been present at that interview, the account of it will please some of your friends in England." With the 1776 campaign over, he promised to speak well of Grant while in England; even though others might not. Finally, Cornwallis wished him "all the pleasures that Brunswic can afford" and "I shall hope to see you in the month of May." General Grant at Brunswick wrote to Donop that while he did not want to "judge rashly" the actions of the "unfortunate" Colonel Rall, he complimented Donop saying that, "If you had been there and had found yourself overpowered by numbers … you would have contrived to retreat across the [Assunpink] bridge to Bordentown." He understood Donop had gone to Allentown and advised him to remain there until Howe gave him further instructions. Not knowing that Donop was at that time heading for Princeton, Grant gave him permission to go there, if necessary.

Grant still underestimated his foe and reassured Donop that, "If I was with you[,] your grenadiers and Jägers[,] I should not be afraid of an attack from Washington's army. Which is almost naked and do not exceed eight thousand men." However, later that day Cornwallis hastily notified Grant that he was rushing back to Brunswick on General Howe's orders, was collecting his men as he came, and was retaking command in New Jersey for the duration of the current crisis.[11] To strengthen his British and Hessian regiments for some kind of attack on Washington, Howe ordered all men recovered or convalescent in New York City belonging to regiments stationed in New Jersey, to be immediately taken over the Hudson to join their regiments.[12]

Early in the morning, John Adlum went to the office of printer Hugh Gaine, publisher of the Loyalist *New York Mercury*, and probably also a secret agent in Washington's spy network.[13] Adlum found Gaine passing out hand bills "as fast as they were struck off" in his very crowded office. Adlum noticed that some people seemed to be pleased, "but others again seemed to be much disappointed and I could hear some of them whispering to each other that there must be some mistake as it was not possible, that the success on our [American] part could not be as great as represented." When almost out of handbills, Gaine approached Adlum and asked, "What business have you here, you rebel you." Then, Adlum later wrote, "he took me by the shoulder as if to turn me out, but he took care to place himself between me and the company in the office and while he kept pushing me gently forward saying, 'Out, out of my office,' [he] very dexterously slipped a small roll of handbills up my coat sleeve. I affected to sneak off highly affronted, thinking at the same time what kind of Tory he was, those in the office laughing at the same time very heartily."

Once on the street, Adlum ran to his quarters but found only two officers up, but "when they saw the contents of the handbills they ran up and down stairs as if mad or crazy, making a great noise which roused everyone in the house. The more steady officers requested them to make less noise for fear of bringing the patrols" and perhaps losing their paroles and being re-imprisoned. They planned another social dinner that day, inviting the guests of the previous day who had stayed all night. The officers sent Adlum out to purchase large quantities of food and wine for the celebration and, after completing his shopping, Adlum ran to Bridewell to give the good news to the prisoners there. Adlum believed that since the embarrassed British acknowledged 900 prisoners taken, the true number was probably twice that many. This news raised hopes among the prisoners that they would be exchanged within a short time.[14] He went back to Bridewell that evening and learned that the prisoners "had drawn whole and sound biscuit for the first time in about twice the usual quantity, and there was an additional barrel of pork; that was three barrels instead of two for the two days' rations, and this was the first day that the bread and meat had been drawn at one and the same day." Adlum observed "there appeared to be considerable confusion in the city all day, the British running backwards and forwards and troops leaving the city in boats for Staten Island and Amboy, and the citizens appeared quite chop fallen."[15]

**In New Jersey, the 17th** Regiment of Foot at Hillsborough dealt with the usual guard and wood cutting duties along with behavior problems. After hearing about Trenton, the officers became more concerned than usual with obtaining accurate information about enemy strength and movements. A local man had lately given false information, causing Lieutenant Colonel Mawhood to order that any person offering information on rebel troops or movements should be brought to headquarters where the person would be rewarded if the information proved true, but punished if it was false.[16]

The 5th and 49th Regiments of Foot marched from Six-Mile Run to Princeton. The 49th Regiment had been at Six-Mile Run to guard provision wagons and escort them to Princeton. Sergeant Thomas Sullivan of the 49th Regiment described Princeton as "a compact tho' small town, in which is a good college, built of stone, sufficient to hold four hundred students, but our army when we lay there spoiled and plundered a good library that was in it. There is a sett of organs, and a nice chapel in this colloge. It is built in a plentiful but woody country, & seen at a great distance."[17]

After mid-night, Captain Ewald at Mount Holly received orders from Donop to "withdraw at once to Black Horse, which was accomplished safely," and escort Donop's abandoned baggage to Crosswicks and protect it from American attacks. Neither Donop nor Ewald knew Washington had re-crossed his army and prisoners to Pennsylvania and that his other forces had failed to cross. Ewald found, "several hundred wagons, carriages, and carioles – all loaded with plundered goods – and I very much wished that the enemy would take it away from me. I formed the rear guard and let the Jägers wander along both sides of the column to prod the drivers on with blows, to keep order, and to make them go faster." The weather deteriorated and "a hard frost set in after the heavy snow and rainy weather which formed slippery ice." Ewald was slowed because the horses did not have proper winter shoes to provide traction in these conditions and did not catch up with Donop at Crosswicks until 10:00am. They marched on to Allentown, arriving in the evening, and "took up quarters in devastated and abandoned houses which numbered about eighty."[18]

Trenton was quiet, but battle damage to buildings and their lots was severe, while the remnants of war, including horse carcasses, gave a somber atmosphere to the previously vibrant town. Hessian Medical Officer Oliva arranged transportation to Philadelphia for the less severely wounded. After that, he could "attend from morning till night to the unhappy wounded who were lying in all corners," including Major Dechow, shot in the pelvis, and Captain Altenbockum with his head wound. Oliva began moving men to houses near the parsonage hospital, but it would take until December 31 to move everyone. He reported there were "58 wounded privates, and 5 officers", and that "Lieuts. Zoll, Schwabe, and Sternickle had to be daily treated by me."[19] Private Friedrich Marcus died during the day[20] and Colonel Rall, died that evening at the Potts house, attended by Oliva, and was buried in the graveyard of the Presbyterian Church.[21]

**As word of Washington's** victory spread, it renewed confidence among Americans that the Continental Army could survive and not be forced to either surrender or disperse to conduct a war of harassment.[22] Pro-independence Americans immediately felt confident that follow-up military action would force the British troops out of New Jersey and back to New York. Congress wrote to Colonel Thomas Fleming of the 9th Virginia Regiment, overdue on its march to join the army, informing him that Washington had made "an unexpected stroke at Trentown where he now reigns master. We hope to drive the enemy out of New Jersey and if you haste up you'l come in for a share of the glory."[23] President of the Pennsylvania Executive Council and Council of Safety Thomas Wharton wrote to John Hancock to let him know that, "we are sending off reinforcements of militia, in hopes that this very important blow may be followed up." The militia had already been turning out, "but this will give them a new stimulus; and we are in hopes our worthy General will not" keep them idle.[24]

News of the victory arriving in Baltimore gave renewed impetus to Congress, trying to do its work with a number of members missing. Delegate Francis Lewis wrote to the New York Committee of Safety that he was the only representative from New York currently at Congress, making New York effectively unrepresented because the other two New York delegates, Philip Livingston and William Floyd, went north when Congress removed to Baltimore. Several delegates had been detached to work on committees, while others, such as Robert Morris, remained in Philadelphia working on government business. Lewis was upset by all these absences, believing "there was never a more urgent necessity for its being full, than at this time."[25]

Congress passed a number of resolutions to accelerate the movement and arming of troops to join Washington and to upgrade army administrative procedures. Washington was authorized "to use every endeavor, by giving bounties and otherwise, to prevail upon the troops, whose time of inlistment shall expire at the end of the month, to stay with the army so long after that period, as its situation shall render their stay necessary." Even though greatly encouraged by the success at Trenton, Congress "having maturely considered the present crisis; and having perfect reliance on the wisdom, vigour, and uprightness of General Washington" gave him power for up to six months to raise "16 battalions of infantry, in addition to those already voted by Congress" to appoint officers, raise 3000 light horse, three artillery regiments, a corps of engineers, and apply to states for militia as necessary. He could form magazines and "take, wherever he may be, whatever he may want for the use of the army, if the inhabitants will not sell it, allowing a reasonable price for the same; to arrest and confine persons who refuse to take the continental currency, or are otherwise disaffected to the American cause." This further extended the expanded the powers granted to Washington on December 10, and delegate to Congress William Whipple believed giving Washington these powers was "absolutely necessary for the salvation of America." Benjamin Rush agreed that "General Washington must be invested with dictatorial powers for a few months, or we are undone. The vis inertiae of the Congress has almost ruined this country." For Samuel Adams, giving Washington such "large powers … for a limited time" became a necessity.[26]

The problems associated with paper money and inflation were perhaps even more alarming than military issues. While individual States were making efforts to maintain the value of paper money, many people, including high ranking officials, were speculating in specie and merchants were investing paper money in commodities. Even though merchants were ordered to accept Continental money, many required specie or old colonial bills that would still have value if Britain won the war, leading to authorizing Washington to seize property not surrendered for Continental paper money.[27] The multi-state convention dealing with the issue of inflated prices conducted its second day of business at Providence, Rhode Island.

**Although he had not yet** heard directly from Washington, Robert Morris in Philadelphia received trustworthy information, that "our Victory at Trenton has been compleat." He knew that Colonel Cadwalader was going to cross his troops to New Jersey from Bristol that morning and that Putnam was sending reinforcements under Brigadier General Thomas Mifflin. Morris must have believed that further military actions would take place and wrote to John Hancock at Baltimore that, "we shall change the face of affairs & I hope soon to see you back here."[28] Delegate to Congress Christopher Marshall heard that the Hessian prisoners had been brought to Pennsylvania.[29]

Doctor and Reverend David Griffith, then in his mid-30s, was chaplain for the 3rd Virginia Regiment and was acting as a surgeon for the Continental troops in Philadelphia. He wrote to his friend Major Leven Powell in Virginia to report on the action at Trenton and indicated that further actions were planned. After Cadwalader and Ewing joined their forces with Washington, "the whole was to march against the enemy and attack them divided in their cantonments." Even though only Washington had been able to cross on the 26th, "the whole design is not yet abandoned" and the troops, including those at Philadelphia, were expected to cross back to New Jersey beginning tomorrow. The action at Trenton alone "has given new life and spirits to the cause, and has lowered the crests of the Tories in this place, who looked upon the matter as settled, and were hourly expecting the King's troops to arrive without molestation." Washington's army was growing and General Mifflin was back in town after recruiting men in the "back counties of this Province" and "he tells me that there is a virtuous disposition in the people, but they have been discouraged by people of fortune and influence, and that their officers have been backward. They are, however, now coming down pretty generally; this good news, I think will hurry and encourage them." He had heard that American troops had been active in northern New Jersey and asked if it was true that 3000 men from Virginia were headed for Washington's army. They were needed because "tho' our fears are a little quieted for the present, yet we have much reason to wish for succor. Militia are precarious as to the time of their stay, and the time of some of the Continental Troops, and some flying camp men will expire on New Years Day. The whole may amount to about 3000 men."[30]

**For Washington's troops**, the return march and river crossing back to Pennsylvania continued into the morning and many troops did not get to their camps until noon or later.[31] Colonel John Haslet of the Delaware Regiment fell into the Delaware River about 3:00am while crossing back. The water reached up to his waist and he developed piles and swelling in his legs that persisted. However, he felt it was no big problem if Washington was able to drive the British back to New York.[32] Twenty-two-year-old Private John Dewey of the 3rd Massachusetts Regiment was one who didn't get across until morning, noting in his diary that "we arrived in camp after a very fatiguing journey of 14 miles. This is a Christmas worthy of remembrance."[33]

After re-crossing the Delaware, Washington and several officers rode from McConkey's Ferry down to the Harvey's house in Upper Makefield Township where he remained that night.[34] On the morning of the 27th, Washington rode over to Newtown and set up his headquarters at "the old yellow house" of widow Hannah Harris and her 11 slaves.[35] The Hessian officers were brought to Newtown by 3rd Virginia Regiment Colonel George Weedon about whom Lieutenant Piel noted, "His lowly origins spoke to his advantage, and thus he won all of our hearts through his friendly treatment toward us." The Hessian officers were quartered in several inns and private houses, while their soldiers were quartered in the Presbyterian Church and town jail.[36] While kept at the Newtown Presbyterian Church, one Hessian soldier is said by an early church historian to have written on a wall with a coal, "In time of war, and not before, God and the soldiers men adore. When the war's o'er and all things righted, The Lord's forgot and the soldier slighted." However, since this is from an English poem, it is more likely to have been written by an American soldier quartered or hospitalized at the church at another time during the war.[37] Dr. William Shippen finally got to Newtown from Bethlehem after the battle was over and the Hessian prisoners were there.[38]

The captured staff officers had their noon meal with General Washington, at which Lieutenant Wiederholdt, probably exaggerating, recalled, "When I dined with General Washington he made the pleasant compliment, and expressly asked to meet me in order, as he said, to get to know such an excellent officer in person. He had asked about my name and character and noted such on his blackboard, and authorized and offered free access to himself at all times, where he might be." Washington asked him questions about the action at Trenton and Wiederholdt gave his opinion that their failure had been caused by the faulty disposition of the Hessian troops about the town. He also listed other mistakes made by Rall and how he would have avoided them. Washington praised him for his vigilance and the defiance he had shown with the few men he had at his outpost when the battle began. Wiederholdt found Washington to be polite, refined, and reserved, a man of few words, and that he resembled in appearance Captain von Biesenrodt of the Knyphausen Regiment. Washington gave Wiederholdt permission to return briefly to Trenton on parole, in order to search for some possessions he had left behind. Although Wiederholdt appears to have had quite a strong ego, he did keep Washington's praise in perspective, saying, "What good did it do me? I am and probably will remain the lieutenant from Capernaum."[39]

JUST HOW MANY MEN and what quantity of weapons and supplies had been captured was difficult to determine and for a week or more there were all sorts of wild numbers circulating about and constantly revised. For example, on December 27, Thomas Wharton, President of the Pennsylvania Council of Safety, wrote to John Hancock that in addition to "the arms mentioned in the enclosed letter to have fallen into our hands we have taken about 200 stand in General Dickinson's house at Trenton."[40] A gallant attempt at very specific numbers of captured soldiers, but admittedly "very rough," was transmitted from Colonel Stephen Moylan to Robert Morris on December 27, giving the total number breakdown as one colonel, two lieutenant colonels, three majors, four captains, eight lieutenants, twelve ensigns, two surgeons, 92 sergeants, 20 drums, nine musicians, 25 officers' servants, and 740 rank and file for a total of 918 prisoners. The numbers were further broken down by regiment, including the separate 38 artillery officers and men. In terms of captured material, Moylan listed "six pieces of artillery brass double fortified three pounders, twelve drums, four standards, and about 1000 stand of arms." Note that wives and children were not mentioned even though there were some.

In contrast, Moylan noted, "Our loss very inconsiderable, two or three killed & as many wounded."[41] Major George Johnston of the Virginia troops mistakenly believed the Americans had about 20 killed and wounded while the Hessians had about 100. He mentioned specifically Lieutenant Monroe and Ensign James Buxton as being wounded.[42] No names of Americans killed in action have survived, if there were any, and the statement about men killed may refer to men who froze to death on the march. Aside from the wounds to Captain Washington, Lieutenant Monroe, and Ensign Buxton, the only recorded wound was to Joseph Brearley. Brearley was from Maidenhead, had been a captain in the 2nd New Jersey Regiment in the Canadian campaign, and had served as a spy for Washington before the battle. A fellow militiaman later deposed that Brearley was struck in the leg by a nearly expended bullet that caused him to be somewhat lame for some time afterwards. Brearley has not been suggested as one of the militia guides, but he could have tagged along in some way.[43] Other early returns noted the six cannon carriages, three ammunition wagons, four wagons of baggage, 40 horses, and "as many muskets, bayonets, cartouch boxes & swords as there are prisoners."[44]

In a letter to Congress describing how he had captured the Hessians, Washington made no mention of follow-up plans.[45] However, in a letter to Major General William Heath he reiterated the importance of "attacking the enemy's detached posts [in northeast New Jersey] when it can be done with a good prospect of success," because "the best of consequences must result from their being harassed on every occasion on that Quarter."[46] Washington was already forming plans to follow-up the Trenton attack and expressed to Cadwalader his "most earnest wish, to pursue every means that shall seem probable to distress the enemy and to promise success on our part." He knew it would be very valuable to "beat up the rest of their quarters bordering on and near the [Delaware] river." He had called a council of war to explore options, but until a plan was formed he recommended that Cadwalader and Putnam should not take any independent actions "till you hear from me." Washington was not sure whether he would cross back at McConkey's or would bring his force down to join with Cadwalader. While a plan was being formed, he requested "frequent information of the state of the river and whether it is to be passed in boats or whether the ice will admit of a passage."[47]

**Believing that Washington** was still in New Jersey, Cadwalader at Bristol had ordered his approximately 1,500 troops to be ready to march to the Neshaminy Ferry about a mile above Bristol the morning of the 27th. After the failure to cross overnight, he wanted to get them across as early as possible to support Washington. At Bristol Ferry that morning, Presbyterian minister John Rosbrugh, of Allentown, Pennsylvania, wrote in a hurried letter to his wife, "you would think it strange to see your husband, an old man, riding with a French fusé slung at his back."[48] Although beyond militia age, he had carried his own musket as a private in the Pennsylvania militia before recently being appointed chaplain. Anticipating the approaching military action, he morbidly speculated, "This may be ye last letter ye shall receive from your husband."[49]

Delaware militia Captain Thomas Rodney got to Bristol about daylight and began about 10:00am to march to the ferry. Once again, the light infantry covered the landing.[50] Charles Willson Peale's company was ordered to march in the fine weather with what they could carry on their backs and crossed to New Jersey with the Philadelphia and Pennsylvania county militias and the New England troops.[51] Sergeant William Young's company, having heard the evening before a rumor about the defeat of the Hessians at Trenton, was up before daylight and got ready to join its battalion, which it did about 9:00am when they set out and crossed to New Jersey.[52] The Rhode Island troops were delayed in order to receive clothing that had arrived from Philadelphia the previous night.[53] Sergeant John Smith got up early, ate breakfast, and was packing things up when Colonel Lippitt came and told them to take everything they could carry because they were going to cross over the river to New Jersey. They marched to town and drew rum and shoes and stockings "for some of the soldiers that had none to wair" and about 2:00pm marched up the river and crossed.[54]

About 1:00pm, when the militia were all over and the Rhode Island troops were about to start, they received word from Washington, through Colonel Hitchcock's paymaster, that his army had returned to Pennsylvania after the Trenton victory. This unexpected news "occasioned much perplexity and a great variety of opinions." Having expected to join with Washington's army at Trenton, Cadwalader now had to decide how to proceed. Cadwalader and some officers argued it would be best to cross back to Pennsylvania because the reason for crossing no longer existed, there were no American troops to support them, they had so few troops and they were in bad shape, and Donop had an equal or greater number of troops and might come back from Mount Holly.

Joseph Reed and other officers strongly disagreed, believing that a retreat back across the river was impracticable and could be fatal. Besides, the militia had now been called out three times, separated from their families, and served a long time without action and if they returned to Pennsylvania without attempting something they would feel useless, might desert in large numbers before completing their actual service term, and would not be inclined to turn out when called in the future. They argued that even though the success at Trenton might have been "brilliant, its effects would depend upon its being followed up; that the shock to the enemy must be very great, and if attacked before they recovered from the panic no one could say to what extent the success might be pushed." Colonel Reed expressed that opinion strongly, and also that the militiamen should seek to match the glory and honor of the Continental troops at Trenton. They should continue with their plan, and Washington might again cross the river to continue on the offensive.[55]

Reed suggested that the troops proceed to Burlington and wait there for further advice – perhaps advancing to Bordentown or Mount Holly, "as intelligence might direct." Reed, along with Colonel John Cox and Major Joseph Cowperthwaite reconnoitered to check on a report that some Hessian Jägers had been sighted, but found the report groundless. They advanced to the enemy outposts about four miles from Burlington and found the Hessians had evacuated them. Reed was told by the local people that Donop had immediately retreated, "in the utmost panic and confusion," the evening of the 26th upon hearing of the disaster at Trenton. Upon learning that the enemy had left Black Horse and Mount Holly, Cadwalader decided to proceed on to Burlington and began to march about 3:00pm, arriving at Burlington about 9:00pm. He took possession of the town and found the British had fled "in great precipitation" from it and nearby areas, pressing into service all the wagons within their reach.[56]

Reed and his group went on to Bordentown and learned that the Hessians and local Loyalists had fled when the British troops escaping from Trenton came to town. Reed observed that most of the houses along the road "had a red rag nailed upon the door, which the inhabitants on this reverse of affairs were now busily pulling down." Reed observed that "Bordentown bore all the marks of a savage enemy – the poor inhabitants terrified, effectually broken and hardly resembling what they had been a few months before."[57] Declaration of Independence signer Francis Hopkinson had suffered the destruction of "all his furniture, cabinet of curiosities and his fine harpsicord" reputed to be "the best that ever came to America."[58]

By the end of the day, Cadwalader's troops needed rest and food after a long day's work so they got both at Burlington. Private Robert Wright of Colonel John Bayard's 2nd Battalion of Pennsylvania Associators had crossed to Burlington and then marched to Bordentown and on to Crosswicks. Wright was a 21-year-old native of Ireland who came to Philadelphia with his father and brothers in 1769 and had completed his seven-year apprenticeship as a breeches maker in June 1776. His unit was drafted to go to Allentown with a "party of riflemen to endeavor to overtake the enemy's rear-guard." This detachment got to Allentown that night in spite of the severe weather and bad road conditions and were told that Donop had divided his force with part headed for Princeton and part to Brunswick.[59]

Joseph Reed and Colonel John Cox were now at Bordentown and Cadwalader was set to march there at 4:00am. The light troops were ordered to be ready to march at 4:00am and the troops were quartered in houses by 11:00pm, giving them about four hours to sleep.[60] Peale's company had marched, with flanking parties, to Burlington and along the way one flanking party captured a supposed spy in the woods, but another got away. They arrived in Burlington that night and secured quarters.[61] Sergeant John Smith had marched seven or eight miles in a roundabout way to Burlington, having heard that some Hessians were there, and it took until about 9:00pm to get there due to the cold, dark, and bad roads. They found no enemy and lodged at the Burlington Barracks. Having no wood, they had to pull down fences to make a fire to warm themselves and cook.[62]

When Cadwalader wrote to Washington at 10:00pm from Burlington to explain why he had proceeded, "tho not quite conformable to your ordrs which I recd on the march this afternoon." He then suggested that if Washington also wanted to cross over, "it may be easily effected at the place where we passed." The enemy troops were in a panic and pursuing them would keep them going. Cadwalader understood many of them had gone to South Amboy and "if we can drive them from West Jersey, the success will raise an army by next spring, & establish the credit of the Continental money, to support it—I shall write you tomorrow, I hope from Trenton." Cadwalader told Washington he had two brass 6-pounders and two iron 3-pounders. Shortly after the letter was completed, Colonel Reed set out with it for Trenton.[63]

Margaret Morris learned about the Battle of Trenton by way of a letter from Colonel Reed to his brother. In noting the significantly greater number of Hessian casualties compared with the American, she erroneously speculated that it was due "to the prevailing custom among the Hessians of getting drunk on the eve of that great day which brought peace on earth and good-will to men," which she did not see as good Christian behavior. Her speculation helped create the myth that the Hessians were drunk or hung-over at the battle. She noted that in the evening, a large group of Pennsylvania militia and other troops "landed in the neck, and marched into town with artillery, baggage, &c., and are quartered on the inhabitants. One company was lodged at J.V.'s [James Verree's] and a guard placed between his house and ours." No soldiers were quartered at her house, but "an officer spent the evening with us, and appeared to be in high spirits, and talked of engaging the English as a very trifling affair – nothing so easy as to drive them over the North [Hudson] River, &c. – not considering there is a God of battle, as well as a God of Peace, who may have given them the late advantage in order to draw them out to meet the chastisement that is reserved for them."[64]

**Washington praised and** thanked his officers and soldiers in the day's General Orders, "for their spirited and gallant behavior at Trenton yesterday." If any fault could be found, it "proceeded from a too great eagerness to push forward upon the enemy." He told his men that the value of the military supplies taken from the enemy would be distributed proportionately among the officers and men "who crossed the river." Laying the groundwork for an appeal to his men to extend their enlistments, he made special mention of Colonel Bradley's Connecticut state troop battalion, many of whom had "overstayed the time for which they were engaged." He thanked them for staying with the army and said they "may be dismissed if they choose it." However, now that they "have begun the glorious work of driving the enemy, he hopes they will not now turn their backs upon them, and leave the business half-finished at this important crisis, a crisis, which may, more than probably determine the fate of America." All the field officers of this regiment were absent sick, prisoner of war, or away on duty, leaving the senior captain in command. Washington then exhorted "the officers and soldiers of all those regiments whose term of service expires in a few days, to remain.[65]

**By the end of the** day, Washington was resting his troops and actively planning further military action in conversations with this officers. He only had four days until many enlistments expired. Would the victory at Trenton prove sufficient to get enough men to extend their enlistments a few weeks so he could make further moves? If not, what else could he offer? Would the changeable winter weather continue to help or hinder his plans? Like many of the people who supported the ideals and efforts of the Revolution, Washington believed that Providence supported them, but that it would take human resourcefulness and efforts to achieve success. It was more than just a military chess game problem. He had to reverse the deep discouragement of those with strong feelings about the righteousness of the cause.

# Chapter 12

## Saturday, December 28, 1776

Word of the battle at Trenton had still not travelled far. In Newport, Rhode Island, the day began with a "gentle frost" and "a scanty allowance" of two bushels of coal was issued for each barrack room. Lieutenant Peebles noted that not enough firewood to keep the troops warm had been provided, with the result that "the old houses & fences suffer." That evening, Peebles was part of about a dozen regimental officers who formed a club to dine together on Wednesdays and "play cards & sup" on Saturday evenings. Peebles was not sure the arrangement would last long because, even though they had not yet heard about the action at Trenton, he "still believed that we shall go to NYork soon."[1] Lieutenant Mackenzie continued his interest in rebel boats that came ashore not knowing the British were now in control of the area. Because the American privateer *Alfred* and her prizes were expected to come into the harbor very soon, "orders have been given to hoist the rebel colours upon the appearance of any vessels. The ships in the harbour have struck their colours, and the commodores their broad pendants." These simple actions would add to the misplaced confidence of approaching American ships.[2]

**In New York City** the morning was very cold and dull and it began to snow about noon. In consequence of Donop's retreat from Burlington, the artillery earmarked to defend it against the river gondolas was now ordered to remain at Amboy.[3] Howe ordered that a picket from each regiment in New York was to make rounds at night and be ready to turn out on the shortest notice. His soldiers must have better appreciated the order that, "Spruce beer will be issued to the troops at Mr. Horsfields Brewery near Maiden Lane from 10 in the morning, to 4 in the afternoon, at the rate of 4 shill[ing]s per barrel of 30 gallons."[4]

Captain Bamford heard largely inaccurate information about the action at Trenton, including that Washington had attacked with a force of about 7,000 men. Already, Colonel Rall was being blamed and Bamford recorded that Rall, "by some misconduct suffer'd himself to be nearly surrounded, without making any disposition for securing his retreat," and had lost about 100 killed and wounded and more than 700 taken prisoner, while between 400 and 500 escaped to Colonel Donop's post. The rebels also captured six cannon and 15 colours. Bamford heard Hessian officers say that Rall's death was "a lucky circumstance for him, for had he liv'd he must have been broke with infamy. At least."[5]

**In Philadelphia, Christopher Marshall** went to the Council of Safety to arrange for wood to be supplied to the wives of the militia Associators who had gone to camp. The news of the victory at Trenton was confirmed and he learned that the Pennsylvania militia had crossed over to the Jerseys the day before and the Hessian prisoners at Newtown were expected in town the next day. In the morning, Major Thomas Proctor's artillery company with two cannon, ammunition, and baggage left the city for headquarters, as did hundreds of militia from the country. Marshall wrote in his diary that, "It's said three thousand went for camp yesterday, headed by Gen. Putnam, all in high spirits and warm clothing."[6] Enthusiasm to support the war effort was clearly improved, even if overstated, virtually overnight.

The Executive Committee of Congress (Robert Morris, George Walton, and George Clymer) wrote to John Hancock that Cadwalader had informed General Putnam that the enemy was panic stricken and they hoped that "our troops will follow them up & not give them time to recover."[7] The Committee then wrote to Washington expressing their sincere joy "in your Excellencys success at Trentown as we conceive it will have the most important publick consequences and because we think it will do justice in some degree to a character we admire & which we have long wished to appear in the world with that brilliancy that success always obtains & which the members of Congress know you deserve." They had stood by Washington when others expressed doubt about his abilities and now expressed their hope that his success "is only the beginning of more important advantages" for the American cause. They believed it very likely, that the enemy troops "are seized with a panic whilst your forces are flushed with success and such precious moments shou'd not be lost." Immediately following up with further attacks, before the enemy has time to recover from its surprise, should result in "clearing the Jerseys of them." Continuing to put offensive pressure on the enemy would make it, "probable that those troops whose times of enlistment are now expiring will follow their successful General altho they wou'd have left him whilst acting a defensive part." Large bodies of Associators were already marching to Washington's assistance, and although they had been "put in motion when our affairs were at the worst … you have given a spring to the tardy spirits & we think their numbers will be greatly augmented." Other reinforcements were expected at camp daily, including Colonel Flemings 9th Virginia Regiment, as well as Pennsylvania Continentals raised in the back counties and additional regiments from Maryland and Virginia.

Regarding the soon-to-expire Continental enlistments, the Committee advised Washington that if any of the seamen in the two New England regiments should "obstinately persist in being discharged from your service on New Years day we think it adviseable to prevail on them to come down here [to Philadelphia] & assist in getting the frigates out." Congress was anxious to get these ships out to sea, but needed crewmen. The Marblehead regiment that had worked so hard during the crossing on the night of the 25th had volunteered even before the crossing to sail the Continental frigates to a New England port on their way home when their enlistments were up. Washington had not taken them up on the offer, hoping to reenlist them in the army or enlist them into the permanent crews for the frigates.[8] Now, he would take what he could get from them. Regarding the Hessian prisoners, the Committee did not think they should be exchanged, but that Washington should separate the officers from their men and take advantage of the "favourable opportunity of making them acquainted with the situation & circumstances" of German immigrants in eastern

Pennsylvania "who came here without a farthing of property & have by care & industry acquired plentifull fortunes which they have enjoyed in perfect peace & tranquility until invaders have thought proper to disturb & destroy those possessions."[9] Instead of looking at the Hessians as vile mercenaries, Revolution leaders were now beginning see them as facilitators of Hessian desertions and even potentially productive American citizens.[10]

Congress was hoping to be able to return to Philadelphia if Washington could drive the British further back towards New York. North Carolina delegate William Hooper wrote to Robert Morris that he wished the Congress could return to Philadelphia without any fear of having to flee again. For one reason, Baltimore was increasingly uncomfortable for the delegates and in general was a "dirty, boggy hole [that] beggars all description." Except when the streets were frozen hard, the delegates had to ride on horseback to get to Congress, because the roads were "so miry that carriages almost stall on the sides of them. When the Devil proffered our Saviour the Kingdoms of the World, he surely placed his thumb on this delectable spot & reserved it to himself for his own peculiar chosen seat and inheritance." As for the people of Baltimore, "the congress can boast no acquaintance with them but what arises from their daily exorbitant claims upon our pockets."[11]

The December 28 edition of the *Pennsylvania Evening Post* published portions of a letter reportedly from "an officer of distinction" at Newtown, Bucks County, dated December 27, 1776 that gave a generally accurate, morale-raising, description of the battle and capture of the Hessians. Other news items and advertisements provided old news from London and news from a few days to a few months old from various other places. Aside from some comments about British atrocities and the need for men to step up and support the cause, there was nothing to indicate that Philadelphia felt threatened with attack.[12]

**General Grant at Brunswick** ordered Donop to have his troops take post at Princeton and, still downplaying the quality of his enemy, told him that should the American forces "make an attempt upon your cantonments ... those rebel gentlemen will have reason to repent it."[13] General Howe wrote to Grant about Trenton stating, "It has been a most wretched business. Much misconduct on the part of Rall according to some particulars that have been reported." He ordered the Light Dragoons at Princeton to rejoin Leslie, and Grant and Leslie must decide whether Donop's brigade and Rall's surviving troops would be enough to garrison Princeton. Howe did not want to have any British troops at Princeton if it could be avoided, just Hessians and Scots. At least for the present, this was now the left wing of the line of cantonments. Not aware yet of Donop's panicky retreat, he said Donop's troops from Bordentown should be moved up quickly and the Hessian 4th Battalion of Grenadiers marched to Princeton. He gave Grant permission to make any alterations in the plan he deemed "most proper & efficient" and, to avoid two of Rall's mistakes, instructed him to create breastworks in the streets of Princeton and take all necessary precautions for defense, including plans for units to support each other in case of attack. Because there were American militia and new Continental regiments being formed in cantonment at Morristown, he might send a battalion of the 71st Regiment of Foot from Newark to Springfield to keep an eye on them. Howe closed by wishing Grant, "Merry Christmas to you notwithstanding all our disasters."[14]

Daily routine orders to the 17th Regiment of Foot at Hillsborough included that there would be the usual wood cutting party and the trees were to be cut close to the ground. The officer commanding the work party would be answerable if the men left their work to go to houses of the local people. Sentries were to be posted "towards the enemy who are to prevent the soldiers pass." General Grant presented "a pipe of Madeira wine to the officers" to make up for his order that no officer could have a leave of absence at present. Two days of forage for the horses would be issued tomorrow at the usual place and four days of flour for the men would be issued when the quartermaster sergeants return. Regimental officers should submit returns of camp equipment and arms needed by their officers and men for the upcoming campaign.[15]

The remnants of the three Rall regiments had been temporarily commanded by Captain Bocking, but now Captain Emanuel von Wilmousky of the Lossberg grenadier company was put in command. The makeshift regiment headed for Princeton where they quartered in town "and in the neighbourhood as comfortably as circumstances permitted, but it was bad enough." Captain Ewald marched his Jägers to Kingston, "a village consisting of about sixty to seventy houses of which only one was inhabited," occupied the town, and patrolled the routes to Rocky Hill, Trenton, and Cranbury.[16]

**Temperatures were below** freezing in the Trenton area and there was a bit of snow when some Americans returned to the town.[17] Colonel Joseph Reed, with Lieutenant Colonel John Cox and Major Joseph Cowperthwaite, arrived about 2:00am. Reed found the town evacuated by the British, with things "in a still more wretched condition" than Bordentown. He wrote to Washington "urging him to cross the river again & pursue the advantages which Providence had presented." He did not mention the paroled wounded Hessian soldiers left in town or how well medical officer Oliva was taking care of them. Private Kurt Mensing of the Lossberg Regiment died from his wounds that day.[18] Reed felt there was a real possibility of catching up with Donop before he reached Princeton or Brunswick and when two parties of light troops requested by Reed marched into Trenton about 2:00pm he directed them to pursue Donop's brigade. He wanted them to harass the Hessian rearguard, and stop them if possible until other American units could join them.[19]

**The American troops that** had crossed into south Jersey were acting to assess any enemy presence. Lieutenant Charles Willson Peale received orders to march at 4:00am and his battalion set off just after daybreak. They had marched about four miles when a party was detached to pursue two Hessians reported in the area. They halted after six miles when word was received that the enemy was just two and a half miles from them and advancing. Half of the 2nd Battalion, Philadelphia Associators, including Peale's company, was ordered back to a crossroad, where they halted for a short time until ordered to rejoin the battalion, which they caught up with at Bordentown.

Peale's company quartered at a house that needed extensive cleaning after its recent occupation by enemy troops. He left some men to clean and then took a walk and came across a storehouse marked "King's Stores" and got some beef and pork. When he heard about some flour being available, he got a barrel and delivered some to Captain Boyd.

Taking some of the flour himself, he asked a family "to let a negro girl make up some bread for us," but the woman of the family said she would make bread for them and bake it in her oven. She was very kind to them because she was a Whig who had found it necessary to be hypocritical and act the Loyalist while the British troops were there. They were not given time to enjoy their cleaned rooms, but were ordered to march and set out about dusk, without their flour since they had no wagons. The ground was very slippery and Peale took a fall that broke the stock of his musket.

They made it the four miles to Crosswicks about bedtime, but Peale noted, "no bed for us, who think ourselves happy to get a plank by the fire." Fortunately, they found quarters with a Mr. Cooke who "made us very welcome." Mr. Cooke had been subject to Hessian plundering and for clothing was left with only the shirt on his back. Peale noted the large extent of plundering, saying of the Hessians that "they have taken hogs, sheep, horses and cows, everywhere; even children have been stripped of their clothes – in which business the Hessian women were the most active – in short, the abuse of the inhabitants is beyond description."[20]

Captain Thomas Rodney left Burlington about 4:00am and marched his company on the Great Road to Bordentown. He recorded, "Along the road we saw many Hessian posts at bridges and cross roads; they were chiefly made with rails and covered with straw, all deserted. The whole country as we passed appeared one scene of devastation and ruin. Neither hay, straw, grain, or any live stock or poultry to be seen." About 9:00am they halted at the foot of a bridge about half a mile from Bordentown and heard the enemy had deserted the town, were about five miles away, would probably return, and some light horse were expected any minute. They took post in a cornfield and set sentry posts on all the roads, waiting for about an hour before learning that the enemy were retreating rapidly rather than attacking. They then marched into town and took possession of the stores the enemy had left behind, went into quarters, refreshed themselves, and were joined by the main body of the army about two hours later.

Rodney described Bordentown as "pleasantly situated on the River Delaware about 10 miles above Burlington, the houses are chiefly brick, and several of them large elegant and neat, but they all look like barns and stables, full of hay, straw, dirt and nastiness, and everything valuable about them destroyed and carried off, and all the inhabitants fled." This had been Colonel Donop's headquarters, but Rodney thought "it looked more like the headquarters of a swine herd." Also, "Mr. Bordens house had some hundred pounds worth of goods, and valuable furniture ruined and broken to pieces."

Cadwalader was informed in the afternoon that enemy troops were at Allentown eight miles away. About dusk the light troops pushed forward followed by two battalions and they soon reached Crosswicks, about four miles away, described by Rodney as a little town of "all wooden houses built at the crossing of several roads." Here they learned that the enemy had left Allentown and gone to "a place called Hide town" about eight miles further away. Some officers wanted their troops to make a forced march that night to intercept them, but they "had then been on duty four days and nights, making forced marches without six hours sleep in the whole time." The company officers "unanimously declared it was madness to attempt it; for it would use up all our brave men, not one of whom had yet given out but all were dreadfully fatigued. However, a few riflemen and fresh men were sent off, and the light troops were to reinforce them in the morning." Taking advantage of the opportunity to get some rest, the men took up "comfortable quarters, and something refreshing to eat and drink, and several prisoners were picked up in the neighborhood that night, one of them a member of the Kings foot guard, a very tall, likely fellow, said that he had been sent on Christmas day from Brunswick to Mount Holly with orders for the troops to retreat."[21]

Sergeant William Young's company loaded their baggage onto a wagon and marched to Bristol where it was unloaded, put on board a "flat bottomed boat," and in spite of the ice taken across the river. Margaret Morris at Burlington noted that early in the morning the "troops marched out of town in high spirits," while snow in the morning "drove the gondolas again down the river." Knowing that the soldiers coming through town would soon be engaged in battle, she was saddened that a number would be killed. Sergeant Young's company got to Colonel Cox's house at Burlington before dark and as soon as the baggage was stored they foraged for firewood, "made a good fire. Got supper, went to sleep." The weather cleared in the afternoon and Margaret Morris, who lived next door to Cox, "observed several boats with soldiers and their baggage making up to our wharf." Then, "a man, who seemed to have command over the soldiers just landed, civilly asked for the keys to Colonel Cox's house, in which they stored their baggage and took up their quarters for the night, and were very quiet." She also sent them two mince pies which accepted gratefully and prayed, "May God Bless all our friends and benefactors." Margaret was surprised that one of the soldiers was her brother-in-law, George Dillwyn. "When I saw the companions he was among, I thought of what Solomon said of his beloved, that she was like an apple tree amongst the trees of the wood. When he came into the house, my kindred heart bade him welcome to the hospital roof – for so must I ever deem that roof which has sheltered me and my little flock – though our joy at meeting him was checked by the prospect before us and around."[22]

Rhode Island Sergeant John Smith's company rose in the morning and ate some beef roasted on their fire coals. They marched for Bordentown and it began to snow "a little modratly," so that "the traviling was slipry & sharp to our feet." They got to within two or three miles of Bordentown and halted, hearing that some enemy light horse was nearby. They built fires to warm themselves and then it snowed. After two hours they went into town where they "stayed in the street for some time until we had houses provided for us to quarter in." One of their scouts took a Hessian prisoner and killed another near town. This Hessian had fired on the scout, but did no damage. In Bordentown they found twelve sick and wounded Hessians that had been left behind at one house and found provisions that had been left in almost every house. The Hessians also left provisions in storehouses and a waggon in the road "with a hogshed of rum & port." They received orders to take up flour and meat wherever found and cook up a three day supply during the night. Sergeant Smith's company were packed into a "verey small roome" all night, where they cooked. [23]

**At Newtown, Lieutenant Piel** noted, "This morning we visited General Lord Stirling, who conducted himself in a very friendly manner toward us. He received us with these words, 'Your General von Heister treated me like a brother when I was a prisoner [captured at the Battle of Long Island], and so, Gentlemen, you shall be treated by me in the same manner.'" After they sat down, "a tall, thin, sad man entered, whom we assumed to be the local pastor, and who directed a long speech at us, in which he sought to convince us of the correct view of the Americans in this war." Piel noted this pastor "scolded" the Hessian officers "so miserably that we finally tired of his idle talk and told him we had not been sent to America to determine which of the parties was in the right, but to fight for the King." Stirling rescued them from the pastor and asked them to accompany him to see Washington, who received them "very politely," but spoke to them only in English. Piel wrote that, "In the face of this man nothing of the great man showed for which he would be noted. His eyes have no fire, but a slight smile in his expression when he spoke inspired love and respect." He kept four of the officers, no doubt including Wiederholdt, for the noon meal while the rest ate with Lord Stirling.[24]

Lord Stirling, on behalf of Washington, and with a lame hand, wrote to New Jersey Governor William Livingston from Newtown reporting that they had captured or killed at least 1200 of the "best of Hessian troops, with their artillery and stores." He exclaimed, "the effect is amazing" and the enemy troops had left Bordentown, Black Horse, Burlington, and Mount Holly to head across the state toward South Amboy and we are now in possession of all those places they abandoned. He asked Livingston to have the militia form small scout parties and harass the Hessian camps and line of march on their retreat. He advised, "now is the time to exert every move and if we do; General Howe's army will be ruined." The prospect of more attacks by Washington on British cantonments with the goal of forcing the enemy troops from the state was very invigorating. The state had been aroused and it was important that the legislature resume business immediately. The Assembly had been called to meet the next Thursday and he hoped the governor and council could be there also to complete the government. Stirling hoped that "we shall soon be in full possession of New Jersey" to raise morale even further. Efforts must be increased to raise the new Continental regiments because, as things now stand, "no man of spirit will serve." Men needed encouragement to enlist and problems with officer appointments needed to be solved so officers could begin recruiting. To encourage officers to accept commissions, it would be important to "let merit in service & not dirty connections" determine appointments and advancement. Suffering from the ill effects of fighting in the cold, snowy weather, Stirling hoped to be well enough soon to help give the enemy another drubbing. He proudly recalled, "I had the honor to make two regiments of them surrender prisoners of war [at Trenton] and so treat them in such a stile as will make the rest of them more willing to surrender than to fight."[25]

Washington received erroneous intelligence that Donop's troops had retreated rapidly towards South Amboy, in actuality Princeton, immediately after hearing of the attack on Trenton. General Mifflin was ready to follow Cadwalader and Ewing and cross the river to New Jersey to pursue them. Washington planned to cross himself as soon as his men were refreshed and recovered from the fatigue of the past few days and with these combined troops he would have a respectable force in New Jersey to make further attacks against British posts. He called on Continental Generals Alexander McDougall and William Maxwell at Morristown, and the New Jersey militia in general, to make harassing attacks on the British flanks and rear. To encourage a larger militia turnout, Washington ordered the men to be informed that he planned to "rescue their country from the hands of the enemy" that had been plundering their homes and farms and mistreating their women. Washington wanted all available troops to be prepared to join up with him to create "a fair opportunity .... of driving the enemy entirely from, or at least to, the extremity of the province of Jersey."[26]

**Two days after taking** the Hessians at Trenton, Washington was still resting his troops and planning how he could force more British forces out of New Jersey. Sergeant McCarty was spending his second day in the Bucks County woods with no shelter from the snow, sleet, and rain. He felt that, "my time was not yet come, bless His name, or I should have been frozen."[27] Private David How of Sargent's regiment spent the day washing his "things."[28] Having just arrived at Newtown the day before, busy doctor William Shippen set off to fix up another hospital and left Washington whom he knew was "preparing for another expedition in ye Jerseys."[29] Washington would have most of his veteran troops for only three more days. While he certainly appreciated the militiamen who were joining him and whose enthusiasm would help greatly, they were not seasoned combat veterans. He was determined to force the British out of the Jerseys, but how would he do that in three days? The bulk of his experienced men were still recuperating in Bucks County. Most of his men were counting the hours until they could depart for home with a discharge and, hopefully, their back pay.

# Chapter 13

## Sunday, December 29, 1776

Word of the battle was still spreading slowly to outlying areas. No ships from New York had arrived in Rhode Island since the British took control of Newport and Lieutenant Mackenzie noted that, "we are totally ignorant of the operations of the army under General Howe."[1] Lieutenant Peebles's company attended church "dress'd in britches for the first time." He noted that there were "some pretty looking girls" in church. The only military action he mentioned was the capture of 10 men from a privateer crew the day before.[2] In Virginia, Nicholas Cresswell's main concern was a violent pain in his breast that he attributed possibly to pleurisy.[3]

General Howe was still absorbing the fragmented information coming in about Trenton when he reluctantly wrote to Lord George Germain to inform him of the incident there. He could not give precise details, but seems to have had at least a sense of what happened. He interpreted it more as a hit and run attack, because "the rebels recrossed the river Delaware immediately with the troops and cannon that they had taken." Like others, he was already blaming Rall and wrote, "this misfortune seems to have proceeded from Col. Rall's quitting his post, and advancing to the attack, instead of defending the village." Downplaying the significance of the encounter, Howe did not give the number captured and typically underestimated the killed and wounded. He also pointed out that "some few officers and about 200 men of the brigade, with the chasseurs [jägers], and a party of dragoons, retreated to Col. Donop's corps at Burdentown, 6 miles distant."[4]

Stephen Kemble's journal entry revealed an incomplete understanding of the Trenton episode, stating that Putnam had been at the attack and that Rall had known the Americans were crossing the river, but "made no disposition for his defence." The number of killed and wounded was unknown, but "about three hundred Hessians" had escaped capture and joined with Donop. He also had heard the "chasseurs [jägers], light horse, and a detachment of light infantry escaped, with the loss [of] one chasseur only."[5] There had been no detachment of British light infantry at Trenton on December 26 and this may refer to the light infantry sent to Donop that had stopped at Trenton and then returned to Princeton.

Captain Bamford described the weather as very fine, but with a hard morning frost.[6] Howe's general orders required a small contingent of guards to report to the Kings Wharf on the Hudson the next morning to escort American prisoners to Paulus Hook for delivery to an officer of the 57th Regiment of Foot.[7] He also wrote to Grant, ordering him to keep the field guns with the troops and to remove the light dragoons from Princeton. Grant had expressed some concern about sufficient ammunition supplies and Howe reassured him that for some days past there had been 800,000 musket cartridges at Amboy, exclusive of 40,000 Grant had alluded to, and all were at Grant's disposal. Howe had long ago ordered ammunition for the British and Hessian artillery and believed that it also must be at Amboy. He acknowledged knowing that a number of troops needed shoes.

Howe inquired if Grant had any plans for changes to the troop cantonments, noting that Donop appeared to be in panic by leaving his sick behind and probably would not be satisfied with the planned number of troops for Princeton. However, Howe felt it was important to continue posting troops at Hackensack, New Bridge, Acquackanonk, and Westfield. He also mentioned keeping troops at Spanktown and the need to protect army baggage at Amboy. Donop's retreat towards Princeton had disheartened the Loyalists south of Trenton, so Howe approved the plan to take Morristown in order to give protection to the many loyal inhabitants he was told lived in that area. To secure it they needed troops at Springfield, Westfield, and Bound Brook. He ordered that troops in the scattered cantonments must, unlike Rall, construct defensive breastworks.[8]

Lieutenant Colonel James Webster of the 33rd Regiment of Foot notified Colonel Elisha Lawrence of the Loyalist New Jersey

Volunteers that the Howes had granted a full pardon to Richard Stockton, the captured signer of the Declaration of Independence who had signed an oath under the provisions of the November 30 proclamation while being held by the British.[9] Stockton was entitled to have his property returned to him, including a horse that had been taken from him. Everything should be returned to him at the house of John Covenhoven in Monmouth County.[10]

Charles Lee wrote a letter of complaint to General Howe by way of General Grant in the hopes of improving his captivity conditions. He asked for "a little air and exercise under a proper guard – as I begin now to feel the effects of close confinement."[11]

The British were receiving questionable intelligence about American actions. Captain Ewald at Kingston was told that Washington had crossed back to New Jersey with 16,000 men, his army had been greatly increased since Trenton, and had "encamped behind Trenton Creek." This told Ewald that Washington was planning to defend Trenton by taking advantage of the high ground on Mill Hill, which Rall had failed to do. From Rocky Hill they heard that the troops of captured General Lee were now under General Lincoln and "approaching our right flank from the mountains of Morristown."[12] Those troops were actually under General John Sullivan and had joined Washington before the Battle of Trenton.

Paroled prisoner John Adlum noted that the British and Loyalists in New York City were "recovering their spirits and I could hear the citizens in the market when conversing together and observing that as soon as the army was concentrated they would march on and take Philadelphia and so put an end to the business at once."[13]

**WHILE WASHINGTON KEPT** his follow-up plans close to his vest, others did not hesitate to speculate and encourage him. Major George Johnston of the 5th Virginia Regiment, a officer in his mid-20s, very understatedly commented to a friend that, "The Gen'l, reflecting that our necessary retreat from the Deleware would perhaps hazard too much the fate of America, determined, at all events, to attempt a change in affairs."[14] Robert Morris encouraged Washington as strongly as he could "say with decency" to pursue the British forces with his entire army. More militia was turning out daily and Morris hoped they would

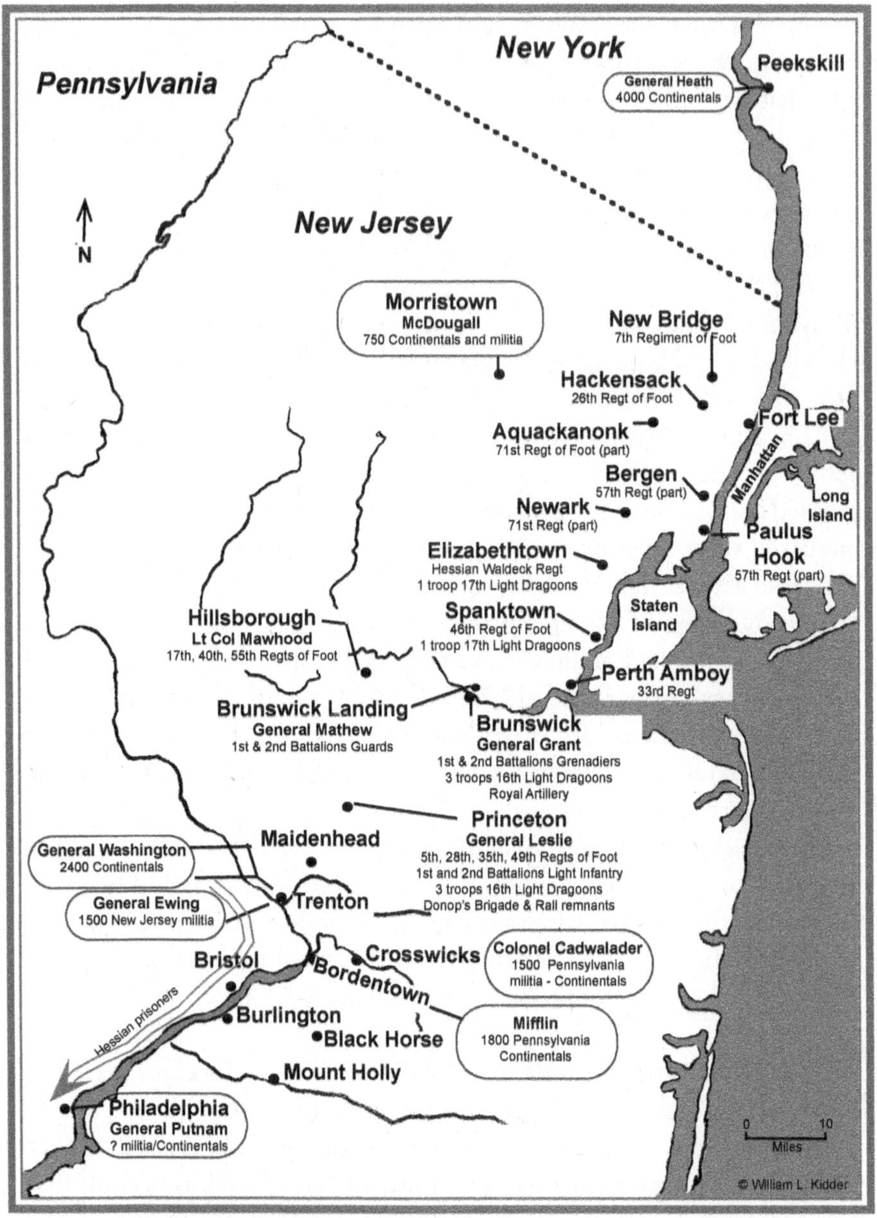


**Map 13: Aftermath of Battle of Trenton, December 29-31**

Washington's troops moved into the areas of Trenton, Bordentown, and Crosswicks while the British began to concentrate troops at Princeton.

make Washington strong enough to drive the British out of New Jersey, because then the Congress could return to Philadelphia.[15] Washington, while appreciating Morris's support, needed no encouragement and demonstrating his "great daring and a penchant for putting everything to the hazard," set out to cross his army once again to Trenton.[16] He was determined to succeed, but knew his men would again face "much fatigue and difficulty, on account of the ice, which will neither allow us to cross on foot or give us an easy passage for the boats."[17]

Two groups of militia light infantry marched into Trenton about 2:00pm and Colonel Reed immediately sent them in pursuit of Donop, ordering them to "harass his rear, till the other troops should come up."[18]

Washington ordered all unnecessary baggage left at Newtown, guarded by small squads of men unable to march or endure much fatigue, and the sick sent to Philadelphia under the direction of doctors Shippen and John Cochran. Lord Stirling found himself temporarily unfit for active duty due to exposure to the severe weather on the 26th that aggravated his rheumatism, so Washington left him in command at Newtown. Before leaving, Washington presented a silver teapot to Mrs. Harris.[19] Still wanting to control the Delaware, Washington ordered all boats to be collected at Easton, Coryell's Ferry, McConkey's Ferry, Yardley's Ferry and the Trenton ferries and put under a militia guard of an officer and 20 men. Colonel Knox assigned artillery and ammunition to each division and General Greene's division with its baggage and supplies was ordered to cross at Yardley's Ferry and General Sullivan's division at McConkey's Ferry.[20]

Washington also sent his Hessian prisoners to Philadelphia and wrote to the Pennsylvania Council of Safety that he did not care where they were quartered, but wanted the officers and men separated. Expecting his prisoners to one day be exchanged, he wanted the officers treated well and the soldiers to "have such principles instilled into them during their confinement, that when they return, they may open the eyes of their countrymen, who have not the most cordial affection for their English fellow soldiers." Unlike many Americans who considered the Hessians to be inhuman beasts, Washington, in spite of what they had done to his men in battle, wanted to treat them well to encourage future Hessian desertions.[21]

Hessian Lieutenant Piel noted that "our non-commissioned officers and privates were taken to Philadelphia today."[22] *The Pennsylvania Evening Post* reported that, "upwards of nine hundred Hessians, who were taken at Trenton, were brought to this city." Ignoring that the Hessians were professional soldiers and some accompanied by family members, it stated, "The wretched condition of these unhappy men, most of whom, if not all, were dragged from their wives and families by a despotic and avaricious prince, must sensibly affect every generous mind with the dreadful effects of arbitrary power."[23] The Executive Committee of Congress noted the Hessians "formed a line of two deep up & down Front Street from Market to Walnut Street, and most people seemed very angry they shou'd ever think of running away from such a set of vagabonds. We have advised that both the officers & men shou'd be well treated & kept from conversing with disaffected people as much as possible."[24]

Christopher Marshall wrote in his diary that it was about 11:00am when about 900 Hessian prisoners arrived in the city "and made a poor, despicable appearance."[25] A British officer later wrote that the captured Hessians, "marched through that city in public shew: the inhabitants, far and near, who did not give credit to the first reports, came in to look at an enemy, the same of whose valour and bravery had spread terror from one end of the continent to the other; which now began to wear off, when they found that manners, language, and habit, made the only difference between those people and themselves."[26]

The commissioned officers remained at Newtown and Lieutenant Wiederholdt took advantage of Washington's permission to go to Trenton to collect some personal belongings he had left behind. He was happy to find, in addition to some cash, "a new uniform and five shirts, all of which I had in a small suitcase, and by chance had left in Major von Dechow's quarters, and which had been protected by the hostess." He stayed overnight and returned to Newtown the next day.[27] While in Trenton he may have visited the wounded Hessians, including Friedrich Hartmann who died that day and belonged to the same company in the Lossberg Regiment as private Mensing who had died the previous day.[28]

Washington planned to pursue and engage the enemy as soon as possible, and "try to beat up more of their quarters and in a word, in every instance adopt such measures as the exigency of our affairs requires and our situation will justify." However, Washington was greatly concerned about being able to feed his troops and feared "it will be extremely difficult, if not impracticable, as the enemy, from every account has taken and collected every thing they could find."[29] Washington ordered General Thomas Mifflin, who also served as Quartermaster General, to procure all the provisions he could, especially flour, and forward them to Trenton.[30]

Washington took time out on this busy day to deal with a prisoner exchange problem and to arrange for General Lee to receive a sum of money to make his life more comfortable while in British custody.[31] Washington wrote to Lee from Newtown, enclosing a letter from Robert Morris with a draft for £116.9.3 sterling, asking him to send information on "the state of your health and your situation, in both of which I hope you are as happy as a person under your circumstances can possibly be."[32]

Rev. David Avery crossed back to New Jersey above Trenton and got into town about midnight, while Sergeant James McMichael's company crossed at Yardley's Ferry at 10:00pm and camped out in six inches of snow with no tents or houses to protect them from the very cold weather.[33] David How's company drew provisions and cooked them "in order for a march and at night we all marchd to Howles Ferry [at Yardley] and crossed it and staid there till morning."[34]

Before he crossed to New Jersey, Major George Johnston wrote a letter at McConkey's Ferry to a friend in Virginia telling him of the Trenton victory. He commented on the morale reversal among both the Americans and the British. Regarding the Americans he wrote, "The presence of Gen'l Washington, and the activity of the other Gen'ls infused such spirit and courage into our men as promised a happy issue to the War, if the men now regaling themselves at home would obey their country's call and turn out." Perhaps not recognizing the unusualness of the fighting at Trenton and at risk of underestimating enemy ability, he proclaimed that if Americans knew "how easy a victory over such men as our enemies are, may be obtained, they would press on to share the honor of saving their bleeding country with us." In contrast, "So much has this attack disconcerted Howe's motions, that his troops quartered in the several Jersey towns, are flying to So. Amboy to seek security in their ships, from which they never could have penetrated so far into the country if they had not been encouraged by the [Loyalist] inhabitants."

This greatly overstated the British actions, but Johnston continued his enthusiasm, stating the Americans were pursuing the British "and doubt not regaining in 10 days all the lost ground. ... They have fled precipitately from Bordentown and Burlington, leaving stores to the value of £12000, now safe with us." He added a post script declaring, "Express this moment from Gen. Mifflin, says he is at the head of 2600 in full pursuit of the enemy, who are flying as hard as they can to their ships. Our whole force is crossing from Philadelphia quite up to this place. The militia are coming in, in large bodies. Everything is in motion to join in full cry."[35]

**Captain Thomas Rodney's** company moved out from Bordentown about sunrise to reinforce some troops sent forward the previous night towards Cranbury. They marched through Allentown, and met the troops returning from Cranbury about half a mile beyond, "with about 30 bullocks and five tories." They all returned to Allentown and took up quarters. Rodney described it as "a little village of wooden houses, but indifferently built on both sides of the road at a mill about 4 miles from Crosswicks." During the afternoon, the body of Isaac Pearson was brought in. Pearson had tried to flee when found in a house with some Loyalists who were captured. Rodney says, "They shot two balls over his head to stop him, but as he persisted in making off, the next two were ordered to fire at him and one of their balls passed thro' his breast and he fell dead on the spot. He is said to have been very active in favor of the enemy."[36]

Isaac Pearson had served in the rebel Provincial Congress and provided lodging for Loyalist Anglican Rev. George Panton who had left Trenton after the Declaration of Independence was passed. Pearson's wife always believed that he was "murdered," and after the war attested that their house was also ransacked by American troops. Only one carpet was saved, and she showed investigators "the remains of the boxes broken open & riffled by the Americans after the murder of her husband."[37] Pearson had been one of the Loyalists who took tea daily with some British and Hessian officers at the home of Mary Field at Whitehill. Upon hearing of the defeat at Trenton on the 26th they had immediately fled town, desperate to reach the protection of the British army. Mary later wrote that Pearson "was unfortunately shot by endeavoring to make his escape from the American army."[38]

Charles Willson Peale also mentioned Pearson in his diary as being brought in dead after attempting to escape. Peale noted some Hessians, "had been here the day before our arrival, but in the greatest hurry and confusion, with a great number of wagons, carrying off plunder. They had planted some cannon on the road, expecting us every moment. Here I got a barrel of flour and some beef, which I ordered to be dressed ready for a march."[39]

After crossing the river at Dutch Neck, about two miles above Bristol, Philadelphia Associator Ensign Philip Hagner's company went to Burlington and then marched the next day to Bordentown where they captured the British stores and wounded. They went to Crosswicks that night and quartered at the Friends meeting house. Four companies of his regiment then went towards Cranbury where they surprised some Loyalists, including Tench Coxe, Peter Campbell, and Edward Shippen, who surrendered. Another was the deceased Isaac Pearson. The three Loyalist prisoners were taken to Crosswicks where Joseph Reed examined them and ordered their confinement. Hagner says, "He treated them with much sternness. I saw them in hand cuffs by whose order I am not able to say. We remained at Crosswicks a few days."[40]

Sergeant William Young, quartered at the home of Colonel John Cox at Burlington, got up early and had breakfast. He set out with his company for Bordentown about 9:00am and reached it about 2:00pm. As they set off, they passed the door of Margaret Morris, who had given them two pies the previous evening, and "stopped to bless and thank" her for them. While there, saw a room full of wounded Hessians, including one who had lost his nose to a bullet and all in "wretched condition." They immediately left for Crosswicks and got there at sunset very tired after the 15-mile march. They put their baggage in the Friends meeting house where they planned to stay that night. On the way to Crosswicks they had met a party of seven Loyalists marching to Bordentown under a strong guard. He learned that an eighth Loyalist who he identified as a merchant of Trenton (Isaac Pearson) had tried to escape through a window from the house where they were caught, but was shot at and killed. The travelling had been very bad that day.[41]

Margaret Morris noted a large number of soldiers were in town and after Sergeant Young's company left the house next door another company moved in. She noted that she received their thanks for the pies "not as my due, but as belonging to my Master who had reached a morsel to them by my hand." The town people were very short of bread and firewood for the soldiers, and Margaret commented, "This seems to be only one of the many calamities of war."[42]

Sergeant John Smith of Lippitt's Rhode Island Regiment went to Crosswicks, about four miles northeast of Bordentown where the Quaker inhabitants had a very "beautiful meeting house built of brick in which was kept our piquet guard all the time we tareyed in town." They got there about 9:00am, when "the sun was about two hours high in the morning." The road had been very slippery. At the meeting house they built some fires for warmth. The residents told them the enemy had come through town the day before about noon. Most of them were Hessians and they numbered 4,000 or 5,000 men. They had a large amount of baggage and left several hundred barrels of salted pork and beef in town. That night the men were ordered to find quarters and while some "went into houses & shops" others were "oblig'd to lie out of doors & to build themselves sheds with boards & burn fences to meak them fires to cook with." A small party was sent out under a lieutenant to capture a Loyalist said to be at his house, but he got away before they got there.[43]

**Only part of Washington's** main army had gotten across the river by the end of the day. Washington clearly wanted to attack more British positions, but with two days left on most enlistments he needed to find a way to get the men to extend them, especially those who did not already have a plan for future endeavours, such as the Massachusetts men who anticipated privateering wealth. Robert Morris encouraged Washington to "prevail on all [seafaring men] that will not continue with him to come down here to man our frigates." They would not be permanent crew members, because the frigates would simply carry them home to New England and, hopefully, on the way impress men from prizes taken by the frigates to fill out the crews. But, at least the frigates would get out to sea.[44]

How many men could Washington convince to remain with him? How could he use them effectively to get the British out of New Jersey?

# Chapter 14

## Monday, December 30, 1776

It would still be weeks before news of Trenton arrived in England. Lord Germain only now received General Howe's letters written on November 30, but the Cabinet would not begin evaluating his thoughts until January 10, 1777. The news had all been positive, leading many people in Britain to expect the war to end very soon, although some less optimistic leaders were concerned that if the costly war continued for very long support for it would evaporate.[1]

**On this cloudy,** freezing day in Newport, Rhode Island, Lieutenant Peebles's company, still unaware of Trenton, conducted a field day at noon, going into the country and performing various battlefield maneuvers. On a visit to the hospital, Peebles was troubled to find "things not as they should be." His military servant was taken ill and his landlady was "very kind to him."[2] Lieutenant Mackenzie was involved with the repair of a redoubt abandoned by the rebels and other measures to improve the British defenses from rebel harassment.[3]

**At Pennyroyal Hill** in Virginia, Nicholas Cresswell heard his first, somewhat inaccurate, news about the attack on Trenton and that General Howe had retreated to Brunswick while Washington "play'd the devil" by harassing him and taking many prisoners.[4]

**Buried in a long list** of miscellaneous items, *The New York Gazette* reported on page three that on "Wednesday morning last one of the Hessian brigades stationed at Trenton, was surprised by a large body of rebels, and after an engagement which lasted for a little time, between 3 and 400 made good their retreat, and the whole loss is about 900 men." As a Loyalist paper, it downplayed the significance of the battle by emphasizing the successful "retreat" of the minority, rather than the capture of the majority. In contrast, it highlighted on page one the November 30 amnesty proclamation of the Howe brothers, with information about its success noted in a later article.[5]

Howe ordered his troops in New York to form a detachment of guards to parade the next morning at the New Bridewell prison to escort a number of prisoners to Kingsbridge where, although bearing visible evidence of their mistreatment, they would be freed.[6] Congress had been deeply concerned over the mistreatment of American prisoners in New York, and Georgia delegate George Walton believed it was due to either a British belief that such treatment was "proper for rebels" or an effort to persuade prisoners to agree to enlist with the enemy. He believed that Congress was "indispensably bound, to comfort and protect them as far as it is in its power," and contrasted their treatment with that of British prisoners by the Americans. He expressed the need for a commissary of prisoners.[7]

In a follow-up to Howe's letter of the previous day, Samuel Cleaveland at New York sent General Grant a list of guns, ammunition, and military stores then at Amboy. He was surprised that General Howe thought there was no ammunition for the Hessian cannon. In fact, for some time there had been 500 cartridges for them and also a quantity for the British cannon. Musket cartridges and flints had recently increased in stock.[8]

**At Brunswick, Grant** received faulty intelligence from General Leslie at Princeton that between 12,000 and 15,000 Americans had crossed back to Trenton and Putnam, with 4,000 men and four cannon was advancing by Crosswicks. While these were greatly inflated numbers, they suggested a threat to Princeton requiring reinforcements to be sent there. Grant also received intelligence that a man coming from Allentown reported 5,000 rebels were expected to march towards Brunswick from there. They had collected flour and were baking bread for that purpose and some had advanced five miles that morning.[9]

**Donop's troops left** Kingston and joined the forces concentrating under General Leslie at Princeton. Ewald found the town consisted of about 320 houses, besides the college, and an entire regiment was quartered in the college building. Six redoubts were constructed "on the heights toward Trenton" and armed with 12- and 6-pounder artillery. Reflecting on the news of Trenton, Captain Ewald expressed the dramatic change in British confidence when he recorded, "Thus had the times changed! The Americans had constantly run before us. Four weeks ago we expected to end the war with the capture of Philadelphia, and now we had to render Washington the honor of thinking about our defense." In addition, "such a fright came over the army that if Washington had used this opportunity we would have flown to our ships and let him have all of America. Since we had thus far underestimated our enemy, from this unhappy day onward we saw everything through a magnifying glass."[10]

Ewald attributed this reversal to several causes including the too long string of cantonments, and also partly to Donop, "who was led by the nose to Mount Holly by Colonel Griffin and detained there by love, and partly to the Jäger detachment under Lieutenant Grothausen, who was posted at the Dickinson house near Trenton." If Grothausen had "patrolled diligently as far as Pennington on the morning when Washington crossed the Delaware, the enemy would have been discovered. He could have thrown himself into the house to cover the road to Trenton, which would have detained General Washington until Colonel Rall could support him, for the colonel did not lack resoluteness."

While Ewald pondered how events had come to the current situation, false reports came into Princeton "almost hourly of the approach of Washington's army." Ewald knew that Lord Cornwallis was preparing to come to Princeton and "planned shortly afterward to give the enemy a beating and thereby repair the damage at Trenton."[11] While the British were concentrating a large force at Princeton to take on Washington's army in a major battle, Washington was planning how he could attack smaller British forces in cantonments in order to force the British out of New Jersey.

**Robert Morris's 28-year-old** wife, Mary, had come to Baltimore with Congress while Robert remained in Philadelphia. She wrote him on December 30 responding to his letter about Trenton "which brought those glad tidings" that were so different from what she was expecting after the army had been so much on the defensive and losing men. She had expected to hear about more retreat. She hoped that "indeed, the tide is turned, and that our great Washington will have the success his virtues deserve." She hoped he would continue on to rout the enemy army that has "prosecuted this cruell war" solely to enslave "this once happy country." She was happy to have spread the exciting news to the many guests she and her father had entertained to celebrate the Christmas season.[12]

The Committee of Secret Correspondence of Congress wrote to the Commissioners at Paris reporting the successful action at Trenton and adding, "We hope this blow will be followed by others that may leave the enemy not so much to boast of, as they some days ago expected, and we had reason to apprehend." Because French and European assistance was essential, Congress "have authorized you to make such tenders to France & Spain, as, they hope, will prevent any longer delay of an event that is judged so essential to the well being of North America." The Commissioners should point out to the French what should be obvious, "that if Great Britain should succeed in her design of subjugating these States, their inhabitants, now well trained to arms, might be compelled to become instruments for making conquest of the French possessions in the West Indies; which would be a sad contrast to that security & commercial benefit that would result to France from the independence of North America." They also gave the Commissioners permission to approach the ambassadors to France from the Courts of Vienna, Prussia, Spain, and the Grand Duke of Tuscany to seek their support also.[13]

John Hancock wrote a circular to the States explaining why Congress had given Washington such extensive powers on December 27, explaining that, "Ever attentive to the security of civil liberty, Congress would not have consented to the vesting such powers in the Military Department …, if the situation of public affairs did not require at this crisis a decision and vigour which distance and numbers deny to Assemblies far removed from each other, and from the immediate Seat of War." He also pointed out the desperate need for the states to fill their new regiments with dispatch.[14] Because state government in New Jersey was so disrupted, Governor Livingston's copy was addressed to him "or the present executive power in New

Jersey." In a post script, Hancock added, "I congratulate you on the success of Genl Washington in the Jerseys the particulars you will find in the papers enclosed."[15]

In an example of the inaccurate reports that were circulating, Charles Coxe, who represented Hunterdon County in the New Jersey General Assembly, wrote to Livingston that there were reports that Bordentown had been retaken, 1500 Hessians captured, and a total of 20 brass field pieces captured at Trenton and Bordentown.[16]

The Executive Committee of Congress wrote to Hancock about the present supply problems and those anticipated for the spring campaign and expressed the hope that the army would finally take up winter quarters in New Jersey. The capture of the Loyalists and killing of Isaac Pearson apparently became transposed to Hessians and they wrote, "A Captn Smith writes from Crosswicks that nine Hessian officers were taken & one killed in that quarter, supposed to be part of those that fled from Trentown. No further Acct yet from Genl. Cadwallader." They expressed concern about British ships in Delaware Bay preventing the ships of Captain Biddle from getting out to sea. They were sending a man to Cape May to keep them informed of British naval movements.[17]

Robert Morris wrote to Washington that he was sending him the hard money he had requested and explained just how he was getting that money.[18]

**The Hessian officers at** Newtown signed a parole promising to obey travel limitations imposed by authority, to behave peaceably, not communicate any intelligence, or speak or do anything disrespectful to the American States. They also agreed to "restrain" their servants, who were allowed to remain with them.[19] Lieutenant Piel wrote, "This afternoon the captured officers, led by Colonel Weedon, began our trip to Philadelphia. We were given five wagons. We spent the night in a pleasant little village by the name of Fourlancends, six miles from Newtown."[20]

**At Burlington, Margaret Morris** saw many "poor soldiers sick and wounded brought into town." They were quartered in the courthouse and in private houses. Several townsmen told the soldiers they would procure firewood for them, but then found that very difficult, since most of the local wagons had been "pressed to take the soldiers' baggage."[21]

The army was receiving reinforcements daily and the troops were impatient to seek revenge for the British atrocities committed in New Jersey. Benjamin Rush wrote to Richard Henry Lee from Crosswicks that, "There is no soil so dear to a soldier as that which is marked with the footsteps of a flying enemy – everything looks well." Rush found that gathering intelligence had been difficult due to the currency problems, people were more inclined to accept hard British money. He asked Congress to send Washington £2,000 or £3,000 in hard money, because "it will do you more service than twenty new regiments. Let not this matter be debated and postponed [in Congress] in the usual way for two or three weeks; the salvation of America, under God, depends upon its being done in an instant." Efforts to convince men to extend their enlistments were already underway and Benjamin Rush optimistically informed Richard Henry Lee that, "two small brigades of New England troops have consented to serve a month after the time of their enlistments expire. There is reason to believe all the New England troops in their predicament will follow their example."[22]

One of those soldiers was Lieutenant Stephen Olney who later recalled, "Our regiment was several days at Crosswicks, where General Mifflin made a harangue to the three regiments of Rhode-Island, which then composed nearly one half of the present army of General Washington, to induce them to stay one month longer than the time for which they were engaged. Our regiment, with one accord, agreed to stay to a man; as did also the others, except a few who made their escape by the enemy at Trenton, the next day, and was not seen in the army afterwards."[23] Charles Willson Peale noted, "This morning General Mifflin came in here, and … had some regiments of New England troops paraded, whose service was just up. He harangued them on the necessity of their continuing in the service one month longer, promising them ten dollars gratuity for their past and present services – with which they showed their ready consent by three cheers."[24]

Sergeant William Young rose before dawn on a very cold night, checked on his men, found them "hearty except 3." He saw some New Jersey light horse going through on a scouting party and during the morning saw General Mifflin come to their camp and convince the

New England forces to "stay till this campaign is over." They spent the day "busy in dressing and packing provision ready to march which I believe will be soon."[25]

Sergeant John Smith recorded that "in the afternoon our brigade was sent for into the field where we paraded befor the general who was present with all the field officers & after meaking many fair promises to them he begged them to tarey one month longer in the service & almost every man consented to stay longer who receiv'd 10 dols bounty as soon as signd their names." At this point, "the Genl with the soldiers gave three Huzzas & was with claping of hands for joy amongst the specttators & as soon as that was over the Genel orderd us to heave a gill of rum pr man." Then, "we was dismisd to goe to our quarters with great applause[.] the inhabitents & others saying we had done honour to our country viz New England." After receiving their rum they paraded and set off for Trenton to tell Washington of their extensions and "meak his heart glad once more."[26]

**Thomas Rodney recounted** a situation that cemented his friendship with the Philadelphia officers of the Light Infantry Regiment. He recorded, "Capt. Francis Wade a vain blustering man of one of the city battallions was appointed quartermaster general." Each light infantry company had a light wagon for its baggage and Captain Wade ordered his wagon master to collect them and send them out for forage. The light infantry officers refused to give up their wagons, so Captain Wade sent them an order to do so. One captain submitted, but the others went to Rodney who "ordered the wagon master, who was putting in the horses to desist, and to inform the Q.M.G. that he should not have one of them, that we were subject, every moment, to be ordered out on parties and should not part with our wagons. The Q.M.G. was much offended, but could not help himself, and the officers were much pleased with my conduct."[27]

**Washington crossed back to** New Jersey in the morning and took post at Trenton while his army, baggage, provisions, and artillery (including the six captured Hessian cannon) crossed at McConkey's, Yardley's, Howell's, and Trenton ferries. Because the ice made the crossing "extremely difficult and fatiguing" not everyone or everything got over until the next day. The weather was rather mild, making the roads very muddy. Private John Dewey recorded that they struck their "tents and turned them into the store, and marched to Trenton; 9 miles." Sergeant James McMichael's company of the Pennsylvania Line broke camp on the New Jersey side of Yardley's Ferry at 8:00am and marched into Trenton two hours later. Washington established his headquarters at the house owned by fugitive Loyalist John Barnes on Queen Street, very near the Assunpink bridge.[28]

Sergeant Nathaniel Root of the 20th Continental Regiment recalled that "three or four days after the victory at Trenton, the American army recrossed the Delaware into New Jersey. At this time our troops were in a destitute and deplorable condition. The horses attached to our cannon were without shoes, and when passing over the ice they would slide in every direction, and could advance only by the assistance of the soldiers. Our men too, were without shoes or other comfortable clothing."[29]

Not everyone got across to Trenton that day. Sergeant McCarty had prepared everything on December 29 so everything was ready on the 30th. His men and the supply wagon marched to the river, but could not cross. They were "up all night and wet, almost froze." They did not get across and join their regiment until the next day.[30] Rev. Avery recorded in his diary that the troops were now over the river.[31] Private David How's company marched with all their baggage down to Trenton from Howell's Ferry where they had crossed the previous evening.[32]

**Some of Washington's** officers doubted his wisdom, believing he was inviting defeat rather than additional success by relocating to Trenton instead of attacking another British cantonment. Major James Wilkinson worried that Washington had placed himself in a very dangerous situation by returning there and putting himself "into a 'cul de sac,'" with the river at this back and with "a corps numerically inferior to that of the enemy in his front," an enemy that until recently had forced him to retreat.[33] Expecting the British to seek revenge for the capture of the Hessians and attack him at Trenton, Washington ordered all his artillery to be posted on Mill Hill, the rising ground behind Trenton Mills on the south side of the Assunpink Creek in Nottingham Township, with two cannon posted specifically to cover the Assunpink Creek bridge. He then formed his troops in three lines behind the artillery, with the baggage wagons behind everything. Guard posts with a captain and 40 men were established on each road leading into town and the captains were ordered to keep mounted patrols out to two miles. Horses for these patrols were supplied by the quartermaster department since the men were infantry. Officers planned out areas to quarter their troops, keeping them together as much as possible. Everyone held himself in readiness to move out at a moment's notice.[34]

Enlistments for many soldiers expired in two days. Washington wrote to the officer in command at Morristown that the New England regiments had, "to a man," extended their enlistments for six weeks upon being offered a bounty of 10 dollars in addition to their pay over that time. He hoped the four regiments at Morristown in a similar situation would do the same and he authorized the same reward. He needed these veteran Continental troops to lead in battle the large numbers of militia joining him. He requested the troops at Morristown to make a strike at Elizabethtown, or that area, and be ready to join with him to drive the enemy out of the state.[35] In addition to troops, Washington needed food for the army and hard money to pay spies. Not all his troops had crossed to New Jersey yet because he was waiting for food and "Jersey has been swept so clean that there is no dependence upon any thing there."[36]

**Nathanael Greene wrote** to Caty, his wife, from Trenton, noting the importance of the battle a few days previously. He wrote, "This is an important period to America, big with great events. God only knows what will be the issue of this campaign, but everything wears a much better prospect than they have for some weeks past. The enimy are collecting their force at Princeton; whether they mean to attack us or to act upon the defensive." Things were turning around for the army and he told Caty, "I am well in health and hope to continue so. In a few weeks I hope to have a fine army together." To raise her spirits he wrote, "should we get possession again of the Jerseys perhaps I may get liberty to come and see you. I pity your situation exceedingly. Your distress and anxiety must be very great; put on a good stock of fortitude."[37]

Joseph Reed led a six man intelligence gathering patrol of the Light Horse of Philadelphia towards Princeton. They were unable to learn much during their ride and could not convince any local person to go into Princeton, because the British had struck so much terror. Even people well disposed towards the cause could not be convinced to go – even if paid. Reed decided to scout on the outskirts of town and perhaps get behind the town where there would be fewer guard posts.

Near the John Flock farm, about half a mile southeast of Clarksville, they emerged from some woods and from a knoll on Quaker Road observed a British soldier "passing from a barn to the dwelling-house without arms." They first thought he was a marauder and two men were sent to capture him, but then another man was seen and then a third. Now the whole patrol charged and surrounded the house. As a result, "Twelve British soldiers, equipped as dragoons, and well armed, their pieces loaded, and having the advantage of the house, surrendered to seven horsemen, six of whom had never before seen an enemy." A Commissary was also captured and only a sergeant escaped and later reported at Princeton that he had to fight his way through fifty horsemen, which was no doubt readily believed. A local resident later said the British soldiers, "instead of being on guard to defend the Commissary and themselves were imployed in a much pleasanter business, that was, in attacking and conquering a parcel of mince pyes."[38]

Sergeant McMichael wrote, "we had the pleasure of seeing seven prisoners brought in by our light horse, from whom we learned that the enemy are at Princeton 7000 strong, and intend to attack us at Trenton in a few days." The prisoners were examined separately and their information "left no doubt of the enemy's superiority, and his intention to advance upon us, which would put General Washington in a critical situation." It appeared to many that occupying Trenton put Washington in a position where retreat was impracticable. And, even if he could retreat, it would renew the discouragement that had existed before the Battle of Trenton. If he took on the British army in full battle, though, he risked "annihilation of the Grand Army, an event the most dangerous of all to the public cause." Defending Trenton appeared to put him in a trap where he was likely to "fight and die, if he could not conquer or extricate himself with honour."[39]

**But, were things really** what they appeared to be? Was Washington hoping for some good luck that would throw the advantage to him? Or, in the spirit of General Heath's philosophy, was he creating an appearance of something which was actually not intended?

# Chapter 15

## Tuesday, December 31, 1776

Still having no knowledge of Trenton, Lord North forwarded letters to the King from General Howe and the Commissary General concerning complaints about the poor quality of bread and flour that had increased when suppliers began obtaining them from Europe. He also stated the French were inappropriately providing aid to American ships and escorting them out of the Bay of Biscay.[1]

Lord George Germain wrote to Undersecretary of State William Knox that the 1776 campaign waged by the Howes had been completed "honourably and advantageously." However, he could not approve the general pardon the Howe brothers had offered in their November 30 proclamation. He felt it discouraged Loyalists who had suffered at the hands of the rebels to see their oppressors go unpunished, and warned, "this sentimental manner of making war will, I fear, not have the desired effect." He then criticized Generals Clinton and Burgoyne for taking the liberty to come home on leave without the King's permission.[2]

**In Paris, Silas Deane** sat down and wrote out a list of the arguments he could use to induce France to join the thirteen colonies in their war against Great Britain. He stated the British Government was prosecuting, without provocation or injury, a war that violated "every principle of humanity and justice." Deane then repeated many of the charges against the King stated in the Declaration of Independence, including hiring German auxiliaries. In addition, he inferred from the "wanton destruction" of towns "only for sake of destruction", that British leaders had given cruel orders to their commanders in America. Deane then outlined the opportunities for European countries, such as France, to trade with an independent America and benefit from the wealth of American resources. Rather than posing a threat to other countries, an independent America would respect their rights.

Acknowledging previous French material aid, Deane declared that the Americans could not hold out long due to lack of essentials such as artillery, small arms, gunpowder, and clothing, and if the colonies were compelled to submit to Britain, "that submission must be such as ought to alarm Europe in general, & France in particular." Reunited with its thirteen colonies, Britain would use their resources to raise money and build an army threatening to other countries – including France and Spain. Although making every effort to end the war in one campaign, Britain was going broke fighting its American war. If the colonies, with foreign help, could keep the war going, the British would be forced to negotiate a peace recognizing their independence, and countries like France would benefit accordingly. But, if its colonies were subdued, Britain would be free to make life difficult for other countries, especially France.

Deane concluded by noting that in representing the United Colonies, he did not possess the advantages of representatives from established and powerful states. He had no money "to offer in subsidies for mercenary troops." However, the worthiness of the American cause should be "sufficient to interest the great lovers & promoters of human felicity to espouse and support it." By supporting the Americans, France would be "relieving the oppressed & humbling the oppressor" and would be the recipient of "the endless gratitude of the numberless millions rising into existence in a new & extensive world."[3] These were idealistic arguments, but American victories were needed to advance them.

**ALSO UNAWARE OF TRENTON** and assuming that General Howe was by that time very likely at Philadelphia and that General Clinton with 10,000 men had taken possession of Rhode Island, Lieutenant Governor Marriot Arbuthnot at Halifax, Nova Scotia wrote an encouraging letter to Germain stating, "The hour, my lord, is approaching with hasty strides in which you will be relieved from future anxiety for your country from the machinations of the disaffected on this side the Atlantic."[4]

**Lieutenant Peebles's regiment** paraded at 11:00am as usual as temperatures moderated to produce a thaw. The news of the capture of General Lee in New Jersey on December 13 arrived in Newport and there was "a buzz of some action there." Peebles was pleased to meet "a lady in the street [who was] well dress'd & had a very genteel appearance, & came afterwards into a shop where I was." He learned that she was a well-known, and respected, woman about 30 years old who ran a house "of pleasure." He declared that Newport "must have arrived to a tolerable degree of modern luxury, when houses of that kind were publickly allowed of, & the manners of the people by no means rigid when subjects of that sort become family conversation." He then closed his diary for the year with, "God knows, if, how, or where we shall end the next."[5] Lieutenant Mackenzie was more interested that the British ship sent to search for a rebel privateer seen off the island a few days previously had not yet returned.[6]

**Captain William Bamford** in New York City found the fine morning weather brought a gentle thaw. He was thankful that the winter weather had been very mild so far and there had been no severe weather of any kind. It had been very favorable for British military operations. He wrote in his diary the prayer, "O Lord God I praise thy holy name for that thou hast been pleased to protect me in the day of danger. Accept my thanks Gracious God." However, very aware of Trenton, he ended his diary for the year on a pessimistic note writing, "This rebellion is most obstinately persisted in, nor do I see that we take proper steps to put an end to it for by our continual blunders, which the enemy never fail to take advantage of, we seem more to encourage than dishearten them. I wish our mismanagement may not produce effects fatal to Great Britain & I greatly fear our neglects are willful & that in the end we shall loose this country."[7]

Lieutenant Colonel Stephen Kemble jotted some diary notes commenting on the conduct of General Howe during his pursuit of Washington across New Jersey and the seeming opportunities that he missed. Kemble's final comment was, "Why post so small detachments as to be in danger of insult, as happened in Rall's affair, upon the frontiers of your line of communication, or why put Hessians at the advanced posts, particularly the man at Trentown, who was noisy, but not sullen, unacquainted with the language, and a drunkard?"[8]

Engineer Archibald Robertson passed over from New York to Amboy at 7:00am and at 10:00am set out for Brunswick where he arrived at 2:00pm. There he heard the report that the rebels were on the Jersey side of the Delaware and he was ordered to leave for Newark the next morning. At 11:00pm an express arrived with the message that the rebels intended to attack Princeton. General Grant ordered two battalions of grenadiers and one battalion of the guards and three regiments of the 4th Brigade and a regiment of Hessian grenadiers to be ready to march there in the morning.[9]

**Assessing the year** now drawing to a close, Nicholas Cresswell in Virginia declared it to have been worse than Egyptian bondage and saw no prospect of making things better.[10] In Williamsburg, Leven Powell wrote to his wife about the unsettled situation he was in as Virginia reorganized its militia and Continentals. He had been an officer in a minuteman battalion and was now angling for a commission in the Continentals, but was concerned about the politics that could get in the way. Whatever happened, he told her, "The desire I have of being instrumental in the relief of my country out-ways every other consideration, tho' I confess I wish the point settled and that I could spend the rest of my days in my family."[11]

**Thomas Paine's** *The American Crisis No. 1* appeared on the first two pages of *The Pennsylvania Evening Post* before the news and advertisements. In the local news the paper reported, "by the last advices from the Jersies, we learn the enemy are every where flying before our army, who frequently take small parties of them. Since the affair at Trenton, it is said, we have taken four hundred, amongst whom are several officers." This was a bit overly optimistic, but in the spirit of the time. Rather than fearing British soldiers taking Philadelphia, the city was now concerned about providing proper care for wounded and sick American soldiers coming into town. There was also an announcement dated December 27 that the Congress had appointed a committee, the Executive Committee of Robert Morris, George Clymer, and George Walton, to "transact such Continental business in this city as may be proper and necessary."[12]

Christopher Marshall saw more released American prisoners coming into town and also more Hessian prisoners arriving in the evening.[13] The Hessian officers had resumed their journey that morning and passed through Frankfurt and Kensington, which Lieutenant Piel described as "two pleasant little cities." They traveled to Philadelphia in covered wagons providing protection from the mud, but were still subject to violent curses from people they met on the road and arrived toward evening, greeted by a large assembly of people who showered them with uncomplimentary catcalls. On their first evening in town, described by Lieutenant Wiederholdt as "large, beautiful and lying between the Delaware and Schuylkill Rivers," they enjoyed a fine meal with plenty of wine and punch at the Indian Queen Tavern, as ordered and paid for by the Congress, and afterwards each officer made individual lodging arrangements.[14]

**James Smith had recently arrived** in Baltimore as a Pennsylvania delegate to Congress and wrote to his wife, Eleanor, that he had been met with "a kind welcome from Congress, & every body here are extremely kind & obliging." This reception "partly forced me out of my gloomy situation, & the agreeable news from Genl Washington has given new life & spirits to every body here." He enclosed a handbill on the Trenton success and reported, "I hear one of Genl. Washington's Aid de Camps is arrived here last night with a Hessian standard. This place is much more sociable than Philada."[15]

William Whipple wrote to fellow New Hampshire delegate Josiah Bartlett, providing information on the battle of Trenton and also the valuable cargo captured at sea by the *Andrew Doria*. Congress had taken measures "to prevent the abuses suffer'd by the soldiers last campaign. I am in no doubt that the greviences so justly complain'd off in every department will be redress'd so far as is possible, & the causes of them remov'd." He recognized that these past grievances had made recruiting for the new regiments very difficult and believed a huge amount of effort must be expended to convince men to enlist. When veteran

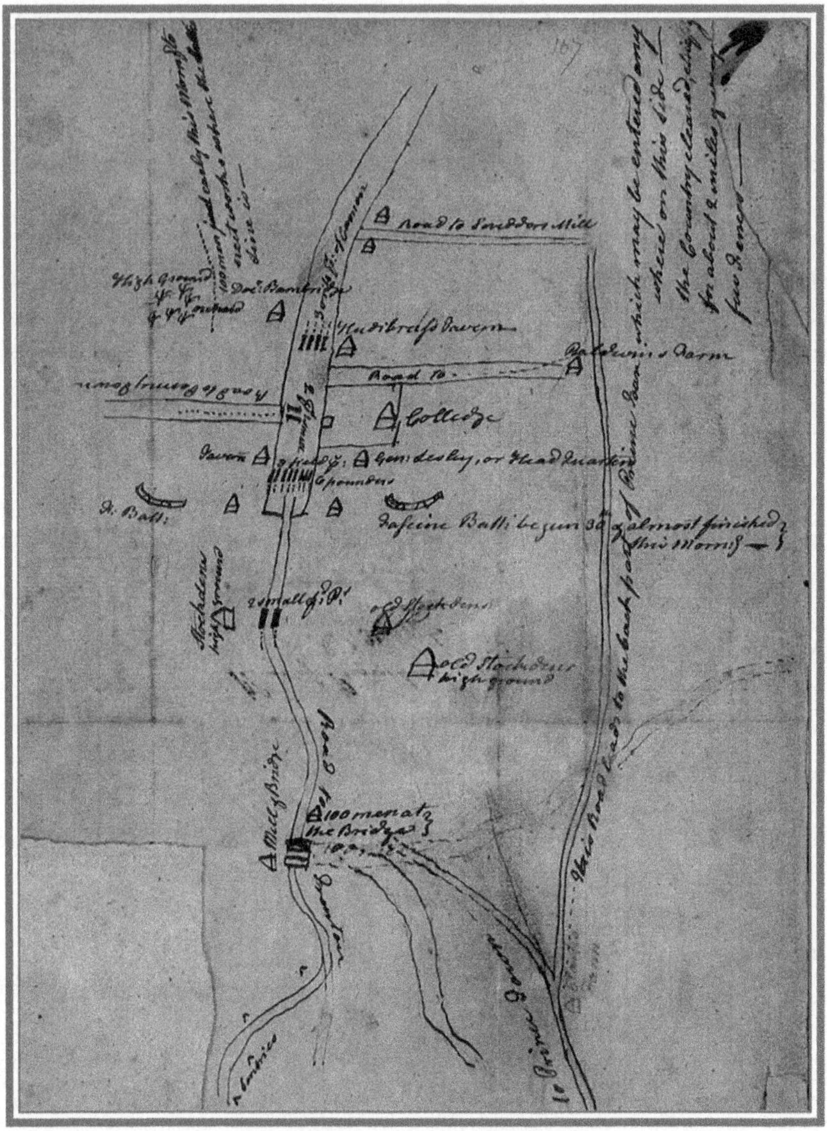

**Map 14: The Spy Map**

Map drawn by "A very intelligent gentleman" from Princeton about December 30 that provided useful information for Washington as he planned how to deal with the British forces at Princeton who might attack him at Trenton.

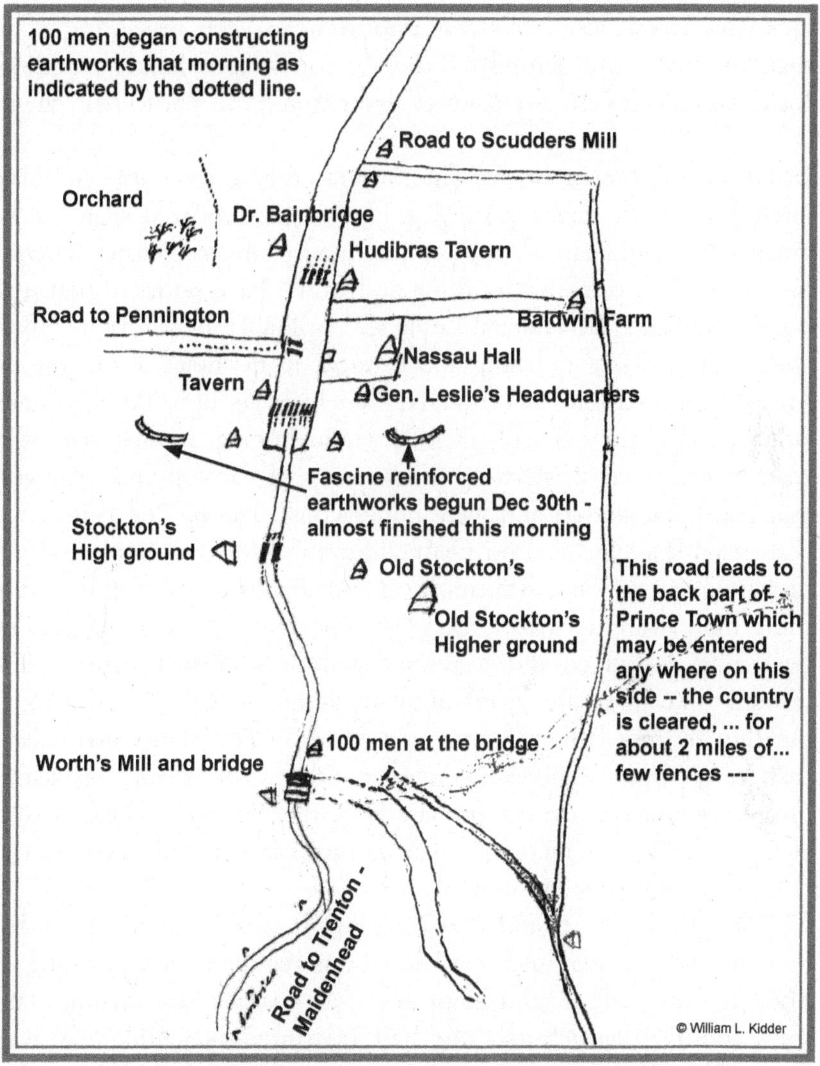


**Map 15: What the Spy Map told Washington about Princeton**

soldiers were asked to reenlist they should be "assur'd that the causes of their [past] complaints will be remov'd." A large number of soldiers were needed, because the British were actively working to further enlarge their forces with troops from other countries, in addition to the Hessians. It was also extremely important to keep reassuring France that Americans fully supported the war for independence, would fight for it, and stand with any country that entered the war to help them.[16]

**Colonel Cadwalader, at Crosswicks**, forwarded some important intelligence from civilians to Washington. He reported that, "A very intelligent gentleman is returned just now from Princeton." The man had set out the previous morning and would have returned that night, but was detained by General Leslie and Colonel Abercrombie. He was able to escape that morning and brought in his news. From the best sources he could find, he estimated there were about 5,000 Hessian and British troops, pretty evenly divided. He had drawn a quick map of the road from Princeton showing the location of cannon and earthworks that had been started and were under construction. The British were convinced that Washington planned an attack on Princeton and were preparing earthwork fortifications in anticipation of it. But, he did not think there were as many troops as reported to him. Forced to stay overnight, he lodged and conversed with some British officers. They wanted to know Washington's numbers and he told them about 16,000, but they did not believe it was more than 5-6,000. They also believed that many of the American soldiers had been forced into service and great numbers were deserting every day. Other British had heard that the American army was increasing daily as men came in with renewed vigor due to the victory at Trenton.

The young spy found that no sentries were posted on the back or east end of town and that the troops paraded each morning one hour before sunrise and slept on their arms some nights. There were about 50 light horse, one half quartered at Scudder's Mill and the other half on the west side of town. The British soldiers were greatly fatigued because they had expected to be attacked for the past several nights and they had consumed very little food until last night, when "a very considerable number of wagons arrived with provisions from Brunswick." Expecting an attack, "all their baggage is sent to

Brunswick, where there are but few men." More troops were on the way from Brunswick. In addition to this information, the young spy also produced a very important hand drawn map that Washington could use to plan an attack on the town.

Cadwalader had received by express rider Washington's letter about Reed's reconnaissance the day before and said his spy had been nearby when Reed captured "the party of chasseurs" and that an assistant quartermaster general or commissary was there also who took word of it to the British. Conveying the news from his area, Cadwalader wrote that a party of 200 Cumberland County militiamen were on their way to join him. He also noted that the former sheriff of Monmouth County, Loyalist Elisha Lawrence, had been collecting about 70 men at Monmouth Courthouse and had put 20 men in prison for refusing to bear arms against the rebels. Major Nicholas of the Marines wanted to attack the Lawrence group, but Cadwalader refused his request, believing it was not a good time for it. But, he would if Washington approved.[17]

Joseph Hodgkins wrote to his wife again expressing the "hardships & fatague" the army had experienced over the previous month and his thankfulness that he was "alive & well & in good spirits at present" and his hopes that this would continue. He then recounted the problems the army had experienced trying to cross the Delaware on the night of December 25 and the great success that Washington had achieved at Trenton.[18] Although Hodgkins had earlier informed his wife that he had "no thoughts" of continuing in the army after his commitment ended at the end of the year, he stayed with the army and in February signed on for three years as a captain in the Continental Line.[19]

Charles Willson Peale entered in his diary that, "At daybreak this morning we were called to parade, and Gen. Cadwalader ordered every captain to parade each morning at the alarm post, at 5 o'clock precisely. Whoever should be wanting would be put under arrest."[20]

Sergeant William Young was still at Crosswicks and had not had a very good night's sleep after going to bed late at his quarters in the meeting house that also served as the guard house for the picket guard. He heard about the Reed scout towards Princeton, a Hessian prisoner was brought in, and a scouting party under Major John Mifflin came through. It looked like rain and his men were busy cutting firewood. He heard that the troops at Bordentown had taken a large quantity of beef, salt pork, and excellent rum. He was extremely fatigued, but still healthy, and jotted in his journal that, "It is melancholy to think what loosness prevails among all our men. There is among the New England men some seriousness. Dined very hearty this day on a good piece of cold beef and pork, a good appetite is always good sauce. Wrote this day to my wife by Mr. Gay, I hope it will find her well."[21]

At Crosswicks, twenty-year-old John Howland, a descendant of Mayflower passenger John Howland, had been convinced to extend his enlistment in Colonel Lippitt's Rhode Island Regiment. The weather turned mild and a thaw began when Howland's regiment was paraded in the evening and ordered to march, although, "None of us knew where we were bound. We only perceived we were going westward."[22] Philip Rodman, age 19, also of Lippitt's regiment was a black man who extended his enlistment for one month "at the request of Washington." Consider Bowen of the same age and regiment also extended.[23] Sergeant John Smith of Lippitt's regiment wrote that before dawn they were "ordred to turn out again with our packs as tho we were to march we then received orders to draw 3 days provisions and to cook it all which we obeyed again hearing the enemy were returning towards us."[24]

**In his Brigade Orders** for the day, General Mifflin gave his "hearty thanks to the brigade for the alertness shown by them" during an alarm the previous evening. He recommended that all officers keep their units ready to march "at a minute's warning, for which purpose they must prevent their men from strolling too far from their quarters." He sent out a party of about 200 men under Majors John Mifflin and Adam Hubley to harass the enemy. Every man was told to always keep with him "dressed provisions for three days" and that deviating from this order "may ruin the best concerted plans."[25]

Rumors were rampant and Margaret Morris heard one about a significant engagement between the two armies in which the British lost 300 killed and wounded and 400 taken prisoner. However, in the evening that rumor was denied and it appeared there had been no battle.[26]

**At daylight, Captain Thomas Rodney** and the light troops were ordered to make a forced march to Brunswick to liberate General Lee, reportedly guarded by just 250 men. They set off for Cranbury, a small village about 12 miles from Allentown, from which they would continue on horseback after dark to carry out the plan. At Cranbury they sent out two spies to reconnoiter Brunswick and any troops headed there from Amboy, and waited for dark. The spies reported that the British were reinforcing Brunswick with 1500 men, making their plan unfeasible, so they decided to return to Allentown. Unfortunately, Rodney related, "This sudden change alarmed the people very much at Cranberry, they expected the enemy were coming and two very beautiful ladies who had been very kind and polite at my quarters, being a whig family, were exceedingly distressed and hung around me in tears until I was obliged to tell them the true reason of our departure."

Rodney and his men "marched back to Allentown through a very dark night and roads half leg deep [in mud] which worried the troops exceedingly." At Allentown he found his quarters full of militiamen "and there was no place to sit or lie down." His room was occupied by three Pennsylvania field officers who "sternly refused" Rodney's polite request to come in "and sit by the fire." Rodney told them he had no other place to go and, as he drew his sword and opened the door, said if they would not admit him and his men, they would have to defend themselves. The Pennsylvanians "begged me to wait until they could light a candle, and upon seeing our dress very politely invited us in and then spread the table, and covered it with good wine and ready dressed provisions of which they had great variety, and we spent the rest of the night in great festivity."[27]

**Hoping to get a greater** turnout of militia, Washington wrote a public letter to "the friends of America in the State of New Jersey" telling them that his army had been greatly reinforced, he had reentered the State, and was preparing to "relieve their distressed State from the depredations of our enemies." He then named several militia officers he had dispatched to gather the militia.[28] To help win civilian support, Washington also ordered that all plunder taken from the enemy forces must be given to quartermaster officers who would see the proceeds distributed equitably among those who took it. To prevent further damage to civilians, any plunder from civilians, including Loyalists, would not count. Both sides were struggling for the hearts and minds of the civilian population, fighting to convince people that one political system was better than another, and while their leaders understood this, the soldiers who made most of the contacts with civilians often did not.

Washington only had a few hours to convince the men whose enlistments expired at the end of the day to extend them. He received the December 27 resolves of Congress granting him virtually dictatorial powers, including the power to offer bonuses for enlistment extensions, something he had been doing anyway even without authorization.[29] Over the previous few days he had been able to convince a number of men to extend their enlistments with promises of "money, movement, and results," and those who agreed displayed those values that developed the professionalism, derived from perseverance through endless hardships, that would keep the army in the field till the end of the war.[30]

The bounty had become a needed incentive when Pennsylvania had offered a ten dollar bounty to its militiamen and a sizeable number agreed to continue for six weeks, while some New Jersey militiamen, such as those from the 1st Hunterdon Regiment, without a monetary incentive continued to serve, no matter how long they had been out, because they were defending their own homes and families.[31] Washington then had promised his Continentals the same ten dollar bounty to stay six weeks, even though he knew "the consequences which will result from it; but what could be done?"

The Continentals knew that they were more valued than militia and Washington was surprised, and genuinely pleased, that they did not demand a higher bounty than the militia.[32] However, the failure to regularly pay soldiers in the past, made the offer seem hollow. Washington wrote to Robert Morris to raise all the money he could and send it quickly. Even if he had to borrow the money, Washington noted that he had used his personal credit and "every man of interest and every lover of his country must strain his credit upon such an occasion. No time my dear sir is to be lost."[33]

To help Washington convince men to extend, Henry Knox, promoted to brigadier general by Congress the day after the battle of

Trenton, addressed the troops in his commanding voice and urged them to stay with the army a few more days, while General Thomas Mifflin came up from Bordentown to speak with the soldiers.[34] Chaplain Avery wrote in his diary that "much pains taken to persuade ye continental troops to tarry six weeks after yr inlistment shall be out, wh will be tomorrow. Colo. Paterson's Regt. agreed, generally, to tarry, havg. 10 dollars bounty each soldier."[35]

Sergeant Nathaniel Root recalled that, "while we were at Trenton, on the last of December, 1776, the time for which I and most of my regiment had enlisted expired." Washington "ordered our regiment to be paraded, and personally addressed us, urging that we should stay a month longer. He alluded to our recent victory at Trenton; told us that our services were greatly needed, and that we could now do more for our country than we ever could at any future period; and in the most affectionate manner entreated us to stay." But, when Washington had the drums beat for volunteers, not one man came forward because, "the soldiers worn down with fatigue and privations, had their hearts fixed on home and the comforts of the domestic circle, and it was hard to forego the anticipated pleasures of the society of our dearest friends."

But, then "the General wheeled his horse about, rode in front of the regiment, and addressing us again said, 'My brave fellows, you have done all I asked you to do, and more than could be reasonably expected; but your country is at stake, your wives, your houses, and all that you hold dear. You have worn yourselves out with fatigues and hardships, but we know not how to spare you. If you will consent to stay only one month longer, you will render that service to the cause of liberty, and to your country, which you probably never can do under any other circumstances. The present is emphatically the crisis, which is to decide our destiny.'"

Then the drums beat again and "the soldiers felt the force of the appeal. One said to another, 'I will remain if you will.' Others remarked, 'We cannot go home under such circumstances.' A few stepped forth, and their example was immediately followed by nearly all who were fit for duty in the regiment, amounting to about two hundred volunteers." So far the soldiers had made only a verbal contract and "an officer enquired of the General if these men should be enrolled. He replied, -- 'No! men who will volunteer in such a case as this, need no enrolment to keep them to their duty.'"[36] While this demonstrated his confidence in them and pleased the men, it kept the extensions as verbal contracts that would complicate army administration.

Private John Dewey wrote in his journal, "by the General's desire we agreed to stay six weeks longer."[37] Rhode Islander Stephen Olney's first child had been born on October 19 and although "he had never seen the face of kindred but once since he first enlisted in the war; yet he resolved to keep at his post." Being so deeply involved in the war, "he realized all the danger that menaced the country at that time, yet unshrinkingly determined to share peril and fatigue."[38] Lieutenant Elisha Bostwick recalled, "by the pressing solicitation of his Excellency a part of those whose time was out consented on a ten dollar bounty to stay six weeks longer & altho desirous as others to return home I engaged to stay that time & made every exertion in my power to make as many of the soldiers stay with me as I could & quite a number did engage with me who otherwise would have went home."[39]

Private Moses Smith of the 26th Continental Regiment, who had helped capture 20 British horses after the battle of Trenton, also extended his enlistment for six weeks.[40] Thirteen-year-old fifer Oliver Corey of Colonel Paul Dudley Sargent's Massachusetts regiment, had been detached to serve as fifer for General Sullivan's Life Guard. For the rest of his life, Corey recalled that when Washington, mounted on his horse, made his plea to the men to extend their enlistments, Corey was near enough to observe tears on the cheeks of Washington and there was "scarcely a dry eye among the soldiers." In contrast "those who left the army for home were hooted at & covered with opprobrium."[41]

Washington estimated that at least half the men whose enlistments ran out consented to stay. He did not expect many men in Colonel Glover's regiment to extend and had planned to "endeavor to procure the rest for the purpose of fitting out the frigates upon the best terms I can."[42] Private Jacob Francis was one man who turned down the bonus and left the army. Francis was from nearby Amwell, about 15 miles from Trenton, and had left home as a boy when his mother, a free black woman, bound him out as an indentured servant to a local farmer. His indenture time was sold several times to other men who took him many places, including the West Indies, and he was living in Massachusetts when his indenture expired on his 21st birthday. He had signed into the army as Jacob Gulick, or Hulick, the surname of one of his several indenture owners, and was really curious about what had happened over the years to his mother and also wanted to know what his real family name was. He was owed seven and a half months pay like others in the regiment, but was given only three month's pay and told to go to Peekskill, New York at a future date to get the remainder of his pay and a discharge. After receiving his three month's pay and permission to leave, he went immediately to Amwell where he found his mother alive, but in poor health, and learned that his family name was Francis whereupon he took that name for the rest of his life. He never did go to Peekskill.[43]

Some men were literally in no condition to remain in the army. Private Ebenezer White did not extend, and was discharged on the west side of the river opposite Trenton where he was "so badly sick and frozen that he was unable to move for six weeks and did not arrive home till the next April."[44] Probably a number of the men who did not extend their enlistments were equally incapacitated.

Officer's commitments also expired and rather than extending, some officers accepted commissions in the new, longer-term army being raised. Glover's regiment did not have many men who extended, but Captain Theophilus Munson accepted a captaincy in the new 8th Connecticut Regiment.[45] At the request of some Massachusetts officers and on the recommendation of Washington, Captain William Hull of Colonel Charles Webb's 19th Continental Regiment was commissioned major of Colonel Jackson's 8th Massachusetts Regiment.[46] Some officers decided to leave. Colonel John Chester, commanding the 6th Battalion of Connecticut State troops declined a Continental colonelcy in the new army and, although committed to the cause of liberty and encouraged by Washington to continue in the service, left the army due to concerns for his family.[47]

After sunset, Washington sent a body of troops north to Eight Mile Run (Shipetauken Creek) about six miles south of Princeton to set up a blocking position to delay any British advance towards Trenton.[48] Major George Johnston wrote that this force consisted of General

Stephen's and General Fermoy's brigades, with two cannon, and they advanced to Maidenhead about four miles from Princeton while two other brigades advanced just two miles north from Trenton to cover their retreat.[49]

**Each soldier had been faced** with a difficult, potentially life endangering, individual decision about extending his enlistment. It was clear that those who extended would not be sitting around in winter quarters for the next six weeks. Would any man have extended without the psychological lift of the Trenton victory? At the end of the day, many of the soldiers who had extended their enlistments must have wondered just what the next six weeks would bring. Knowing that a very large British army was expected to attack them at Trenton, it must have occurred to many that they might very soon become martyrs on Trenton's Mill Hill.

# Chapter 16

## Wednesday, January 1, 1777

Robert Grant in London read about the capture of Fort Washington over a month previously. He kept expecting to receive news that his friend General James Grant was about to embark on his return to England, and assumed the delay was due to army slowness in getting into winter quarters. Reporting to James on the mood in England he commented, "when the last news arrived from America an abstract of it was carried to Lloyd's Coffee House, and read publickly." The reader ended by joyously declaring there would be "no Republican Government, no American Independency thanks to the officers & troops for their gallant behavior & success to His Majesty's Arms." The more than 300 merchants at the coffee house responded with three cheers. Robert noted that, back in March when the British evacuated Boston, "a man would have gotten himself knocked down who had proposed such a thing." Then, referring to disparaging remarks about the American soldiers made by Grant and the Earl of Sandwich in 1775, Robert noted, "It is now generally allowed that Lord Sandwich's speech in the House of Lords & yours in the House of Commons truly described the Yankee warriors."[1]

Responding to the argument being put forth that conquering America was impracticable, Sandwich had declared, "Suppose the colonies do abound in men, what does that signify? They are raw, undisciplined, cowardly men. I wish instead of 40 or 50,000 of these brave fellows, they would produce in the field at least 200,000, the more the better, the easier would be the conquest; [because] if they did not run away, they would starve themselves into compliance with our measures."[2] Grant had regaled British audiences in 1775 with anecdotes belittling the Americans besieging Boston, such as, "tis not astonishing they were sickly–for they had their provisions in one corner of the tent, a barrel in the other which served for a necessary house which likewise for a table, when the head was put upon it." In a speech before Parliament, Grant related that American soldiers sanctimoniously criticized the regulars as "heathens" because "they drink, they whore, they swear," but still "they live," whereas, "we don't drink, we don't whore, we don't swear but we pray and we dye." But, he was not so blinded by contempt for the Americans that he lost all perspective. "I don't mean to say," he told Parliament, "that the Americans from their numbers may not become formidable and I don't mean to say that they cannot be made soldiers. But I say Sir they are not soldiers at present."[3] Shortly after the Battle of Long Island in 1776, he wrote that "if a good bleeding can bring those bible-faced Yankees to their senses, the fever of independence should soon abate." He predicted that, "they may from compulsion become dutiful subjects for a time, but they will never be cordial and affectionate." However, he expected that "in the course of the winter the [peace] commissioners will probably be able to bring things to an accommodation, for I don't look for another campaign."[4]

King George wrote to Lord North about the continuing problems encountered in supplying the troops with food. He believed those problems would soon cease because, "Sir William Howe is now in possession of so extensive a country [including New Jersey] that he will not require to be entirely provided from Europe; I have seen a private letter from the General that his posts will extend from the river Delawarr to Rhode Island, consequently my opinion seems well grounded."[5]

Ambrose Serle in New York wrote to the Earl of Dartmouth congratulating him on the successes of the 1776 campaign, and noted that from all accounts "the rebellion is nearly broken, and beyond any apparent probability of resource or recovery. The most intelligent of the rebels themselves are of this opinion, as we learn both by intercepted letters and by other channels of communication." However, this meant that his time was "exceedingly taken up in making out pardons for rebels, who are coming in for them by hundreds." Serle hoped that Philadelphia would be taken in the early spring, the warships there either be taken or destroyed, and the war settled in the next campaign. He had observed that many people "have lowered their tone; and though their late advantage in surprising a post of Hessians will undoubtedly flush them with a sort of triumph (for of all vain men I believe the people of this country are the vainest); yet their satisfaction, as I understand, is likely to be very short-lived, and we may soon expect to hear of their being rewarded with a proper chastisement."[6] From these words it appears he knew of the plans to attack Trenton very soon.

**Apparently unaware that they were** already at Princeton, Howe ordered his Deputy Quartermaster General to provide vessels to receive the "remains," i.e., the men who escaped capture, of Colonel Rall's Brigade at Amboy, and take them to New York City, where the Barrack Master was to prepare barracks for them.[7] He wrote to Grant with wishes for "a happy new year," and advised him to make sure he secured Brunswick during his absence to attack Washington at Trenton. Regarding troop placements, Howe advised, "I think you should leave the whole of the guards there & the post at Hillsborough and Kingston & I should wish the 40th Regt there in place of Kohler's Grendrs who might join the guards. The drawing off the 46th will expose Spanktown too much." Howe approved of the "breastwork redoubts" being erected at Princeton and hoped that Donop would not object to posting his four battalions and Jägers there. Howe expected that, in working with Cornwallis, "your situation will enable you to keep the Jersies as quiet as any commander in this situation."[8] Rather than personally take field command to gain his revenge, Howe had cancelled Cornwallis's leave and sent him back to New Jersey to retake command from Grant. Cornwallis immediately marched toward Princeton, collecting troops for the attack on Trenton as he went.[9]

**A group of American prisoners** released by Howe from the terrible conditions in New York arrived at Milford, Connecticut after a "tedious passage of several days" on the British ship Glasgow that had left New York on December 24. Evidence of the poor treatment the men had received while imprisoned was evident in their "rueful countenances." Two dozen or more had died on the short voyage and 50 more would die over the next few months at Milford.[10]

**John Peebles in Newport,** Rhode Island, initiated his diary for 1777 with best wishes for a happy New Year and the hope that "peace & plenty" would prevail and "civil discord cease when Britain stretches forth her hand to give her children peace." The grenadier officers dined on board ship with Peebles's friend Willie Dunlop and they "had a very good dinner & sat drinking till it was late. He gave some very good songs."[11]

**At Pennyroyal Hill** in Virginia, Nicholas Cresswell began his 1777 diary by writing, "This is the first day of the New Year, which I am afraid will be spent, by me, to as little purpose as the two last have been. I am now in a disagreeable and precarious, situation, I dare do nothing to get bread. Cannot return to my Native Country. The meanes of my support depends on the whim and caprice of a friend." Regarding the war, he wrote that he was "in feare of going to jail every day on account of my political principles. And no prospect of this unnatural rebellion being suppressed this year. Am determined to make my escape the first opportunity." However, he put aside these negative thoughts and spent the day with friends, "danceing and makeing ourselves as merry as whiskey toddy, and good company will afford."[12]

**The Moravian Congregation** at Hebron, Pennsylvania spent the day with "everyone in town … rejoicing over the victory gained by the Provincials" at Trenton.[13]

**Margaret Morris in Burlington** found New Year's Day observed without the "usual rejoicings, etc." and believed it would "be the beginning of a sorrowful year to very many people." Yet, she still had hope to "look forward with confidence to Him who can bring out of this confusion the greatest order."[14]

**William Eddis, a 38-year-old** solidly Loyalist Englishman living in Annapolis, Maryland since 1769 where he was surveyor of the customs, wrote a letter to friends in England stating, "The year opens with the most dreary prospects. The recent event of Trenton will add strength to the sinews of war and cruelly procrastinate the wished return of peace." He briefly recounted the British successes in the fall campaign and before the battle at Trenton saying, "the general disposition of the colonies tended to a reconciliation, and even the submission of some of the provinces was daily expected."

But, Eddis recognized the dramatic psychological impact of the Trenton victory commenting, "trifling as this maneuver might have been considered in the prosecution of a regular war, it has been in this instance attended with the most prejudicial and alarming consequences to His Majesty's arms." Only a few days after the affair he noted, "to many it has appeared extraordinary that the advanced post was occupied by Hessian regiments who might reasonably be supposed less competent than British to determine on the authenticity of intelligence or the disposition of the colonists with respect to political attachment." While explaining the improvements for raising the new American army Eddis noted, "It is confidently asserted, and it appears to be universally believed, that General Washington will quickly be enabled to repossess the Jerseys, and to contract the British posts into a very limited sphere of action," and eliminate any imminent threat to Philadelphia. Like many others, he saw the problem of inflation as a serious impediment to the successful prosecution of the war by Congress and the states. As was probably true in many of the other new states, he noted that "the internal government of Maryland is not yet perfectly adjusted, but the arrangements under the new constitution are in great forwardness, and will speedily take place in the various departments." This would no doubt result in his losing his job, making him free to shape his future, including returning to England.[15]

In 1775, Eddis had written a newspaper column under the pseudonym "A Friend to Amity" and declared the real problem between Britain and her American colonies was determining just how to redress the American grievances. He warned the Americans not to seek freedom for themselves while imposing tyranny on others. "While we contend for the inestimable blessing of British subjects, let us not assume a tyrannical authority over each other. In a word, let reason and moderation hold the scale in every important determination, so shall we be firm in the cause of honour and true patriotism – so shall every real grievance be effectually redressed – every man shall sing the song of gladness under his own vine, and we shall at once be FREE – be LOYAL – and be HAPPY!"[16]

**As the New Year began,** Congressional delegates had mixed feelings about still being in Baltimore instead of Philadelphia. Samuel Adams was pleased that "business has been done since we came to this place, more to my satisfaction than any or every thing done before, excepting the Declaration of Independence which should have been made immediately after the 19th of April 75."[17] William Hooper, however, still found Baltimore to be a "dirty infamous extravagant hole, where with all possible economy we live at the rate of 50/ per day, every necessary of life being double what they cost us in Philadelphia," where everything was already very expensive.[18] New Englander Oliver Wolcott also criticized Baltimore for being "infinitely the most dirty place I was ever in. No one can walk about here but in boots. The air and paths are in the same condition that they are with us [in New England mud season] the latter end of March and beginning of April. This weather I suppose will continue near two months. The place is said to be healthy but I am sure it is extremely uncomfortable."[19] Whatever their opinion of Baltimore, a number of delegates simply felt cut off from their States. New Hampshire delegate Matthew Thornton had not heard any official news from his state for some time and only knew what he read in newspapers, which was often inaccurate.[20] William Hooper was not only exhausted from his work in Congress, but without information from the North Carolina Convention he was not even sure he was still an official delegate.[21]

Congress wanted to eliminate any doubt about the people's commitment to independence, given greater life by Washington's victory at Trenton. The representatives to France and Spain had been instructed to push this message, to overcome "the artful and insidious representations of the Emissaries of Britain to the contrary."[22] Not knowing that its commissioners in Europe had designated Arthur Lee to negotiate a treaty of friendship and commerce with Spain, the Committee of Secret Correspondence wrote to Benjamin Franklin appointing him to that position. But, Congress later confirmed Lee's appointment.[23]

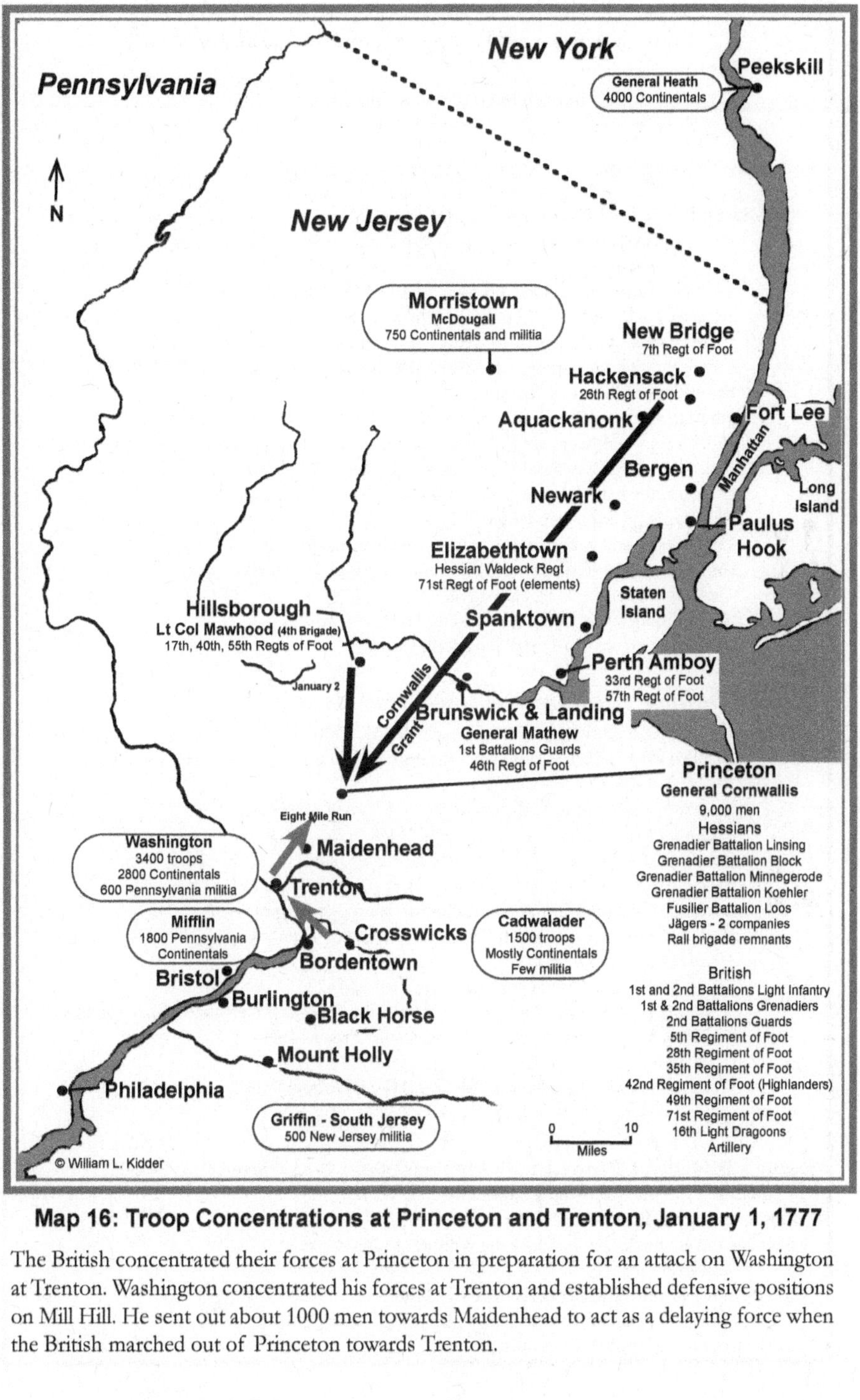


**Map 16: Troop Concentrations at Princeton and Trenton, January 1, 1777**

The British concentrated their forces at Princeton in preparation for an attack on Washington at Trenton. Washington concentrated his forces at Trenton and established defensive positions on Mill Hill. He sent out about 1000 men towards Maidenhead to act as a delaying force when the British marched out of Princeton towards Trenton.

**Table 6: American Troops at Trenton - January 1, 1777**

**Light Horse of Philadelphia** (*Captain Samuel Morris*)
*Corent John Lardner, Corporal James Hunter*

**Sullivan's Division** (*Major General John Sullivan*) – 1200-1400

**St. Clair's Brigade** (*Brigadier General Arthur St. Clair*) - less than 100 men per regiment.
1st New Hampshire Regiment (formerly 5th Continental ) (*Colonel John Stark*)
*William Chamberlin*
2nd New Hampshire Regiment (formerly 8th Continental ) (*Colonel Enoch Poor*)
3rd New Hampshire Regiment (formerly 2nd Continental ) (Colonel Alexander Scammell)
1st Massachusetts Regiment(formerly 15th Continental )(Colonel John Paterson)
[These regiments took their new designations January 1, 1777]
**Remnants of Glover's Brigade**
4th Massachusetts Regiment (Colonel William Shepard) [created Jan 1, 1777]
14th Continental Regiment (Massachusetts) (*Colonel John Glover*, absent)
19th Continental Regiment (Connecticut) (*Colonel Charles Webb*)
23rd Continental Regiment (Massachusetts) (Colonel John Bailey)
**Remnants of Sargent's Brigade**
13th Continental Regiment (Massachusetts) (Colonel Joseph Read)
16th Continental Regiment (Massachusetts) (*Colonel Paul Dudley Sargent*)
*David How, Oliver Corey, Ebenezer White*
Ward's Connecticut Regiment (Colonel Andrew Ward)
Connecticut State Troops (Colonel John Chester)

**Greene's Division** (*Major General Nathanael Greene*) - 1400
**Mercer's Brigade** (*Brigadier General Hugh Mercer*) - 300
Smallwood's Maryland Continental Regiment (Lieutenant Colonel John Stone) - c50
*Captain Maynard, Cornelius Wells*
Miles's Pennsylvania Rifle Regiment (*Major Ennion Williams*) – 200
*Captain John Marshall, Sergeant James McMichael, Cary McClelland*
Rawling's Maryland and Virginia Rifle Regiment (Colonel Moses Rawlings) – 75
Eastern Company New Jersey State Artillery (*Captain Daniel Neil*), 2 guns
**Stirling's Brigade remnants attached to Mercer's Brigade – 50**
Haslet's Delaware Continental Regiment (*Colonel John Haslet*) – 5
*Captain Thomas Holland,*
Read's 1st Virginia Regiment (Capt. John Fleming) -20
*Captain Graham, Lieutenant Abraham Kirkpatrick, Lieutenant Bartholomew Yates, Jonathan Grant*
Weedon's 3rd Virginia Regiment (*Colonel George Weedon*, absent)
*Sergeant Thomas McCarty,*
Williams's 6th Maryland Regiment (Colonel Otho Holland Williams, absent)
[created Dec 10, 1776]

**Ewing's Brigade of Pennsylvania Militia** (*Brigadier General James Ewing*) – 600
Cumberland County Regiment (Colonel Frederick Watts)
Lancaster County Regiment (Colonel Jacob Klotz)
Cumberland County Regiment (Colonel William Montgomery)
*Thomas McGee,*
York County Regiment (Colonel Richard McAllister)
Chester County Regiment (Colonel James Moore)
Bucks County Regiment (Colonel Joseph Hart)

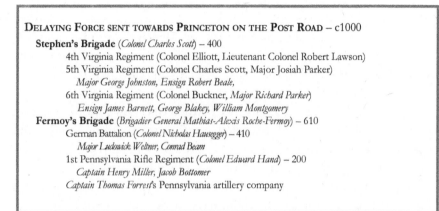

**Delaying Force sent towards Princeton on the Post Road** – c1000

**Stephen's Brigade** (*Colonel Charles Scott*) – 400

4th Virginia Regiment (Colonel Elliott, Lieutenant Colonel Robert Lawson)

5th Virginia Regiment (Colonel Charles Scott, Major Josiah Parker)

*Major George Johnston, Ensign Robert Beale,*

6th Virginia Regiment (Colonel Buckner, *Major Richard Parker*)

*Ensign James Barnett, George Blakey, William Montgomery*

**Fermoy's Brigade** (*Brigadier General Mathias-Alexis Roche-Fermoy*) – 610

German Battalion (*Colonel Nicholas Hausegger*) – 410

*Major Ludowick Weltner, Conrad Beam*

1st Pennsylvania Rifle Regiment (*Colonel Edward Hand*) – 200

*Captain Henry Miller, Jacob Bottomer*

*Captain Thomas Forrest's* Pennsylvania artillery company

Congress was highly encouraged by the victory at Trenton, but now expected more of them. Matthew Thornton wrote hopefully that, "Congress expects every moment the news of a Grand engagement."[24] Elbridge Gerry believed, "The middle States are roused from their late supine state, & are exerting themselves to reinforce the army; I hope a proper spirit will be exercised on this occasion & the enemy be driven from the Jersies." He now believed that with hard work "we shall see the Independence of America established on a foundation that cannot be shaken by the arms of tyranny." He was even considering how to deal with the defeated Loyalists, believing they must be expelled and "bonds will not answer the purpose," prisons could not hold them all, and "they are not worth hanging."[25]

William Hooper was encouraged that Trenton had produced "a fine effect upon our recruiting service, one Reg't whose term of enlistment was expired having reenlisted to a man since that event." As for the enemy, "from what we can learn they are pannic struck. Certain it is that 2000 which were at Bordentown moved towards Princeton with great precipitation and carried off all their stores with them." He expected that Washington would "attempt to drive the enemy back to New York." Hooper also believed that Washington was in danger at Newtown, "where a plot was formed against him and his [military] family, happily defeated by an early discovery of the Tories intentions."[26] Other Congressmen knew of this plot and one wrote that, "The General was inform'd a few nights ago, that a conspiracy was form'd by some people in Bucks County near his camp to kidnap him as poor Lee was, but he has more prudence than to be caught in that manner, however the disposition of the inhabitants of that county appears to be inimical to our cause, which you knew before."[27]

**Christopher Marshall in Philadelphia** saw more Hessian prisoners, including many wounded, come to town during the day and evening.[28] Lieutenant Piel wrote, "We visited General [Israel] Putnam. He shook hands with each one of us and we had a glass of Madeira. This gray-haired, old fellow might well be an honorable man, but hardly anyone but the rebels would have made him a general. We were quartered in private houses, for which we had to pay a high price."[29]

**George Inman reflected** on British garrison life at Princeton after the battle of Trenton. He says, "The season of the year being severe, snow on the ground and for nights having no other bed than hard frozen earth or ice and no other covering than a cloak oftentimes induced me to reflect on past times when I used to sleep in soft downy beds and with every comfortable necessary around me, amongst them friends whom I left, and wch perhaps if I had remained might still have enjoy'd."[30]

At about daybreak a force consisting of British light infantry and mounted and dismounted Hessian Jägers marched toward Maidenhead under Lieutenant Colonel Abercrombie to force back the American troops at Eight Mile Run (Shipetaukin Creek). The British and Hessians called this area the Pass where the river banks rose 60 feet on either side where the road cut through. The Americans held their ground until grenadiers were sent against them. Casualties were believed to have been 140 men on both sides, including several Jägers.[31] During the morning engagements, two American men were apparently murdered by a British soldier who may have been acting under the influence of General Howe's order to hang men who engaged in ambushes while not in uniform. Without having time to hang them, the soldier simply shot them and left their bodies on the field. It also appears that a British dragoon was wounded when an American accidentally shot his iron ramrod at him. The mounted man apparently leaned back and the ramrod entered under his chin and exited at his nose. He suffered for several days before dying.[32]

Also during the morning, Captain Ewald took two English dragoons and twenty of his Jägers to Rocky Hill to secure the bridge across the Millstone River. This put him in position to cover the right flank of General Grant's approximately 1,000 men as they marched from Brunswick to Princeton. At 11:00am, Grant began the march to Princeton and it became extremely difficult and unpleasant when the weather turned much warmer and rain set in.[33]

Grant left only about 600 men at Brunswick to guard the military stores and the war chest containing £70,000 sterling, arrived at Princeton at 1:00pm, and ordered Donop to take some Hessian grenadiers and the British 12th Regiment of Foot to reconnoiter the road towards Trenton. He then began preparing to attack the Americans at Trenton the next day. The British troops at Princeton expected a major American attack after a skirmish was fought near one of their pickets, during which they killed four rebels.

As soon as he arrived in Princeton, engineer Archibald Robertson, accompanied Sir William Erskine and Donop on a reconnaissance of about three miles toward Maidenhead. While getting extremely wet, they saw no enemy. The 42nd Regiment of Foot, three Hessian grenadier battalions, and the Jägers bivouacked about a mile outside Princeton.[34] The Jägers made patrols towards Maidenhead, protected by 125 grenadiers, to reconnoiter the rebel positions. They encountered a rebel force and then fell back several miles, in accordance with their orders, and the enemy did not pursue them.[35] Donop's Hessians had come to Princeton after retreating from the Burlington area when Trenton was taken, and now Donop was looking for revenge and according to Sergeant Thomas Sullivan of the 49th Regiment of Foot, "he therefore went thro' the ranks and declared openly to his men, that any of them who would take a rebel prisoner would receive 50 stripes; signifying to them they were to kill all the rebels they could without mercy."[36]

Having ridden 50 miles while gathering several thousand troops, Cornwallis arrived late in the day.[37] He decided to attack Trenton directly by marching his troops down the main road through Maidenhead (modern Route 206) and disregarded Donop's sound advice to send part of the army by way of Crosswicks to turn the American right flank.[38] Donop's experiences throughout December had given him a clear understanding of how that flanking attack would work, and he also knew how difficult it would be to march so many men on one, very muddy road. But Cornwallis, knowing that he outnumbered Washington's rabble with the cream of the British army, adamantly rejected Donop's advice and ordered his troops to be ready to march at daybreak, even though many would have a short night because they were camped up to five miles outside Princeton. The army's baggage and the 4th Brigade under command of Lieutenant Colonel Mawhood would remain at Princeton.

The British advanced guard posts had frequently been receiving enemy fire in the night, forcing them to post an additional 100 men on the Allentown (Quaker) Road and the men lay on their arms for three consecutive nights. On the night of January 1 they made many fires along the Trenton-Princeton Road and across Stony Brook and up the rise on Cochran's Hill, but apparently did not post guards on the Quaker Road.[39]

**New Jersey weather** began the New Year with a major thaw, with low-40s temperatures in the morning rising into the low-50s in the afternoon, which turned the frozen roads and fields to deep mud that made travel both unpleasant and extremely difficult.[40] Washington's roughly 5,000 men were a mixture of recently recruited Continentals, militia, and veteran troops in mere remnants of regiments, debilitated by long marches, hard battles, and great suffering.[41]

Private David How of Colonel Paul Dudley Sargent's regiment had not extended his enlistment and during the morning drew wages and food money before setting out for home in Massachusetts in the afternoon, with his captured Hessian musket and knapsack.[42] Washington continued to promise bounties to men who would extend their expiring enlistments. Robert Morris, in response to Washington's plea the day before, arose very early in the morning and sent Washington $50,000 collected on his own credit from his friends in Philadelphia and from his own resources. He had sent funds several days earlier and pledged to exert his efforts should additional amounts be necessary in the future.[43] Washington received "two parcels of hard money, which I suppose will turn out agreeable to the list, having not had time to count

**TABLE 7: AMERICAN FORCES AT CROSSWICKS – JANUARY 1, 1777 – 1500**

**Cadwalader's Brigade** (*Colonel John Cadwalader*) – 1150
- 1st Battalion Philadelphia Associators (Colonel Jacob Morgan)
- 2nd Battalion Philadelphia Associators (Colonel John Bayard)
- 3rd Battalion Philadelphia Associators (Colonel John Nixon)
  - *Major Thomas Mifflin, Sergeant William Young,*
- 5th Rifle Battalion of Philadelphia Associators (Colonel Timothy Matlack)
- Philadelphia Light Infantry Company (*Captain George Henry*)
- Chester County Militia Regiment (Commander unknown)
  - *James Johnston,*
- Dover [Kent County, Delaware] Light Infantry Company(*Captain Thomas Rodney*) - 35
  - *Martinas Sipple,*
- Continental Marines (Major Samuel Nicholas) - 50
  - *William Shippen*
- 2nd Company of Artillery, Philadelphia Associators (*Captain Joseph Moulder*)
  - Two 6-pounders, two 3-pounders
  - *Zebulon Applegate,*

**Hitchcock's Brigade** (*Major Israel Angell*) - 353
- 4th Continental Regiment (Massachusetts) (Colonel John Nixon) - 63
- 9th Continental Regiment (Rhode Island) (Colonel James Varnum) - 7
- 11th Continental Regiment (Rhode Island) (*Colonel Daniel Hitchcock, Major Israel Angell*) - 120
- 12th Continental Regiment (Massachusetts) (*Colonel Moses Little*) - 3
- Rhode Island State Regiment (*Colonel Christopher Lippitt*) - 160
  - *Captain Loring Peck, Sergeant Daniel Smith, Preserved Buffington, John Howland,*

**AMERICAN FORCES AT BORDENTOWN – JANUARY 1, 1777 – 1800**

**Mifflin's Brigade** (*Brigadier General Thomas Mifflin*) - 1500
- 2nd Pennsylvania Regiment (Colonel Philip De Haas)
- 4th Pennsylvania Regiment (Colonel Daniel Brodhaed)
- 10th Pennsylvania Regiment (Colonel Joseph Penrose)
- 11th Pennsylvania Regiment (Colonel Richard Humpton)
- 12th Pennsylvania Regiment (Colonel William Cooke)

it." He was also hoping for money to be sent down from Ticonderoga, unless it was needed there.[44]

Continuing his efforts to win back civilian support for the Revolution, Washington posted notices forbidding both Continentals and militia from "plundering any person whatsoever, whether Tories or others." The notices stated that the property of Loyalists would "be applied to public uses in a regular manner," and he "expected that humanity and tenderness to women and children will distinguish brave Americans, contending for liberty, from infamous mercenary ravagers, whether British or Hessians."[45] But, he had no sympathy for men who had joined the Loyalist military forces. Two Trenton men, Charles Harrison and Peter Campbell, who had left town to take commissions in the Loyalist regiment raised by Trenton's Isaac Allen, were now prisoners of war and Washington wanted them "closely confined."[46]

**Sergeant William Young** rose just before 4:00am at Crosswicks, having slept well, and at 5:00am his men paraded under arms. Rev. George Duffield's service at the Quaker Meeting House was cancelled when they got the orders to parade instead. During the rainy afternoon they were "under orders to march at a minutes warning." found he was "obliged to put up with the disagreeable company of a mixed multitude, our own people are very loose in their conversation. I mean the Malitia. The New England men are a quiet set of men." noted that the previous New Year's Day he had had the pleasure of dining with his entire family, but this year "the Providence of God orders it another way."[47] Thomas Rodney's company at Allentown were allowed to rest during the day.[48]

**General Mifflin at** Bordentown dealt with basic organizational issues while anticipating imminent action. Washington had sent Captain Thomas Holland of Haslet's Delaware Regiment, an experienced military officer formerly of the Royal Welch Fusiliers, to "assist in forming and arranging the Brigade, which consists of many small Corps, and of course requires general arrangement.[49] Unavoidable difficulties and much danger would arise from leaving them in their present state. "The officers and men are, therefore, to pay great attention to the arrangement, to know their places, and to be able to form, when occasion requires, in an instant." He was also dealing with his troop's poor response to drum signals to turn out. Responding to a recent failure to respond, he declared, "had the enemy advanced towards this Town at that time, the army here might have been, to their eternal disgrace and the ruin of their Country, made prisoners of war." Putting things to rights was important because Mifflin heard that Washington had sent a large force towards Princeton, "which in all probability will bring on a General Action." After the morning brigade orders were written, Mifflin received an express from Nathanael

Greene at Trenton informing him that the British were in motion and their suspected target was Cadwalader's forces, so he should keep his men in readiness to support Cadwalader at a moment's notice and send out reconnaissance patrols to learn what he could, and send the information to Trenton.[50]

**Sergeant McCarty was sick** at the Trenton barracks on a day of "rain, snow, and what not." He had orders to be ready to fight, but even though he was "always willing" for a fight, only scouting parties were sent out.[51]

**Washington had received** on December 31 the resolves, passed by Congress on December 27, giving him near dictatorial powers and recognized that Congress had high expectations for what he would accomplish with them. He wrote to assure Congress, "that all my faculties shall be employed, to direct properly the powers they have been pleased to vest me with, and to advance objects and only those, which gave rise to this honourable mark of distinction." He beseeched the members that if his "exertions should not be attended with the desired success" that Congress would recognize the cause to be "the peculiarly distressed situation of our affairs, and the difficulties I have to combat, rather than to a want of zeal for my country, and the closest attention to her interest, to promote which has ever been my study."[52] Washington also wrote to the Committee of Congress at Philadelphia (Morris, Clymer, and Walton) assuring them that, "Instead of thinking myself freed from all civil obligations, by this mark of their confidence, I shall constantly bear in mind, that as the sword was the last resort for the preservation of our liberties, so it ought to be the first thing laid aside, when those liberties are firmly established." He also acknowledged receipt of "two parcels of hard money" to pay the bounties for enlistment extensions.[53]

It is likely that Washington's actions had been calculated to make Cornwallis believe that he intended to make a stand at Trenton, while his real intention was to attack any rearguard the British left at Princeton and then continue on to Brunswick to capture their supplies and move on to Morristown. From there, in the relative safety of the Watchung Mountains he could harass any British troops remaining in eastern New Jersey. The British would be removed from western New Jersey.

But he did not spread that idea yet, even to his top officers. Washington must have had multiple conversations during the preceding days with Joseph Reed and others who knew the area well and were aware of a little used road (that still had low tree stumps in it) that would allow him to skirt the British troops he enticed to Trenton and get to Princeton undetected. On the evening of January 1, he sent out four troopers of the Light Horse of Philadelphia and one of them, John Lardner, later stated that "on the evening of 1 Jany 1777 a party of the Troop George Campbell, James Caldwell, myself & I think another, were posted as a patrole on this very road. We remained on it the whole night, occasionally going as high as Quaker bridge. We found that the Enemy had no patroles there, and that apparently they had no knowledge of it."[54] Washington needed everyone, including any British spies, to believe he meant to make an all or nothing stand at Trenton. It even appeared to many of his officers that he had decided his only choice was to delay and punish the British for as long as he could and make them pay an unacceptably heavy price when attacking him on Mill Hill; i.e. make it another Bunker Hill.

To delay and weaken the British when they marched on Trenton, Washington had sent out the force under General Fermoy to establish a defensive post at Five Mile Run and place pickets through the village of Maidenhead, with orders to harass the enemy soldiers, slow their advance, and not allow them to reach Trenton before evening, too late for a full-scale battle.[55] He would not make the mistake that Rall had made and try to defend the town, but instead form up his troops on the southeast side of the Assunpink.

Washington hinted at his plan to deceive Cornwallis, telling Hancock that "we are now making our arrangements, and concerting a plan of operations, which I shall attempt to execute as soon as possible, and which I hope will be attended with some success." He told the Committee in Philadelphia that "we are devising such measures, as I hope, if they succeed, will add as much or more to the distress of the enemy, than their defeat at Trenton, and I promise myself the greatest advantages from having engaged a number of the eastern troops to stay six weeks beyond their time of enlistment, upon giving a bounty of ten dollars."[56] He was clearly not planning to sacrifice his army in a glorious stand at Trenton, but his latest intelligence, of uncertain value, was that the British "have collected the principal part of their force, from Brunswic and the neighboring posts, at Princeton, where they are throwing up some works. The number there is reported to be from five to six thousand; and it is confidently said they have sent the chief part of their baggage to Brunswick. It is added, that General Howe landed at Amboy a day or two ago with a thousand light troops, and is on his march from thence." Washington had not been able to obtain returns of his own force, but believed it was now reduced to about 1500 to 1600, in addition to about 1800 at Bordentown with General Mifflin and about the same at Crosswicks under Colonel Cadwalader, for a total of about 5000. He said it was useless to try to estimate the number of troops from the number of regiments because, "many of 'em by reason of sickness cannot turn out more than a hundred men."[57]

In what was perhaps an extreme example, Delaware Colonel John Haslet, still suffering from swollen legs injured during the re-crossing of the Delaware the night of December 26-27, wrote to Delaware militia General Caesar Rodney that, "Capt. Holland, Ensign Wilson, Dr. Gilder, and myself are all [of the Delaware battalion] who have followed the American cause to Trenton, two privates excepted. On Genl. Washington being informed of this, he declared his intention of having officers and men bound neck and heels and brought back as an example to the army."[58]

Early in the day, Dr. Benjamin Rush rode up from Crosswicks to Trenton to visit several Continental officers and went to General St. Clair's quarters at Alexander Douglass's house in Kingsbury near the Assunpink Creek bridge. He met with General Mercer and Colonel Clement Biddle to learn details about the previous week's battle. Mercer impressed him during their conversation with his determination that "he would not be conquered, but that he would cross the mountains and live among the Indians, rather than submit to the power of Great Britain in any of the civilized states."[59]

That evening, Dr. Rush heard that British troops were collecting at Princeton under Cornwallis and planned to attack Trenton and Crosswicks. Washington called a council of war to debate whether

Cadwalader's troops at Crosswicks, seven miles from Trenton, should remain there, join the army at Trenton, or be ordered to attack Brunswick, by way of Cranbury, assuming that post was significantly weakened after sending troops to Princeton. When the council could not agree, General Knox suggested Dr. Rush, who was serving with Cadwalader's militia, be invited to the council. Rush accepted the invitation, although he did not feel competent to give military advice. However, he did tell Washington "that all the Philadelphia militia would be very happy in being under his immediate command." Rush then left the meeting, only to be called back within a few minutes and given a letter to deliver immediately to Colonel Cadwalader. Rush set off for Crosswicks at 10:00pm, escorted by a Philadelphia light horseman.[60]

**General Leslie's Loyalist spy**, John Williams, who had been going out at night and reporting back to Leslie each day since the battle at Trenton, went out the night of January 1 to get information on the advanced enemy forces encamped near Maidenhead. His luck ran out and he was taken prisoner about midnight and carried to Trenton where he was immediately tried by a court martial and found guilty of spying. He was sentenced to be executed only a few hours later at 10:00am.[61]

# Chapter 17

## Battle of Assunpink, Thursday, January 2, 1777

After negotiating the muddy roads from Trenton to Crosswicks as rapidly as possible on that dark, damp, cold night, Dr. Benjamin Rush and his escort arrived at Colonel Cadwalader's quarters about 1:00am and had him awakened. Cadwalader got up, read Washington's letter, and immediately ordered his troops to march to Trenton.[1] Washington had decided to concentrate virtually all his forces at Trenton and reinforce the belief among his men and the British that he intended to make a stand, hoping to survive by creating another Bunker Hill.

**During that night march**, Charles Willson Peale found the going "very tedious" because of "the number of troops, badness of the roads, so many runs [creeks] to cross, and fences to remove."[2] Sergeant William Young became "a good deal fatigued on account of the deepness of [the] road," and in the darkness, "I could not see my way, the moon gave some light, but it being on my back I could not see so as to get the best road."[3] John Howland found the deep mud of the roads and darkness led to "accidents to the artillery carriages, or the falling of a horse, &c."[4] Captain Samuel Massey of the 4th Battalion of Philadelphia Associators said the roads were so bad, "they were frequently halted – to assist the horses in drawing the artillery – [which] retarded the march so much."[5]

**About the same time** the first exhausted troops from Crosswicks began arriving in Trenton at daybreak, Jäger Captain Ewald arrived at Princeton with his company from Rocky Hill and was ordered to draw

## Table 8: British and Hessian Troops January 2, 1777

### On march to Trenton under Lieutenant General Charles Cornwallis

**Vanguard** (*Colonel Carl von Donop*)
1 company Hessian Jägers (foot) (*Captain Johann Ewald*)
1 company Hessian Jägers (mounted) (*Captain Friedrich Lorey*)
2 troops 16th Light Dragoons

**Light Infantry Brigade** (*Major General James Grant*)
1st Light Infantry Battalion (MajorThomas Musgrave)
2nd Light Infantry Battyalion (Major John Maitland)
Grenadier Battaion Koehler (Lieutenant Colonel Johann Koehler)
42nd Regiment of Foot (Royal Highland) (Lieutenant Colonel Thomas Stirling)
71st Regiment of Foot (Scotch Regiment)

**Royal Artillery Detachment**
Possibly four light 12-pounders, ten 6-pounders, eight 3-pounders, and two 5½-inch howitzers
(Source: Duncan, Major Francis. *History of the Royal Regiment of Artillery*, London: John Muray, 1879, I:311)

**British Grenadiers and Guards Brigade** (Lieutenant Colonel the Hon. Henry Monckton)
1st British Grenadier Battalion (Lieutenant Colonel William Medows)
2nd British Grenadier Battalion (Lieutenant Colonel Henry Monckton)
1st Battalion Foot Guards (Brigadier General Mathew)
*Captain Thomas Dowdeswell, Ensign Thomas Glyn*

**Hessian Brigade Grenadiers and Fusiliers**
Grenadier Battalion Linsing (Lieutenant Colonel Otto von Linsing)
Grenadier Battalion Block (Lieutenant Colonel Henrich von Bloch)
Grenadier Battalion Minnegerode (Lieutenant Colonel Friedrich von Minnegerode)
Battalion of remnants of the Rall Brigade (Captain Wilmousky)
Fusilier Battalion Loos (Colonel Johann von Loos)

### Detached at Maidenhead

**Second British Brigade** (*Brigadier General Alexander Leslie*)
5th Regiment of Foot (Lieutenant Colonel William Walcott)
28th Regiment of Foot (Lieutenant Colonel Robert Prescott)
*Captain William Hall*
35th Regiment of Foot (Lieutenant Colonel James Cockburne)
49th Regiment of Foot (Major Cornelius Cuyler)
*Sergeant Thomas Sullivan*

### Reserve Troops remaining at Princeton (see: Table 9 page 296)

**British and Hessian Troops at other posts in New Jersey**

**Brunswick and Raritan Landing garrisons -**
46th Regiment of Foot (General Vaughan)
2nd Battalion Foot Guards (Lieutenant Colonel James Ogilvie)

**Elizabethtown garrison**
Waldeck Regiment (Hessian)
71st Regiment of Foot (elements)
2 troops of the 17th Regiment of Light Dragoons

**Amboy garrison**
33rd Regiment of Foot
57th Regiment of Foot

**Hackensack-New Bridge garrison**
7th Regiment of Foot
26th Regiment of Foot

**The New York garrison**
1st British Brigade - 4th, 27th, and 45th Regiments of Foot
Some Hessian troops

biscuit and brandy for his men and then set off for Maidenhead.[6] Early in the day, the reinforced guard post on the Quaker Road that had lain on its arms for three nights, left their fires and joined the march to Trenton. They were not replaced.[7] Collecting thousands of troops marching on muddy roads from a variety of distances in the pre-dawn hours resulted in delays, so Cornwallis sent off troops as they became ready, producing gaps in the column that engineer Archibald Robertson feared put them at risk to be "cut up in detail." Robertson was one British officer who, after the impressive action at Trenton, expected well-planned, aggressive moves from the Americans rather than ragged defensive ones.[8] Donop was to lead the troops and says, "at 8 o'clock in the morning of the 2nd the two battalions of Light Infantry joined me, and I set out to march for Trenton."[9] Like many British officers, 22-year-old Captain Thomas Dowdeswell of the 1st Battalion, Brigade of Foot Guards, who had arrived the previous night from Brunswick, optimistically marched his company "towards Trentown, expecting either to engage the rebels, or drive them over the Delaware with considerable loss to them."[10]

**Temperatures rising to about** 40 degrees during the morning and afternoon kept the roads and fields in deep mud that made any kind of movement unpleasant and fatiguing for the men of both armies.[11] The mud and cold slush clung to everything it touched, making every step difficult and exhausting for the marching men and the horses pulling artillery pieces and wagons. Ravines and streams cutting the road also slowed progress while the British troops constantly kept alert for American ambushes.

**While the British marched** out of Princeton, the American troops from Crosswicks and Bordentown arrived in Trenton over a period of several hours during the morning. Nineteen-year-old private James Johnston of the Chester County militia arrived about daylight, and his company was ordered to occupy General Dickinson's disheveled greenhouse, the former Jäger outpost, about a mile from the center of Trenton.[12] When John Adams visited the Dickinson home nine months later he described the farm, gardens, and greenhouse as "a scene of desolation." The greenhouse floor had been dug up, supposedly by Hessians searching for money. In one room there was "a huge crash of glass bottles" presumed to have been broken by the Hessians.[13]

Peale's company got to Trenton about an hour after sunrise and found "the difficulty of getting quarters kept us a long time under arms. At last we were provided, and had made a fire. I took a short nap on a plank, with my feet to the fire."[14]

When Sergeant Young got to Trenton about 9:00am, he saw the six Hessian cannon captured the week before and called on Mrs. Brown, "the old lady at whose house I lodged when I first got to Trentown, December 5" at the end of the retreat across New Jersey. His company was also posted at Dickinson's greenhouse.[15]

Presbyterian militia chaplain John Rosbrugh arrived from Crosswicks, went to a tavern, tied his horse in a shed, and entered the tavern for some refreshment.[16]

Dr. Rush got back to Trenton about 7:00am and "went to Genl. St. Clair's quarters, and begged the favor of his bed for a few hours." Rush recalled, "Just as I began to sleep, an alarm gun was fired at the General's door. I started up, and the first creature I saw was a black woman crying and wringing her hands in my room. She was followed by Genl. St. Clair with a composed countenance" who announced the enemy was advancing. Rush asked, "what do you intend to do?" and St. Clair answered with a smile, "Why, fight them." Rush then watched him take down his sword and tie the scabbard to his thigh "with a calmness such as I thought seldom took place at the expectation of a battle." Rush followed him out, mounted his horse, rode to meet some Philadelphia militia still on the road just below town, and rode slowly back with them. On the way, he asked a militiaman how he felt, to which the man bravely replied, "as if I were going to sit down to a good breakfast."[17]

John Howland's company had taken quarters in houses recently occupied by Hessians and "kindled our fires, got on our kettles, and were collecting from our knapsacks or pockets, a stray remnant of bread or tainted pork, when the drums beat to arms. Hungry, tired and sleepy, we swallowed our half cooked food, placed the camp kettles in the wagons, and leaving the comfort of houses which we had not lately enjoyed, formed the line for marching."[18] Cumberland County, New Jersey militiaman Thomas McGee arrived at Trenton after an all-night march from Bordentown and was called to arms "before we could receive our rations."[19] At 10:00am, Pennsylvania Rifle Sergeant James McMichael "received news that the enemy were advancing, when the drums beat to arms and we were all paraded on the south side of the bridge [over Assunpink Creek]."[20]

That creek was a natural defensive barrier and the troops dug in on Mill Hill overlooking it. To prevent the British from attacking them across the creek and cutting off retreat routes, Washington's troops needed to take advantage of the high ground and concentrate their fire on the limited crossing points at the creek's narrow stone bridge and several fording points. Joseph Reed knew the area well and went out with several horsemen to reconnoiter the two primary fords. They found the ford at Samuel Henry's Mill "scarcely passable for horses, the water being rapid and high," while at the Phillips Mill, a mile or so higher up the creek, they found the ford to be "in very good order; and had the enemy taken the opportunity of passing it, the consequences would probably have been fatal," because they could have outflanked the army on Mill Hill.[21] John Dewey recalled, "after our army had got posted in the best manner for their own defense, our brigade, with

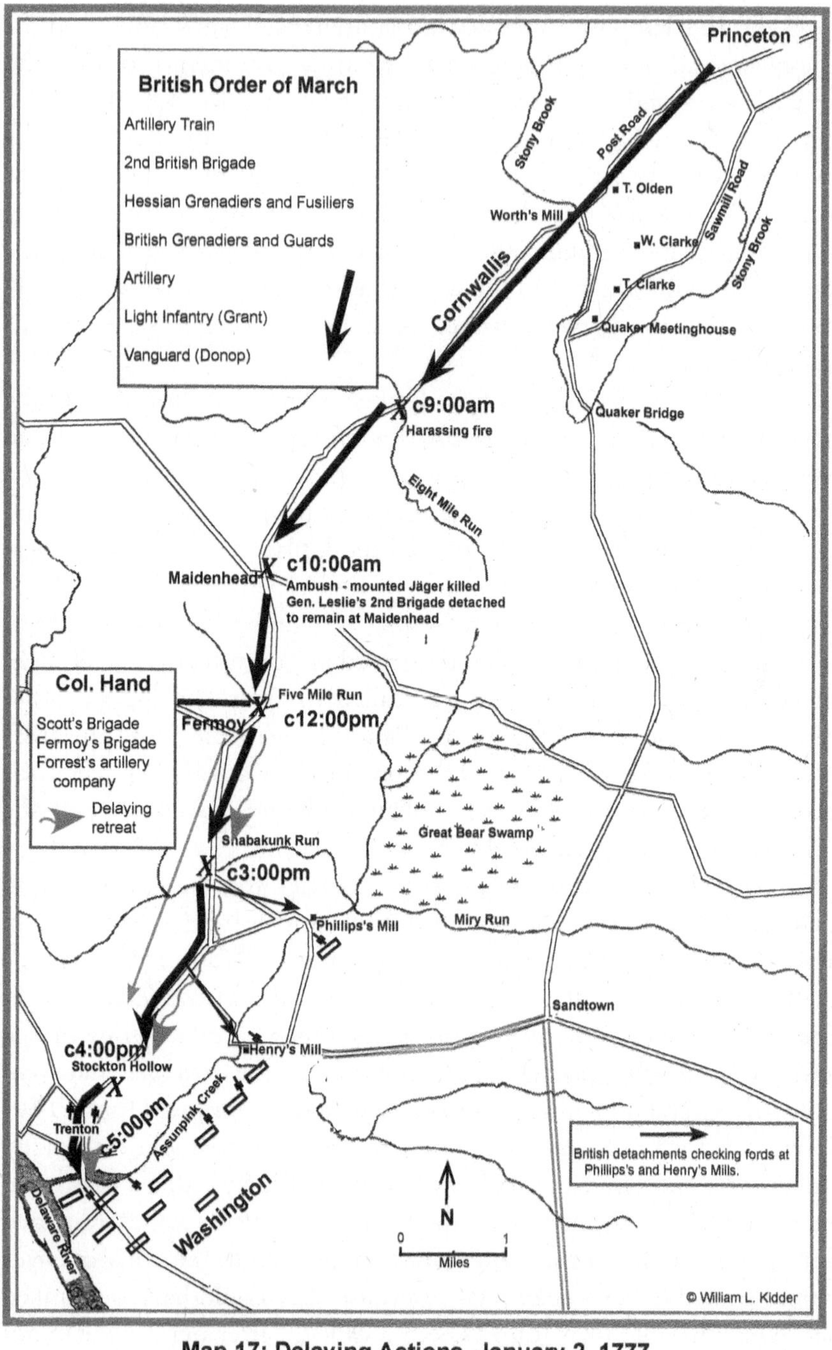


Map 17: Delaying Actions, January 2, 1777

some other troops, was ordered to march up the river to a certain fordway, to prevent the enemy crossing the river."[22]

To reduce the danger of a flanking attack, a brigade was placed at the Phillips Mill ford, about two miles above the Trenton bridge and on the extreme right of the army. Troops were also stationed in a field opposite Samuel Henry's mill and ford, about a mile from the bridge. A brigade and an artillery company were posted on the high bank of Mill Hill just east of the Assunpink Creek bridge. The American left was on the Delaware River and the troops had constructed small earthworks on the ridge and across the road below the Queen Street bridge. A line of reserves was placed behind them.[23] A New Jersey militiaman described the American disposition on Mill Hill as "the troops were placed one above the other so that they appeared to cover the whole slope from bottom to top, which brought a great many muskets within shot of the bridge. Within 70 or 80 yards of the bridge, and in front of and in the road, as many pieces of artillery as could be managed were stationed."[24] Major George Johnston of the 5th Virginia Regiment believed that altogether there were at least 30 cannon on Mill Hill and the south side of the Assunpink.[25] Henry Knox described Mill Hill as completely commanding Trenton "with 30 or 40 pieces of artillery in front." He felt the position was strong, but also hazardous, because "had our right wing [covering Henry's and Phillips's fords] been defeated[,] the defeat of the left would almost have been an immediate consequence & the whole thrown into confusion or push'd into the Delaware."[26]

Lieutenant Peale was startled awake from his nap by drums beating the call to arms and paraded with his regiment at their alarm post. Looking about him, Peale was "greatly struck with the appearance of so fine an army. At least a brigade paraded in the same field below the town" across the Assunpink in Kingsbury.[27] When the alarm gun fired at about 10:00am, Sergeant 's company hurried to pack up their baggage and make ready at their assigned position across the Assunpink Creek for the oncoming British.[28] James Johnston's militiamen at Dickinson's greenhouse were preparing breakfast when they heard the alarm, hurried back to town, crossed the Assunpink Creek bridge, and formed up with the army on Mill Hill. Johnston recalled Washington ordered about 12 pieces of artillery to be placed behind Trenton Mills.[29]

John Cowell admired his family's friend William Morris, a 23-year-old tailor serving as drummer for the Trenton militia company. Throughout his life, Cowell could visualize "Morris standing at the head of the main street in this city beating the troops to arms in consequence of the approach of the British army." Cowell told his mother "what a good drummer Morris was" and then followed him across the Assunpink bridge to where the army was forming on Mill Hill, "being pleased with his dexterity as a musician."[30] Men recalled hearing alarm drums at different times, so they probably beat several times in response to updated information coming in from the series of delaying actions taking place on the road to Princeton. When an alarm was sounded about 11:00am, Rev. Avery saw the army form up on the south side of the Assunpink Creek with Sullivan's division guarding several fording places.[31] Philadelphia Associator John Hood, reported two cannon were placed back of Mr. Waln's house opposite his mill and some riflemen were placed in the mill and additional artillery along the creek.[32]

Captain Thomas Rodney got to Trenton from Allentown about 11:00am and "found all the troops from our different posts in Jersey, collected and collecting there under Gen. Washington himself; and the regular troops were already properly disposed to receive the enemy, whose main body was then within a few miles and determined to dispossess us."[33]

**Due to the alarms,** Loyalist spy John Williams's 10:00am execution was cancelled. Instead, he was marched with several other prisoners to Trenton Ferry, taken across the river, and jailed at Newtown. In the confusion of the rapidly changing situation, his death sentence apparently did not follow him.[34]

**Henry Knox sat down** and, finding an express rider was about to leave, wrote hurriedly to Lucy telling her that "we are collecting our force at this place & shall give battle to the enemy very soon. Our people have exerted great fortitude & staid beyond the time of their inlistments in high spirits[,] but want arms & clothing." He then joyously announced that he had been promoted to brigadier general and put in command of the artillery, but lamented that the recent "attack on Trenton [on December 26] was a most horid scene to the poor inhabitants – War my Lucy is not a humane trade & the man who follows at such will s[uffer] with his proper demerits in another world." As he wrote those words, Knox was within hours of experiencing more battlefield horrors.[35] However, even under the pressure of impending combat, he also took the time to write to artillery officer and prisoner of war John Lamb, captured at Quebec, with the good news that he was to be exchanged.[36]

**Twelve-year-old Nancy Shippen,** from a very prominent Philadelphia family, sat down at her boarding school in Trenton, Mrs. Rogers' School for Young Ladies, and penned her mother a short letter conveying family news, greetings, and statements of affection. Her father was Continental Army surgeon William Shippen and her mother, Alice, was one of the Virginia Lees, sister of Declaration of Independence signers Richard Henry and Francis Lightfoot Lee. However, whether trying to protect her mother from fear for her safety, or simply absorbed by other things besides the war, Nancy did not say anything about the recent events in Trenton or that a great battle was approaching that could potentially negate the successful capture of the Hessians.[37]

**While people in Trenton awaited** the inevitable arrival of the British, the fighting on the Princeton road was heard in town with increasing clarity and loudness as the armies grew nearer. Civilians in Trenton, such as Nancy Shippen and her schoolmates, sought cover, while the American army consolidated its position on the south side of the Assunpink Creek. Preserved Buffington, 17 years old, of Captain Loring Peck's Company of Lippitt's Rhode Island Regiment was getting his equipment ready to confront the British when he was seriously "wounded in the hand by the bursting of a musket" during the morning preparations.[38] Sergeant McCarty was still sick, but upon receiving orders in the morning to make ready for battle, he served his men some flour and meat before the alarm sounded about noon.[39]

Stephen Olney arrived at Trenton about sunrise and said "we took quarters in the houses and began to prepare for breakfast; but before it was ready, the drum beat to arms." This surprised them because, "the enemy whom we supposed at Princeton, twelve miles off, or at Brunswick, twenty four miles off, were near at hand and double our number." Olney paraded on the south side of the Assunpink Creek on Mill Hill with other units, including Sergeant McMichael's.[40] Philadelphia Associator Ensign Philip Hagner reached Trenton about 8:00am and when the alarm guns fired was under arms on the commons in Kingsbury.[41]

**Shortly into his march**, Donop found that at Eight Mile Run, "at the approach of my advance guard the rebels retired without firing a musket and destroyed the wooden bridge between Maidenhead and Princeton, but I had it soon repaired. On the height on the other side of the bridge we pulled up cannon and muskets one next to the other but that did not last long since the enemy retired toward Trenton in good order, putting itself under the protection of its cannon on the other side of the bridge."[42]

The exhausting road conditions, and periodic halts made to scatter American pickets, greatly slowed their march. As the head of the British column approached the village of Maidenhead late in the morning, the advance squad of mounted Jägers spotted what seemed to be a mounted farmer who bolted down the road towards Trenton when he saw them. The Jägers gave chase. The fastest of them gained on the American and raised his sword to strike a blow, but before he could strike he was wounded by a shot fired by a hidden American picket near the Maidenhead Presbyterian Church. When he attempted to turn around at the sound of a bugle from his unit, two additional American shots killed him and his horse. The "farmer" they chased was not the simple civilian he appeared to be, but was First Lieutenant Elias Hunt of the 1st Hunterdon Regiment of militia who lived on the temporarily abandoned farm where the Jägers had spotted him. He was perhaps a scout for the picket or bait to lure someone like the Jäger into the ambush. After disrupting the British advance, the Americans melted back into the landscape they knew so well. Another Maidenhead militiaman, John Phillips, was with this "advance part of the army in the village" of Maidenhead and retreated "with the army to Trenton when the British Army advanced a second time on that place."

The British paused to eliminate the gaps between marching units to discourage further ambushes. They buried the dead Jäger in a patch of woods on 1st Hunterdon County Regiment's Major Joseph Phillips's farm, across the road from the Presbyterian Church and over the years a local tradition developed claiming that the ghost of the Jäger appeared from time to time in those woods. After closing up their column, the British and Hessians continued their march to Trenton about noon, still about five miles from Trenton and with only about five hours of daylight remaining.[43] The British continued at a slow pace while frequently exchanging fire with the stubborn, retreating enemy.

For the past two days and nights, Ensign James Barnett and Private William Montgomery of the 6th Virginia Regiment had been part of the American delaying force of about 1000 men posted near Maidenhead at Five Mile Run.[44] These troops consisted of Charles Scott's Virginia brigade, Edward Hand's Maryland and Pennsylvania Riflemen, Hausegger's Pennsylvania and Maryland German Battalion, and Captain Thomas Forrest's Pennsylvania artillery company with its two guns.

As the British column approached the Americans waiting for them at Five Mile Run, the American commander, General Fermoy, inexplicably mounted his horse and rode off rapidly towards Trenton without saying a word to any of his subordinates. At this point he basically disappears from the record until March. What he did between January 2 and mid-March is not known. Lacking orders from Fermoy, Colonel Edward Hand, now the senior officer present, had to take command. Hand was a talented and highly respected commander of his backcountry riflemen; also remembered by them as a trained doctor who prescribed medications for his men.[45] Demonstrating his respected leadership qualities, Hand took charge and placed Captain Henry Miller of his riflemen, another man known for his bravery and skill, in command of his advanced guard of skirmishers. Aware of the orders to engage the British at every suitable point, to delay them as long as possible, Hand's troops successfully slowed the British advance from Maidenhead, past Five Mile Run, and finally to the Shabakunk Creek.

About 1:00pm, Colonel Hand deployed his men within the mile-deep woods on the right side of the road at the Shabakunk, posting

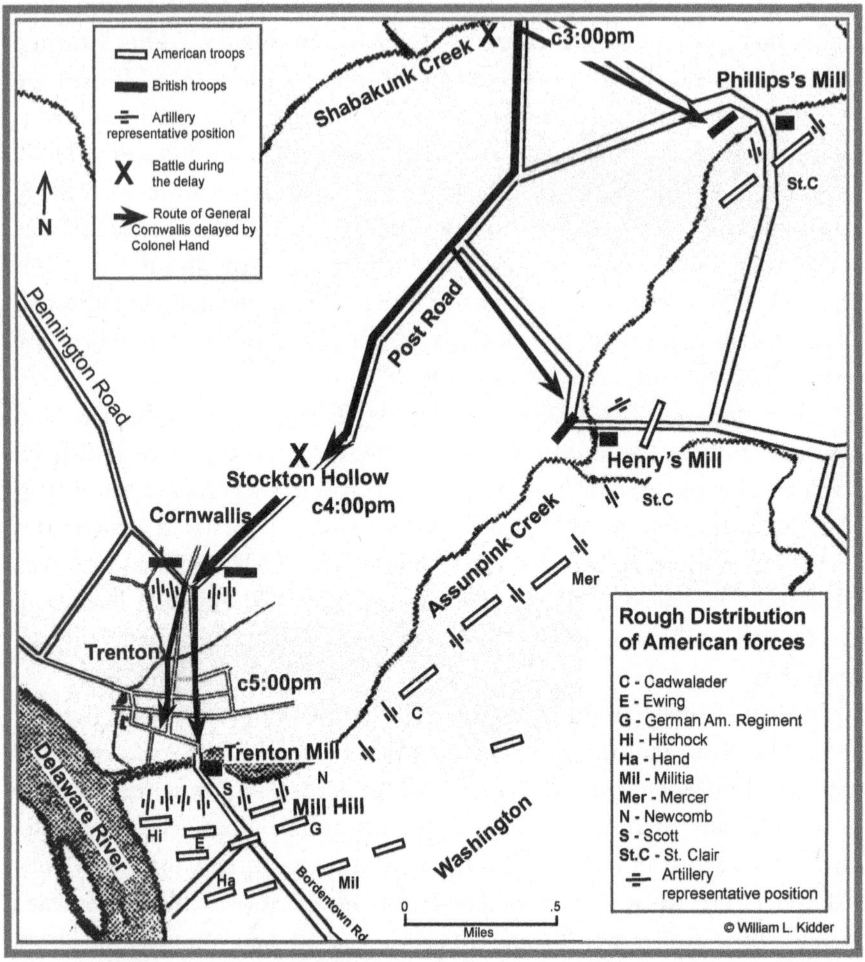


**Map 18: Battle of the Assunpink Creek - January 2, 1777**

Washington placed his troops on Mill Hill across the Assunpink Creek to use it as a barrier when the British got to Trenton to attack him. This gave him the advantage of high ground and a concentration of artillery fire, however, he was vulnerable to having his forces attacked on the right flank if the British crossed troops at Henry's or Phillips's Mills. While there were several places that could be forded on the Assunpink, the main crossing point was the stone bridge at Trenton Mill. This is where the British focused their attack late in the day after being delayed by the forces under Colonel Hand. American artillery focused on the bridge and each attempt by the British to storm across the bridge was beaten back.

For the British and Hessian troops in this engagement see Table 8 (page 254) and for the American troops see Tables 6 (page 242) and 7 (page 247).

himself on the right and Miller on the left, and quietly awaited the British. When the British advance guard came within extremely close range, the Americans fired a deadly and unexpected volley that broke the British and forced them to retreat back to their main force in some confusion. Then, preparing for full battle, Cornwallis formed his column into a line of battle on the soft, muddy earth, and ordered up artillery that fired into the woods for about thirty minutes before he advanced his troops.[46] Jäger Captain Ewald noted that Lieutenant von Grothausen was seriously wounded in this fight. He had commanded the fifty Jägers that had escaped across the Assunpink Creek bridge on December 26. During the course of the day, the British took some American prisoners and Ewald learned from them how Washington had positioned his troops on Mill Hill and that the British could expect to continue meeting resistance throughout their march to Trenton.[47]

During these actions on their approach to Trenton, the British learned of the American troops stationed at Phillips's Mill and Henry's Mill that threatened their left flank. Their concern was relieved when the Americans proved more intent on defense than offense.[48] James Wilkinson recalled, "the enemy's flankers reconnoitered those fords, but finding them guarded, [re]joined their main body: my station gave me a fair view of the left flank of the enemy's column, after it had passed the wood from Shabbakong, and wheeled to their right on the margin of the high ground, which leads to Trenton."[49] Some British troops remained at the fords and John Dewey's company was posted at one of them "where the enemy upon the other side took much advantage of the ground, which [they] improved, to cannonade us very severely when there was nothing to cover us from their shot but the open air."[50] Fortunately, the British did not cross troops at the fords to flank the Americans.

Outnumbered about six to one, Colonel Hand had persistently delayed the British for an additional two hours. It was now 3:00pm, with only about two hours of daylight remaining, and the British were still about two miles from Trenton. Hand slowly withdrew his troops about a mile and half to a ravine or depression known as Stockton Hollow, where they could again significantly retard the British advance. He placed Captain Forrest with his cannon at the back of the ravine, where they had a clear field of fire over the road, and the three small Virginia

Regiments under Colonel Charles Scott on the right where they could defend the ground between the road and the fords on the Assunpink.[51]

UNDER ARMS ON THE Kingsbury commons during the delaying action, Philadelphia Associator Ensign Philip Hagner and his company were ordered into a wood and then to march back to the commons and light their fires. Before they could obey those orders they heard a sudden firing near the Mill on the Assunpink. Colonel Joseph Reed came up and rode over to the mill to investigate and returned to let them know there was no immediate danger and they could ground arms. Hagner remembered Reed as being very active throughout the battle.[52]

HENRY KNOX'S LETTER TO Lucy left town about 3:00pm and about the same time, he later wrote her, "the column of the enemy attacked a party of ours which was stationed about one mile above Trenton. Our party was small & did not make much resistance."[53] The exhausted, mud covered retreating troops were now only about half a mile from Trenton and Washington, along with Nathanael Greene and Henry Knox, rode out to talk with them. Washington thanked them for the fine job they had done all day and told them how important it was to delay the British until nightfall, so the defenses on the south side of Assunpink Creek could be completed. He ordered them to make "as obstinate a stand as could be made on that ground, without hazarding the pieces [cannon]," then left and returned to the defensive positions just beyond the Assunpink.[54]

The exhausted and mud covered British troops felt continued pressure from their officers to push forward against the fierce resolve displayed by the retreating Americans. As the British column advanced into range, Captain Forrest's guns opened fire with round shot, bringing it to a halt. Once again, Cornwallis deployed into a muddy line of battle, advanced his field artillery, and his men inexorably marched forward to take the high ground at the north entrance to town. As the enemy approached town, Stephen Olney's company, heading for the same spot, "marched with a view to take possession of an eminence the north side of the town, as I then supposed, to get into a better situation, so if we were obliged to retire to the north and hilly part of Jersey, we could get there with better safety; but the enemy got possession of these hills before we did, and commenced a smart fire upon us." Olney heard General Greene at the head of the column give the order to retreat, whereupon "the first platoon wheeled, some others turned about, as we had been taught on parade duty, so that we passed Trenton bridge in great disorder." When they formed up in order again, "the men were at arm's length apart, so as to make a numerous and formidable appearance, (none but a Yankee would have thought of that.) Thus we remained until dark, without firing much, and but little from the enemy. A few scattering balls were passing each way, most of the time."[55]

Knox commented that the British force, led by Hessian grenadiers and Jägers, "enter'd the town pell-mell pretty much in the same manner as we had driven the Hessians seven days before."[56] Some of the British officers also made this observation. Archibald Robertson arriving on the outskirts of Trenton saw, "the heights and woods on our right were soon forced with little loss and our troops followed them into Trenton where their main body was drawn up, about 6 or 7,000, with the creek and bridge in front and [a] number of field pieces." The cannonade with the Americans only cost the British a few men, but they felt they could not attack the American position. As Robertson said, "They were exactly in the position Rall should have taken when he was atack'd[,] from which he might have retreated towards Borden's Town with very little loss."[57]

While the British charged down the main streets of town towards the bridge, Captain Moulder's 4-pounders and other artillery fired on them with great effect "being well placed and skillfully manned by as hardy, fearless and energetic set of youths as the army could produce."[58] In response, John Hood said, "the enemy threw a number of shells, … and one cannon ball passed through the 3d Batallion [of Associators] & killed 2 Men."[59]

Captain Ewald says, "Toward evening we reached the heights [at the head of town], which were occupied by the enemy with an infantry corps, some cavalry, and several guns. The Jägers and light infantry, supported by the Hessian grenadiers, attacked the enemy at once, whereupon he withdrew through Trenton across the bridge to his army after slight resistance. But the rear guard was so hard pressed by the Jägers and light infantry that the majority were either killed or captured." Once in town, "The Jägers and light infantry immediately attempted to occupy the houses of the town on this side of the bridge. Since the enemy had likewise occupied the houses on the other side, which lay in front of the enemy army, a stubborn outpost fight occurred here whereby many men were killed and wounded on both sides. During this fighting the army deployed upon the heights before the town." The light infantry and Scots were then ordered "to occupy the right bank of Assunpink Creek to keep a sharp eye on the movements of the enemy."[60]

The Linsing and Block Hessian grenadier battalions and the Jägers were the first of Cornwallis's troops to enter Trenton. Donop placed the Minnegerode Battalion along with the remnants of the Rall brigade "on the height on the left since a rebel corps was beyond the river which is there. Inside and outside Trenton we had to suffer a rather strong cannonade from the enemy, but we only posted Jäger and Light Infantry piquets in the city and retired the other troops into the woods on the height so that we would not suffer any more losses from the mortar cannon of the enemies." Following Donop's brigade came British grenadiers who were placed next to the Minnegerode Grenadier Battalion on the left wing.[61]

John Howland believed that the next hour, or less, would decide whether "we should be independent states, or conquered rebels!" If Cornwallis's troops managed to cross the bridge or ford the Assunpink, it would take a miracle to prevent complete defeat. Howland believed anyone who doubted him was not aware that the American army then consisted of "a few half-starved, half-frozen, feeble, worn out men, with old fowling pieces for muskets, and half of them without bayonets, and the states so disheartened, discouraged, or poor, that they sent no reinforcements, no recruits to supply the places of this handful of men, who, but the day before had volunteered to remain with their venerated and beloved commander, for thirty days more."[62]

Ensign Robert Beale of the 5th Virginia Regiment had been fighting the delaying action all day and was just entering Trenton in retreat when his unit was ordered to turn around and press back against the advancing British. They had only taken a few steps, though, when word was frantically shouted to "shift for yourselves, boys, get over the bridge as quick as you can." The men turned around and took off running toward the bridge under heavy British fire. Several men were killed and "a very clever young man, who had but a few days before been made an ensign by Colonel Parker, carried the colors. He was shot down in the street with his thigh broken, but the colors were brought off."[63] Refusing to panic, the Americans continued to harass and delay the British and Hessian advance through town, impressing the Hessians with how they "withdrew in the most perfect order."[64] Henry Knox observed, "the enemy pushed our small party thro' the town with vigor tho not with much loss."[65] While retreating, 17-year-old private Isaiah Crandall took a British musket ball in the back that knocked him to his hands and knees. The bullet had hit his knapsack and put 33 holes through his folded up blanket, but a hard lump of bread stopped the force of the bullet and probably saved his life.[66]

**When notified that the** British were entering town, Rev. Rosbrugh hastily left the tavern, but found his horse gone. Hurrying on foot to escape across the Assunpink Creek bridge, he could not get to it and tried to ford the creek, but found it impossible. Turning to hide in a grove of trees, he ran into some Hessians commanded by a British officer. He surrendered as a prisoner of war and offered his gold watch and money to the soldiers, asking them to spare his life for his wife and family. The items were taken, but the soldiers, possibly in response to Donop's order to take no prisoners, prepared to put him to death. He knelt down under a tree and prayed for his enemies, who proceeded to make him a martyr with bayonet thrusts and sabre slashes.[67]

**John Howland's company** of Lippitt's regiment was ordered to cross the bridge back into Trenton and march up the main street to provide cover for the retreating troops. When they reached the retreating Americans, Howland's men opened their ranks to let them pass and then closed back up into a solid, compact column in the narrow street. The British pressed down a parallel street and poured fire into the American right flank from spaces between houses. At this point, according to Howland, "When what was now our front, arrived near the bridge we were to pass, and where the lower, or water street [Front Street] formed a junction with the main street, the British made a quick advance in an oblique direction to cut us off from the bridge." The

Americans were closer to the bridge and, supported by artillery fire from Mill Hill that caused the British to fall back, avoided being cut off.[68] Americans on the Mill Hill side of the Assunpink Creek waved at the small groups of Americans racing through town to the bridge to get out of the street so they could fire at the British further up it.[69] Just like the battle on December 26, this was street fighting among the buildings in Trenton, a number of which took damage from the bullets and artillery rounds. In this fight, however, the muskets of both armies were not hindered by the weather and the artillery fire on the town from both armies was much heavier.

Pennsylvania militiaman James Johnston recalled that the enemy came down Queen Street, driving the Americans before them and inflicting casualties, while receiving heavy and effective fire from behind houses. When the British reached the intersection of Queen and Second Street, they began to receive artillery fire from the cannon posted on Mill Hill, causing them to recoil.[70] Another British force marched rapidly down King Street and opened fire on the Americans at Front Street, but could not prevent their crossing the bridge. The skirmishers who had been fighting all day to slow the British advance got across the bridge and joined the main army on Mill Hill. When crossing the bridge they passed General Washington who had stationed himself on horseback at one end, where his display of personal courage and confidence under fire inspired his men.[71]

John Stevens's company of 1st Hunterdon County Regiment militiamen was ordered, with others, to assist a company of artillery defending the bridge and militiaman Titus Mershon also participated in fighting the British "across the Bridge."[72] George Johnston observed that the British "passage into the town was disputed every inch," by "the advanced parties, who resolutely maintained their ground with much loss to the enemy till the General ordered 'em all into the main body [across the bridge], which they effected with but little loss."[73]

From their position in a Kingsbury field, Charles Willson Peale's company watched as the British fought their way through town and one of the American cannon and a howitzer "played on the town."[74] The guns of Moulder's and other artillery companies had been stationed to concentrate fire on the Assunpink Creek bridge and fired on British troops coming through Trenton towards it.[75] Twenty-one-year-old Zebulon Applegate of Captain Moulder's company later said, "near sun down when the Americans came in sight on a retreat and the British or Hessians were pursuing them with their artillery[,] We kept our post & reserved our fire until the Americans went down into a hollow by a mill & we then fired our artillery over the heads of the Americans at the British and they got into the houses & fired out of them and at us when they could get a chance at us – they fired right fast out of the jail (until we gave them a load of grape shot right at them and stopt them)."[76] The jail was the first floor of the Hunterdon County Courthouse on the lower part of King Street between Front and Second Streets.

Private Jacob Bottomer of Colonel Hand's regiment was wounded in the left side during the delaying action. His lieutenant immediately ordered several soldiers to bring him along and told Bottomer not to cry out. Bottomer fell down just before reaching the bridge and was trampled by an estimated 50 retreating soldiers. After his company crossed the bridge and formed in battle formation along the creek, Bottomer came crawling along, very weak from loss of blood. His wound was thought to be mortal, but he was placed under the care of army surgeons and survived.[77]

Americans crossing the narrow stone bridge crammed together, providing the pursuing British with a tempting target. John Howland was impressed that "the noble horse of Gen. Washington stood with his breast pressed close against the end of the west rail of the bridge, and the firm, composed, and majestic countenance of the general inspired confidence and assurance in a moment so important and critical." Howland crossed the bridge next to the west rail and at the end of it was "pressed against the shoulder of the general's horse, and in contact with the general's boot. The horse stood as firm as the rider, and seemed to understand that he was not to quit his post and station." When Howland was about halfway over the bridge, Washington ordered his commander, Colonel Hitchcock, to form his men as quickly as possible in a field he pointed to on the south side of the creek on the Kingsbury farm. Hitchcock obeyed the order and then advanced his men to the edge of the creek, where they hastily built a temporary breastwork and forced the British to fall back and take cover among the houses in town.[78]

Dr. Rush saw "a brave and sensible American colonel" who asked his troops as "they came within sight of the enemy who they were. They answered, 'Hessians, sir.' He asked them what they were. They answered, 'Men, sir;' and 'What are you, my lads?' asked the Colonel. 'Why, men, sir.' 'Then,' said the Colonel, 'let not one man be afraid of another.'"[79] Dr. Rush recalled that "in the afternoon a cannonade began in which several soldiers were wounded. All was now hurry, confusion and noise. General Washington and his aids rode by the Philadelphia militia in all the terrible aspect of war. Genl. Mifflin, in a blanket coat, galloped at the head of a body of Pennsylvania militia. He appeared to be all soul. I recollect the ardor with which he called to them to quicken their steps. His command was not without effect. They ran after him." General Knox "was cool, cheerful, and was present everywhere."[80] In passing Rush, he cried out, "your opinion last night was very fortunate for us."[81]

Delaware Captain Thomas Rodney found that "after sunset this afternoon the enemy came down in a very heavy column to force the bridge. The fire was very heavy and the light troops were ordered to fly to the support of that important post, and as we drew near, I stepped out of the front to order my men to close up; at this time Martinas Sipple was about 10 steps behind the man next in front of him; I at once drew my sword and threatened to cut his head off if he did not keep close, he then sprang forward and I returned to the front."[82]

The three-regiment Virginia brigade that had been fighting the delaying action all day, including Ensign Beale's company, "was ordered to form in column at the bridge and General Washington came and in the presence of us all, told Colonel Charles Scott of the 5th Virginia Regiment to defend the bridge to the last extremity." Colonel Scott, renowned for his colorful swearing, answered with an oath, followed by, "Yes, General, as long as there is a man alive."[83] By one account, Washington, with a small detachment, then moved off a bit on his horse but turned back and looked at Scott and his men, appearing to ponder the importance of what Scott and his men must accomplish. Thinking Washington had departed, Scott told his men, "Well, boys, you know the old boss has put us here to defend this bridge; and by G-d it must be done, let what will come. Now I want to tell you one thing.

You're all in the habit of shooting too high. You waste your powder and lead; and I have cursed you about it a hundred times. Now, I tell you what it is, nothing must be wasted; every crack must count. For that reason boys, whenever you see them fellows first begin to put their feet upon this bridge, do you shin 'em." Taking this in, Washington could not help chuckling and when Scott saw him they exchanged "a pleasant glance."[84] Colonel Scott was known both for swearing and for advising his men to aim low so they would not miss the enemy completely by firing too high.[85] Washington also told Major Richard Parker of the 6th Virginia Regiment, "that this bridge must be defended to the last extremity," to which Parker replied, "Sir, we intend to sleep on it."[86]

While it was typical for Washington to be in the thick of the fighting, some of his officers urged him to post himself in a safer position behind the lines on Mill Hill rather than stay so near the bridge. Washington refused on the grounds that his presence would encourage his troops, but some could not help thinking he was wishing for a cannon ball to end his life, because he appeared to be facing almost certain defeat.[87]

The bridge over the Assunpink was now the doorway for the British troops advancing on the American positions in Kingsbury and on Mill Hill. Major James Wilkinson saw the enemy continue "to advance until he forced our corps to retire by the bridge across the Assanpink, I had a fair flank view of this little combat from the opposite side of the Assanpink, and recollect perfectly the sun had set, and the evening was so far advanced, that I could distinguish the flame from the muzzles of our muskets."[88]

Immediately after the last American troops got over the long, two-arched stone bridge, Sergeant White's guns and all the other American cannon fired together on the advancing British columns. John Howland recalled, "the cannon which had been drawn aside, to leave us a passage, were again placed at the end of the bridge and discharged into the front of the enemy's column, which was advancing towards it; at the same time several pieces placed at the right and left of the bridge, with musketry at the intervals, took them partly in flank."[89] Henry Knox later wrote that after the Americans got over the bridge, "the enemy advanced within reach of our cannon who saluted them with great vociferation and some execution."[90]

Sergeant Daniel Smith of Stonington, Connecticut, serving in Lippitt's Rhode Island Regiment, recalled that as soon as the Americans finished crossing the bridge, "the artillery which was stationed at the end of the bridge opened up on the enemy's van and swept them from the bridge as often as they attempted to cross with grape shot." Each time the enemy was forced back, "Genl Washington rode up and ordered the Army to cheer, which they did several times."[91] On the third British attempt, according to White, "we loaded with canister shot, and let them come nearer" before firing together and making the bridge look "red as blood, with their killed and wounded, and their red coats. The enemy beat a retreat, and it began to grow dark." The cannon fire went both ways for about 12 minutes, and one enemy cannon ball killed two men on Mill Hill.[92]

When darkness caused the British to call off the assault, Henry Knox's artillery continued with "a few shells we now & then chucked at them to prevent their enjoying their new quarters . . . ."[93] Donop later reported, "in and outside Trenton we had to suffer a heavy cannonade from the enemy, through which however the loss is not great."[94] The cannonade continued at intervals in the dark with American artillery fire striking several buildings in Trenton. Charles Axford, Jr.'s home was damaged by at least one cannon ball that entered his house and destroyed a walnut tea table. By tradition, the building on the corner at Queen and Second Street was struck by cannon balls and the courthouse and jail lost part of a wall. Jonathan Richmond's tavern on Mill Hill was hit by a 3-pounder British cannon ball that embedded in the mortar.[95]

Most of the British troops withdrew to the high ground on the Beakes farm just above the town, although a number of soldiers milled about in the town streets. The exchange of artillery fire had been so pronounced and characteristic of the battle that participants often later referred to the encounter as the cannonade at Trenton, rather than the battle.[96]

James Wilkinson described the situation at the end of the day saying, "after forcing our advanced party, the enemy took post in our front, at about 1000 yards distance, with the intervention of the village (now city) of Trenton, and the Assanpink creek, which was every where fordable below the mill: a cannonade ensued between the two armies with little effect, during which Lord Cornwallis displayed his columns, and extended his lines, to the westward, on the heights above the town. If there ever was a crisis in the affairs of the revolution, this was the moment; thirty minutes would have sufficed to bring the two armies into contact, and thirty more would have decided the combat; and, covered with wo [sic], Columbia might have wept the loss of her beloved chief and most valorous sons."[97]

**General Leslie had departed** Princeton mid-morning with his troops at the end of Cornwallis's column to march to Maidenhead where his brigade would encamp as a reserve for Cornwallis and Lieutenant Colonel Mawhood arrived in Princeton late in the day with his cold, hungry men of the 4th Brigade and took over the occupation of the town to guard the military stores there and protect the lines of communication. During the night, British Lieutenant Inman of the 17th Regiment of Foot noted "we were ordered ... from Prince Town as an Escort to Stores." Mawhood was to bring the supplies guarded by two regiments from his brigade, along with some cavalry, artillery, and replacements early in the morning to support him in the decisive battle he expected to fight there.[98]

**An overnight rain in** Newport had made the streets dirty and the ground muddy, but Lieutenant Peebles's regiment still paraded at 11:00am and "did a few manouvres in the field." The big news of the day was about a frigate that came into port with several prizes.[99]

**In Providence, Rhode Island,** delegates to the multi-state convention tackling the issue of inflated prices ended their meeting on January 2 after fixing prices on many items, restricting the mark-up on imported goods, but did not control war munitions and left a number of decisions to the states. The price of labor had been so high that it caused discontent among soldiers and discouraged enlistments, so labor prices were set. The convention recommended to cease printing paper money, unless it bore interest at four percent, and that funds for the war be raised by taxation. These suggested policies, crafted during the ten crucial days of revolution, were not approved by Congress until February 1777.[100]

**Near Monmouth Court House,** Lieutenant Colonel John Morris, a former British lieutenant now raising the Loyalist 2nd Battalion of New Jersey Volunteers, became the target of troops under Majors John Mifflin and Adam Hubley who had been ordered to harass the British. Mifflin and Hubley arrived at Monmouth Court House that evening and learned of a party of about 200 Loyalists under Lieutenant Colonel Morris. The Americans, about 120 in number, formed up intending to attack the Loyalists at the town. However, shortly before their arrival, Lieutenant Colonel Morris ordered his men and their supply wagons to head towards Middletown. Mifflin and Hubley set off after them and engaged them shortly before sundown. The skirmish lasted about eight minutes with a "very heavy fire" kept up by both sides until the Loyalists gave way and retreated rapidly in the dark. Mifflin and Hubley took 23 men prisoner, along with seven wagon loads of stores and 12 horses, that they brought to Bordentown. The Americans marched into town and took up lodgings for the night, unaware of the battle at Trenton that day.[101]

**Not yet aware of the day's action** and still reflecting on the December 26 battle at Trenton, Delegate to Congress Thomas Nelson in Baltimore wrote, "Our affairs have had a black appearance for the two last months, but they say the Devil is not so black as he is painted. We have at last turn'd the tables upon those scoundrels by surprise, as you will see by the enclos'd paper. It was very unfortunate for us, that Ewing and Cadwalader could not get over the river, for it is almost certain, that they would have surprised a large detachment of Hessians at Mount Holly, and most probably they would have taken the greatest part of them. The number of prisoners exceeds what the General makes them by 500. He is always very moderate. Could we but get a good regular army we should soon clear the continent of these damn'd invaders."[102]

**Washington's army was still** in relatively good shape after a day of masterful delaying actions set up by Washington and carried out by Colonel Hand. Washington, however, still seemed to be trapped by Cornwallis who expected to finish him off the next day. But, was Washington actually trapped or had he planned something other than what seemed so obvious? Had he created a mask to deceive Cornwallis that the proud general could not yet see through? Cornwallis demonstrated his contempt for his enemy by not advancing to outflank Washington during his approach to Trenton and, although no documentary evidence can prove it, Cornwallis is reported to have expressed his overconfidence that evening with words to the effect that "We've got the Old Fox safe now. We'll go over and bag him in the morning."[103] Washington's soldiers at the end of their second day of a six week extension must have wondered whether they, or their comrades who had declined the extension and departed for home, had done the sensible thing. Would they ever get an opportunity to spend their ten dollar bonus for extending? Had it been a moment of weakness when they agreed to extend because of their deep love fand respect or their commander, as well as the ten dollars?

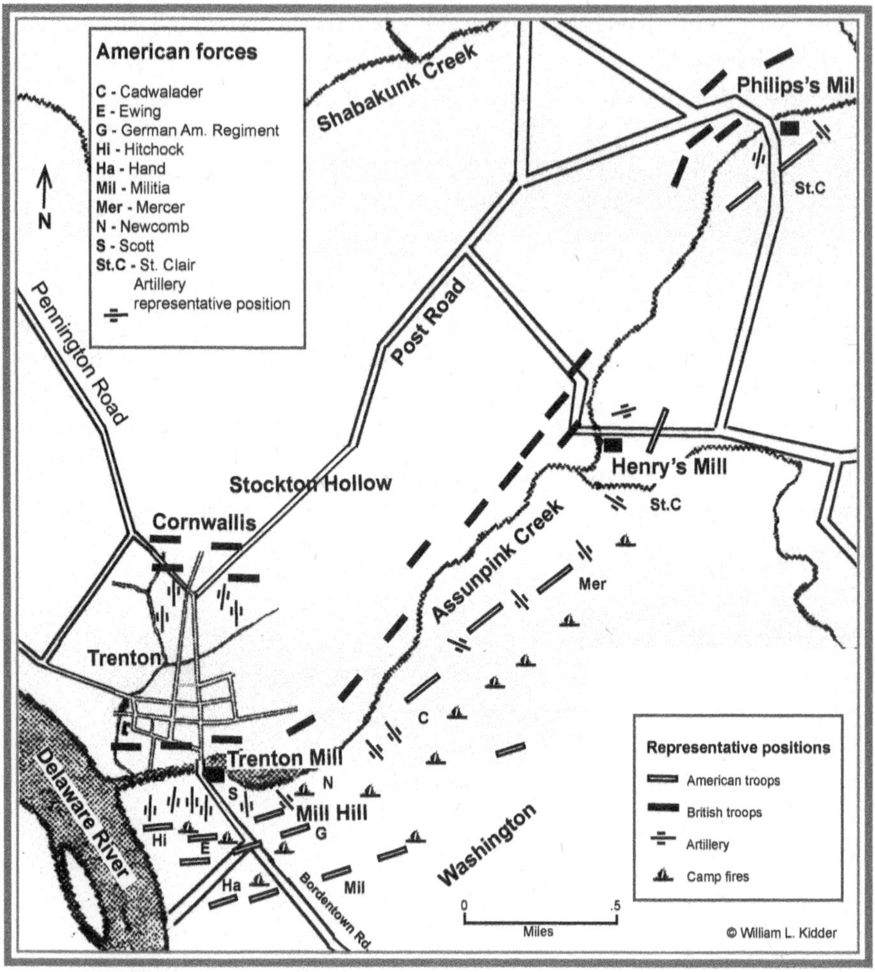


**Map 19: Troop Dispositions night of January 2, 1777**

After the firing ceased, the troops of both armies settled in for the night, built fires, cooked rations, set up sentries, withdrew from cannon range, and generally prepared to resume fighting the next morning. The British established units at the upstream fords to prevent an American flanking attack and the Americans did likewise.

# Chapter 18

## Overnight March to Princeton, Friday, January 3, 1777

Believing that his enemy was cornered and could easily be disposed of in the morning, Cornwallis called off the attack after dark to avoid the complications of night fighting and because his greatly fatigued troops needed to rest after their long day slogging through deep mud while constantly engaging with an enemy force of about 6,000 men.[1] Picket posts, without fires, were established in town, while "the remainder of the troops were withdrawn to the hills in the wood [above the northeast end of Trenton], so that there should be no further loss through the fire from the enemy's howitzers."[2] Pennsylvania rifle Sergeant James McMichael celebrated that "our artillery fire was so severe, that the enemy retreated out of town" and encamped on the high ground on the north side of town. "We continued firing bombs up to seven o'clock P.M., when we were ordered to rest, which we very commodiously did upon a number of rails for a bed."[3] John Dewey's company stationed at a ford, after exchanging cannon fire with the British "retreated a small distance to a grove of wood, in which we built our fires; the enemy encamped right against us upon the other side of the river."[4] Sentries were posted by both armies within 150 yards of each other along the Assunpink and soldiers behind the picket posts made up fires and began cooking supper. George Blakey of the 6th Virginia Regiment saw that units of the American army "encamped near the bridge," while "the British encamped on the battleground near the bridge on the opposite side, so that the sentinels of the one army were posted at one end of the bridge & of the other at the other end."[5]

Captain Thomas Rodney's men retired to the woods, encamped, and kindled fires. Rodney stated, "I then had the roll called to see if any of our men were missing and Martinas [Sipple] was not to be found, but Lieut. Mark McCall informed me, that immediately on my returning to the head of the column, after making him close up, he [Martinas] fled out of the field."[6] Sergeant White's men were "dismissed for an hour or two, to pull down all the fences we could find, to build fires with them – and get some refreshment."[7]

Lieutenant Peale reported that his company "marched to the skirts of the field, grounded our arms, made fires with the fence rails, and talked over the fatigues of the day; and some, after eating, laid themselves down to sleep." Peale also had new responsibilities because his commander, Captain Lawrence Bernie, had injured his leg some time before and had ridden on horseback rather than march on foot with the company on the overnight march from Crosswicks. During the long day of fighting on foot, though, he had suffered through his pain, but now told Peale he could no longer lead the company and had recommended him to Cadwalader to take command. Peale's first orders to his men were to take some of the baggage from the wagons and send the rest away. Peale gave each of his men a gill of rum, from a quarter cask he had in his baggage, along with a quarter of beef. He was unable to lay down to rest because of his over active mind, and in that condition "wonderfully escaped going with a surgeon of his acquaintance [most likely Dr. Rush] to assist in cuting off the limbs & dressing the wounds of those unfortunate men of that day."[8]

Stephen Olney says, "after dark, we were dismissed a little while to get our breakfast, dinner, and supper. As the night advanced it became extremely cold, and it seemed to me extravagant that our men should pull down such good cedar fences to augment our fires, and they were replenished by some stragglers, as we afterwards understood, who were ordered for that purpose."[9]

THE LONG DAY OF FIGHTING was the first time many of the American soldiers had experienced serious combat, and for Dr. Rush, "the scene which accompanied and followed this combat was new to me." During the day a number of Americans had been killed, including some men of the Cumberland County, Pennsylvania militia, and one or two men of the 3rd Philadelphia Battalion killed by a cannon shot.[10] There were also a large number of wounded who needed attention. Lesser wounds were treated by regimental medical personnel while the most severely wounded were sent to Rush, who noted that, "the first wounded man that came off the field was a New England soldier." This was probably Moses Smith of the 26th Continental Regiment who only two days before had extended his enlistment for six weeks, and now "his right hand hung a little above his wrist by nothing but a piece of skin. It had been broken by a cannon ball." Rush took him under care and got him to a house commandeered as a hospital close to the river. Smith had also received a wound shattering his thigh bone from knee to hip and he recalled being taken to a house with other wounded men, where the surgeons, thinking he would not live, removed a large number of limbs from other men before dressing his wound. Miraculously, he did live and was taken to the Philadelphia hospital where he remained until being discharged on April 1.[11] A cannon ball wound also necessitated amputation of the left hand of David Jackson, a private in the 4th Battalion Chester County Militia.[12] Private George Tilson of the 1st Pennsylvania Regiment received such a severe wound from a shot through the left leg that he was still recovering at an army hospital in September 1778, and as late as October 15, 1785, Dr. Bodo Otto attested that Tilson's wound would require a long time to completely heal, if it ever did.[13] Forest Belanger of Captain Zephaniah Steelman's company of the Gloucester County militia was mortally wounded and died that night.[14]

During the evening, Doctors Rush and Cochran, with several young men they were teaching, treated about 20 wounded men. Rush praised Cochran as one who "possesses humanity as well as skill, and is dear to all who know him." Exhausted after working into the early morning, they lay down on some straw in the same room with their patients. According to Rush, "it was now for the first time [that] war appeared to me in its awful plentitude of horrors. I want words to describe the anguish of my soul, excited by the cries and groans and convulsions of the men who lay by my side." He slept for only two or three hours.[15]

This experience at Trenton motivated Rush to study the effects of combat on soldiers. When battles commenced, he observed "thirst to be a very common sensation among both officers and soldiers. It occurred where no exercise, or action of the body, could have excited it." Officers, at the beginning of battles, even in very cold weather reported they "felt a glow of heat, so universal as to be perceptible in both their ears." He observed that soldiers bore surgery immediately after battles "with much more fortitude than they did at any time afterwards." At Trenton, he noticed that Philadelphia militiamen, accustomed to city life, suffered very little illness when sleeping hungry and poorly clothed in tents, barns, or the open cold air and displayed "patience, firmness, and magnanimity." As a strong supporter of the revolution's ideals, Rush could only attribute this "to the vigour infused into the human body by the victory of Trenton having produced insensibility to all the usual remote causes of diseases" and "an insensibility of body produced by an uncommon tone of mind excited by the love of liberty and their country."[16]

**While Rush and Cochran** treated the wounded and the British, Hessian, and American fighting men rested and prepared to renew combat the next morning, Washington called a council of war at the house of Alexander Douglass, where General St. Clair had his quarters.[17] At some point during the day, Washington had moved his headquarters from the John Barnes house to Jonathan Richmond's tavern on the south side of the Assunpink Creek bridge, but had abandoned that building as well when it came within range of British artillery fire.[18] St. Clair later wrote that, "notwithstanding the army was in a very unfavourable position, the general summoned a council of the general officers at my quarters, and after stating the difficulties in his way; the probability of defeat, and the consequences that would necessarily result if it happened, desired advice."

Even though Washington probably knew exactly what he wanted to do, he invited discussion of the possible courses of action. St. Clair later said he felt pleased that he "had the good fortune to suggest the idea of turning the left of the enemy in the night: gaining a march upon him, and proceeding with all possible expedition to Brunswick." It is possible that Washington had prepared him in previous conversations to propose the plan so it would seem more collegial than if Washington had simply ordered it. St. Clair says, "General Mercer immediately fell in with it, and very forcibly pointed out both its practicability, and the advantages that would necessarily result from it." Not surprisingly, Washington "highly approved it; nor was there one dissenting voice in the council, except as to some of the details, of little moment."[19] The army would march overnight to Princeton, avoiding detection by Cornwallis, and defeat the small garrison left there before moving on to Brunswick to take or destroy British supplies. They could then move on to a defensible position at Morristown and the British would have to abandon most of New Jersey. By re-occupying Trenton to entice a British attack and then fighting the day-long delaying action, Washington had Cornwallis just where he wanted him. But, Washington had skillfully insured that his top officers felt they were part of the decision on how to extricate the army from danger.

In reality, there were no other workable options. Retreating south to Bordentown would have been difficult and very likely unsuccessful, and crossing the river back to Pennsylvania was not an option. Taking on a frontal assault at Trenton in the morning, while it might prove very costly for the British, would have almost inevitably resulted in disaster for the Americans, especially if they were flanked by British troops crossing at the Henry's and Phillips Mill fords.

Given Joseph Reed's reconnaissance towards Princeton on December 30 and the January 1 all-night guard post on the very road he would take, who saw no enemy patrols, Washington had a good idea of how he was going to proceed. Private John Lardner of the Light Horse of Philadelphia believed that Washington decided on the route he would take before the council met, because he had sent out the patrol the night before and it was "along this road Washington led his army the following night, on the memorable retreat, & with which he must have been made acquainted or the patroles would not have been placed there." He also believed that Adjutant General Joseph Reed was well acquainted with this road. Lardner also reported, "I well remember the circumstance of the Council sitting near to where the Troop was station'd, on the evening of the 2d Janry, and to have heard it confidently mentioned the next day & repeatedly afterwards as the universal sentiment -- that the thought of the movement that night originated entirely with Washington -- solely his own manoeuvre."[20] So, this may not have been a plan to extricate himself from a self-

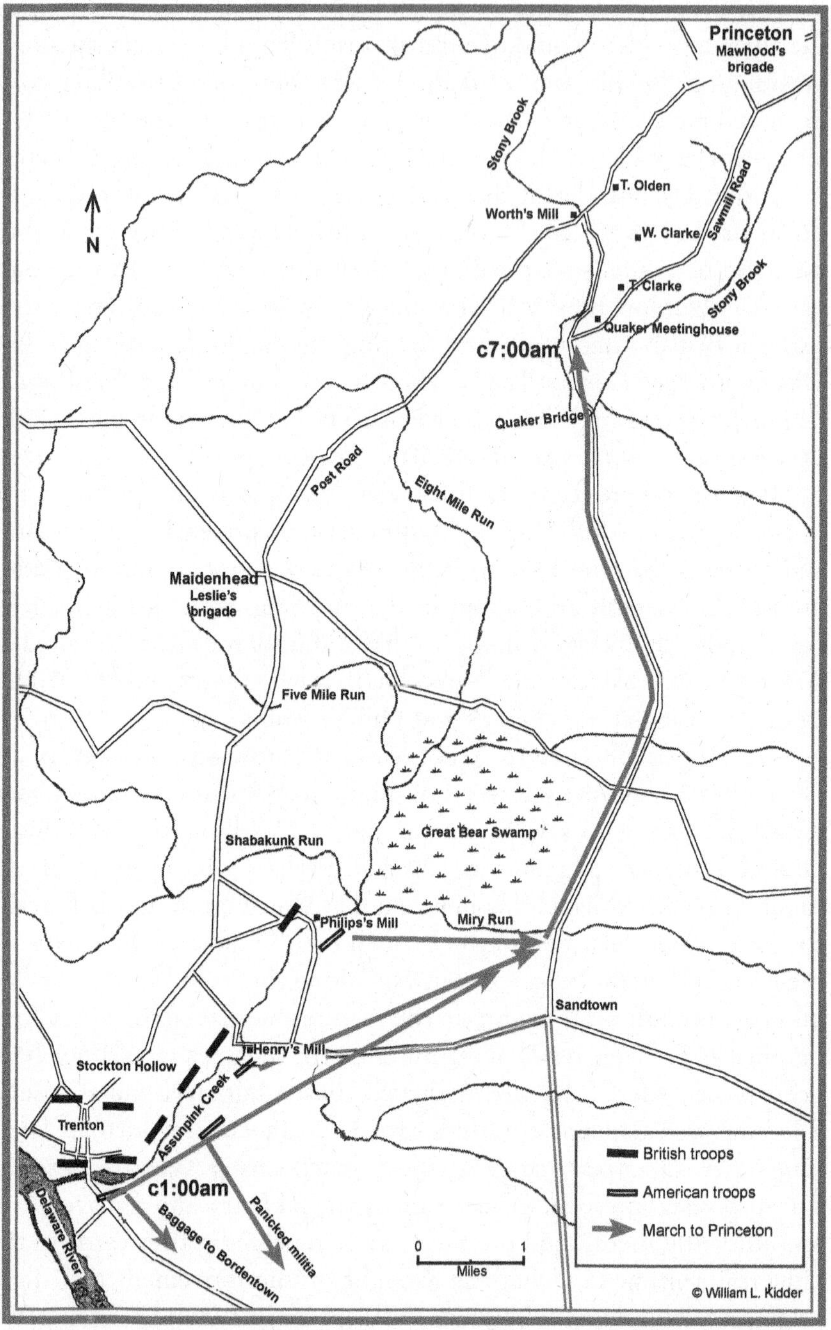


**Map 20: Washington's Night March to Princeton, January 2-3, 1777**

imposed trap, but part of Washington's overall plan to force the British from New Jersey by taking advantage of the weaknesses in their chain of cantonments and avoiding a large pitched battle with the full British army, such as Cornwallis eagerly anticipated the next morning. By not revealing the plan earlier he also avoided word of it leaking out to the British.

A British officer later concluded that, "Mr. Washington, whom we have already seen capable of great and daring enterprise [at Trenton] … and surprising the intermediate posts of communication by unexpected and rapid movements, … conceived the idea of stealing a march on the royal army" which was at that time "harassed and jaded by the long march, and the bad roads." He believed Washington was encouraged in this plan because his men, apart from those involved in the day-long delaying actions, were relatively fresh, "his intelligence good, and his knowledge of the country, through all the cuts and bye-roads, perfect."[21] Ensign Martin Hunter of the 52nd Regiment of Foot bought into Washington's deception and believed that he intended to "recross the river into Pennsylvania" when the fighting broke off. Therefore he noted, "We remained all night lying upon our arms, in expectation that he would attack us if he had not recrossed the Delaware, but he certainly made a much better manoeuvre than either, by marching during the night to Princetown."[22]

Chaplain David Avery of Connecticut stated in a sermon a year later that after the battle at Trenton on the 26th and the retreat of Donop's forces from Burlington, "this was not to be brooked by those, who seem to have imagined they were ordained to triumph, without control. As soon as those affrighted troops [of Donop] could be rallied Cornwallis advanced upon us at Trenton, his heart full of wrath, and swords in his lips, breathing forth slaughter, and cruel, dire revenge! – But the great Lord of Lords, who sitteth in the heavens, laughed at him, and had him in derision! His progress was checked, with a spirit becoming the grand cause depending." Washington had protected his army by the day-long delaying retreat and now showed his true importance to the cause when, "at this juncture, nothing contributed so much to our advantage, as 'one of those stratagems of war, which fall to the lot of great abilities only to invent:' when in the dead of night, leaving the enemy unalarmed, by their own fires, on the opposite side of Trenton-Creek, we marched to Princeton."[23]

**Unaware of Washington's plan**, the American soldiers believed, as Stephen Olney put it, that they were in "the most desperate situation I had ever known it; we had no boats to carry us across the Delaware, and if we had, so powerful an enemy would certainly destroy the better half before we could embark. To cross the enemy's line of march, between this and Princeton, seemed impracticable; and when we thought of retreating into the south part of Jersey, where there was no support for an army, that was discouraging." However, "the men and officers seemed cheerful, and in great spirits; I asked Lieutenant Bridges what he thought now, of our independence. He answered cheerfully, 'I do n't know; the Lord must help us.'" Olney felt, "We must stop one moment to admire the cheerfulness and composure of the soldiers in the most trying and critical situation. … The whole American army must have seen their danger, but they seemed to feel too that the mighty mind of their commander was equal to the event."[24] They were about to find out if it was.

**Throughout the day,** although the temperature hovered around 40 degrees, a cold front came through ending the rain, clearing the skies, and bringing a shift in wind direction to the northwest. As an experienced farmer and outdoorsman, Washington knew that this signaled the onset of an overnight freeze. The temperature dropped overnight into the 20s and the muddy roads froze into a hard, though bumpy and slippery, surface on which to march troops and artillery the roughly 13 miles to Princeton.[25] According to one British officer, "The weather was at this time extremely severe; both armies lay on their arms in the snow, without tents or cover – ours, with a determination of beginning the attack at day-break."[26]

Three local 1st Hunterdon County Regiment militiamen, Elias Phillips, Patrick Lamb, and Ezekiel Anderson, who were familiar with the chosen route, were interviewed and selected to be guides for the army that night.[27] Alexander Douglass, the owner and resident of the house, was also a New Jersey militiaman and volunteered to help pilot Cadwalader's brigade.[28] Great efforts were made to keep the plan secret, but there were many rumors afoot. Major George Johnston of the 5th Virginia Regiment heard a rumor that General Howe himself was heading towards Trenton with a reinforcement of 3000 men for the attack the next morning and later erroneously felt this was why Washington decided to leave Trenton "so privately as not to be observed, [and] filed off to the left."[29]

For Washington's plan to work, the British must not become suspicious either from their own observation or intelligence from deserters or local spies. No orders could be shouted that revealed their leaving. To keep the British unaware of the withdrawal, "the sentinels paced their rounds as though nothing was about to happen. The laugh of the relieved guard was heard above the din of both armies, 'all's well' rang above the night."[30] Stephen Olney recalled, "the roads which the day before had been mud, snow, and water, were congealed now, and had become hard as a pavement and solid, and our army was ordered to parade in silence, and leave those comfortable fires. The orders for our march were given in so low a tone, that some of the colonels were at a stand which way to move their regiments."[31]

Sergeant White recalled that the fires were kept going "to deceive the enemy; to make them suppose that we were there encamped."[32] Trenton militiaman George Yard was detailed to stay back with other men and told "to keep up the fires in order to deceive the British General and induce him to believe the American army was still lying before him."[33] Troops used fence rails to keep campfires burning brightly during the night, while fatigue parties created earthworks by the old mill and strengthened those at the lower ford. The noises from constructing these defenses were intended to give the British pickets the idea that the Americans were digging in for the morning's battle. Guard posts at the fords and the bridge were strengthened and maintained through the night.[34] Twenty-six-year-old Cornelius Wells of Smallwood's Maryland Regiment had returned to Trenton that morning from his duties guarding the Hessian prisoners taken on December 26 and joined his company encamped on the Assunpink Creek. After dark, he helped build "double" the usual number of fires that Pennsylvania rifleman Cary McClelland remembered were ordered built "about two rods [33 feet] apart."[35]

In the opinion of one British officer, "it must be allowed, the deception was admirable, and it was conducted in a masterly manner; it deserves a place amongst distinguished military achievements, and was worthy of a better cause." However, this same officer noted in his 1780 history of the war that Washington's movement was in fact observed, even though it "was masked under the veil of night, and with all possible secrecy." The advanced sentries "heard the rattling of carriages, and the patroles, in going their rounds, made their reports of an uncommon hurry in the enemy's camp, that indicated they were in motion, which was visible also at times through the glimmering of their fires; and though these reports were confirmed, and carried to head-quarters, where some officers had communicated their suspicions of the enemy's forming some design, yet both the one and the other were disregarded, and the enemy permitted to proceed in the execution of their plan."[36]

British engineer Robertson, a keen observer, was one of those who picked up movements behind the fires. He noticed the Americans filing off to the left as though they might attack the British flank. He wrote in his diary that "I observed distinctly this evening the rebels filing of[f] to their left, which made Sir William [Erskine] post the 2d Battalion Grenadiers and Guards with a Battalion Hessian Grenadiers to secure that flank [at Phillips's and Henry's mills]. At the same time were apprehensive they meditated a blow on Prince Town which was but weak. Two of the 3 regiments have been order'd to join us after we saw the rebels force." However, Cornwallis could not be convinced and looked forward to crushing Washington the next morning, so the British troops lay out all night in the hard frost.[37] To Washington's benefit, Cornwallis completely misinterpreted his actions, dismissed the idea that the Americans were threatening Princeton, and instead believed they were preparing to attack his flank sometime during the night with a surprise attack, similar to the attack on Trenton on December 26.[38]

Joseph Reed wrote at midnight to General Putnam in south Jersey, giving him a brief report on the day's battle and noting that he was writing from the east side of the creek running through Trenton. His main message was that, "it was resolved to make a forced march & attack the enemy in Princeton. We are to do this with the greatest security. Our baggage is sent off toward Burlington. His Excell. begs you would march immediately forward with all the force you can collect to Crosswicks where you will find a very advantageous post –

[and place] your advanced party at Allen Town. You will also send a good guard for our baggage wherever it may be. Let us hear from you as often as possible we shall do the same by you."[39]

Sergeant Young was ordered at 1:00am to "move out with the baggage and proceed to Burlington," causing "such a hurry skurry among all our waggoners."[40] In addition to the baggage, Preserved Buffington was sent south due to his wounded hand.[41] He was just one of many sick and wounded sent to Bordentown. Sergeant McCarty had been sick for several days and "about two hours in the night" was also "ordered off with the baggage."[42]

Peale's company began to march about 1:00am and went through woods onto a road and turned north. Somewhat like Cornwallis, Peale expected they were going to surround the British and only after marching several miles learned they were taking an indirect road to Princeton and "marching pretty fast."[43]

Christopher Burlingame of Captain Oliver Pond's Company was in a party of men ordered to guard one of the fords on the Assunpink and "whether through mistake or by design I never knew we were in open sight of the enemy." They did not march initially when the army began to leave, but, "when it was ascertained the army had gone, we marched after them."[44] James Johnston's company had been detailed for the main guard and shortly after being relieved sometime later found the army was about to move out. He said, "many of the soldiers thinking they were about to be led against the enemy threw away their knapsacks. General Washington inquired at the rear of the column, who commands here? Major Bell, of Colonel Evans regiment, announced himself as in command, and received orders to remain behind for two hours, carefully observing the enemy." Johnston was one of a party sent forward with Major Bell "to reconnoiter the enemy." As they moved forward "they had a full view of the Hessians sitting round their fires smoking their pipes." When suddenly challenged by a British sentry, Johnston "and the others dropped to the ground, and lay quiet until the centinel was heard to resume his walk. They then cautiously retrograded and made report. At the expiration of the two hours Major Bell proceeded to join the main army."[45]

At some point that night, 17-year-old Chester County, Pennsylvania militiaman William Hutchison, along with militiaman Hugh Coppell, examined the battlefield near the bridge and saw that the dead bodies of the enemy "lay thicker and closer together for a space than I ever beheld sheaves of wheat lying in a field over which the reapers had just passed."[46]

According to Joseph Reed, "a working party was detached to the lower ford near the bridge in Trenton, with orders to continue busily and noisily at work till daybreak, and fires were lighted on the lower bank of the Assanpink near which the American sentinels were to be seen during the night." When the army withdrew, the advance was led by General "Mercer with the flying camp" while the main body was primarily Pennsylvania troops under Washington's command. About daybreak, 6:50am, they neared the point where Reed had captured the dragoons on December 30.[47]

When Thomas Rodney's company began its march to Princeton no one knew exactly whether they were moving out to attack the enemy in his rear or go on to Princeton. During the march, Rodney's Dover Company and the Red Feather Company of Philadelphia Light Infantry led the van while three companies of Philadelphia light infantry were at the rear. While the van marched on in good order, there was confusion in the rear and when an erroneous cry was heard that they were surrounded by Hessians, a number of militia panicked and fled towards Bordentown, while the rest of the army remained under control.[48]

Colonel Cadwalader reported that upon departure from Trenton around midnight of 2/3 January 1777, "about five hundred men, and two pieces of iron cannon, were left to amuse the enemy." That left the Continental artillery with around 33 to 35 guns to make the march to Princeton.[49]

John Howland commented on the indirect road to Princeton, noting "a considerable part of it was by a new passage, which appeared to have been cut through the woods, as the stubs were left from two to five inches high. We moved slowly on account of the artillery, frequently coming to a halt, and when ordered forward again, one, two or three men in each platoon would stand, with their arms supported, fast asleep. A platoon next in rear advancing on them, they, in walking or attempting to move, would strike a stub and fall."[50]

**The British leaders were not the only ones** unaware of the American army's departure. About 4:00am, Dr. Cochran exited his make-shift hospital and discovered the army had left. No one had thought to alert the doctors about the march to Princeton. He and Dr. Rush quickly found wagons, put their patients in them, and guessing the army had retreated to Bordentown, set off in that direction. After some hours on the road they heard distant firing, but weren't sure where it came from. Had Lieutenant Peale gone with Dr. Rush to tend the wounded, he later knew "he would have been left behind on the march of the army which took place at 12 O'clock."[51]

After the battle across the Assunpink had ceased, a small group of New Jersey militiamen not serving in organized regiments somehow obtained permission to leave camp for the night, planning to return before sunrise to be in position when the British attacked. Militia Private John Stevens of the 1st Hunterdon County Regiment, along with several militia officers including Colonel Van Cleve, General Nathaniel Heard, Colonel David Brearley and Captain Benjamin Van Cleve, "went after dark about a mile into the country to a farmer whom we all knew to procure refreshment and lodging." They ate and turned in, but well before sunrise made their way back to where they had left the army in Trenton. However, the army was gone, and Stevens says, "we were unable to find where they had gone to." They learned the baggage had been sent down towards Bordentown so they set out and soon heard the distant sounds of cannon and gunfire in the direction of Princeton which Stevens says, "assured us the army was at that place." Many years later, Stevens confessed this in his pension application noting, "This will account for my not being in the battle of Princeton."[52]

Stevens had no reason to fabricate this story, especially since it did no credit to him or the other men he mentions, and it illustrates the disorganized state of the New Jersey militia at that time, as well as the secrecy of Washington's plan. These men seem to be serving ad hoc with the army rather than in any formal capacity. They were in-between their volunteer full-time service with the five-month New Jersey militia levies which disbanded on November 30 and rejoining their regular Hunterdon and Monmouth County part-time militia regiments. These men fully intended to participate in battle on January 3, expecting it to be at Trenton, just as the British did. This story confirms it was a well-kept secret indeed. Another militiaman who missed the Battle of Princeton for a similar reason was drummer William Morris, who says, "My family lived on the route, near the Bear Swamp, and I was allowed to sleep there which I did." Returning after the army left, he "rejoined the company next morning at Princeton, after the battle was over."[53]

Another attempt to make the British believe the American army remained in Trenton apparently was made on the morning of January 3. James B. Green remembered hearing his father, a 1st Hunterdon County Regiment militiaman, and other veterans of the war talk about their experiences, including how his father received orders early on the morning of the 3rd, probably about the time the march began, to "attend at the Ferry" and appear to be readying to "cross over Washington's army[,] which was a feint."[54]

While occupying Trenton since December 30, some of the American troops were stationed at the "houses and stores belonging to William Richards, at Lamberton, near Trenton, for barracks, hospitals, and slaughter houses." At some point before the troops left, the Richards "dwelling-house was burnt down (supposed by accident) with a large quantity of mustard seed, some household goods, and a chocolate mill, &c. &c."[55] Near the same place, "a little black horse, marked on the buttock CA [Continental Army], belonging to the states, with bridle, saddle, and saddle bags" was "taken from the door of the provision store [at Lamberton] near Trenton, on the evening of the second instant." The saddle bags contained "between ten and twelve thousand dollars Continental Money, mostly in sheets of one hundred and thirty dollars. Also a few pair of stockings, a shirt, and a pair of black breeches lined with shammy, belonging to the Commissary. Also an account book with a blue cover." A newspaper advertisement several weeks later offered a $200 reward for the horse and baggage and a special note reminded readers that, "as the above is public money, it is hoped every friend to the states will use means to have it restored." If the thief returned the horse and all items, "he shall be free from farther trouble."[56]

**Early in the morning** two British officers came to the house of merchant Samuel Tucker near the head of King Street and asked for breakfast. They had learned about daybreak that the American army was gone and were "filled with astonishment" wondering how Washington could have gotten his army back across the river without being discovered.[57]

AFTER THEIR ALL-NIGHT MARCH on the frozen mud roads, the American forces approached Princeton believing that the town was occupied by a British brigade similar in size to the garrison they had defeated at Trenton. The men must have been relieved they were no longer dug in on Mill Hill awaiting an overwhelming British assault, but were on the move probably into some situation that would be better. Washington's army was larger, although very different from the one he had at Trenton the previous week. Veteran regiments were mostly now just remnants, made up of men who had extended their enlistments, while large numbers in other regiments were inexperienced militiamen who had joined the army after Trenton and only fought in the short battle and cannonade over Assunpink Creek the previous evening. Washington's forces significantly outnumbered the British at Princeton and he expected to take them by surprise, much like he had surprised the Hessians at Trenton. But, could he surprise the British in Princeton without the cover of a storm, such as the one that had luckily shielded his approach to Trenton?

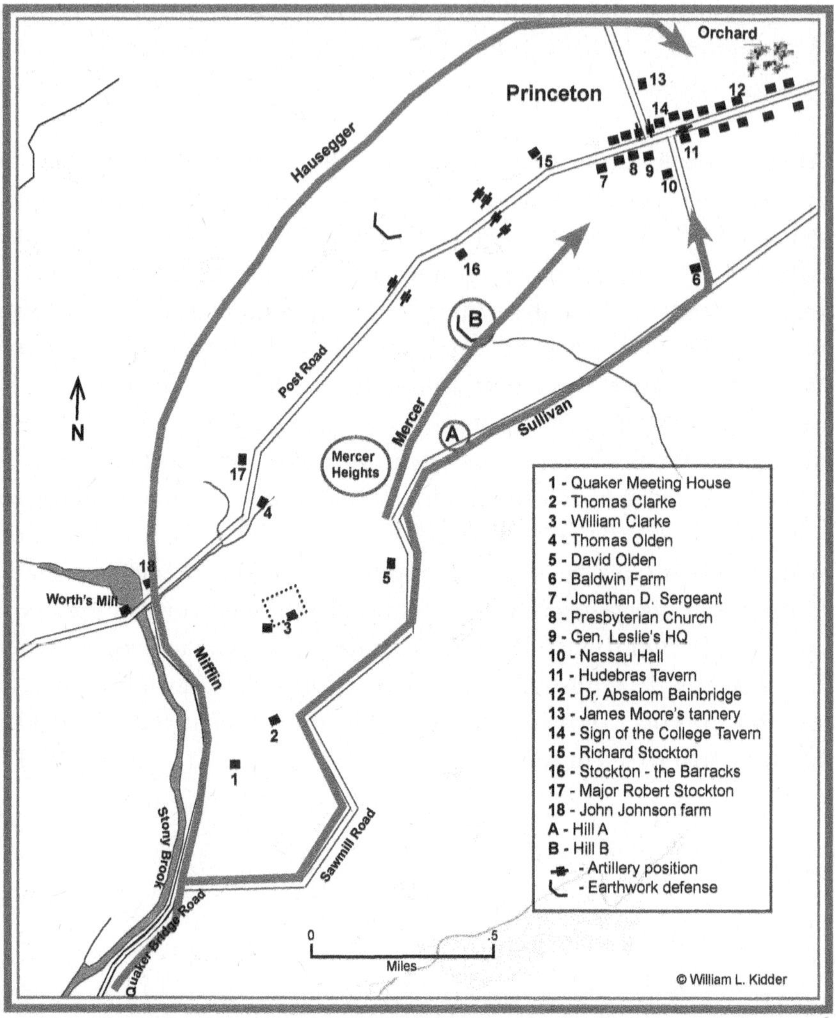


**Map 21: Washington's Plan for attacking Princeton, January 3, 1777**

Washington planned to attack Princeton with a pincers envelopment similar to what he had done at Trenton. This time there would be a third force going directly to the center of town. Compare the upper right hand corner of this map with the spy map of Princeton (Map 14 and 15 - pages 224 and 225) to see how Washington was able to use it to create his plan. This plan had to be quickly modified just as it was beginning because of the departure of most of the British troops early on the morning of January 3 to reinforce Cornwallis at Trenton.

# Chapter 19

## Battle of Princeton, Friday, January 3, 1777

In the early morning daylight, 84-year-old Robert Lawrence at Thomas Olden's house near Princeton saw British regulars from the Princeton garrison marching toward Trenton on the Trenton-Princeton Post Road (modern State Route 206).[1] Lieutenant Colonel Charles Mawhood, commanding them, was obeying orders received the previous night from Lord Cornwallis and was unaware that Washington's army was no longer at Trenton, but was actually quite close by. Captain Thomas Trewren with a troop of the 16th Light Dragoons led this force marching to support Cornwallis in his attack on Trenton with needed supplies and additional troops. The dragoons were followed by the 17th Regiment of Foot, a number of supply wagons, the 55th Regiment of Foot, four cannon and artillerymen, a squad of dismounted 16th Light Dragoons, and a number of convalescents, stragglers and recruits on their way to join their units. The 40th Regiment of Foot remained in Princeton to guard the town. The British troops on the road combined with those remaining in Princeton were similar in number to the Hessian garrison defeated at Trenton.[2]

**ABOUT 7:00AM, SOME 20 MINUTES** before sunrise, unaware that these British troops were marching south on the Post Road, Washington halted his army at a wooded area along Stony Brook about two miles from Princeton, close to the British picket position that had been

**Table 9: British Troops at Princeton, January 3, 1777**

**4th Brigade** (*Lieutenant Colonel Charles Mawhood*)
55th Regiment of Foot - 250
*Captain James Taylor Trevor*
17th Regiment of Foot (*Lieutenant Colonel Charles Mawhood*)- 246
*Lieutenant William Leslie, George Inman, Peter McDonald, Captain Lieutenant John McPherson*
40th Regiment of Foot - 333
*Captain Robert Mostyn*
16th Light Dragoon troop (dismounted) - 60
16th Light Dragoon troop (mounted) - 30
*Lieutenant Simon Wilmot, Cornet Evatt,*
Artillery - 4 guns - 30

**Troops in transit to units at Trenton**
Grenadiers - 1 company (from 43rd and 52nd Regiments) - 32
*Captain Thomas Williamson*
Light Infantry - 1 company (44th Regtiment?) - 50
42nd Regiment of Foot - 1 company - 50
Miscellaneous convalescents, recruits - 100

discontinued the day before.[3] Washington explained to his officers how they were going to surprise the garrison, using a strategy reminiscent of the previous week's plan for attacking Trenton, by enveloping the town from several directions.

Troops under General Sullivan would approach Princeton on the little known Sawmill Road, shown on the spy's map, turn left at the Baldwin farm road and attack the town, focusing on Nassau Hall known to quarter a number of the British troops. Sullivan had about 2,300 men of St. Clair's brigade of New Englanders, the Virginia brigade, Hitchcock's New England brigade, and Colonel Hand's Pennsylvania riflemen and about 13 pieces of artillery. These were some of Washington's best troops, about half of his Continentals and artillery, and about the same number of men Washington had at the Battle of Trenton.

About 500 men of Colonel Hausegger's German Battalion and the 3rd Battalion of Philadelphia Associators would march along Stony Brook and across the Post Road, then head north to the back of Princeton, cross the road to Pennington (today's Witherspoon Street), neutralize the cannon at the Hudibras Tavern, and cut off any British retreat to New Brunswick, while capturing or destroying as many of

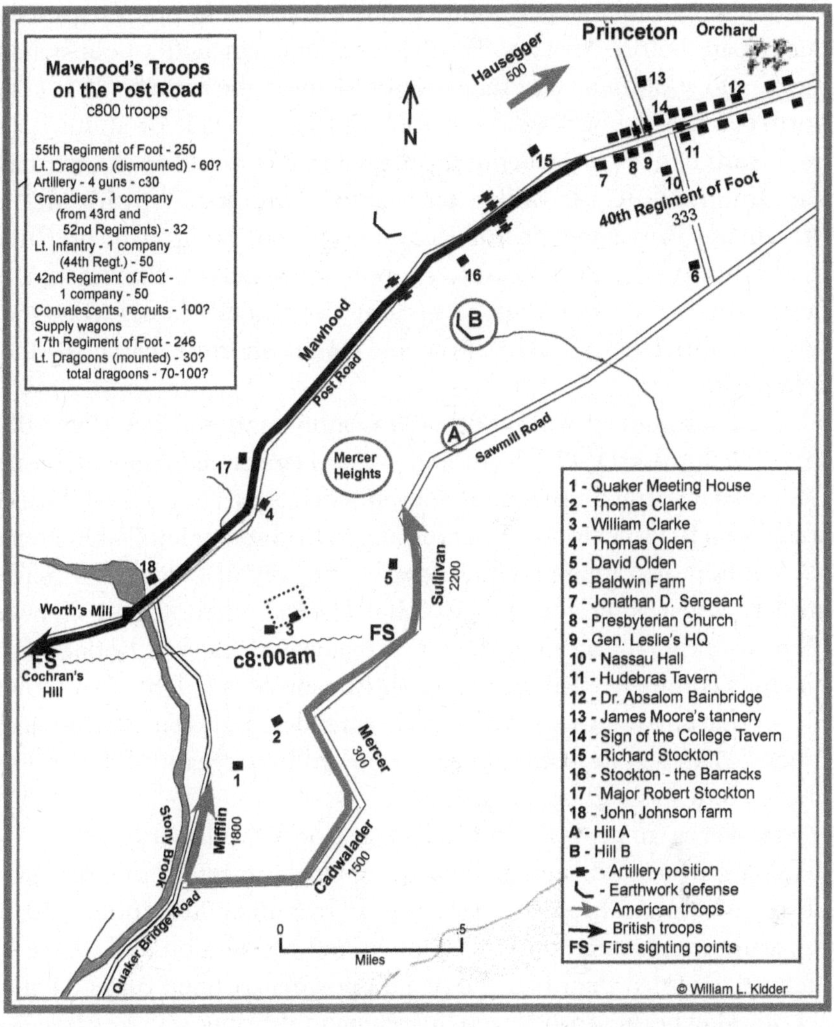


**Map 22: Battle of Princeton, January 3, 1777 - Initial Sightings c8:00am**

This map shows how Washington's plan had to be modified because of unexpected developments. The two armies were moving in opposite directions when they spotted each other about 8:00am. Neither army understood the nature of its opponent at first.

the British troops at Princeton as possible. Having the longest march, Hausegger's troops set off immediately along Stony Brook, crossed the Post Road, before Mawhood's advanced units reached a point where they could spot them, and then, out of sight of the main road, headed north towards the back of Princeton.[4] Mifflin's Brigade of about 1,500 men from five depleted Pennsylvania regiments would soon after take the same route to the bridge across Stony Brook at Worth's Mill to prevent any British troops from escaping towards Trenton, be prepared to advance on the Post Road to support the attack on Princeton, and destroy the Stony Brook bridge to delay Cornwallis's forces when they arrived from Trenton.[5] Theirs's would be the shortest march, so they held back.

General Mercer, with about 400 Continentals and between 1,000 to 1,300 New Jersey, Delaware, and Pennsylvania militia under Colonel Cadwalader formed up behind Sullivan's division. They would "march straight on to Princeton without turning to the right or left." Mercer had two cannon of Captain Neil's Eastern Company of New Jersey militia artillery and Cadwalader six. Colonel Haslet, on foot, and General Mercer, on horseback, led Mercer's brigade and Captain Rodney says his small company "flanked the whole brigade on the right in an Indian file so that my men were very much extended and distant from each other; I marched in front and was followed by sargeant McKnatt and next to him was Nehemiah Tilton."[6]

However, since most of the British troops were out of town and marching to Trenton rather than occupying Princeton, this plan was obsolete before it began. Sunrise was at 7:20am and by about 7:30am the army was formed up and the men had rested a bit and, those so inclined, downed their half gill of gun powder fortified rum.[7] As they set off, Mawhood's troops were marching in the opposite direction out of sight, but not far away.

**By around 7:50am,** Sullivan's division had turned onto Sawmill Road, marched northeast past Thomas Clarke's house, and was marching toward David Olden's house. Possibly because their eyes were diverted by the sun flashing off some metal equipment, several officers at the rear of Sullivan's division spotted two or three British dragoons to their left about a mile away on the high ground of Cochran's Hill on the Post Road.[8] Sergeant Nathaniel Root of the 20th Continental Regiment wrote that from the hill crest east-north-east of Thomas Clarke's house and a bit north of Sawmill Road, "we observed a light-horseman looking towards us, as we view an object when the sun shines directly in our faces."[9]

The British had just crossed Stony Brook at Worth's Mill where they saw and undoubtedly discussed the marks left by Hausegger's 500 troops who had recently crossed the dirt road. This should have been a clear warning that unknown troops were in the area and likely heading towards Princton. Why they neglected the duty to investigate is unknown. But, when the lead dragoons got to the top of Cochran's Hill, Cornet Henry Evatt of the 16th Light Dragoons, keeping an eye out for any trouble, spotted some unknown troops, Sullivan's column, in the distance, about the same time he was spotted by them. Evatt's troop commander, Lieutenant Simon Wilmot, immediately informed Mawhood, who "in the grey of the morning," thought the troops might be Hessians, but sent Wilmot with a trooper down "to the edge of the wood to see what they were." Wilmot shortly returned to Mawhood and reported he thought the troops were a detachment of the rebel army marching in line towards Princeton and parallel to them.[10] But, he could not accurately estimate their numbers because of the distance and the intervening tree branches. Several days later, Henry Knox wrote to Lucy that, "you may judge of their surprise when they discovered such large columns marching up. They could not possibly suppose it was our army, for that they took for granted was cooped up near Trenton. They could not possibly suppose it was their own army returning by a back road; in short, I believe they were as much astonished as if an army had dropped perpendicularly upon them. However they had not much time for consideration."[11]

Mawhood had to quickly decide whether to carry out his orders and proceed to Trenton expeditiously to support Cornwallis, or engage this enemy force of unknown size. He could have destroyed the Stony Brook bridge after his troops all crossed, to delay any pursuit while he continued on to Trenton, but this would leave the 40th Regiment of Foot vulnerable to falling into the enemy's hands. He also could not justify to himself "the idea of a flight, before the people he had long since been accustomed to conquer and despise – [and] these considerations determined him to make a stand, and put it to the issue of an action."

Mawhood decided to reverse his march and try to intercept the unknown troops on some high ground, today called Mercer Heights, before they got to town. Mawhood's troops and horse-drawn equipment awkwardly turned around on the frozen dirt road and marched back towards Princeton in reverse order with part of the 55th Regiment of Foot now in the lead, followed by the wagons, the 17th Regiment of Foot and the 16th Light Dragoons. The convalescents, transfers and recruits had been organized for this march into temporary, make-shift, company-size units under junior officers and posted between the 17th and the 55th Regiments. While turning around, Mawhood sent orders to the 40th Regiment of Foot to come to his aid. He then advanced his regiment with the light dragoons and the 55th Regiment toward Mercer Heights to intercept the Americans and sent Lieutenant Wilmot back out to learn more.[12]

Washington likewise could not see the entire British force due to trees partially blocking his view and, believing the horsemen to be merely a morning patrol sent out from Princeton, ordered Mercer's brigade to leave the line of march and attack them, while he rode on to Sullivan's division.[13] Mercer expected the British to stay on the Post Road while returning to town, so he turned his brigade to the left near Thomas Clarke's house and headed for the road in a direction that would take him past William Clarke's house and then Thomas Olden's.[14]

About that time, Wilmot had advanced to a spot, where "his retreat [would be] hazardous and difficult," within rifle range of Mercer's men, where he now also saw Cadwalader's column and realized this was a larger force than he originally had seen. When Mercer spotted Wilmot making his reconnaissance, he ordered his riflemen "to pick him off." Visibility was now good, about 8:00am, but the temperature was only around 20 degrees with a light wind and the riflemen standing in the middle of a field near Thomas Clarke's house were cold and tired from their all-night march. Several riflemen made ready to fire, but just then, Wilmot "wheeled about, and was out of their reach," and galloped off to report to Mawhood that there were two more columns in addition to the first one sighted.[15] Knowing that the escaping horseman would

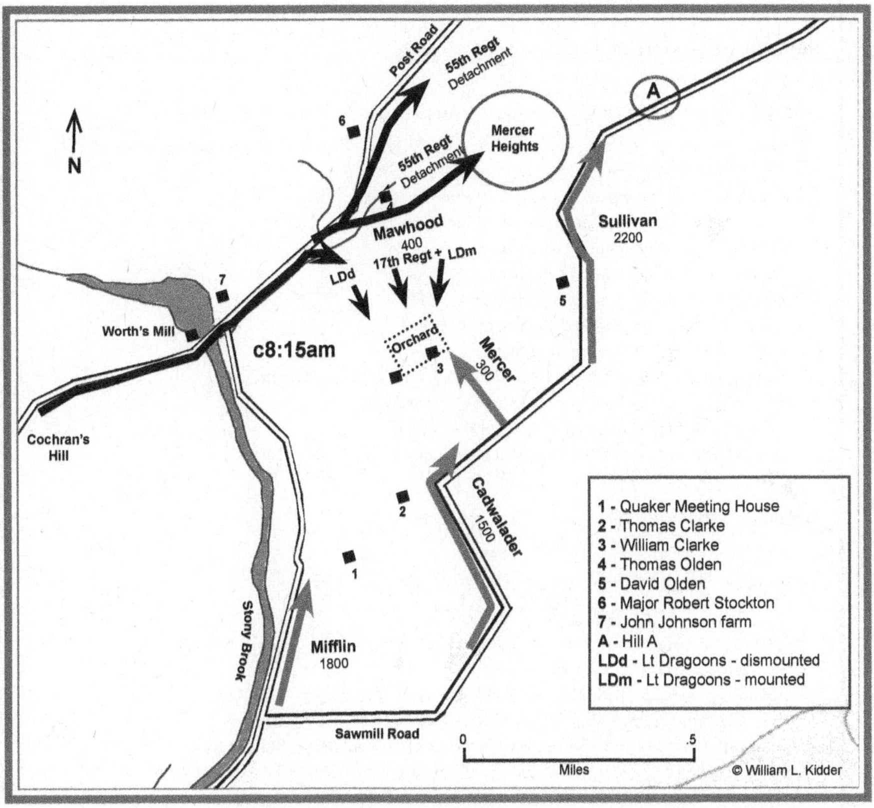


**Map 23: Battle of Princeton, January 3, 1777 - c8:15am - 8:20am**

Washington believed the British force was just a morning patrol out of Princeton and Mercer was sent to intercept it. Mawhood sent out scouts and prepared to intercept the American force before it got to Princeton. Mawhood's and Mercer's forces engaged at the beginning of the battle in the vicinity of William Clarke's orchard. During a British bayonet charge General Mercer was mortally wounded and his troops, having few bayonets, broke.

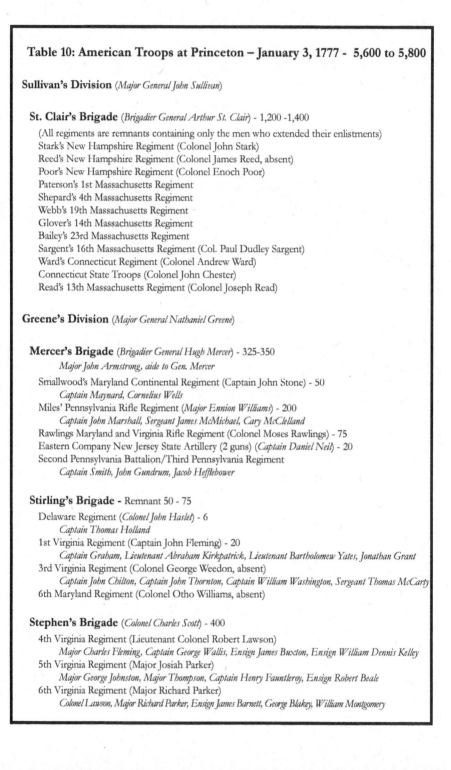

**Table 10: American Troops at Princeton – January 3, 1777 - 5,600 to 5,800**

**Sullivan's Division** (*Major General John Sullivan*)

**St. Clair's Brigade** (*Brigadier General Arthur St. Clair*) - 1,200 -1,400

(All regiments are remnants containing only the men who extended their enlistments)
Stark's New Hampshire Regiment (Colonel John Stark)
Reed's New Hampshire Regiment (Colonel James Reed, absent)
Poor's New Hampshire Regiment (Colonel Enoch Poor)
Paterson's 1st Massachusetts Regiment
Shepard's 4th Massachusetts Regiment
Webb's 19th Massachusetts Regiment
Glover's 14th Massachusetts Regiment
Bailey's 23rd Massachusetts Regiment
Sargent's 16th Massachusetts Regiment (Col. Paul Dudley Sargent)
Ward's Connecticut Regiment (Colonel Andrew Ward)
Connecticut State Troops (Colonel John Chester)
Read's 13th Massachusetts Regiment (Colonel Joseph Read)

**Greene's Division** (*Major General Nathaniel Greene*)

**Mercer's Brigade** (*Brigadier General Hugh Mercer*) - 325-350
*Major John Armstrong, aide to Gen. Mercer*

Smallwood's Maryland Continental Regiment (Captain John Stone) - 50
*Captain Maynard, Cornelius Wells*
Miles' Pennsylvania Rifle Regiment (*Major Ennion Williams*) - 200
*Captain John Marshall, Sergeant James McMichael, Cary McClelland*
Rawlings Maryland and Virginia Rifle Regiment (Colonel Moses Rawlings) - 75
Eastern Company New Jersey State Artillery (2 guns) (*Captain Daniel Neil*) - 20
Second Pennsylvania Battalion/Third Pennsylvania Regiment
*Captain Smith, John Gundrum, Jacob Hefflebower*

**Stirling's Brigade** - Remnant 50 - 75

Delaware Regiment (*Colonel John Haslet*) - 6
*Captain Thomas Holland*
1st Virginia Regiment (Captain John Fleming) - 20
*Captain Graham, Lieutenant Abraham Kirkpatrick, Lieutenant Bartholomew Yates, Jonathan Grant*
3rd Virginia Regiment (Colonel George Weedon, absent)
*Captain John Chilton, Captain John Thornton, Captain William Washington, Sergeant Thomas McCarty*
6th Maryland Regiment (Colonel Otho Williams, absent)

**Stephen's Brigade** (*Colonel Charles Scott*) - 400

4th Virginia Regiment (Lieutenant Colonel Robert Lawson)
*Major Charles Fleming, Captain George Wallis, Ensign James Buxton, Ensign William Dennis Kelley*
5th Virginia Regiment (Major Josiah Parker)
*Major George Johnston, Major Thompson, Captain Henry Fauntleroy, Ensign Robert Beale*
6th Virginia Regiment (Major Richard Parker)
*Colonel Lawson, Major Richard Parker, Ensign James Barnett, George Blakey, William Montgomery*

**Fermoy's Brigade** (*Brig. Gen. Mathias-Alexis Roche-Fermoy* - absent) - 610

German Battalion [4 Maryland and 4 Pennsylvania companies] (*Colonel Nicholas Hausegger*) – 410

*Major Ludowick Weltner, Conrad Beam*

1st Pennsylvania Rifle Regiment (Colonel Edward Hand) - 200

*Captain Henry Miller, Jacob Bottomer, George Tilson*

**Cadwalader's Brigade** (*Colonel John Cadwalader*) - 1,150

1st Battalion Philadelphia Associators (Colonel Jacob Morgan)

*Major Joseph Cowperthwaite, Ensign Anthony Morris*

2nd Battalion Philadelphia Associators (Colonel John Bayard)

*Lieutenant Charles Willson Peale, Ensign Philip Hagner, Robert Wright*

3rd Battalion Philadelphia Associators (Colonel John Nixon)

*Sergeant William Young, John Hood, John Keen*

Philadelphia Rifle Battalion (Colonel Timothy Matlack)

Philadelphia Light Infantry Company (Captain George Henry)

Chester County Militia Regiment

*Colonel Evans, Major Bell, Captain Thomas Strawbridge, Hugh Coppell, William*

Dover [Kent County, Delaware] Light Infantry Company (*Captain Thomas Rodney*)

*Lieutenant Mark McCall, Sergeant McKnatt, Mark Coudratt, Jonathan Lowber, Martinas Sipple, Nehemiah Tilton*

United States Marines (Major Samuel Nicholas) - 58

*Captain William Shippen*

2nd Company of Artillery, Philadelphia Associators (*Captain Joseph Moulder*)

*Second Lieutenant Anthony Cuthbert, Sergeant Godfrey, Zebulon Applegate*

*Captain Jehu Eyre*'s Pennsylvania militia artillery company - 67

**Hitchcock's Brigade** (*Major Israel Angell*) - 353

Lippitt's Rhode Island Regiment (Colonel Christopher Lippitt) - 160

*Captain Loring Peck, Sergeant Daniel Smith, Sergeant John Smith, Consider Bowen, Preserved Buffington, Isaiah Crandall, John Howland, Philip Rodman*

1st Rhode Island Regiment (Colonel James Varnum) - 7

2nd Rhode Island Regiment (Colonel Daniel Hitchcock) - 120

*Major Israel Angell, Captain Jeremiah Olney, Lieutenant James Bridges, Lieutenant Stephen Olney, Ensign Oliver Jencks*

4th Massachusetts's Regiment (Colonel John Nixon) - 63

12th Massachusetts's Regiment (Colonel Moses Little) - 3

*Lieutenant Joseph Hodgkins*

Massachusetts's Company of Continental Artillery (Captain Lieutenant Winthrop Sargent)

**Mifflin's Brigade** (*Brigadier General Thomas Mifflin*) - 1,500

2nd Pennsylvania Regiment (Colonel Philip De Haas)

4th Pennsylvania Regiment (Colonel Daniel Brodhead)

10th Pennsylvania Regiment (Colonel Joseph Penrose)

11th Pennsylvania Regiment (Colonel Richard Humpton)

12th Pennsylvania Regiment (Colonel William Cooke)

Northumberland County (PA) militia (Col. James Potter)

*Major John Kelly, George Espy*

Northhampton County (PA) militia

*Ensign John Hendy*

report his position, Mercer sped up his advance. He had about 120 men followed by another 200, but neglected to send out a screen of riflemen in advance. Cadwalder's brigade would follow and support him.[16]

Lieutenant Wilmot reached Mawhood on the Post Road and told him there were at least three columns of rebels marching toward Princeton on the Sawmill Road, only about half a mile from his troops on the Post Road. Mawhood decided there would not be time to intercept the first column, Sullivan's, or to try and reach Princeton before it did. The 40th Regiment of Foot would have to defend Princeton as best they could. Mawhood decided to intercept Mercer's column and immediately ordered his 17th Regiment and the dragoons up a slope to take position behind the orchard on William Clarke's farm. The speed with which the British reacted and deployed for combat displayed Mawhood's outstanding leadership and the discipline of the British soldiers. They would be well prepared to receive Mercer's troops.[17]

Robert Lawrence at Thomas Olden's house now saw the same British troops he had seen marching out of town about half an hour earlier "comeing back faster then they went." Lawrence saw a party of the 17th Regiment come into the field at his house and lay down their packs before forming up "at the corner of our garden about 60 yards from the door and then march away immediately to the field of battle which was in William Clarkes wheat field and orchard round about his house and how much further to the westward I know not [but] it was plain within sight of our door at about 400 yards distance."[18] Altogether, Mawhood had about 450 men and two cannon.[19]

Lawrence could plainly see the field where the battle was about to take place and, before hearing any gunfire, saw a man fall and immediately afterward "the report and smoke of a gun was seen and heard," followed by so much gunfire that the shots could not be counted and "we presently went down into the cellar to keep out of the way of the shot." A neighbor woman was also down in the cellar and was "so affrighted that she imagined that the field was covered with blood." He later heard that at the beginning of the battle, a woman living near the bridge on the Post Road on the Princeton side of Stony Brook had lost her leg when a cannon ball, thought to be from an American cannon, smashed her ankle.[20]

John Hood of the 3rd Battalion of Philadelphia Associators with General Hausegger had arrived near Princeton about daylight when they came through some woods and a field at the back of the town and from the orchard covered hill behind the house of Dr. Bainbridge was able to see Mawhood's column ascending Cochran's Hill, its reversal of direction, and then the beginning of the battle with Mercer's men. They undoubtedly saw the earthworks that Mawhood had begun to construct just days before.[21]

Apollos Morris wrote of Mercer's troops that, "coming near the summit of the declivity a fence between an house and a barn presented itself." They rushed through a gate "without [first] reconnoitering into a thick planted orchard and were soon surprised to find themselves in presence of a well up line of infantry with a flanking piquet and two pieces of cannon. This line was in an open field, separated from the orchard only by a two bar fence." They "pushed across the orchard (which was narrow tho' it extended a good way to the right and left) to get possession of the fence[,] hoping from the appearance of a little bank at bottom, that it would afford some shelter."[22]

Lieutenant John Armstrong, aide-de-camp to General Mercer, says, the "march was rapidly made and without seeing an enemy till gaining a position between [William] Clarke's house and barn, a British regiment already in line and greatly out-flanking us presented itself."[23] Sergeant Root in Mercer's forces described it "as we were descending a hill through an orchard, a party of the enemy who were entrenched behind a bank and fence, rose and fired upon us. Their first shot passed over our heads cutting the limbs of the trees under which we were marching." They were ordered to wheel and had just started to obey the order when the corporal standing at the left shoulder of Sergeant Root "received a ball and fell dead on the spot."[24]

Sergeant James McMichael of Miles' Pennsylvania Rifle Regiment recorded, "Gen. Mercer with 100 Pennsylvania riflemen and 20 Virginians, were detached to the front to bring on the attack. The enemy then consisting of 500 paraded in an open field in battle array. We boldly marched to within 25 yards of them, and then commenced the attack, which was very hot."[25] Jacob Hefflebower of Captain Smith's Company of the 3rd Pennsylvania Regiment encountered British fire upon reaching high ground and his regiment kept the high ground

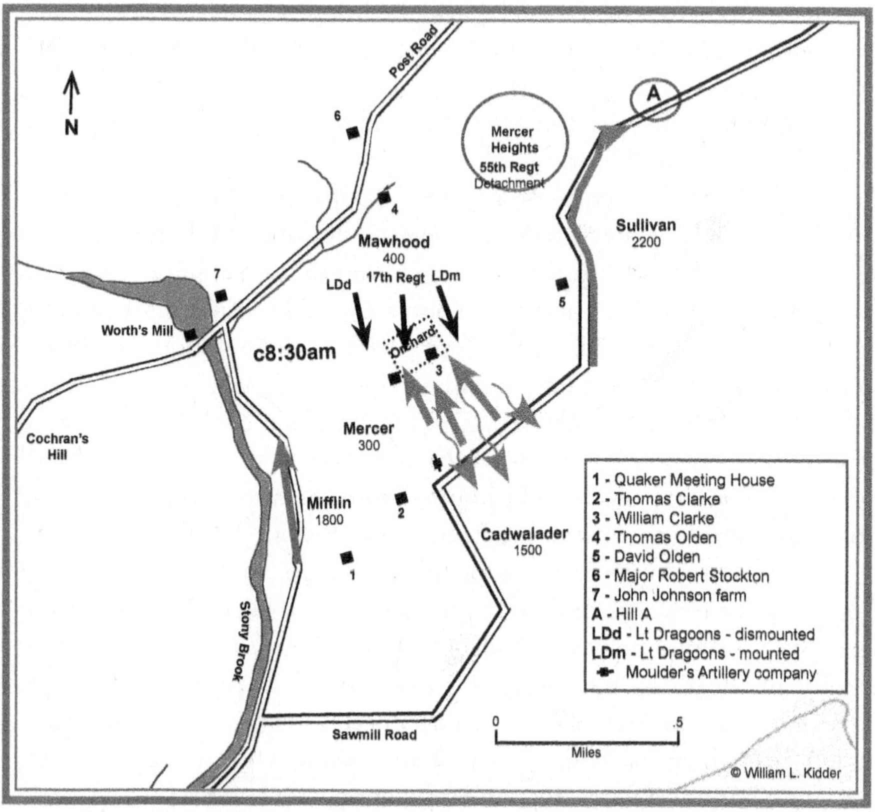


**Map 24: Battle of Princeton, January 3, 1777 - c8:30am - 8:40am**

Cadwalader's troops attempted to support Mercer's men retreating from the British bayonet charge, but also were forced to retreat in some disorder. Moulder's artillery company provided important defensive fire, but the outcome of the battle looked grim for the Americans.

advantage with the smoke from their own guns blowing towards the enemy, so that the British shots fell short.[26] After the initial British volley Sergeant Root says, "we formed, advanced, and fired upon the enemy. They retreated eight rods [44 yards] to their packs, which were laid in a line." Root recalled that he, "advanced to the fence on the opposite side of the ditch which the enemy had just left, fell on one knee and loaded my musket with ball and buckshot."[27]

Some of the miscellaneous troops travelling with Mawhood to join their regiments at Trenton were with the 17th Regiment. British Lieutenant William Hale recorded that, "the [American] advanced guard of 800 reserved their fire till we advanced within 40 yards, and then gave us a very heavy discharge, which brought down 7 of my platoon at once, the rest, being recruits, gave way. I rallied these with some difficulty, and brought them on with bayonets, the rebels poured in a second fire, and killed Capt. [Thomas] Williams[on] of the 52nd Grenadiers and Leslie of the 17th which advanced in a most excellent order, and at length we drove them through the railings, barns and orchards."[28] Captain Williamson was one of the men returning to their regiments, and a few days before had been ordered to march the men who had been in the hospital to join their regiments. Ensign Martin Hunter of the 52nd Regiment of Foot noted that Williamson was "a most accomplished man and was the third captain of the 52nd Grenadiers killed in the war."[29]

Twenty-five-year-old Captain William Leslie, a good friend of Dr. Rush, took musket balls in his left breast and side and fell on his back, with his right arm extended as he dropped his sword. His servant, Peter McDonald, rushed up to him and found him still alive, but unable to speak. Before Leslie died in McDonald's arms a few seconds later, he gestured to McDonald to take his pocket watch. McDonald placed Leslie's body in a baggage wagon and stayed close by to protect it until his own safety was threatened.[30] Lieutenant William Armstrong of the 17th Foot believed of Captain Leslie that, "a more amiable man never existed."[31]

Thomas Rodney found that the British "returned the fire and charged bayonets." Sergeant Root "heard Gen. Mercer command in a tone of distress, 'Retreat!'" but Rodney found the British "onset was so fierce that Gen. Mercer fell mortally wounded and many of his

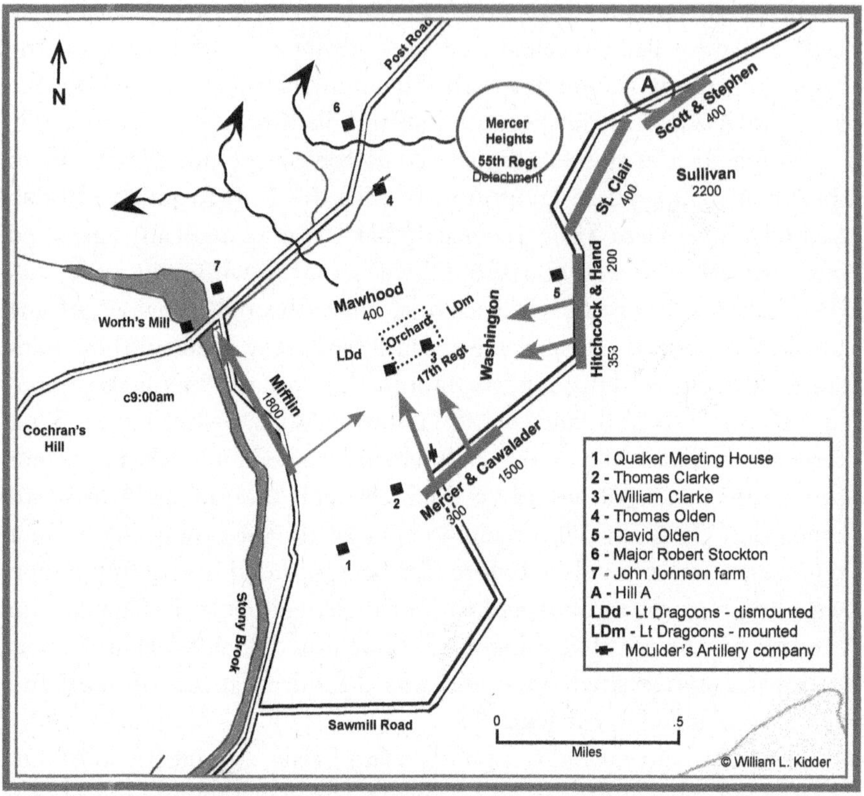


**Map 25: Battle of Princeton, January 3, 1777 - c8:40 - c9:00am**

Before the British could finish off Mercer and Cadwalader, Washington spotted what is going on and ordered Hitchchock's and Hand's brigades to follow him and attack the British from across Maxwell's Field. A portion of Mifflin's brigade, on its way to destroy the bridge at Worth's Mill, peeled off to join in the fighting. Displaying remarkable personal bravery, Washington inspired his troops to stand firm against the British and caused Mawhood's forces to retreat from the battlefield and head for Maidenhead or Princeton.

officers were killed, and the brigade being effectually broken, began a disorderly flight."[32] John Chilton of the 3rd Virginia Regiment saw that Mercer had his horse shot from under him as "he staid too much behind to conduct our retreat and was inhumanly murdered with bayonets." Cary McClelland of Captain John Marshall's company of Pennsylvania rifles saw, "Gen. Mercer had the hoof shot off his horse with a three pounder; and was himself wounded in the groin and fell. After that we had to push bayonets at the right and left wings and G Mercer was stabbed 7 times with bayonets."[33] Mercer's aide-de-camp, Major John Armstrong, was briefly pinned under his wounded horse before being rescued.[34] Also, Captain John Chilton of the 3rd Virginia Regiment recorded, Major Fleming was killed and Lieutenant Yates fell into enemy hands after receiving a "slight wound in the thigh" and the enemy "immediately butchered him with the greatest barbarity."[35] Among those killed in the heavy fighting was Captain Daniel Neil, commanding the two gun artillery company of New Jersey State militia. British Lieutenant Hale believed they kept possession of the orchard for about 20 minutes and turned one of the cannon captured from Neil's company on the Americans.[36]

Virginia rifleman Jonathan Grant in Captain Graham's company had his colonel, major, and many other officers killed and when Lieutenant Kirkpatrick fell wounded, Grant carried him from the battlefield.[37] Jacob Hefflebower of the 3rd Pennsylvania Regiment was severely wounded in the forehead by a bullet. Fortunately, he was wearing his grenadier cap with a brass plate on the front and the bullet struck the plate and helped save his life, although he fell to the ground and was carried from the battlefield by John Gundrum after the battle.[38] In the confusion of battle, Sergeant Root says he, "looked about for the main body of the army which I could not discover – discharged my musket at part of the enemy, and ran for a piece of wood, at a little distance where I thought I might shelter."[39]

**Back in Trenton, just as** Samuel Tucker poured coffee, about 8:00am, for the two British officers who had come to his house, they heard loud cannon fire and brisk small arms fire and immediately departed the house thinking that Washington had renewed the fighting. For another British officer, "a heavy cannonade, a little after day-break, effectually roused us from our slumbers, and announced the rebels attack on Prince Town."[40]

British Captain William Hall of the 28th Regiment of Foot later wrote that when Cornwallis heard the cannon fire coming from near Princeton, "there remained no room to doubt of the enemy's design, and excited apprehensions that we had not yet felt the full weight of the blow: for though the sacrifice of the three regiments at that place appeared more than probable, and became an object of momentous concern, yet it sunk, on the reflection of the loss of Brunswick, which was an event much to be dreaded, from its defenceless [sic] situation, and the weakness of the garrison, now exposed to the ravages of the rebel army, which, by a stolen march of five hours, had outstripped the King's forces."[41] Hessian Colonel Donop was not surprised, because he believed that Washington always had "sound information of our smallest movements," and must have been able to march "5 or 6 thousand" men around them and "thus surprised the garrison at Princeton."[42]

Cornwallis put his army in motion about 8:00am.[43] The soldiers from Rall's brigade who had fled town on the 26th were now re-occupying "almost all of the houses of Trenton" and no doubt had searched for any personal items they may have left behind when they escaped that battle. They may also have visited their wounded comrades being cared for by Hessian medical officer Oliva. When Donop advanced into Trenton the previous evening, he had visited the Rall brigade wounded and noted that they "had been treated very well there." The 1st Battalion of Guards led Cornwallis's troops while Donop's brigade formed the rear-guard. Donop had to leave behind Jäger Lieutenant Grothausen with his fatal chest wound. Grothausen had been severely criticized for his hasty retreat on the 26th and Ewald believed that he, like Rall, was fortunate to die from combat wounds before being court-martialed.[44]

**After the British left Trenton**, John Hayes, one of Rev. Rosbrugh's parishioners, buried Rosbrugh's body somewhere in Trenton and it was later moved to the Presbyterian churchyard, although the grave is not marked. Rosbrugh became an important martyr to the cause and, among other notices of the tragedy, Dr. Benjamin Rush wrote to Richard Henry Lee on January 14 about Rosbrugh that, "the savages [Hessians] murdered a clergyman, a chaplain to a battalion of militia, in cold blood, at Trenton, after he had surrendered himself and begged for mercy."[45] Rev. George Duffield saw the corpse before it was interred in the burying ground and observed "besides the strokes which had been given him on the head with some edged weapon, he had been stabbed with a bayonet in the back of the neck, and between his ribs on the right side, which last appeared remarkably deep, and from which, even then, there issued a large quantity of blood."[46]

**Additional assistance for the troops** at Princeton was put in motion when most of the troops still at Brunswick were ordered to march when they heard of the gunfire there and correctly believed that Cornwallis was at Trenton.[47]

**As Mercer's men retreated** on the William Clarke farm, they ran into Cadwalader's troops coming onto the field from near Thomas Clarke's house to support them. After overrunning Mercer, the 17th Regiment advanced on Cadwalader's militia "just then leaving out of a wood[,] which they likewise put in some disorder."[48] As Cadwalader lined up his forces, he saw "about fifty light infantry of the enemy [who] posted themselves behind the fence, about an hundred yards distance."[49] To counter that threat, he sent Captain Henry with about 100 light infantry.[50] Henry's men, assisted by an artillery barrage from Captain Joseph Moulder's two cannon placed on high ground to the right of the Thomas Clarke house, stopped the advance of the 17th Regiment when, "the first discharge from our field pieces on the left, drove them up to the main body."[51]

Zebulon Applegate of Moulder's artillery company says, "after we got into the field we formed a line with the artillery in the center and the other troops on each side." They had gone about three or four hundred yards "when we saw the British run out 2 pieces of field pieces from behind a large barn and orchard and fired at us." Moulder's cannon "returned the compliments and kept a heavy fire until they retreated [when] we advanced. When the battle first begun we had a bad piece of ground going down the side of a hill and after one or two rounds" we received orders to retreat and "as soon as we began to retreat the British huzzaed all along the line – we retreated about twenty or thirty yards" until told "not to go any further but to dispute the ground."[52] The British fired high over the heads of Moulder's men, while Moulder "mowed them down in rows as if they had lain down to rest."[53] Thomas Rodney noted that even British prisoners captured at the battle believed the American artillery was better served than the British and that "almost every shot from ours was placed in the thick of them while theirs flew harmless o'er our heads."[54]

**Lieutenant Peale, serving with** Cadwalader's militia, wrote that Mercer's battalion, "just ahead of us, began an exceedingly quick platoon firing, and some cannon. We marched on quickly and met some of the troops retreating in confusion. We continued our march towards the hill where the firing was, though now rather irregularly. I carried my platoon to the top of the hill, and fired, though unwillingly, for I thought the enemy too far off, and then retreated, loading. We returned to the charge, and fired a second time, and retreated as before. Coming up the third time, the enemy retreated."[55] At the time Mercer's Brigade was retreating into Cadwalader's militia, a supporting attack from the 55th Regiment of Foot could have defeated them. However, repeated calls from Colonel Mawhood to that regiment were not answered, apparently because they saw "such a slaughter among the first rank of the 17th that their commander felt it was over." During the battle, a woman who had experienced a recent miscarriage was bed ridden in her home. After a shot came through a window of her room, her husband and nurse had to carry her to the cellar for her safety.[56]

**The van of Sullivan's column** had advanced past Mercer Heights to a small hill nearer town when Washington realized the magnitude and disarray of Mercer's engagement near the Thomas Clarke farm. Virginian Robert Beale recorded, "A severe fire of musketry commenced on our left clearly within sight. When we saw our men run, they were rallied and brought to the charge, and we saw them run the second time."[57] Washington ordered Hitchcock's and Hand's brigades to go to Mercer's and Cadwalader's assistance. Colonel Hitchcock was ill, so Major Israel Angell, as the senior officer present, gave the men an inspiring short speech "encouraging them

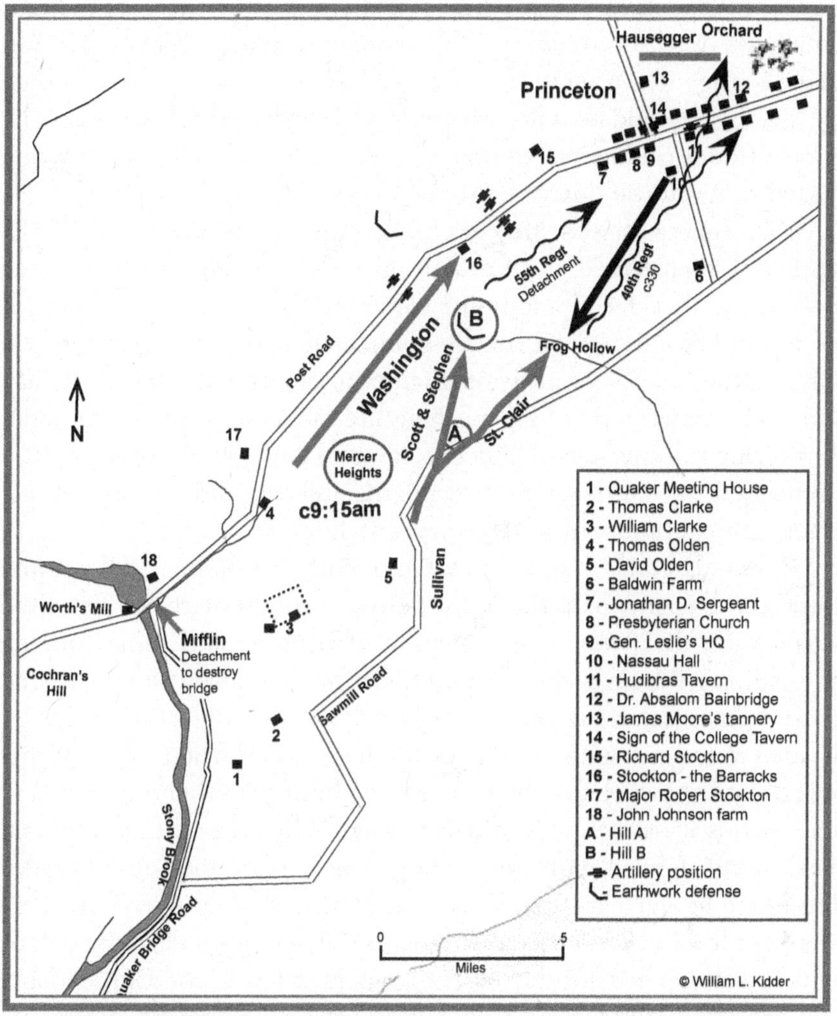


**Map 26: Battle of Princeton, January 3, 1777 - c9:00am - c9:15am**

After Mawhood's retreat, Washington's troops pressed the remaining British troops in Princeton and defeated them in several mop-up actions. There was no formal British surrender, just individuals and small groups becoming captured while others managed to escape. At that point Hausegger's troops were positioned to pick up retreating British soldiers, even though General Hausegger himself had either been captured by retreating British soldiers or had deserted to them.

to act the part that became brave soldiers, worthy of the cause for which we were contending."[58] Personally leading Hitchcock's and Hand's brigades, Washington galloped across what is today known as Maxwell's Field to rally Mercer's and Cadwalader's troops. The forces under Sullivan's command, still 1,600 to 1,800 men strong, halted to await the outcome of the battle.

The enemy chased Mercer's troops "as far as the brow of the declivity," then halted and brought up their own artillery. They were now aware they faced additional forces and given the frantic retreat of the militia, that could not be completely stopped by Washington himself, they sent a company of infantry to overrun Moulder's artillery. However, between receiving a galling fire of grapeshot from Moulder and seeing the advance of Hitchcock's men and Hand's riflemen, they exchanged "a few long shots with the militia" and then retreated, leaving their artillery behind for want of horses.[59]

After marching a short distance, Lieutenant Stephen Olney first noticed the enemy near them just before 30 or 40 of the British fired a volley on the front of the column who broke and came running through the Rhode Islander's ranks. Captain Jeremiah Olney ordered these men to join his ranks and about a dozen did, while the remainder headed for the woods. Lieutenant Olney says, "when clear of the woods and other obstructions, our column displayed and marched in line; at this instant the enemy made a full discharge of musketry and field-pieces, loaded with grape shot, which made the most horrible music about our ears I had ever heard, but as they overshot, there were but few but what continued the march, looking well at the colors, which were carried steadily by Ensign Oliver Jencks, of Cumberland, (no fool of a job to carry colors steady at such a time.)" The enemy was surprised that, "we were not all dead and that we continued to advance in order with a reserved charge for them, [and] turned their backs and fled in disorder."[60]

According to Morris, what "contribut'd to restore order was the alertness of the Philadelphia light infantry which ran up on the right flank of the pursuers and the good countenance of a New England battalion which advanced in good order in front, and some rounds of grape fired from two [of Moulder's] field pieces opportunely advanced on their left flank."[61] Cadwalader recorded that at that moment,

"I just then saw a considerable party of horse [mounted dragoons under Cornet Staples] moving off to our right, to take advantage of the confusion, but a discharge or two from the [Moulder's] cannon immediately dispersed them. I asked the General if it would not be proper to form about an hundred yards in the rear."[62]

As Sergeant Root was seeking shelter, he saw Washington at the head of the troops coming on to help the retreating men from Mercer and Cadwalader's troops and heard him yell, "Parade with us, my brave fellows, there is but a handful of the enemy, and we will have them directly." Root, along with others, "immediately joined the main body, and marched over the ground again."[63]

James Read with the Philadelphia Associators later commented to his wife, "O my Susan! It was a glorious day and I would not have been absent from it for all the money I ever expect to be worth. I happened to be amongst those who were in the first and hottest of the fire and I flatter myself that our superiors have approved of our conduct." Then he could not help writing, "I would wish to say a few words respecting the actions of that truly great man Gen. Washington, but it is not in the power of language to convey any just idea of him. His greatness is far beyond my description. I shall never forget …, when I saw him brave all the dangers of the field, and his important life hanging as it were by a single hair with a thousand deaths flying around him. Believe me I thought not of myself. He is surely America's better Genius and Heaven's peculiar care."[64] Read was referring to how Washington, after crossing Maxwell's Field, rode between the British and American lines encouraging his men, leading many to fear he would be killed.

During the fighting, John Keen of Captain Richard Humphreys's company of Cadwalader's division was slightly wounded when a cannon ball hit and splintered a fence rail while Washington was receiving some information about the enemy.[65]

So far most of the action had taken place between the houses of Thomas and William Clarke and Cadwalader's men never reached the orchard. The reforming of his forces about 100 yards in the rear took place under the cover of the hillside on the south side of Sawmill Road toward the wood. As Cadwalader reformed his troops, he "collected some of the brigade and some New Englandmen, and advanced obliquely to the right, passed a fence, and marched up to the left of the enemy. Two small parties were formed on the left, and advanced at the same time, and bravely pushed up in the face of a heavy fire. The enemy then left their station and inclined to the left, and gave us several heavy fires, in which two were killed and several wounded."[66]

**When the fighting began** between Mercer and Mawhood, Mifflin's brigade had been advancing along the Stony Brook in a ravine that cut off their view of the battlefield, although they certainly could hear what was going on. Mifflin ordered some of his units to climb out of the ravine and head for the battle, while the majority continued on to destroy the Stony Brook bridge. With Hitchcock's and Hand's forces led by Washington closing in on Mawhood from the north-east, Cadwalader, the remnants of Mercer's brigade pushing in their front, and the arrival of Mifflin's small force on his right flank created a threat of encirclement for Mawhood. As British forces disintegrated, the defeat threatened to turn into a rout. Wilkinson recalled that, "Colonel Hand endeavoured, by a rapid movement, to turn the enemy's left flank, and had nearly succeeded when they fled in disorder ... up the north side of Stoney brook." The "fox chase" was on. "We then pushed forward towards the town spreading over the fields and through the woods to enclose the enemy and take prisoners."[67] Sullivan, Stephen, and St. Clair watching the battle from afar saw that the tide of the battle had turned, and resumed their advance towards Princeton.

As his troops retreated, Mawhood ordered his cavalry to the front where they kept the Americans occupied and slowed down their pursuit. The Americans pursued those horsemen, believing they were the rear guard. This, plus a thickly wooded area, prevented the Americans from quickly discovering the escape route of the 17th Regiment.[68] In spite of very gallant behavior, the 17th Regiment and the 50 mounted dragoons retreated rapidly, leaving behind their casualties. While pursuing them, Washington came upon wounded 17th Regiment Captain-Lieutenant John McPherson, shot through the lungs, and assured him that even the privates in the 17th Regiment would be treated like officers "on account of their gallant behaviour."[69]

George Inman of the 17th Regiment, among those who escaped to Maidenhead by various routes, later wrote that, "We suffered much,"

... and "sustained a loss of 101 rank and file, killed and wounded and much the greater part by the first fire received, I being the only officer in the right wing of the battallion that was not very much injured receiving only a buck shot through my cross belt wch just entered the pit of my stomach and made me sick for the moment."[70]

By this time the 55th Regiment of Foot was hurrying towards Princeton to defend the town. Mawhood ordered a detachment of the 55th to defend a hill ("Hill B") in the path of the Americans while the rest of the regiment hurried toward Mercer Heights.

**During Hausegger's march north** towards the back of town, he sent out reconnaissance scouts who discovered Mawhood's troops marching out of Princeton, while remaining undetected. This surprise presence of British troops led to a heated discussion between Colonel Hausegger and Major Weltner. Unable to inform Washington of his discovery, Hausegger wanted to attack, but Weltner urged caution because their gunfire could disrupt Washington's battle plan and they did not yet know the strength and location of the enemy forces. Colonel Hausegger was not convinced and ordered his regiment to leave the back road and head for the enemy forces on the Post Road, with Hausegger riding ahead. By then American forces were fully engaged with the 17th Regiment.

As the battle raged in and around William Clarke's orchard, Sullivan, still on the Sawmill Road, tried unsuccessfully to get word to Hausegger to forego his mission beyond the town and rejoin the army. On his own, Hausegger, with a ten-man squad, rode into a woods heading towards the firing and was surprised and captured by a party of enemy troops, possibly some men retreating from the battlefield. The story of Hausegger's capture was controversial at the time and continues so today. It is unclear whether he was captured or deserted, as was generally believed at the time, although he always maintained his innocence, even demanding a court martial, which Washington denied him. At some point that morning, there was apparently fighting at the Princeton orchard between Hausegger's men and men from either the 40th Regiment of Foot or troops retreating from the main battle during which 24-year-old Jacob Saylor of Hausegger's battalion was cut on the face by a British bayonet, a wound that eventually cost him the sight of one eye. Saylor often played his fiddle for the diversion of his battalion and was a favorite among the men.[71]

By this time, Captain James Taylor Trevor's detachment of the 55th Regiment occupied "Hill B" and another detachment took a position on Mercer Heights. From their respective positions, Sullivan and Trevor could watch the main battle unfold in the triangular area formed by the houses of Thomas Clarke and Thomas Olden and the elevated ground occupied by Lieutenant Wilmot's dismounted dragoons on Mawhood's right flank.[72] While Sullivan and Trevor kept a frustrated eye on each other, they found themselves unable to move. Trevor was not strong enough to attack Sullivan by himself, but neither could he go to Mawhood's aid because that would open up Princeton and the 40th Regiment to attack by Sullivan. Sullivan dared not march on Princeton without better knowledge of British strength there, but neither could he go to the aide of Mercer as long as the British kept troops on Mercer Heights.

However, when it became clear that the momentum of the battle favored the Americans, Colonel Scott's Virginians headed for the fray. Scott called out to his men: "boys there are 250 red coats on yonder hill & about 250 of us, we can beat them." Ensign Beale's men, with a great "Huzzah" rushed from their position on "Hill A" to "Hill B", but found Trevor's detachment had already left it. They had seen Mawhood retreating, so Trevor proceeded to Princeton to support Captain Robert Mostyn of the 40th Regiment in command there. Approaching town, Beale's men saw a small defensive earthwork that had been thrown up along the Post Road to protect the road into town, but found it empty. They continued on to the college and looked back down the hill and saw the British running.[73] Near the end of the battle, Robert Lawrence at the Olden house says, "seven regulars was seen from our door to fall at once."[74]

As Beale's men hurried off to attack the troops they thought were on Hill B and then the earthwork at the entrance to Princeton, Sullivan's and St. Clair's brigades continued to march along Sawmill Road to the northern edge of Frog Hollow ravine, described by Wilkinson as "somewhat deep and steep," where Captain Mostyn briefly delayed Sullivan's advancing troops with some men of the 40th and 55th Regiments that he had collected.[75] Apollos Morris reported that "some of the 40th appeared pouring out of the back gate of the college and taking possession of a dike [Frog Hollow] which extended from thence down the hill." The Americans attacked, crossed the ravine, and while they were ascending "the opposite side within sixty or 80 yards of the enemy, who were still concealed from our view by the acclivity," the British turned around and headed for the college.[76] Mostyn's small force was hopelessly outnumbered and, according to Morris, was "soon removed by the fire of two field pieces," which killed Mostyn.[77]

Moulder's men, hauling their cannon toward the college, encountered British wounded begging for quarter and told them they were safe, because "we are after live men," and then handed the grateful wounded their canteens of whiskey.[78]

While British soldiers streamed back into Princeton as a disorganized mob of fugitives, some fled out what is today Witherspoon Street, passed through Rocky Hill and headed toward Brunswick. Some occupied Nassau Hall, knocking out glass window panes, and stationed themselves at windows to resist an American assault. When the Americans brought up their artillery and fired a shot or two, a cannonball came through a Prayer Hall window and destroyed the portrait of George II. Sergeant Root says that, "after two or three discharges, a white flag appeared at the window, and the british surrendered" and according to Peale, "we huzza'd victory." Root found the British prisoners to be "a haughty, crabbed set of men, as they fully exhibited while prisoners, on their march to the country."[79] One local tradition is that it was Princeton tanner and militia Captain James Moore, with several of his men, who burst open the door to Nassau Hall and demanded the British surrender, which was given.[80]

The skirmishes in the town of Princeton were simply mop-up actions after the primary defeat of the 17th Regiment on the Clarke farms was secured by Washington's heroic charge across Maxwell's Field which dispersed Mawhood's troops, many of whom were captured. The time was a little after 9:00am. In about two hours Washington's army had struck another chip from the myth of British invincibility, but their stay in Princeton would be short.[81]

**With the main British army** pursuing him, would Washington be able to achieve even more victories? Washington was no longer retreating from battlefield defeat, but was achieving victories by choosing his battles to avoid major actions, even when he seemed to be inviting them, as at Trenton the previous day, and defeating enemy forces he outnumbered, as he had just done at Princeton. Still wanting to force the British completely out of New Jersey, what could he do next? He had asked a lot of his men, could they do more? Could he continue to combine sound planning with good luck and enemy mistakes?

# Chapter 20

## Aftermath of Battle, Friday, January 3, 1777

As soon as the fighting ended, American soldiers came to Thomas Olden's house on the Post Road where Robert Lawrence says, "though they were both hungry and thirsty some of them [were] laughing out right, others smiling, and not a man among them but showed joy in his countenance." The sight stirred Lawrence's "old blood with love to those men that but a few minutes before had been courageously looking death in the face in relieving a part of their Country from the barbarous insults and ravages of a bold and daring enemy." When the neighbor woman who had retreated so frightened to their cellar came out, "she called earnestly to us to look out and see how all the field was quite red with blood. When none was to be seen at that distance. This I mention only to show into what strange mistakes sudden frights with the fear of death may put us into."

Soon, the "house was filled and surrounded with Genl Washington's men, and himself on horseback at the door. They brought in with them on their shoulders, their clothes besmeared with blood, two wounded regulars, one of them was shot in at his hip and the bullet lodged in his groin, and the other was shot through his body just below his short ribs." He was in great pain and died that afternoon. The other man was at their house for several days before being taken away. The Americans helped tend wounded British soldiers after the battle and "caryed them in large numbers into other houses that was near; not regarding the spoiling of their cloaths."

General Mercer was carried to the Thomas Clarke house with several other wounded men. Pennsylvania militia Ensign John Hendy later testified that he was one of those who carried Mercer to Thomas Clarke's house and that "this brave officer exclaimed as he was carried along 'Cheer up my boys the day is ours'." Local people estimated that above 20 men were carried into William Clarke's house, while 60 were carried to Princeton, possibly both Americans and British.[1]

**When Washington entered Princeton**, Mercer's and Cadwalader's brigades under Nathanael Greene remained about a quarter-mile out of town, while Sullivan's division occupied it. Sergeant Joseph White came into town with the first units and upon entering Nassau Hall discovered a fine breakfast ready to eat in one of the rooms. He went in, locked the door to keep the bounty for himself, and sat down and ate it. He also found and took from the same room a pair of shoes, a Bible, and a British officers' coat that he later sold to an American officer, since he was not permitted to wear it. Leaving the room, he saw other Americans picking up fresh British blankets and throwing away their old dirty ones, so he took one. White saw men outside Nassau Hall filling wagons with as many barrels of flour from the British stores as they could hold, and smashing the remaining barrels. At least one American soldier found a box containing hard money, and kept it for himself rather than dividing it among his company. Washington's December 31 orders, that enemy plunder was to be divided equally among those who took it, went largely unenforced.[2] Continental prisoners and about 30 men accused of being or assisting rebels were liberated from their confinement in Nassau Hall.[3]

After the battle, Sergeant Root's experiences caused him to exclaim, "O, the barbarity of man!" He was particularly struck by the barbarous treatment of the American wounded during the battle. He says, "On our retreat, we had left a comrade of ours whose name was Loomis from Lebanon, Ct., whose leg was broken by a musket ball, under a cart in a yard; but on our return he was dead, having received several wounds from a British bayonet. My old associates were scattered about groaning, dying and dead. One officer who was shot from his horse lay in a hollow place in the ground rolling and writhing in his blood, unconscious of anything around him. The ground was frozen and all the blood which was shed remained on the surface, which added to the horror of this scene of carnage."

At some point during the battle, Sergeant Root had lost the end joint of a forefinger to a musket ball, but was completely unaware of it until after the battle an officer saw blood on his clothes and his finger was "bleeding profusely." Checking himself out, he also found bullet holes in the skirt of his coat and noted, "my pack, which was made fast by leather strings, was shot from my back, and with it went what little clothing I had. It was, however, soon replaced by one which had belonged to a British officer, and was well furnished. It was not mine long, for it was stolen shortly afterwards."[4]

Ensign Anthony Morris, Jr. of the Pennsylvania Associators died three hours after being wounded. Dr. Jonathan Potts noted that he received three wounds, one on the chin, one on the knee, and the third, the mortal wound, on the right temple by a grape shot and also that the wounded General Mercer was robbed, "as he lay unable to resist on the bed, [by British soldiers] even to taking his cravat from his neck, insulting him all the time." However, Potts was able to revengefully and positively declare that the British had "never been so shamefully drubbed and out generaled in every respect. I hourly expect to hear of their whole army being cut to pieces or made prisoners."[5]

Others, not killed after being wounded, died on the field or soon after. Captain William Shippen, 27 years old, had joined the Continental Marines and, returning from a cruise shortly before the battle, had gone to camp and joined Washington. Only a few days earlier he had been described as a "smart little fellow" by Margaret Morris, after threatening to shoot her son as a Loyalist spy. He was one of 50 some marines who probably fought at Princeton and was the first United States Marine to die in a land battle. He left four children. Lieutenant Thomas Parsons of the 1st Battalion of Philadelphia County militia was wounded in the knee and died soon after, leaving a widow and two children.[6]

But, the killing of wounded men brought strong reactions from the men who witnessed it. Sergeant Young noted that after an officer was wounded in one leg, "a soldier came and knocked his brains out with the butt end of his gun. A lad that was wounded they stabbed 3 times in his side with his bayonet, which so exasperated our men that seeing two Hessians behind a tree ran at them, shot one and run the other through and that the militia behaved to [a] miricle."[7]

In contrast to British actions, a newspaper notice several weeks later stated that, "General Washington perceiving a wounded soldier belonging to the enemy laying on the field, came up to him, and after enquiring into the nature of his wound, commended him for his gallant behaviour, and assured him that he should want for nothing that his camp could furnish him. — After the General left him an American soldier who thought he was dead, came up in order to strip him; the General see[ing] it, bid the soldier begone, and ordered a sentry to stand over the wounded prisoner till he was carried to a convenient house to be dressed."[8]

After about an hour, it was apparent that the van of Cornwallis's army was getting near and orders were given to be ready to march in half an hour. This caused plundering to speed up and items taken divided among nearby soldiers, while items that could not be carried off were simply destroyed, even including rum from the local store. Before leaving town, the American forces had to be reorganized and gathered together, whether from self-motivated looting or ordered pursuit of individual British soldiers still hiding out in the area.[9]

After the battle, some individuals and groups deserted, even though it had been a victory. Some militia companies deserted bodily; in one case a whole company ran away except "a lieutenant and a lame man."[10] Jonathan Lowber and Mark Coudratt of Thomas Rodney's Delaware militia volunteers deserted.[11]

**Shortly after about 300 British troops** had surrendered and been taken prisoner, Stephen Olney heard that "our cannon, which we had left at the [Stoney Brook] bridge, west of Princeton, began to play at the enemy we had left at Trenton, who having lost sight of us last night, were in pursuit of us this morning." William McCracken of Captain Thomas Strawbridge's Company of the Chester County militia in Mifflin's brigade heard firing from muskets as his company marched to assist the Northumberland County militia to break down and set fire to the Stony Brook bridge.[12] These were the two guns of Captain Forrest's company which were protecting the Northumberland County militia party, led by Major John Kelly, ordered by Colonel James Potter to dismantle the Stony Brook bridge to delay the British forces approaching Princeton.[13]

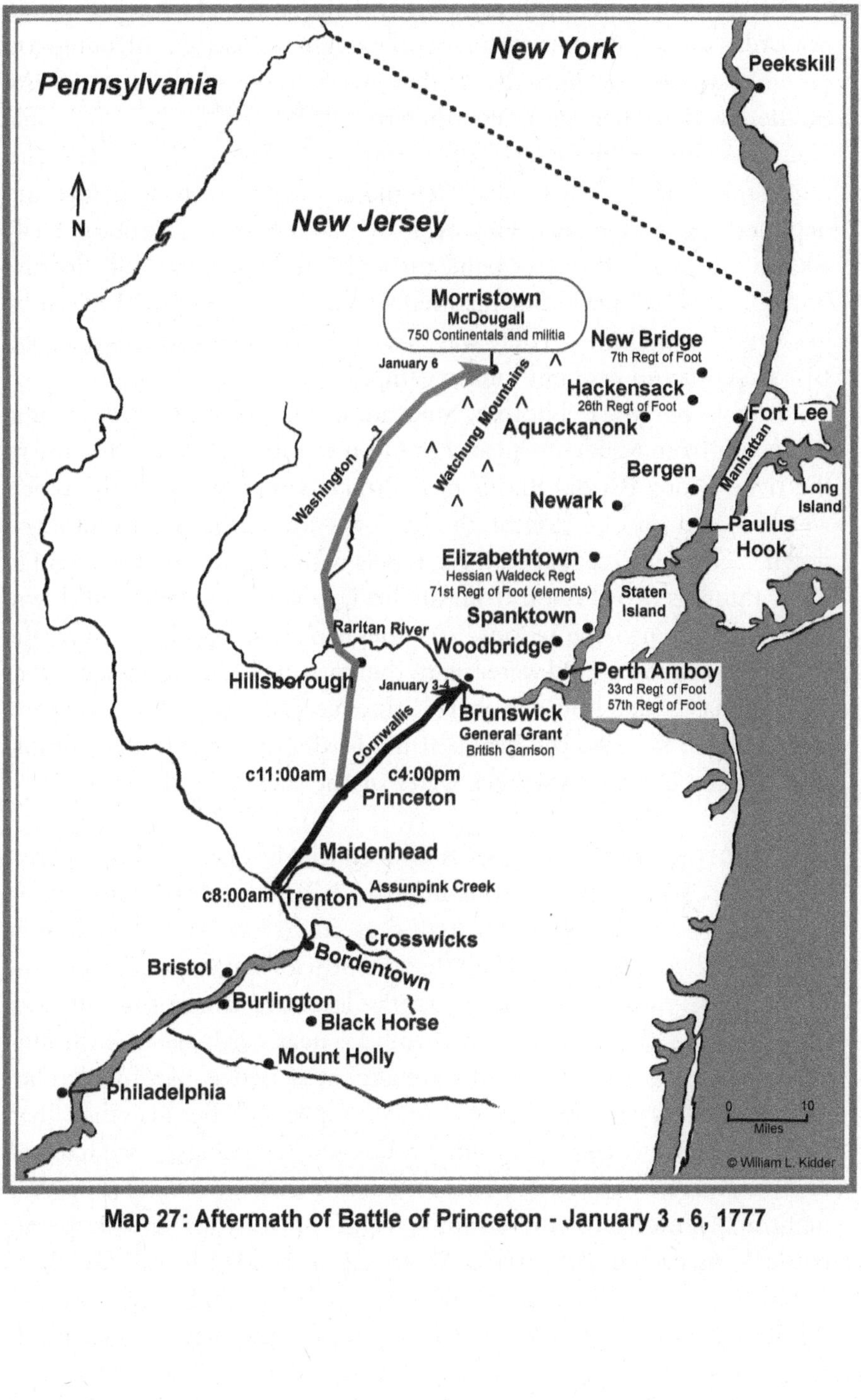


Map 27: Aftermath of Battle of Princeton - January 3 - 6, 1777

Major Kelly personally labored with his men, because he would not order men to do something people might accuse him of being too cowardly to take on himself. As they worked, the enemy opened fire on them with artillery and, according to militiaman George Espy, while Kelly was cutting "the sleeper of the bridge," it fell and Kelly "fell with it into the creek." Kelly's militiamen did not expect him to survive and departed the bridge area. However, by making great exertions, Kelly was able to reach the river bank through the high water and floating timbers, and followed after his men. Even though weighted down by his wet, frozen clothes, Kelly was even able to take prisoner an armed British scout and brought him to camp.[14]

British Sergeant Thomas Sullivan in the column approaching Princeton from Maidenhead and Trenton reported, "when we came to the river [Stony Brook] that is near Princetown, a party of the rebels were formed on one side of the bridge, and another party cutting it down." The British engaged these rebels with two 6-pounders, "and in a few minutes drove them from the bridge, which they had cut down, and retreated into the woods." As they slowly crossed the river, the British waded in icy cold water up to their waists. From his viewpoint at the Thomas Olden house, Robert Lawrence also saw that "the regulars were obliged to cross the brook at the ford with their artillery almost middle deep in water (the back water of the mill being then up)."[15]

**Washington's original plan had** been to advance with his superior force on to Brunswick to further hurt the British by destroying supplies. However, as Stephen Olney noted, they could have done this if they had 400 or 500 fresh troops, but that the previous nights' marches, "the first through mud, snow and water, the last over frozen ground, with the hardships of the day, seemed to have nearly exhausted both men and officers – some of whom were almost as bad as barefoot." They were also short of food, but "no one complained" because they "had been too busily engaged to think of hunger." In general, "we rejoiced to find ourselves so much better situated than we were the preceding night at Trenton" on the seeming verge of a major and desperate battle.[16] Instead of Brunswick, Washington decided to go directly to Morristown, over the next few days, where he would be able to watch the British during the winter and prepare for the next campaign. He would also post troops at Trenton and Princeton to keep an eye on the British at Brunswick and facilitate the movement of newly formed regiments from the south to Morristown. The Americans would then have a solid presence in New Jersey after the ten day campaign.

Sullivan's division marched out for Kingston to take position on high, defensible ground between Kingston and Rocky Hill. As they left, supplies the British had left in Princeton were burning to prevent them being used by the returning enemy. Sullivan's division was followed by Cadwalader's and Mercer's brigades which did not stop in town. Cadwalader's brigade had captured several artillery pieces, but not all could be carried off due to lack of horses. However, to upgrade his weapons, one nice brass 6-pounder was taken by Major Thomas Proctor in exchange for a less desirable iron 3-pounder. One cannon left behind was thrown into a well by the departing Americans, but another gun and ammunition wagon were later recovered by the British from the portion of the battlefield where Mercer and the 17th Regiment had engaged.[17] According to Colonel Jesse Root, the Americans could not take many of the British wagons that "were left behind by reason of the enemy's [40th Regiment] cutting the traces, and taking the horses out before our people got up."[18] When it was reported that the British were nearing, Captain Rodney was ordered to march out with "a number of carpenters … and break up the bridge [over the Millstone], which was done."[19]

Captain John Polhemus of the New Jersey Continentals, a local man serving with Washington between service in the first (1776) and second (1777) Continental Army establishments recalled, "I was left behind with a rear guard to secure stores and bury the dead, which we did by hauling them in sleds to great holes and heaping them in. I was then relieved by Colonel Chamberlain & his regiment," the 2d Hunterdon County Regiment of militia.[20] A local woman, Amy Cheston, was at Princeton that afternoon where she saw her husband, John, for the first time since he had left for Canada a year before with Polhemus.[21] Fifteen Americans and 21 British regulars were buried the next day in a stone quarry. Three that lay dead in and near the main road had been ordered by Washington to be placed in wagons and carried to town. Other dead, predominantly British, were buried by local people in other places.[22]

**Moulder's company was assigned** to the rearguard and ordered to cover the army's retreat by keeping the enemy "in check as long as safe to his men, then spike and leave his guns, and save his men by following with all speed after the main body of the army." Zebulon Applegate of Moulder's company recalled that one of their guns and 17 of Moulder's men, including him, were put on the road "close by Princetown & ordered us to stay there until the British army came up from Trenton and fire three rounds before we retreated" and moved off with the army. However, it was not long before Sergeant Godfrey "swore he would not stay there." Godfrey declared that, "he had fought that morning with anyone in the field and would do it again." But, "to stand and be slaughtered he would not." Captain Moulder told Godfrey that he would notify Washington if he disobeyed orders. However, Moulder's men refused to abandon their gun and earn the name "grass-combers" and as soon as Moulder left to find Washington, a horse and the artillerymen dragged the cannon up the road. The Light Horse of Philadelphia, under Captain Samuel Morris, successfully protected them from the pursuing British. Applegate says, "when we got about three miles we found some of the Americans tearing up a bridge [on the Millstone] that the army had gone over & we got there just in time to get over before the bridge was torn up" and "at night we overtook the main army." If they had been a few minutes longer "it would have been a lost case with us."[23]

**The night march of the** American baggage wagons to Burlington was very difficult, the horses stalled often, and when they finally reached Burlington about 12:00pm, Sergeant Young found himself "a good deal tired[,] Blessed God am very well. Got to Mrs. Annes at Burlenton. Mrs. Annes and Mrs. Bullock received me & sons kindly. Lay down and slept as soon I got to Mrs. Annes's, as did my two sons."[24]

**About the same time,** General Leslie entered Princeton, after Washington had left about 11:00am. He had marched up from Maidenhead, reached Stony Brook about 10:30am, but decided not to advance into town without support. Cornwallis's troops "marched back at quick step," but once again the road was sloppy due to warmer temperatures and it took until about 4:00pm for all the troops to reach Princeton. Ensign Thomas Glyn of the Brigade of Guards recorded that Cornwallis's column had "marched with all possible dispatch through Maidenhead[,] forded the Rivulett [Stony Brook]," and "came to the ground where the action had commenced." Captain Ewald recorded, "we found the entire field of action from Maidenhead on to Princeton and vicinity covered with corpses. … In the afternoon the entire army reached Princeton, marching in and around the town like an army that is thoroughly beaten. Everyone was so frightened that it was completely forgotten even to obtain information about where the Americans had gone. But the enemy now had wings, and it was believed that he had flown toward Brunswick to destroy the main depot, which was protected by only one English regiment."[25]

When Cornwallis's soldiers came to William Clarke's house, they questioned him, while his sick, feeble wife was insulted and robbed of her bed cloak. When she objected, she was threatened with bayonetting. The British used their bayonets to prod her bed for hiding rebels. While this was going on there were 20 wounded British soldiers lying on straw in the next room, where they had been brought by Washington's troops after the battle. Several died soon after, abandoned with no care from their fellow soldiers. Washington had ordered that the packs left in the field by Mawhood's men were to be left alone and not plundered. However, when the British came back through they plundered them.[26] Cornwallis visited both the British and American wounded and left Mercer as a prisoner on parole and assigned "five privates and one surgeon" to stay behind to tend the wounded.[27] The British found none of the enemy in town, but several companies sent into a wooded area found several wounded men from 17th Regiment, an artillery piece, and an ammunition wagon, which they secured. As they approached town they saw that "the [military supply] magazines at Prince Town were burning."[28]

The troops sent out to Princeton from Brunswick did not arrive in time to engage Washington's troops before they left town. However, they secured the cannon lost in the battle and were soon joined by the rest of the army.[29] Remnants of the 17th Regiment who had escaped to Maidenhead passed back over the field of battle about 4:00pm.[30] After Donop's rear guard from Trenton arrived back in Princeton,

Cornwallis was ready to advance and, as reported by Ensign Glyn, "having left a Flag of Truce with the sick and wounded in Prince Town was determined to make a forced march to relieve Brunswick had Genl. Washington marched to possess it or to recover General Lee. We marched at five in the evening a very hard frost and snow on the ground."[31] Before his main force left Princeton, Cornwallis sent some infantry and carpenters towards Kingston to monitor Washington's movements and repair any damage to the Millstone bridge. He also sent "a strong party of horse [up] … the road to the left of the Millstone" toward Rocky Hill.[32]

Ewald reports, "Hurriedly, the army was issued three days' rations of biscuits and brandy, left behind the stores, all the sick, the wounded, and the greater part of the baggage, and moved with such haste toward Brunswick that, although it was only a five-hour march, over one thousand wagoners first reached Brunswick toward evening on the 4th. If the enemy had pursued them with only a hundred horsemen, one after another would have been captured."[33]

Ensign Martin Hunter of the 52nd Regiment of Foot noted, "We only halted two hours at Princetown, and continued our march all night in hopes of coming up with Washington, but he was too far before us, and got into the Blue Mountains. I never experienced such a disagreeable night's march in my life. It was as dark as possible, and a very cold hard frost, and the horses being tired, the guns got on so slowly that we did not arrive at Brunswick before ten the next morning. We had been eighteen hours in marching sixteen miles." Hessian Captain Bocking noted that the men were extremely tired from the pressures of the past two days and several men stayed behind at Princeton "because of great fatigue. They could barely totter, and the march was very difficult, very cold and dark all night. We stopped several times as the baggage was between and in front of us, and at each halt somebody dropped to the ground; it was quite a job to get the men on their feet again."[34]

**While in Princeton, British** troops searched for belongings left behind when they had marched to Trenton the previous day and some plundered the town, especially the homes of anyone they considered to be a rebel supporter. By one description, they turned the town into "a deserted village; you would think it had been desolated with a plague and an earthquake, as well as with the calamities of war; the college and church are heaps of ruin; all the inhabitants have been plundered; the whole of Mr. [Richard] Stockton's furniture, apparel, and even valuable writings, have been burnt; all his cattle, horses and hogs, sheep, grain, and forage, have been carried away." A British soldier even took the shoes a blacksmith was wearing, to put on his own feet.[35] This was apparently not uncommon, because as Captain Thomas Dowdeswell wrote about that time, "The first thing our English soldiers look for is shoes, we are much in want of them, many of our men not being able to march with us, on that account."[36]

The Quaker Meeting House, the College, and the Presbyterian Church had all sustained significant damage during the occupation and battle. Pews in the Presbyterian Church were burned as kindling and a fireplace was built in the meeting house with a chimney running up through the roof.[37] The library of John Witherspoon was burned and a friend noted, "It grieves him much that he has lost his controversial tracts. He would lay aside the cloth to take revenge of them. I believe he would send them to the Devil if he could, I am sure I would."[38]

Princeton symbolized much of New Jersey that Thomas Rodney described as, "almost totally ruined & nothing can equal the brutal cruelty of the savage slaves of Brittain – what they cannot carry away they burn & destroy – nothing is sacred to their unhallow'd hands. The infirmaties of old age, the innocent weakness of babes, and the delicate form of the female, it is their sport to insult and distress – in no form has distress been seen to meet from them one humane act."[39]

**Various people arrived in Princeton** after the battle and saw its results. When Doctors Rush and Cochran had heard about the battle they, "set off immediately for Princeton and near the town passed over the field of battle still red in many places with human blood."[40] James Giberson, age 30, came to town with his Gloucester County militia company and was struck by the dead horses on the battlefield.[41]

A Somerset County militia company was on the road to Trenton when they heard the sounds of battle at Princeton and turned around and headed towards Pennytown. They "made two or three movements and lay in wait some time in the woods, for the enemy; but [the retreating British] having got intelligence of us by some Tory, returned another road, and so escaped us." The militiamen then went to the farm of Levy Hart, a 1st Hunterdon County Regiment militiaman, where they cooked provisions and rested. One militiaman recorded in his campaign journal that when they got to the Princeton battlefield, it "had a most dismal prospect of a number of pale mangled corpses, lying in the mud and blood. I felt gloomy at the awful scene. Returned in a rough tedious march to Hopewell."[42]

**Washington arrived at Rocky Hill** about 1:30 or 2:00pm and halted to allow his men a short rest. Captain John Polhemus was able to check on his house and mill at Rocky Hill that he co-owned with John Hart, his father-in-law and a signer of the Declaration of Independence. At the mill he found "at least 50 of the British which Morgans Rifles had killed, belonging to the 55th British Regiment. We buried them and going to the house I found a British Seargent in my bed with a part of his face shot off. Also a number of sick and wounded soldiers. As there was no way by which we could take them with us, I swore every man of them not to take up arms against the Independence of America, unless exchanged according to the rules of war and left them."[43]

Washington met with his officers to discuss again whether to try to get to Brunswick ahead of Cornwallis, perhaps liberate General Lee and the British supplies there, or continue to a safe place for the night. But, it was obvious to all that the men were exhausted and some had even dropped out and gone to sleep during the march from Princeton.[44] For example, John Hood, "went to a farmer's to get some refreshments [and] fell asleep" not waking until the next morning after the army had left.[45] The idea of attacking Brunswick had to be abandoned.

The army then marched off towards Somerset Court House and arrived between dusk and 8:00pm when the men got their first real rest. British prisoners were put up at the courthouse and the American troops slept either outdoors or in houses, taverns or barns. Lieutenant Peale settled his company, "into a loft amongst a fine heap of straw ... and were asleep in a few moments," too tired to even care about food. Peale did go looking for food, though, and "purchased some beef, which I got a good woman to boil, against I should call for it in the morning." He also "got a small kettle of potatoes boiled" at another house, so that his men were able to eat their first meal in two days the next morning.[46]

**A few days after the battle** at Princeton, General Howe reflected on what had happened in December and the first three days of January. To General Grant who had felt disdain for Washington's army he wrote, "You say Washingtons army is trifling to yrs. when collected, but formidable when you are divided in Cantonments – No doubt – But Cantonments are only occupied when ye Enemys army is not collected, when it is, the Cantoned army must also collect. An army you well know does not go into Cantonments to fight, but with intentions to be left quiet, & being no fortifyed Places here, we have no other resource untill we can get to Philadelphia. At ye same time I think ye Enemy will be as much tired of a winter Campaign as we can possibly be."[47] While these comments show some insight, they certainly do not reflect how he had ordered things in December.

**British Captain Thomas Dowdeswell** was about 22 or 23 years old and after the campaign suffered from eye problems caused by exposure to the cold and damp. Eventually he would lose his sight. Two weeks after the battle of Princeton, he described Cornwallis's army in the Jersey's as living in "miserable cantonments" between Amboy and Brunswick but in strong enough numbers not to fear the American troops at Morristown. His own living conditions were such that, "six or seven officers with their servants are obliged to lay upon the floor in the same room for want of quarter's, nor have we had our cloaths off since the 31st of last month [Dec]." He found the Continental Army prisoners taken at Princeton well clothed, while the militia on the other hand were "a miserable set of being's almost naked, & as the weather is now setting in severe with a fall of snow, I think they must soon quit the field." He was also aware that the rebels only had until the end of January to take advantage of Howe's amnesty proclamation. He expressed the conflicted feelings that many British officers must have struggled with that, "as a soldier, I hope they will refuse to make any terms with us. But, as a citizen, I sincerely wish the contrary."[48]

**The evening of the battle,** John Adlum learned of the results from the same man who had told him about Trenton. Regarding the people in New York, Adlum observed "their astonishment may be imagined easier than described when instead of General Howe marching to Philadelphia, we heard of the Battle of Princeton."[49]

The news at Newport, Rhode Island that day was the confirmation of the capture of General Lee on December 13, but also the first news that "900 Hessians are taken prisoners by the rebels in the Jersey, & Colo Rall kill'd in fighting his way thro' with a few men that stuck by him." Lieutenant Peebles went to a concert that night.[50]

**Captain John Chester,** while traveling home from the army to Connecticut early in January, wrote at the end of the trip, "You cannot conceive the joy and raptures the people were universally in as we passed the road[.] 'T is good to be the messenger of Glad Tidings." Passing on the victory stories of the ten crucial days as he travelled, he commented, "they make an amazing alteration in the faces of men & things."[51] Even a year later, Chaplain David Avery recalled about Trenton and Princeton that "the tidings flew upon the wings of the wind – and at once revived the hopes of the fearful, which had almost fled! How sudden the transition from darkness to light; from grief to joy!"[52] The people supporting independence were relieved from their anxiety and gained confidence in ultimate victory, taking the stories as proof that it was God's will that America should be independent no matter how strong a force Britain used against them, so that Washington's victories were both miracles and inevitable happenings.[53]

**Looking back on the ten crucial days,** Washington's British enemies acknowledged both his great qualities and the mistakes of their own leaders resulting from overconfidence. Captain Ewald wrote that while they had intended to continue the January 2nd battle at Trenton the next morning, "Washington spared us the trouble. This clever man, who did not doubt that Lord Cornwallis would realize his mistake and would dispatch a corps to the left beyond Crosswick, whereby he would be forced by circumstances to surrender, had decamped at nightfall. Since he could not risk returning across the Delaware, he made such a forced march under cover of darkness that he arrived at daybreak at Princetown." This action contributing to the rise of Washington's reputation as an "excellent general" was "simply and solely" Cornwallis's refusal to march his army in two columns from Princeton to outflank Washington at Trenton. The reason for this refusal was simply that, as at Trenton on December 26, "the enemy was despised, and as usual we had to pay for it."[54] This judgement was also made by Archibald Robertson shortly after the Princeton battle when he wrote, I "hope it will serve us as a lesson in future never to despise any enemy too much."[55]

Lieutenant Colonel Mawhood had found himself in an untenable position, heavily outnumbered by Washington's troops. His bravery, and that of his troops, as noted by Washington, was also clear to General Howe who acknowledged him in his orders at New York on January 8. He declared, "General Howe desires Lieut.-Col. Mawhood will accept his thanks for his gallantry and good conduct in the attack made upon the enemy on the 3d. Instant. He desires his thanks may also be given to the officers and soldiers of the 17th. Foot, to part of the 55th. Regiment, and other detachments on their march, who on that occasion supported the 17th. Regiment and charged the enemy with bayonet in the most spirited manner." He also acknowledged, the spirited defense of the British baggage wagons on the retreat from Princeton by men under Captain William Scott of the 17th Regiment.[56] Although defeated by a much larger force, the 17th Regiment of Foot enhanced its fine reputation.

Washington had audaciously and decisively used the important elements of "ambuscade, surprise and stratagem," valued by General William Heath, to insure the survival of his army, the War for Independence, and his own position as head of the army. Washington became confirmed in his belief that destiny had called him to command the army, and in his immediate communications with Congress may have understandably exaggerated his contributions to the successes while putting blame on others for the things that did not work out so well.[57]

Lieutenant Samuel Shaw expressed what many of the common soldiers under Washington felt after the ten crucial days. He wrote in a letter four days later, "Our army love our General very much, but yet they have one thing against him, which is the little care he takes of himself in any action. His personal bravery, and the desire he has of animating his troops by example, make him fearless of any danger. This, while it makes him appear great, occasions us much uneasiness. But Heaven, who has hitherto been his shield, I hope will still continue to guard so valuable a life."[58]

With the victory at Princeton at the end of the ten crucial days, the spectre of defeat no longer loomed large, but the war was destined to continue for another six and a half years before ending in ultimate victory. Without the successes of those ten days, the war would likely have ended in 1777 with a British victory. In saving the Continental Army, the ten crucial days forced debate to continue over whether a long-term, professional army was necessary for victory. The belief that independence was inevitable and supported by Providence made the army seem unimportant to many people, and there was still great fear in the potential tyranny of a standing, professional army and the hierarchies it promoted. Others, however, advocated for a strong army as Providence's very necessary tool and expected their leaders to have high expectations for its quality and support. Conflicting feelings about the army, and a fluctuating willingness to support it, continued throughout the remainder of the War for Independence.[59]

**Americans who believed the** War for Independence had been on the verge of failure in the final month of 1776 now had renewed enthusiasm and faith in both its righteousness and ultimate success, along with enhanced confidence in Washington's ability as commander to lead the Continental Army to ultimate victory. Washington had proven to have the necessary decisiveness, organizational skills, personal bravery, and either the approval of Providence or the extremely good luck needed to achieve victory. The army being raised for the 1777 campaign was now better able to secure recruits throughout the states, although never enough to completely fill the regiments. The New Jersey government resumed normal functions, with the legislature often meeting at Trenton or Princeton. Many citizens renounced the oaths of loyalty to King and Parliament they had felt pressured to sign for protection from British and Hessian depredations and took oaths of loyalty to their state government. Over the winter, in what became known as the Forage War, encounters occurred between British troops from Brunswick out on foraging parties and American troops who harassed them and prevented their success. These were largely local militiamen feeling renewed support from the Continental Army wintering at Morristown.

British leaders who believed that they had all but put down the rebellion in December, were now assessing whether and how the colonial uprising could ever be defeated. Lord Germain commented to Parliament in 1779, that things had looked very positive in December 1776, "But all our hopes were blasted by that unhappy affair at Trenton." And, Trenton had been just the first action of those ten crucial days that completely changed the psychology of the war.[60] General Howe had wanted to take Philadelphia before the end of the 1776 campaign and now became convinced he must take that city before sending troops north in the spring of 1777 to join with troops from Canada and take control the Hudson River Valley to cut off New England from the other colonies. As the war continued, British leaders continued to struggle unsuccessfully to find a strategy and commander that would bring victory.

The towns of Trenton and Princeton had been shattered by the British and Hessian occupation of December and the ten days of troop movements and battles. However, beginning immediately after the battle of Princeton they became critical locatons for components of the Continental Army support systems (quarter master, commissary, hospital, etc.). During the remaining six and half years of war, Washington and elements of his army would spend much of that time in New Jersey, and although the British army made additional forays into the state and several of them resulted in significant battles (Short Hills, Monmouth, Springfield, Connecticut Farms), it never again occupied New Jersey as it had in December 1776.

New Jersey endured more military encounters than most other states, especially in the north, during the War for Independence, largely because of the intense civil war between Patriots and Loyalists and the continuing presence of the British army at New York. Having suffered the string of defeats attempting to prevent British occupation of New York City in the campaign of 1776, Washington persisted throughout the war in his hope to retake it. Even while employing troops for other objectives, for the next several years he kept troops in position to attempt an attack should it become feasible, possibly in conjunction with French allies. While the Trenton and Princeton victories certainly helped the American commissioners in Paris to back-up their argument that the Americans were fully committed to winning independence, it would take the critical 1777 victory at Saratoga to convince France, and later Spain, to form an open alliance with the thirteen states and become a critical element in their final victory. However, when the French finally joined the war, they were not enthusiastic about a New York City campaign, partly because the sand bar at the approach to New York harbor was too shallow to allow their warships passage, unlike the shallower drafted British ships.

In the fall of 1781, Washington hoped once again to commence a campaign to take New York and finally complete the counter offensive he had envisioned and begun during the ten crucial days, but he had to abandon that idea and instead took much of his army, along with the French army, to Virginia. There, the French navy had made his long-time opponent, Lord Cornwallis, vulnerable to being trapped in a siege at Yorktown where the French controlled the sea to prevent British escape or resupply and the French army assisted him on land with a large number of professional troops. Trenton and Princeton had reinforced the need for the long-term, professional army that Washington now employed successfully, beside his professional French allies, because he had saved the War for Independence in those New Jersey battles with his ragged Continental remnants and untested, but enthusiastic, militia who served as a gallant stopgap to allow for, and encourage, the creation of the new and more professional Continental Army.

The ten crucial days had been an important turning point in the course of the war, but additional crisis points followed that had to be dealt with decisively, with a combination of skill and luck, in order to win independence. When those critical times occurred, Americans could always look back and take heart from the brilliant and decisive actions Washington and those with him had taken over ten crucial days between December 25, 1776 and January 3, 1777 at Trenton and Princeton.

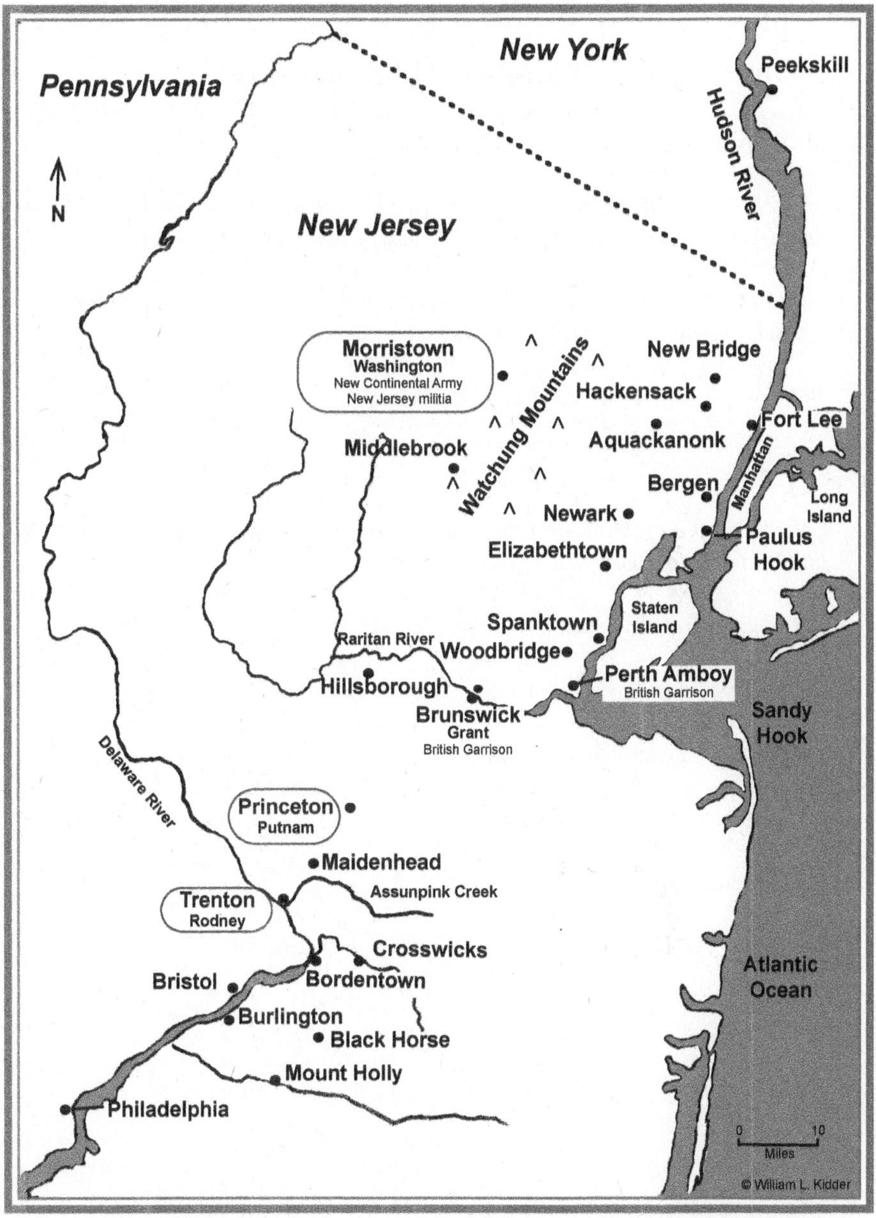


**Map 28: New Jersey - January 1777 after Battle of Princeton**

A comparison with Map 2 (page 22) shows just how much the actions of these ten crucial days removed most of the British presence from New Jersey. Instead of a long line of cantonments, the British were restricted to Brunswick and Perth Amboy. Throughout the remainder of the winter, American forces made life miserable for the British troops by harassing their foraging parties in what became known as the Forage War.

# Citation Abbreviations

Microform identifications - r – roll, i – image, p - page, f – frame

*AO12* - Great Britain, Exchequer and Audit Department. *American Loyalist Claims.* Series 1, 1776-1831, AO 12 [microform] Exchequer and Audit Department

*AO13* - Great Britain, Audit Office. *American Loyalist Claims.* Series 2, 1780-1835, AO 13 [microform] Exchequer and Audit Department

*BPMP* – Battle of Princeton Mapping Project.
Selig, Robert A., Matthew Harris, and Wade P. Catts. *Battle of Princeton Mapping Project: Report of Military Terrain Analysis and Battle Narrative, Princeton, New Jersey.* West Chester, PA: John Milner Associates, 2010.

*GWPLOC* – *George Washington Papers at the Library of Congress, 1741-1799*, available on line at memory.loc.gov

*JCC* – *Journals of the Continental Congress*

*NJSA* – New Jersey State Archives

*PA Archives* – Pennsylvania Archives

*PCC* – *Papers of the Continental Congress*

PF - Pension application file

*PMH&B* - Pennsylvania Magazine of History & Biography

# Notes

**Introduction**

1 Heath, *Heath's Memoirs,* 115-116.

2 We use the word provincials, instead of colonists, to designate those people living in the British colonies in North America. Each colony was essentially a remote province in the minds of the people who lived there.

3 Runes, *Selected Writings of Benjamin Rush,* 325-326, 333.

**Chapter 1**

1 Ferling, *Almost a Miracle,* 189; Palmer, *Washington's Military Genius,* 12, 38, 40, 49.

2 O'Shaunessy, *Men Who Lost America,* 11.

3 Ibid., 84.

4 The Battle of Bunker Hill on June 17, 1775 had resulted in a British victory, but at a tremendous cost in British lives. British officers felt that more victories of this type would be fatal to the war.

5 Anon., "A Second Appeal to the Justice and Interests of the People on the measures respecting America." Excerpted in *New England Chronicle,* May 23, 1776 (Boston, Massachusetts), 1.

6 Lord Sandwich to the King, December 17, 1776; King to Lord North from Queens House, December 17, 1776, in: Fortescue, *Correspondence of King George, III*: 408-409.

7 Nelson, *General James Grant.* Robert Grant, London, to James Grant, New York, December 20, 1776, *James Grant of Ballindalloch Papers,* reel 36. Robert Grant's father had been the business agent for James Grant's father and had mentored young James after the early deaths of his parents. James Grant's mother died when he was 10 and his father when James was 16.

8 O'Shaunessy, *Men Who Lost America,* 132, 135, 142, 143, 144.

9 Ibid., 8, 9, 53.

10 O'Shaunessy, *Men Who Lost America,* 84, 189-191; Almon, *Parliamentary Register,* I: 135.

11 O'Shaunessy, *Men Who Lost America,* 19-22.

12 Guttmacher, *America's Last King,* 129-134.

13 O'Shaunessy, *Men Who Lost America,* 27-30.

14 Palmer, *Washington's Military Genius,* 138.

15 Bowler, *Logistics and the Failure of the British Army,* 66.

16 Ritcheson, *British Politics and the American Revolution,* 211.

17 Herman, *To Rule the Waves,* 314. The common myth is that he invented them for sustenance during his card games.

18 O'Shaunessy, *Men Who Lost America,* 330-331.

19 Herman, *To Rule the Waves,* 310-311, 313.

20 Ferling, *Almost a Miracle,* 187-188.

21 Ritcheson, *British Politics and the American Revolution,* 208-209.

22 Herman,*To Rule the Waves,* 312.

23 Aitken, *Life of James Aitken.* See also: Paul, *Unlikely Allies,* 208-215.

24 Ritcheson, *British Politics and the American Revolution,* 212-213.

25 O'Shaunessy, *Men Who Lost America,* 7, 47-53, 60.

26 Ibid., 167-170, 177.

27 Brown, *American Secretary,* 63-65, 79.

**Chapter 2**

1 Bamford, "Diary," 23.

2 O'Shaunessy, *Men Who Lost America,* 88-89.

3 Smith, *Whispers Across the Atlantick,* 12. He had received word on December 15 that he was granted membership in the Order of the Bath. Ibid., 167.

4 Ambrose Serle to the Earl of Dartmouth, New York, August 12, 1776, in: Stevens, *Facsimiles,* XXIV no. 2041.

5 *New-York Gazette, and Weekly Mercury*, December 23, 1776, 3.
6 O'Shaunessy, *Men Who Lost America*, 96, 101: Fischer, *Washington's Crossing*, 161.
7 Fischer, *Washington's Crossing*, 185.
8 Davies, *Documents of the American Revolution*, XII: 266-269.
9 O'Shaunessy, *Men Who Lost America*, 101.
10 Dwyer, *The Day is Ours!*, 45.
11 Smith, *Whispers Across the Atlantick*, 172.
12 O'Shaunessy, *Men Who Lost America*, 84.
13 Howe's Orderly Book, *Early American Orderly Books, 1748-1817* [microform], r4, number 40. See December 12 for these orders.
14 Sullivan, *From Redcoat to Rebel*, 92.
15 O'Shaunessy, *Men Who Lost America*, 99-100.
16 Williams, *Biography of Revolutionary Heroes*, 148.
17 Fischer, *Washington's Crossing*, 165.
18 O'Shaunessy, *Men Who Lost America*, 102; Howe, *Narrative*, 101; Kwasny, *Washington's Partisan War*, 97.
19 Howes to Germain, December 22, 1776 from New York, Davies, *Documents of the American Revolution*, XII: 274.
20 *New-York Gazette, and Weekly Mercury*, December 23, 1776, 3.
21 Royster, *A Revolutionary People at War*, 116-117; Ambrose Serle to the Earl of Dartmouth, August 12, 1776; Unknown person to William Eden, [1778?], Stevens, *Facsimiles*, XXIV, 2041, 2102.
22 Serle, *American Journal*, 162.
23 Governor William Tryon to Germain, December 24, New York, Davies, *Documents of the American Revolution*, XII: 275.
24 Fischer, *Washington's Crossing*, 116.
25 O'Shaunessy, *Men Who Lost America*, 96.
26 Bowler, *Logistics and the Failure of the British Army*, 64-66.
27 Howe, *Narrative*, 9; Lundin, *Cockpit*, 171.
28 Luzader, *Saratoga*, 1-3; Davies, *Documents of the American Revolution*, XII: 264-266.
29 Fischer, *Washington's Crossing*, 160, 172-173, 181; Gruber, *Howe Brothers*, 345, 354; Anderson, *Command of the Howe Brothers*, 216. See also: Quartermaster Gamble's Circular, Burdentown, December 24, 1776 in Stryker, *Trenton and Princeton*, 343.
30 Ewald, *Diary of the American War*, 18-19, 25.
31 O'Shaunessy, *Men who lost America*, 13; Lutnick, *American Revolution and the British Press*, 95.
32 For more information see "Notes on the composition of the Crown Forces transfers and recruits on 3 January 1777" in Appendix III of *BPMP*.
33 O'Shaunessy, *Men Who Lost America*, 97-100. Historians debate whether the extreme casualties experienced at Bunker Hill in June 1775 played a part in Howe's efforts to prevent high casualties.
34 Smith, *Whispers Across the Atlantick*, 159, 161, 168; Howe, *Narrative*, 9-10.
35 Luzader, *Saratoga*, 1-3; K.G. Davies, *Documents of the American Revolution*, XII: 264-266.
36 Luzader, *Saratoga*, 5-8. The December 20 letters did not reach England until February 23, 1777. Davies, *Documents of the American Revolution*, XII: 266-269.
37 Howe, *Narrative*, 7-9.
38 O'Shaunessy, *Men Who Lost America*, 96, 249-250; Fischer, *Washington's Crossing*, 117-119, 121, 128, 131; Wickwire and Wickwire, *Cornwallis*, 74-78; Howe to Germain, December 20, 1776, Davies, *Documents of the American Revolution*, XII: 266.
39 Davies, *Documents of the American Revolution*, XII: 266-268; O'Shaunessy, *Men Who Lost America*, 252.
40 Dwyer, *The Day is Ours!*, 100. Quoting Clinton.
41 Serle, *American Journal*, 162; *JCC*, VI: 1018-1020.
42 Robertson, *His Diaries and Sketches in America*, 117; William Howe, New York, to James Grant, December 20, 1776, *James Grant of Ballindalloch Papers*, r36; Muenchhausen, *At General Howe's Side*, 8.
43 Oliver Woodruff, NARA M804, PF S14885.
44 Graydon, *Memoirs*, 224-225.
45 Adlum, *Memoirs*, 98-99.
46 Burrows, *Forgotten Patriots*, 62-63.

47 O'Shaunessy, *Men Who Lost America*, 11, 212, 216.
48 Fischer, *Washington's Crossing*, 126. See: Clinton, *The American Rebellion*, 115-121; Gruber, *Howe Brothers*, 135-6; Robertson, *His Diaries and Sketches in America*, 114.
49 Dwyer, *The Day is Ours!*, 46 - quoting Clinton report before he left for Rhode Island.
50 O'Shaunessy, *Men Who Lost America*, 218.
51 Peebles, *Diary*, 74. Although his 42nd Regiment was stationed with von Donop in New Jersey, the grenadier company was detached as part of the 3rd Battalion of grenadiers under Clinton.
52 Mackenzie, *Diary of Frederick Mackenzie*, I: 130.
53 Nelson, *General James Grant*, 105-108; Fischer, *Washington's Crossing*, 182-185, 188, 198.
54 William Howe at New York to James Grant, December 20, 1776; William Howe to James Grant, December 23, 1776; William Howe at New York to James Grant, December 24, 1776, in: *James Grant of Ballindalloch Papers*, r36.
55 Nelson, *General James Grant*, 108-109.
56 Collins, *A Brief Narrative*, passim, for a number of details on the suffering.
57 17th Regiment Orderly Book; Howe's Orderly Book, *Early American Orderly Books, 1748-1817* [microform] r4, Numbers 40, 41.
58 Rodney, *Diary of Captain Thomas Rodney*, 46-47.
59 Gilchrist, "The Tragedy of Captain William Leslie," 28, citing William Leslie to Lady Leven, Hillsborough, New Jersey, 25 December 1776, *Leven & Melville Papers*, Scottish Records Office, Edinburgh, GD 26/9/513/11.
60 Rush, *Autobiography*, 129.
61 17th Regiment Orderly Book; Howe's Orderly Book, Head Quarters, New York, 25th December 1776, *Early American Orderly Books, 1748-1817* [microform], r4, Numbers 40, 41

**Chapter 3**

1 Alexander McDougall at Morristown to George Washington, December 22, 1776, *GWPLOC*.
2 Lundin, *Cockpit*, 158. For more on John Hart see: Hammond, Cleon E., *John Hart: The Biography of a Signer of the Declaration of Independence*, Newfane, VT: The Pioneer Press, 1977.
3 Lundin, *Cockpit*, 163-164; *NJSA*, New Jersey Council of Safety Records, 1776-1778, Loose Records, Box 2, #21 – State of New Jersey against John Lawrence, Esq. of Upper Freehold: affidavit of Gilbert Barton, April 5, 1777; #22 – Affidavit of Thomas Farr against John Lawrence Jr., April 5, 1777; #23 – State of New Jersey against John Lawrence of Upper Freehold, Deposition of Abraham Hendricks, April 5, 1777.
4 Jones, *Life of Ashbel Green*, 121-122.
5 Royster, *A Revolutionary People at War*, 111.
6 Ramsay, *History of the American Revolution*, 314-315.
7 Lundin, *Cockpit*, 157.
8 O'Shaunessy, *Men Who Lost America*, 11, 96.
9 Ramsay, *History of the American Revolution*, 313-315.
10 Benjamin Rush to Richard Henry Lee, December 21, Rush, *Letters of Benjamin Rush*, I: 121.
11 Joseph Reed to Charles Lee, Hackensack, November 21, 1776; Charles Lee to Joseph Reed, Camp, November 24, 1776, Lee, *The Lee Papers*, II; 293-294, 305-306.
12 Samuel B. Webb to Joseph Trumbull, HQ in Bucks County on Delaware, December 16, 1776, Webb, *Correspondence and Journals*, I: 174-175.
13 William Tudor at Makefield, Pennsylvania to Delia Jarvis, December 24, 1776, *Tudor Family Papers*, Massachusetts Historical Society collections online.
14 Adam Stephen to Thomas Jefferson, December 1776 from Camp on Delaware 30 miles from Philadelphia (written between December 13 and 25 – probably about December 20), Boyd, *Papers of Thomas Jefferson*, I: 659-660.
15 George Washington to Robert Morris, HQ, December 25, 1776; George Washington to Congress, December 24, 1776, Fitzpatrick, *Writings of George Washington*, VI: 436-438, 453.
16 Rush, *Autobiography*, 117-119.
17 Royster, *A Revolutionary People at War*, 119-120.

18 This would later cause problems of its own. Some men apparently signed on for three years, some for the duration of the war, and some for three years or the duration. At the end of three years disagreements over what each man had agreed to led to much ill feeling and was one of the main issues in the mutiny of the Pennsylvania Line in January 1781.

19 Ferling, *Ascent of George Washington*, 119-120. The quoted words are Ferling's and the pages noted contain his excellent analysis of how Washington was effected by these events.

20 *JCC*, December 12, 1776, VII: 1027.

21 Elbridge Gerry to James Warren, Baltimore, December 23, 1776, Smith, *Letters of Delegates to Congress*, V: 641.

22 Samuel Adams to James Warren, Baltimore, December 25, 1776, Ibid., V: 660.

23 Burnett, *The Continental Congress*, 228-231, 235-236.

24 Rush, *Autobiography*, 123-124. Pennsylvania had no permanent, government mandated militia units, largely due to its pacifist Quaker population. The Associators were members of voluntary military groups, Associations, that had existed in the colony since before the Revolutionary War. Volunteers were called out to serve in ad hoc numbered battalions of Associators.

25 Robert Morris to John Bradford, Philadelphia, December 24, 1776, Smith, *Letters of Delegates to Congress*, V: 658.

26 Robert Morris to John Hancock, Philadelphia, December 23, 1776, Ibid., V: 647.

27 Holt, "Continental Currency," 106.

28 Robert Morris to Council of Safety, Philadelphia, December 21, 1776, Hazard, *PA Archives*, Series 1, V: 126; Robert Morris to George Washington, Philadelphia, December 23, 1776 (not sent until December 24 due to lack of way to send it.), Smith, *Letters of Delegates to Congress*, V: 648-649. See also: William Whipple to John Langdon, Baltimore, December 24, 1776, Ibid., V: 659-660, for more on the concerns about shipbuilding and need for ships.

29 Holt, "Continental Currency," 106.

30 Wilson, *Book of the First Troop*, 9.

31 Robert Morris to John Bradford, Philadelphia, December 24, 1776, Smith, *Letters of Delegates to Congress*, V: 658

32 Benjamin Rush to Richard Henry Lee, December 21, Butterfield, *Letters of Benjamin Rush*.

33 William Whipple to Josiah Bartlett, Baltimore, December 23, 1776, Smith, *Letters of Delegates to Congress*, V: 652.

34 Samuel Adams to James Warren, Baltimore, December 25, 1776, Smith, *Letters of Delegates to Congress*, V: 661-662. See also: William Ellery to Nicholas Cooke, Baltimore, December 24, 1776 (misdated December 25), Ibid., V: 655, for more on British raising foreign troops.

35 *New-York Gazette, and Weekly Mercury*, December 23, 1776, 4.

36 *Philadelphia Evening Post*, December 24, 1776, 609-610.

37 John Hancock to Robert Treat Paine, Baltimore, January 13, 1777, Paine, *Papers of Robert Treat Paine*, III: 339.

38 William Ellery to Nicholas Cooke, Baltimore, December 24, 1776 (misdated December 25), Smith, *Letters of Delegates to Congress*, V: 654, 656.

39 Oliver Wolcott to Laura Wolcott, Baltimore, December 25, 1776, Ibid., V: 667-669.

40 Benjamin Harrison to Robert Morris, Baltimore, December 25, 1776, Ibid., V: 664-5.

41 William Whipple to Josiah Bartlett, Baltimore, December 23, 1776, Ibid., V: 652.

42 William Ellery to Nicholas Cooke, Baltimore, December 24, 1776 (misdated December 25), Ibid., V: 653.

43 Elbridge Gerry to James Warren, Baltimore, December 23, 1776; Matthew Thornton to Meshech Weare, Baltimore, December 25, 1776, Ibid., V: 641, 666.

44 Benjamin Rush to Richard Henry Lee, Bristol, December 25, 1776, Ibid., V: 666.

45 Robert Morris to John Bradford, Philadelphia, December 24, 1776, Ibid., V: 658.

46 Ramsay, *History of the American Revolution*, 314-317.

47 Benjamin Rush to Richard Henry Lee, Bristol, December 25, 1776, Smith, *Letters of Delegates to Congress*, V: 666.

48 Matthew Thornton to Meshech Weare, Baltimore, December 25, 1776, Ibid., V: 667.

49 Ramsay, *History of the American Revolution*, 316-318.

50 William Whipple to Josiah Bartlett, Baltimore, December 23, 1776, Smith, *Letters of Delegates to Congress*, V: 652.
51 John Adams to Antoine Marie Cerisier, Paris, January 14, 1783, *Papers of John Adams*, XIV, Adams Papers Digital Edition, Massachusetts Historical Society.
52 *Dunlap's Maryland Gazette or The Baltimore General Advertiser*, December 24, 1776, 1. Only two pages.
53 *JCC*, VI: 1027, 1037-1039.
54 Cresswell, *A Man Apart*, xxiv-xxvi, 135; Cresswell, *Journal*, 178.
55 Watson, *Men and Times of the Revolution*, 24.
56 *Freeman's Journal or New Hampshire Gazette* (Portsmouth, New Hampshire), Tuesday, December 24, 1776, 1-4.
57 Smith, *Whispers Across the Atlantick*, 159.
58 Collin, *Journal and Biography*, 236-237. The term "naked" is found frequently in period writings, but it should be interpreted as inadequately clothed for the current conditions, rather than completely lacking clothing. "Army fever" was the general term for any feverish condition associated with a variety of illnesses.
59 John Hancock to Certain States, Baltimore, December 25, 1776, Smith, *Letters of Delegates to Congress*, V: 663 – for more on need for replacement troops
60 Anthony Wayne to General Gates, Ticonderoga, December 1, 1776, Force, *American Archives*, Series 5, III: 1031-1032.
61 Hamilton, *Fort Ticonderoga*, 166-167; Thacher, *A Military Journal*, 82-83.
62 Jordan, "The Military Hospitals at Bethlehem and Lititz," 142; Dr. William Shippen, Sr. to his Brother, January 4, 1777, *PMH&B*, XXI (1897), 497-498.

**Chapter 4**

1 A good description of this is found in Hans Huth, "Letters of a German Mercenary," 491-492. The German mercenary is Colonel Donop. Huth says, "In judging the mental attitude of the German troops that fought in the foreign service, most writers have failed to draw a distinction between the soldiers' and the officers' conceptions of that service. Certainly the majority of the soldiers were sent off under compulsion and conducted themselves accordingly. With the officers, it was different; they burned with ambition to demonstrate their valor and to win martial successes which they would not have found possible in the tedious parade-ground service of garrison duty at home. This conception of the trade of the soldier as a profession must be understood if one is to judge rightly the thought-processes of the officers of that period. Since it was generally impossible for the German officer to advance his career at home, he took service wherever a better future seemed to beckon him; but that did not at all signify the complete abandonment of his "fatherland." He goes on to say, "To the Hessian officers who, in the service of England, were to fight the rebels in America, the war seemed to offer the finest prospects of success. They did not doubt for an instant that the disturbance would soon be ended. Indeed Donop even dreamed that when that victory had been won a new war would be declared, to wit: "against all the powers in this part of the new world," for which resources would be found in Mexico and Peru. That idea did not seem to him at all fantastic, since the army numbered 60,000 men and was supported, furthermore, by the British fleet."
2 Jägers were special Hessian units based on foresters, gamekeepers, and hunters who carried rifles instead of muskets and served as light infantry and skirmishers. Some were mounted and some on foot.
3 The 42nd Regiment was then called the Royal Highland Regiment and later the Black Watch.
4 The huge number of horses employed in various capacities by all the forces in the Revolution required food to keep them healthy and in shape for their work. Working horses needed more than grass, or hay, to keep healthy. They also required grain, such as oats, for its protein and calories. Hay was usually referred to in the records as long forage, since it included the whole plant – stems, leaves, and developing seeds, and the grain as short forage, since it was essentially just the mature seeds. The animals, of course, could also eat plant material in pastures or grass lands, when available. But, keeping horses healthy was about as complex as it was for humans with the armies.

5 *James Grant of Ballindalloch Papers*, r36, frame 044. No date – orders to Donop. The exact units to be stationed at each place was modified from the original orders.
6 Lundin, *Cockpit*, 189. Donop asked for heavy artillery to be sent to Burlington to counter the galleys and efforts were underway to do this in the days before the battle at Trenton on December 26. Meunchhausen, *At General Howe's Side*, 8.
7 Jackson, *Margaret Morris*, 48-49, 57-58.
8 Fischer, *Washington's Crossing*, 198-199 – citing Donop Papers.
9 Colonel Samuel Griffin to General Israel Putnam, Headquarters Mount Holly, December 21, 1776, *PA Archives*, Series 1, V: 127.
10 *Philadelphia Evening Post*, December 24, 1776, 610; August 5, 1777, 412) (See the following pension files for soldiers involved in these actions. Colonel Richard Somers 3rd Gloucester Regiment: NARA M804, PF 2767 Ensign Cornelius McCollum of Captain David Wetherby's company; Ibid., PF S2178 Edward Dowers of Captain Samuel Snell's company who was put under Colonel Joseph Ellis of the 2nd Gloucester County Regiment and marched to Mount Holly; Ibid., PF S5686 Jeremiah Leeds of Captain Zephaniah Sherman's company; Ibid., PF S4868 David Somers of Captain John Somers company.
Lieutenant Colonel Elijah Clark's 2nd Gloucester County Regiment: Ibid., PF S4576 Simon Lucas of Captain Joseph Estell's company - Brother wounded at Petticoat Bridge.
David Potter's 2nd Cumberland County Regiment: Ibid., PF S4660 Richard Sayres. Major Westcott was among those wounded at Mount Holly.
Colonel Joseph Ellis' Regiment: Ibid., PF S28912 Richard Tice of Captain Williams's company. Also: Ibid., PF S2768 Patrick McCollum; Ibid., PF R3661 Stephen Ford wounded in the knee at battle of Petticoat Bridge; Ibid., PF R4950 Lieutenant Isaac Hickman who joined General Griffin at Moorestown; Ibid., PF S5752 Thomas McGee with friend Ephraim Seely in militia.
11 Jackson, *Margaret Morris*, 54.
12 Ewald, *Diary of the American War*, 39.
13 John Cadwalader to Colonel Donop, December 25, 176, from Bristol, *Papers of Joseph Reed* [microform]
14 Ewald, *Diary of the American War*, 39-42. Reynolds later appears on a return of prisoners on Long Island dated August 15, 1778 with the rank of Lieutenant Colonel. NARA M881 Compiled Service Records of Soldiers Who Served in the American Army During the Revolutionary War, Roll 0646. In his pension application file, John Peters, NARA M804, PF R8147 mentions the capture of Reynolds at his home and then being sent to New York. He was on parole while on Long Island.
15 Ewald, *Diary of the American War*, 18.
16 Dwyer, *The Day is Ours!*, 20-21.
17 Kwasny, *Washington's Partisan War*, 98-99.
18 [Field], "A Recently Discovered Letter," 119, 121-122
19 *NJSA*, Legislative Series, Inventories of Damages by the British and Americans in New Jersey, 1776-1782, Damage Report Claim No. 45 Elizabeth Pearson, Burlington; AO13, bundle 92.
20 Davies, *Documents of the American Revolution*, XII: 266-269; Slagle, "The von Lossberg Regiment," 89 - citing Heusser journal manuscript. For information on how the quartermasters were able to get these supplies to the men made prisoner on December 26 see: Kidder, *Crossroads of the Revolution*, 196.
21 Tucker sworn statement of February 15, 1777, *Votes and Proceedings of the General Assembly of the State of New Jersey, Session beginning August 27, 1776*, 69; Samuel Tucker to John Hart, Speaker of the Assembly, January 20, 1777, *NJSA*, BAH Box 5-02, #113.
22 *NJSA*, Legislature, Petitions, Resolutions, Transactions, Accounts and Misc papers 1700-1845, #89 – Report of private committee respecting papers in the hands of [Samuel] Tucker, 1778
23 Tucker sworn statement February 15, 17777; Randle Mitchel sworn statement, February 14, 1777; Samuel Abbot sworn statement, *Votes and Proceedings of the General Assembly of the State of New Jersey, Session beginning August 28, 1776*, 69-70; Samuel Tucker sworn statement, February 15, 1777, *NJSA*, BAH Box 5-02, #115, #117; John Abbott protection paper, NJSA, Department of Defense, Adjutant General's Office (Revolutionary War), Copies of Miscellaneous Records, 1774-1837,

Box 1, #19. Signed by M. Fox, Aid de Camp to the Commander in Chief, Headquarters, Trenton, December 9, 1776 – von Munschhausen, Adjutant. AO12 Daniel Coxe statement in Brereton Poynton file, vol 13, 302-14. See also: *NJSA*, BAH Box 5-02, #116. Some of the money that Tucker did not sign got into circulation. The law required three signatures and these bills only had two – John Hart and Samuel How. In early 1777 newspapers carried warnings that these bills were not legal tender and should not be accepted. They had been plundered by the British from the person appointed to sign them, i.e. Samuel Tucker, before he could do so. Warnings appeared as far as Baltimore. See: *Dunlap's Maryland Gazette*, Tuesday, March 4, 1777, 3; and, *The Pennsylvania Journal*, February 26, 1777, in William S. Stryker, *New Jersey Archives*, Second Series, Trenton: John L. Murphy, 1901), I: 295-296. Mary Field, "Letter," 121.

24 Tucker sworn statement, February 15, 1777, *Votes and Proceedings of the General Assembly of the State of New Jersey, Session beginning August 28, 1776*, 60, 69. For more on this story see: Kidder, *Crossroads of the Revolution*, 116-117, 360.

25 Davis, *Trial of Abraham Hunt*, 40-42.

26 Fischer, *Washington's Crossing*, 182-83.

27 Burgoyne, *Enemy Views*, 126. Burgoyne, *The Diary of Lieutenant von Bardeleben and Other von Donop Regiment Documents*, 82.

28 Smith, *Battle of Trenton*, 27.

29 Kipping, *Hessian View of America*, 22 – citing Hessian Field Jaeger Corps Journal. The Journal of the Knyphausen Regiment also mentioned attacks by parties of "farmers with rifles" on Hessian wagons. The "farmers" were actually militiamen and may have been armed with muskets, and perhaps some rifles since each man was to supply his own weapon.

30 *Hessian Documents of the American Revolution*, Morristown National Historical Park, von Donop Journal, C. 13-14; Fischer, *Washington's Crossing*, 189.

31 Smith, *Battle of Trenton*, 27.

32 [Hall], *The History of the Civil War in America*, I: 253.

33 *Hessian Documents of the American Revolution*, Morristown National Historical Park, von Donop Journal, C24, C. 25-26 – in the translation the Colonel is given as Climber of Hunterdon.

34 Stryker, *Trenton and Princeton*, 110-111; Dwyer, *The Day is Ours!*, 220; Slagle, "The von Lossberg Regiment," 215; Eelking, *German Allied Troops*, 64-65.

35 Atwood, *The Hessians*, 92.

36 Fischer, *Washington's Crossing*, 171-172.

37 Stryker, *Trenton and Princeton*, 78, 343-344; Lundin, *Cockpit*, 162. Similar orders appear in *James Grant of Ballindalloch Papers*, r36, 044 [original plan for cantonments?]

38 Nelson, *General James Grant*, 108.

39 Burgoyne, "Diary of the Hessian Lieutenant [Jacob] Piel, 1776 to 1783," 14.

40 New York, December 24, to Rall from Gen Howe, *James Grant of Ballindalloch Papers*, r36.

41 Stryker, *Trenton and Princeton*, 109.

42 Baurmeister, *Confidential Letters and Journals*, 78 – commenting on a letter from Rall to Colonel von Donop the day before the battle of Trenton.

43 Stryker, *Trenton and Princeton*, 108, 117-123; Dwyer, *The Day is Ours!*, 221-222; Lundin, *Cockpit*, 195; Journal of the Regiment von Alt Lossberg, 1776-83, *Hessian Documents of the American Revolution*, Morristown National Historic Park, Section M, Fiche 249, M.52; Account of First Lieutenant Andreas Wiederholdt of Fusilier Regiment von Knyphausen in a letter from Dumfries, Virginia April 15, 1777, Burgoyne and Mayer, "The Battle of Trenton, 26 December 1776: Reports from the von Jungkenn Papers," *Journal of the Johannes Schwalm Historical Association* V no 4 (1996), 22.

44 Wiederholdt, "Rall at Trenton," 465.

45 Stryker, *Trenton and Princeton*, 122-125.

**Chapter 5**

1 Ferling, Ascent of George Washington, 114; General Charles Lee to Colonel Joseph Reed, November 24, 1776, Lee, *Lee Papers*, II:305-307.

2 Royster, *A Revolutionary People at War*, 116. A Fabian strategy is one that avoids large pitched battles in favor of skirmishes, hit and run, wearing down of the enemy, etc. The name comes from Roman general Fabius who employed this type of strategy against the Carthaginians in the Second Punic War.

3 George Washington to John Augustine Washington, caNovember 19, 1776, Fitzpatrick, *Writings of George Washington*, VI: 242-247.

4 George Washington to John Augustine Washington, Camp near the falls of Trenton, December 18, 1776, Ibid., VI: 396-399.

5 Royster, *A Revolutionary People at War*, 117-118.

6 Kwasny, *Washington's Partisan War*, 98.

7 George Washington to Governor Jonathan Trumbull, December 14, 1776, *GWPLOC.*

8 George Washington to President of Congress, Trenton, December 5, 1776, Fitzpatrick, *Writings of George Washington*, VI: 330-333.

9 George Washington to Gov. Jonathan Trumbull, HQ, Bucks County, December 21, 1776, Ibid., V: 409-412.

10 Wilkinson, *Memoirs*, I: 123. Wilkinson is not always a reliable source and this story may be apocryphal. He only joined Washington's forces a few days before the crossing. However, the sentiments expressed seem in line with those of others recalling this time.

11 Stryker, *Trenton and Princeton*, 64. Apparently from a letter written by Armstrong to William Bradford Reed when preparing his oration for the re-internment of the remains of General Mercer. See: William Bradford Reed, Oration Delivered on the Occasion of the Re-interment of the Remains of General Hugh Mercer, Press of A. Walde, 1840, 29. Also apparently reprinted in Washington and the Generals of the American Revolution, Philadelphia: Carey & Hart, 1848, I: 229. Original letter may be Joseph Armstrong to William B. Reed, July 8, 1839, in Reed, *Papers of Joseph Reed*, r3.

12 George Washington, HQ at Keith's, to Major General William Heath, December 14, 1776, Fitzpatrick, *Writings of George Washington*, VI: 373.

13 George Washington, HQ Bucks County, to Governor Jonathan Trumbull, December 14, 1776, Ibid., VI: 365-367.

14 George Washington, HQ at Keiths, to Major General Horatio Gates, December 14, 1776, Ibid., VI: 371-372.

15 Marshall, *Passages from Diary*, I:122.

16 Showman, *Nathanael Greene Papers*, XIII: 712. If this note was indeed sent to Ewing, it raises the question of where the Durham boats and flats were. Were they still across from Trenton where they had been used to cross the troops and supplies to Pennsylvania several weeks earlier? Or, had the boats been moved north nearer to Coryell's Ferry and now were to be brought "down"? Were other boats also brought to McConkey's by others?

17 Nathanael Greene to Governor Nicholas Cooke, Coryell's Ferry, December 21, 1776, Ibid., I: 374-376.

18 Robert Morris to George Washington, Philadelphia, December 21, 1776, *GWPLOC.*

19 Reed, *Life and Correspondence*, I: 271-273; Joseph Reed to George Washington, Bristol, December 22, 1776, Force, *American Archives*, Series 5, III: 1360-1361. Washington had used similar language when explaining why he temporarily sought more personal power in a letter to Congress on December 20.

20 George Washington, Head Quarters at Keith's, to the General Officers, December 14, 1776, Fitzpatrick, *Writings of George Washington*, VI: 368-370. Pennsylvania Council of Safety, Philadelphia, to George Washington, December 25, 1776, *Papers of George Washington*, Revolutionary War Series, VII: 441. Several companies of the "back country militia" have asked to serve as scouting parties of irregulars instead of regular service. This from the known "divided state of the enemys army and the confidence they have gaind by their late successes." It is unclear whether the letter was ever sent to or received by George Washington.

21 Bonk, *Trenton and Princeton*, 45. While several locations claim to be the spot where Washington planned his attack on Trenton, it seems clear that the planning process took place over time in a number of locations with individuals and groups of officers and elements of the plan even finalized at several locations. The Merrick House seems to have the strongest argument, because

it was apparently the last place where plans were finalized. George Washington, Camp above Trenton Falls, to Joseph Reed, December 23, 1776, Reed, *Life of Joseph Reed*, 274.

22 Fischer, *Washington's Crossing*, 224-225; Weller, *Guns of Destiny*.

23 Henry Knox, "A Plan for the Establishment of a Corps of Continental Artillery, Magazines, Laboratories," December 18, 1776, *GWPLOC*.

24 George Washington to Continental Congress, December 20, 1776, Ibid.

25 Weller, *Guns of Destiny*, 1-8.

26 "Journal of a Pennsylvania Soldier: July-December, 1776," *New York Public Library Bulletin* 1904, VIII, 547-549. Smith, *Historical Collections*, (typescript), Book 1, 51.

27 Smith, *Historical Collections*, Book 2, 87-88.

28 Davis, *History of Bucks County*, II: 121-123. Smith, *Historical Collections* (typescript), Book 1, 45, 47-48, 51, 53, 55, Book 2, 87.

29 Major Ennion Williams, Thompson's Mill, near Coryell's, to Council of Safety, December 17, 1776; Major Ennion Williams, Thompson's Mill, near Coryell's, to Owen Biddle, December 17, 1776, *PA Archives*, series 1, vol 5, 115-117.

30 Major Ennion Williams, Thompson's Mill, to Council of Safety, December 21, 1776, Ibid., 127-128; Smith, Historical Collections, (typescript), Book 1, 54; Statement of William Montgomery in James Barnett NARA M804, PF W391. The "itch" was the extremely uncomfortable condition we call today scabies, caused an infestation of the Sarcoptes scabiei, var. homini mite.

31 George Washington, HQ Bucks County, to the New York Legislature, December 16, 1776; George Washington, HQ Bucks County, PA, to Governor Jonathan Trumbull, December 16, 1776; George Washington, HQ near Coryell's ferry, to Major General William Heath, December 16, 1776, Fitzpatrick, *Writings of George Washington*, VI: 382-385.

32 George Washington, HQ Bucks County, to Major General William Heath, December 18, 1776, Ibid., VI: 392-394. See Abbatt, *Memoirs of Major-General William Heath*, 91-97 for Heath's account of his activities during this time.

33 George Washington, Camp above Trenton Falls, to the President of Congress, December 20, 1776, Fitzpatrick, *Writings of George Washington*, VI: 400-409. Washington had first made his headquarters at "Summerseat" across the river from Trenton in today's Morrisville and after a week or so moved them up the river about 14 miles to the house of William Keith. By December 20 he had moved them to Lord Stirling's headquarters about four miles below, calling his headquarters, "Camp above Trenton Falls."

34 Kwasny, *Washington's Partisan War*, 97.

35 NARA M804, PF S18,305 Philemon Baldwin.

36 Ibid., PF S11170 Rowland Cotton.

37 Ramsay, *History of the American Revolution*, 312-313.

38 Davis, *Life and Character of John Lacey*, 39-42. He accepted another commission to help organize the Bucks County militia soon after in March 1777 and in January 1778 he was appointed a brigadier general of Pennsylvania militia.

39 Dwyer, *The Day is Ours!*, 138; Chamberlin, "Letter," 500.

40 Avery, "Battle of Trenton," 154.

41 Davis, *Life of John Davis*, 8-11. These are today's Thompson-Neely house and mill. See NARA M804, PF S22134 John Borrows, for an example of a militiaman who apparently crossed with the army.

42 Magee, "Major John Polhemus," 289 – citing his journal.

43 NARA M804, PF W906 John Cheston.

44 Charles G. McChesney letter of support dated Heights Town, April 7, 1838 in NARA M804, PF W5944 Joseph Brearley. Brearley was the brother of David Brearley who later played a significant role in developing the US Constitution. He had been a captain in the 2nd New Jersey Regiment in the Canadian campaign and at the time of the battle of Trenton that regiment had disbanded and a new version of it was being recruited. Brearley turned down a commission in the new regiment and instead became First Major of the 1st Hunterdon County militia regiment for the remainder of the war. For more on him see: Kidder, *A People Harassed*, passim.

45 Graydon, *Memoirs*, 147; Billias, *General John Glover*, 101.

46 Billias, *General John Glover*, 4-7.

47 Haven, *Thirty Days in New Jersey*, 11, 44.

48 Philemon Dickinson, Yardley's Farm, to George Washington, December 24, 1776, *GWPLOC*; General Orders, December 25, 1776, *Papers of George Washington*, Revolutionary War Series, VII: 434. Stryker, and subsequently other historians, have misidentified the Captain John Mott who helped secure the guides for Washington. The correct man is Captain John Mott of the 1st Hunterdon County Regiment of the New Jersey militia and not the Captain John Mott in the New Jersey Continental Line. Many accounts of the crossing and battle describe the guides as local farmers who volunteered to guide Washington. In fact, they were militiamen serving on active duty who were recruited before the crossing. For info on the names and identities of the guides, and Captain Mott, see: Kidder, *A People Harassed and Exhausted*, 210-213

49 Fischer, *Washington's Crossing*, Appendix K, 401; Philemon Dickinson, Yardley's Farm, to George Washington, December 24, 1776, *GWPLOC*. This mission would have been similar to the one of David Lanning a few days earlier. Or, it could refer to Lanning. This is a good indication that Dickinson was able to find men to go across to the Trenton area to gather intelligence even though he had earlier written of his trouble finding such a man. It is also an indication that a number of sources were supplying information and the popular legend of John Honeyman, while possibly true that he was one who provided information, is probably exaggerated regarding the significance of the information he provided.

50 NARA M804, PF S10, 376 Elisha Bostwick.

51 Smith, *Battle of Trenton*, 18; Fischer, *Washington's Crossing*, 207-209; Stryker, *Trenton and Princeton*, 129.

52 Wilkinson *Memoirs*, I: 126-127.

53 Smith, *Historical Collections*, Book 1, 50, 89.

54 Alexander Hamilton to the Convention of the Representatives of the State of New York, March 6, 1777, *Papers of Alexander Hamilton*, I: 200. Moore's grave site is now part of Washington Crossing State Park in Bucks County, Pennsylvania near the Thompson/Neely House. He is buried along with 22 other American soldiers who died about the same time.

55 Fischer, *Washington's Crossing*, 191.

56 NARA M804, PF W3830 David Lanning; Barber and Howe, *Historical Collections*, 296; Stryker, *Continental Army at the Crossing*, 16. This is a story that is difficult to prove beyond local tradition. However, it is not improbable and Lanning was known to be active with the militia at this time and would be a likely man to have been sent over. He was also reputed to be a militia guide the night of the crossing and attack.

57 Fischer, *Washington's Crossing*, 209; According to the pension application of John Borrows (NARA M804, PF S22134), the Bucks County company of Captain John Wood's, "being most convenient to the ferries in the neighborhood of Trenton, we were again called out and divided into small parties to guard the different ferries and the boats on the Pennsylvania shore."

58 Eyre, "Memorials of Col. Jehu Eyre," 415-417.

59 Reed, *Life and Correspondence*, I: 275; George Washington, Head Quarters at Trenton Falls, to Colonel John Cadwalader, December 12, 1776, Fitzpatrick, *Writings of George Washington*, VI: 362-363; Fischer, *Washington's Crossing*, 191; For an example of a pension application for one of the Associators, see: NARA M804, PF S3620 Robert Wright of Colonel John Bayard's 2nd Battalion Pennsylvania Associators.

60 Joseph Hodgkins, Buckingham in Pennsylvania, to wife, December 20, 1776, Wade and Lively, *This Glorious Cause*, 227-229; Also see NARA M804, PF S32864 Joseph Hodgkins.

61 Rau, "Sergeant John Smith's Diary of 1776," 266-268. Smith gives a vivid description of their hardships and efforts to forage for food, etc., including plunder

62 Whitfield J. Bell, Jr. and L.H. Butterfield – introduction to Benjamin Rush, *My Dearest Julia*; Runes, *Selected Writings of Benjamin Rush*, introduction; Benjamin Rush to Julia Stockton, January 5, 1776 in Rush, *My Dearest Julia*, 45. See also the introduction; Benjamin Rush to Richard Henry Lee, Philadelphia, January 14, 1777, Butterfield, *Letters of Benjamin Rush*, I: 129.

63 Rush, *Autobiography*, 124.

64 Rodney, *Diary of Captain Thomas Rodney*, 1.

65 Muster Roll, Light Infantry Company of Dover, Delaware Public Archives Commission, *Delaware Archives*, III: 1243. This was apparently made when the company left Morristown in mid-January, 1777 and contains information from December 14, 1776.

66 Rodney, *Diary of Captain Thomas Rodney*, 12-17, 21-22.

67 Private Nehemiah Tilton of Captain Rodney's company to his brother, December 24, 1776 at Neshaminy Creek two miles above Bristol at 3:00pm, *Delaware Archives*, III: 1475. The Coxe family also had Loyalist tendencies, although William Coxe was not a vocal or active Loyalist. Both families were very prominent and wealthy.

68 Rodney, *Diary of Captain Thomas Rodney*, 17; Lundin, *Cockpit*, 167.

69 Dwyer, *The Day is Ours!*, 212.

70 Rodney, *Diary of Captain Thomas Rodney*, 20-21.

71 George Washington, from camp above Trenton Falls, to Joseph Reed or John Cadwalader at Bristol, December 23, 1776, Reed, *Life and Correspondence*, I: 274. Reed was apparently on his way with Dr. Rush to visit with Washington when this dispatch was sent off, so he no doubt heard the information directly from Washington.

72 George Washington to Colonel John Cadwalader, HQ, December 24, 1776, Fitzpatrick, *Writings of George Washington*, VI: 429.

73 George Washington, Camp above Trenton Falls, to Colonel Samuel Griffin, December 24, 1776, Ibid., VI: 429-430.

74 Reed, *Life and Correspondence*, I: 275; Reed, "General Joseph Reed's Narrative," 393.

75 Rodney, *Diary of Captain Thomas Rodney*, 21.

**Chapter 6**

1 For more on the Johnson Ferry see: Osborne, *Where Washington Once Led*, 33, 56-58.

2 Tunis, *The Tavern at the Ferry*, 29; Lane, *From Indian Trail to Iron Horse*, 68-70.

3 Stryker, *Trenton and Princeton*, 129-130; these would include the 16 boats ordered down on December 19, Showman, *Nathanael Greene Papers*, VIII: 712. Much has been written and spoken about identifying the men who collected the boats for Washington's Crossing, especially concerning Daniel Bray. Documents pertaining to collecting boats on the Delaware virtually all refer to getting Washington's and then Lee's troops across to Pennsylvania and securing all boats on the river from British use, rather than specifically for the crossing back to New Jersey on December 25/26. For a detailed analysis of the debate see: Marfy Goodspeed, "Who Collected the Boats?" Goodspeed Histories: New Jersey History and Genealogy, August 20, 2016 and a very detailed comment by Bill Schleicher, March 2, 2017 at https://goodspeedhistories.com/who-collected-the-boats.

4 For more on this type of ferry operation see: Tunis, *The Tavern at the Ferry*, 16-17, 34-36, and, Lane, *From Indian Trail to Iron Horse*, 45-46.

5 See: Kidder, *A People Harassed and Exhausted*, 180.

6 Davis, *History of Bucks County*, II: 124.

7 McCarty, "Revolutionary War Journal," 40.

8 How, *Diary of David How*, 41. NARA M804 PF S29912 David How.

9 Smith, *Historical Collections*, Book 1, 50, 89.

10 Order of Attack, in Powell, *Biographical Sketch of Col. Leven Powell*, 46.

11 Wilkinson, *Memoirs*, I: 127-128. Gates has been charged by historians with leaving the army to lobby for himself with Congress, because of cowardice, or because he was ill. Gates was not known for cowardice, before or after, and participating in the action against Trenton would have improved any lobbying he wanted to do during the winter. His biographer, Paul Nelson, believes that, despite lack of hard evidence, Washington approved of his leaving due to his poor health. David Hackett Fischer counters that he was healthy enough to make a long trip to Baltimore. However, he did not reach Baltimore until December 28 when John Hancock, and others, found him "in a very poor state of health." For example see: Hancock to Schuyler, December 30 – Force, *American Archives*, series 5, III: 1478. Nelson rejects entirely the Wilkinson account, but Fischer does not. Nelson says that Washington never reprimanded Gates and this is evidence that he had approved his departure. Nelson, *General Horatio Gates*, 75-77.

12 Washington to Gates, December 23, 1776, *George Washington Papers*, Revolutionary War Series, VII: 418. This letter is misidentified as written to Colonel Samuel Griffin in Fitzpatrick, *Writings of George Washington*, VI: 428.

13 Greenwood, *Wartime Services*, 80-81; Avery, "Battle of Trenton," 154-155. This could have been a Durham boat because it was flat bottomed, but perhaps more likely a ferry "flat" that was more accurately a scow because it was flat and had box ends. British Officer Thomas Anburey crossed on a ferry at Frenchtown in 1778 and writed, "We crossed the river in scowls [sic], which are flat bottom boats, large enough to contain a wagon and horses; they are a safe conveyance." This is evidence that ferry boats could be known as scows in addition to flats.

14 Wilkinson, *Memoirs*, I: 128.

15 Stryker, *Trenton and Princeton*, 130, 136-137. The author appreciates the discussions with William Welsch and Clay Craighead on the idea that Knox made several round trips.

16 Breck, *Recollections of Samuel Breck*, 208-210. Breck was not present at the crossing as he was only a child then. His description of Knox developed during the 1790s when he knew him as Secretary of War. In his book of recollections he draws portraits of a number of men from the Revolution whom he met in Boston and Philadelphia.

17 Wilkinson, *Memoirs*, I: 128.

18 Fischer, *Washington's Crossing*, 221-222; Smith, *Battle of Trenton*, 20, 32 - Washington's General Orders, December 25, 1776. Ketchum, *Winter Soldiers*, mistakenly states the advance troops were cavalry, probably due to the fact that William Washington later in the war commanded a cavalry unit. At this point he was clearly infantry. Powell, *Biographical Sketch of Col. Leven Powell*, 45-46. There is no documentary evidence of militia guides, but it makes sense given their use with other units and the nature of the mission.

19 Smith, *Battle of Trenton*, 19; Stryker, *Trenton and Princeton*, 113-115; *Papers of George Washington*, Revolutionary War Series, VII: 436-436; Powell, *Biographical Sketch of Col. Leven Powell*, 45-46.

20 Stryker, *Trenton and Princeton*, 135-136.

21 Haven, *Thirty Days in New Jersey*, 14; Brewster, *Rambles About Portsmouth*, 263. Stryker, *Trenton and Princeton*, 134-136, writes that Captain John Blunt of Portsmouth, New Hampshire served by "guiding the boats," assisted by Lieutenant Cuthbert of Captain Moulder's artillery company. Blunt had sailed on the Delaware Bay and river and Stryker says this made him "familiar with the navigation of the Delaware River." However, McConkey's Ferry was well above the head of navigation on the Delaware so it is unlikely that Blunt knew that part of the river. He might have been more useful to Cadwalader at Bristol. However, when Washington visited Portsmouth in November 1789, Tobias Lear, his secretary, noted that he saw an old acquaintance identified as Captain John Blunt, "the helmsman of the boat during the famous crossing of the Delaware." This may be an implication that it was the boat Washington crossed in. In a footnote it is noted that this was according to family tradition, although there was "no reason to doubt" it. See: Decatur, *Private Affairs of George Washington*, 84. Davis, *History of Bucks County*, II: 124, credits Captain Blount with taking helm of the first boat, probably based on Stryker.

22 Billias, *General John Glover*, 66; Roads, *History and Traditions of Marblehead*, 344; Haven, *Thirty Days in New Jersey*, 44-47.

23 Stryker, *Trenton and Princeton*, 133. See: Rodney, *Diary of Captain Thomas Rodney*, 22-23 for description of conditions at that time at Bristol.

24 Stryker, *Trenton and Princeton*, 137-138.

25 Wilkinson, *Memoirs*, I: 122; Washington to John Hancock, December 27, 1776, *George Washington Papers*, Revolutionary War Series, VII: 454..

26 Chamberlin, "Letter," 500.

27 Stryker, *Trenton and Princeton*, 138. For a detailed discussion of the crossing see: William M. Welsch, "Christmas Night 1776: How Did They Cross?, " in Todd Andrlik, Hugh T. Harrington, and Don N. Hagist, *Journal of the American Revolution allthingsliberty.com*, volume 1, Yellow Springs, OH: Ertel, 2013, 100-109.

28 Joseph Hodgkins, Crosswicks, to wife, December 31, 1776, Wade, *This Glorious Cause*, 228-229.

29 Young, "Journal of Sergeant William Young," 259.

30 Rodney, *Diary of Captain Thomas Rodney*, 22.

31 Colonel John Cadwalader, Bristol, to George Washington, Morning of December 26, 1776, *George Washington Papers*, Revolutionary War Series, VII: 442-443. Dunk's Ferry crossed to where today's Beverly, New Jersey is located.

32 Rodney, *Diary of Captain Thomas Rodney*, 22; Reed, "General Joseph Reed's Narrative," 393-394.
33 George Washington, Head Quarters, to Colonel John Cadwalader, December 25, 1776, in *George Washington Papers*, Revolutionary War Series, VII: 438-439; George Washington, McConkey's Ferry, to Cadwalader at Bristol, 6:00pm December 25th, 1776, Stryker, *Trenton and Princeton*, 132.
34 Widmer, *The Christmas Campaign*, 18-19. Reed was actually a colonel, but is often referred to as general in retrospective statements because he filled the office of adjutant general.
35 Philip Hagner's account of the movements of the Am Army in & a[bout] 1776-1777 [apparently dated 1826] Reed, *Papers of Joseph Reed*; Reed, "General Joseph Reed's Narrative," 393-394.
36 Reed, "General Joseph Reed's Narrative," 393-394.
37 Rodney, *Diary of Captain Thomas Rodney*, 23; Smith, *Battle of Trenton*, 19; Colonel John Cadwalader, Bristol, to George Washington, Morning of December 26, 1776, *George Washington Papers*, Revolutionary War Series, VII: 442-443.
38 Philip Hagner's account of the movements of the Am Army in & a[bout] 1776-1777 [apparently dated 1826] Reed, *Papers of Joseph Reed*; Reed, "General Joseph Reed's Narrative," 393-394
39 Colonel John Cadwalader, Bristol, to George Washington, Morning of December 26, 1776, *George Washington Papers*, Revolutionary War Series, VII: 442-443; Smith, *Battle of Trenton*, 19.
40 Rodney, *Diary of Captain Thomas Rodney*, 23; For similar accounts see also: Rau, "Sergeant John Smith's Diary of 1776," 268; Young, "Journal of Sergeant William Young," 259.
41 Widmer, *The Christmas Campaign*, 18-19.
42 John Cadwalader, Bristol, to Pennsylvania Council of Safety, December 16, 1776, Force, *American Archives*, Series 5, III: 1441. Two letters of same date.
43 Stryker, *Trenton and Princeton*, 125.

**Chapter 7**

1 Greenwood, *Wartime Services*, 80-81; Avery, "Battle of Trenton," 154-155.
2 Fischer, *Washington's Crossing*, 225, 355; Weller, *Guns of Destiny*, passim; Henry Knox to Lucy Knox, December 28, 1776, in Stryker, *Trenton and Princeton*, 371-372.
3 Stryker, *Trenton and Princeton*, 145-146. This militia captain John Mott should not, as most historians have, be confused with Captain John Mott of the New Jersey Continentals. They are completely different men. See: Kidder, *A People Harassed and Exhausted*, 210 for details on the identity of Mott.
4 NARA M804, PF S13914 Joab Mershon; Washington's General Orders, December 25, 1776, *Papers of George Washington*, Revolutionary War Series, VII: 434; Smith, *Battle of Trenton*, 20; Order of Attack, in Powell, *Biographical Sketch of Col. Leven Powell*, 445 – a slightly different version of December 25 General Orders.
5 Washington's General Orders, December 25, 1776, *Papers of George Washington*, Revolutionary War Series, VII: 434; Smith, *Battle of Trenton*, 20; Fischer, *Washington's Crossing*, 222-223.
6 Greenwood, *Wartime Services*, 39; Wilkinson, *Memoirs*, I: 128.
7 Powell, "Elisha Bostwick's Memoirs," 102.
8 The road followed today's modern Washington Crossing/Pennington Road, Mercer County Route 546. It passes on the border of Washington Crossing State Park and roughly parallel to a previously labeled "Continental Lane" inside the park that was long thought to have been the original road used by the troops, but this has been disproven. – See Osborne, *Where Washington Once Led*, 37-44.
9 For information on the Bear Tavern and the building there today – see: Osborne, *Where Washington Once Led*, 65-67.
10 Lane, *From Indian Trail to Iron Horse*, 38-41. See also: *New Jersey Historic Roadway Study*, Prepared for New Jersey Department of Transportation and Federal Highway Administration, New Jersey Historic preservation Office, prepared by KSK Architects Planners Historians, Inc. With Armand Corporation, Inc., and Michael Baker, Jr. Inc., January 2011, HPO Log #03-1895-6, Chapter 6.
11 Fischer, *Washington's Crossing*, 226-227; Powell, "Elisha Bostwick's Memoirs," 102.
12 Powell, "Elisha Bostwick's Memoirs," 102.
13 Greenwood, *Wartime Services*, 81-82.

14 Today the road to Howell's Ferry is called Upper Ferry Road and the hamlet of Birmingham is called West Trenton, a crossroads cluster of businesses and homes in Ewing, Township. The army approached the Birmingham intersection on what is today Bear Tavern Road and Sullivan's division departed on today's Grand Avenue that shortly becomes Sullivan Way. At the writing of this book several new constructions in West Trenton have incorporated the name of Birmingham in recognition of the historical name.
15 Powell, "Elisha Bostwick's Memoirs," 102.
16 Fischer, *Washington's Crossing*, 228; Kidder, *People Harassed and Exhausted*, 216; Stryker, *Trenton and Princeton*, 141; NARA M804, PF1307 Jesse Moore.
17 Captain William Hull, 7th Connecticut Regiment, to Andrew Adams, Trenton, January 1, 1777, Stryker, *Trenton and Princeton*, 375-376 - for statement about setting watches. Also, Bonney, *A Legacy of Historical Gleanings*, I: 57. He was later Major General William Hull who surrendered Detroit to British General Brock during the War of 1812.
18 The river road was roughly today's Grand Avenue, Sullivan Way, and West State Street rather than Route 29 along the river.
19 NARA M804, PF W25323 Conrad Beam.
20 See: Fischer, *Washington's Crossing*, 230 and 516n24 for a discussion on this story and how it has been used erroneously. Greenwood, *Wartime Services*, 83.
21 Washington's General Orders, December 25, 1776, *The Papers of George Washington*, Revolutionary War Series, VII: 434–438; Powell, *Biographical Sketch of Col. Leven Powell*, 45-46 – for another version of the orders.
22 Fischer, *Washington's Crossing*, 231; Thompson, *History of Long Island*, 534; Wickes, *History of Medicine in New Jersey*, 371-372; Monroe, *Autobiography*, 25-26.
23 Fischer, *Washington's Crossing*, 231-233, 517n29 for ways this story has been misinterpreted in other works.
24 Dwyer, *The Day is Ours!*, 252, mistakenly gives it as the house of Dr. David Cowell and his brother Ebenezer. Wilkinson, *Memoirs*, I: 129.
25 George Johnston to Leven Powell, December 29, 1776 in Powell, *Biographical Sketch of Col. Leven Powell*, 42. Johnston was the son of a Virginia lawyer who had represented Washington before the war. Shortly after the battle of Princeton, Washington named him as one of his aides-de-camp.

**Chapter 8**

1 Fischer, *Washington's Crossing*, 236 - citing Wiederholdt diary and 1778 testimony, etc.; Stryker, *Trenton and Princeton*, 147.
2 Wiederholdt, "Rall at Trenton," 465-466; Account of First Lieutenant Andreas Wiederholdt of Fusilier Regiment von Knyphausen in a letter from Dumfries, Virginia April 15, 1777, in: Burgoyne and Mayer, "The Battle of Trenton, 26 December 1776: Reports from the von Jungkenn Papers," *Journal of the Johannes Schwalm Historical Association* V no 4 (1996), 22; Fischer, *Washington's Crossing*, 235; Smith, *Battle of Trenton*, 22. There are several stories of the first encounter that are commonly told, but to this author don't ring true. The story of encountering an early morning woodcutter and asking him to point out the Hessian guard post seems unnecessary because Washington had local men guiding his troops who would have known its location. The story of David Lanning confronting a Hessian picket also seems to be an embellishment, even though Lanning was one of the guides, because it contradicts Lieutenant Wiederholdt's account.
3 George Johnston to Leven Powell, December 29, 1776, in Powell, *Biographical Sketch of Col. Leven Powell*, 42.
4 Weller, *Guns of Destiny*, 10.
5 Fischer, *Washington's Crossing*, 239 – citing several Hessian accounts. Stryker, *Trenton and Princeton*, 150-151; Dwyer, *The Day is Ours!*, 251; Smith, *Battle of Trenton*, 22.
6 White, *A Historical Account and Archaeological Analysis of the Eagle Tavern*, 2-2.
7 Stryker, *Trenton and Princeton*, 151-152, 189; Dwyer, *The Day is Ours!*, 251. Quotes Wilkinson who says the early fugitives going over the bridge were joined by some of the musicians, the surgeons, and some of the women. This is very questionable because the Trenton Prisoner List includes the musicians, medical officers, and some wives. It does not list any Jägers.

8 John Cadwalader, Bristol, December 26, 1776, to Pennsylvania Council of Safety, Force, *American Archives*, Series 5, III: 1441. Commenting on the report of a Mr. M. Lane and his observations from Trenton Ferry that morning. Cadwalader had tried to cross the night of the 25th at Dunks' Ferry, but it was impossible to get their cannon across so they had returned to Bristol about 4:00am. From Trenton Ferry, Pennsylvania side, Lane had heard heavy firing on the River and Pennytown Roads leading to Trenton that he said was heavy for about an hour and then moderate for about three quarters hour.

9 Greenwood, *Wartime Services*, 82-83. This cannon must have belonged to either Neil's or Hugg's New Jersey artillery company.

10 NARA M804, PF W459 Jacob Francis.

11 Stryker, *Trenton and Princeton*, 167-168, 186.

12 Avery, "Battle of Trenton," 155.

13 Stryker, *Trenton and Princeton*, 152-153; Dwyer, *The Day is Ours!*, 252 – He quotes an unidentified aide to Washington.

14 *Hessian Documents of the American Revolution*, Morristown National Historic Park – enclosed with Heister to Landgrave Frederick, New York, February 9, 1777, Fiche 11, page 26. Heister says he heard excellent reports on Bockum including from "a nearby resident, at whose house he was posted with his detachment." This may have been Barnes. Also, Barnes, *AO13*, 108. Presumably, Barnes found a way to avoid capture during or after the day's battle.

15 Atwood, *The Hessians*, 93; Washington to Hancock, December 27, 1776, *GWPLOC*.

16 Account of First Lieutenant Andreas Wiederholdt of Fusilier Regiment von Knyphausen in a letter from Dumfries, Virginia April 15, 1777, in: Burgoyne and Mayer, "The Battle of Trenton, 26 December 1776: Reports from the von Jungkenn Papers," 23, 25; Stryker, *Trenton and Princeton*, 149-150; *Dwyer, The Day is Ours!*, 252;

17 Smith, *Battle of Trenton*, 20; Stryker, *Trenton and Princeton*, 148, 153.

18 Wiederholdt, "Rall at Trenton," 465-466.

19 Stryker, *Trenton and Princeton*, 153-154.

20 Embury, *A Grandmother's Recollections*.

21 Dwyer, *The Day is Ours!*, 263. Dwyer does not give a citation for this, but simply attributes it to one report of several stories about close encounters among the people of Trenton.

22 Ibid., 253 – today known as five points, and the location of the battle monument.

23 Weller, *Guns of Destiny*, 9.

24 Now Princeton Avenue. Wilkinson, *Memoirs*, I: 129-131.

25 Stryker, *Trenton and Princeton*, 154-156.

26 Account of First Lieutenant Andreas Wiederholdt of Fusilier Regiment von Knyphausen in a letter from Dumfries, Virginia April 15, 1777, in: Burgoyne and Mayer, ""The Battle of Trenton, 26 December 1776: Reports from the von Jungkenn Papers," 25.

27 Wiederholdt, "Rall at Trenton," 465-466. It is important to keep in mind that Wiederholdt was not a fan of Rall's and because of his own involvement throughout the battle, needed to defend his actions in the defeat. Because Rall died from his battle wounds, he could not defend himself or criticize Wiederholdt.

28 George Washington to John Hancock, December 27, 1776, *GWPLOC*.

29 Stryker, *Trenton and Princeton*, 154-155; *Pennsylvania Gazette*, Sunday, November 22, 1750, 4; Thursday, September 26, 1765, 6. The buildings included a bark house, mill house, bark mill, beam house, stone currying shop, leather house, stable, and chaise-house.

30 Stryker, *Trenton and Princeton*, 154-156; Smith, *Battle of Trenton*, 22

31 Canister was a cluster of small projectiles in a container and firing it essentially made the cannon a large, powerful shotgun.

32 Stryker, *Trenton and Princeton*, 157, 162-163.

33 George Johnston, at McConkey's Ferry, to Leven Powell, December 29, 1776, in Powell, *Biographical Sketch of Col. Leven Powell*, 42.

34 Dwyer, *The Day is Ours!*, 253 – quoting a Washington aide who should have said "hitching" rather than "harnessing."

35 Nathanael Greene, Trenton, to Catharine Green, December 30, 1776, Showman, *Nathanael Greene Papers*, I: 377.

36 Account of Lt Col Franciscus Scheffer, May 5, 1778 at Philadelphia, in: Burgoyne, "The Battle of Trenton, 26 December 1776: Reports from the von Jungkenn Papers," 21-22.
37 Henry Knox to Lucy Knox, December 28, 1776, in Stryker, *Trenton and Princeton*, 371-372.
38 Patrick Duffey, from McConkey's Ferry, to Colonel Proctor of Artillery, December 28, 1776, Hazard, *PA Archives*, V: 141. Apparently it was known that Proctor was being advanced to colonel.
39 NARA M804, PF W5858 John Boudy.
40 NARA M804, PF 1258 Cornelius Sullivan; Thomas Forrest to Col. Proctor, December 29, 1776 from McConkey's Ferry, Hazard, *PA Archives*, I, V: 142. His comments were made about Hessian prisoners.
41 Stryker, *Trenton and Princeton*, 156-158, 162-164; Wilkinson, *Memoirs*, I: 129; White, "The Good Soldier White," 77. NARA M804, PF W11805 Joseph White – contains copy of his book narrative – seems most proud of taking off the damaged cannon at Trenton; Adam Stephen to Jonathan Seaman, January 5, 1777, Ward, *Major General Adam Stephen*, 152. Jonathan Seaman was the overseer of Stephen's plantation. Monroe, *Autobiography*, 25-26.
42 Smith, *Battle of Trenton*, 23. Some have speculated that Washington's and Monroe's wounds may have been from "friendly fire," because Mercer's men were shooting in that direction.
43 Wilson, *Book of the First Troop*, 11.
44 Stryker, *Trenton and Princeton*, 162-164; Wilkinson, *Memoirs*, I: 129.
45 Account of First Lieutenant Andreas Wiederholdt of Fusilier Regiment von Knyphausen in a letter from Dumfries, Virginia April 15, 1777, in: Burgoyne and Mayer, ""The Battle of Trenton, 26 December 1776: Reports from the von Jungkenn Papers," 25; Fischer, *Washington's Crossing*, 243.
46 Stryker, *Trenton and Princeton*, 176-182.
47 Smith, *Battle of Trenton*, 23.
48 Ibid.
49 Stryker, *Trenton and Princeton*, 168-172; Barth, Dorneman, Schwalm, "The Trenton Prisoner List," 18, 22.
50 *Vermont Republican* (Windsor, VT), March 31, 1832, 4.
51 Muhlenberg, *Journals*, II: 771; Dwyer, *The Day is Ours!*, 259.
52 Burgoyne, *Defeat, Disaster, and Dedication*, 20.
53 Muhlenberg, *Journals*, II: 771 – journal entry for December 31, 1776. The Hessians may have mistaken for civilians any American riflemen, or men not in complete uniform, who got into houses and fired on their enemy.
54 Stryker, *Trenton and Princeton*, 168-172; Barth, Dorneman, Schwalm, "The Trenton Prisoner List," 18, 22.
55 Stryker, *Trenton and Princeton*, 190.
56 Loyalist Joseph Galloway later said that a number of Hessian soldiers were "more attentive to the safety of their plunder than their duty, and engaged in putting horses to and loading their wagons, became deaf to all orders." While doing this, he says they were surrounded and taken and there is no evidence that any wagons left the village. Galloway was not an eyewitness and was probably seeking a reason for the defeat. No eyewitnesses give any indication of this kind of behavior. Stryker, *Trenton and Princeton*, 172.
57 Ibid., 174.
58 Weller, *Guns of Destiny*, 9-10.
59 George Johnston, McConkey's Ferry, to Leven Powell, December 29, 1776, in Powell, *Biographical Sketch of Col. Leven Powell*, 42.
60 Watts, "A Memoir of General Henry Miller," 431.
61 Stryker, *Trenton and Princeton*, 175.
62 Smith, *Battle of Trenton*, 24-25.
63 Stryker, *Trenton and Princeton*, 176-182; Smith, *Battle of Trenton*, 25.
64 NARA M804, PF W6287 Benjamin Titus.
65 NARA M804, PF W459 Jacob Francis.
66 Stryker, *Trenton and Princeton*, 176-182.
67 Smith, *Battle of Trenton*, 25; NARA M804, PF W459 Jacob Francis.
68 Stryker, *Trenton and Princeton*, 182-184. On December 27, Washington ordered that the swords and knapsacks that had been taken from officers and sergeants were to be returned.

69 Dwyer, *The Day is Ours!*, citing Major Apollos Morris.
70 McCarty, "Revolutionary War Journal," 41.
71 Burgoyne, *Defeat, Disaster, and Dedication*, 20. Virtually the same words appear in: Journal of the Regiment von Alt Lossberg, 1776-83, *Hessian Documents of the American Revolution*, Morristown National Historic Park, section M, fiche 249, M.53.
72 Stryker, *Trenton and Princeton*, 185, 187 – Stryker considers the various estimates from Hessian officers. Wilkinson, *Memoirs*, I: 131.
73 Smith, *Historical Collections*, Book 1, 47.

**Chapter 9**

1 Stryker, *Trenton and Princeton*, 192. When the Potts house, later the City Tavern, was demolished in 1857, newspapers noted that the pane of glass with the bullet hole was then in possession of one of the citizens and that curiosity hunters had taken pieces of the old-fashioned painted Dutch tile from under the mantle pieces. See: *Newark Daily Advertiser*, June 11, 1857, 2. The glass pane with the bullet hole is now part of the collections of the Old Barracks Museum in Trenton.
2 Carleton. *British Headquarters Papers*, item 7445.
3 *AO12*, vol 15, 110-116; *AO13*, bundle 20, 210-219. He continued to serve the British as a Deputy Commissary in New York, then in Virginia and South Carolina. He had to leave the army when he became ill and returned to New York until the evacuation in 1783. After the war he settled in Nova Scotia.
4 Young, "Journal of Sergeant William Young,"260, footnote 2 cites *Shippen Papers*, 256.
5 Chamberlin, "Letter," 501.
6 Powell, "Elisha Bostwick's Memoirs," 107. For more on the numbers of Hessians who escaped, see: Zellers-Frederick, Andrew A. "The Hessians Who Escaped Washington's Trap at Trenton," *Journal of the American Revolution* (https://allthingsliberty.com), April 18, 2018.
7 Embury, *A Grandmother's Recollections.*
8 Death notice, *Boston Herald*, January 20, 1862, 2. She was 96 at the time of her death. The article noted that Joshua Richard then lived in the house in 1862 where her parents had lived in 1776. The clock reputedly still stood in the same corner of the same room.
9 On his way home after discharge he sold it to a young officer for $8. White, "The Good Soldier White," 77.
10 Jones and Kloster, *Captain Oliver Pond's Hessian Fusiliercap.* Presents the story of this cap which is now in the National Museum of American History, The Smithsonian Institution., Washington, DC.
11 Dwyer, *The Day is Ours!*, 261; Greenwood, *Wartime Services*, 42.
12 NARA M804, PF S23925 Moses Smith.
13 Ryan, *A Salute to Courage*, 56.
14 Reed, "General Joseph Reed's Narrative," 391.
15 Fischer, *Washington's Crossing*, Appendix K, 401; Stryker, *Trenton and Princeton*, 206; Extract of a letter from an officer in the American Army from Newtown, Pennsylvania December 27, 1776. In Force, *American Archives*, Series 5, III: 1442-1443.
16 *NJSA*, Legislature Series, Inventories of Damages by the British and Americans in New Jersey, 1776-1782, Jacob Benjamin Damage Claim No. 13 Hunterdon County.
17 NARA M804, PF W459 Jacob Francis.
18 John Cadwalader, Bristol, December 26, 1776, to PA Council of Safety, Force, *American Archives*, Series 5, III: 1441. Two letters both of same date.
19 Wilson, *Book of the First Troop*, 11.
20 Stryker, *Trenton and Princeton*, 207, Gibson, *Dr. Bodo Otto*, 127-28.
21 Chamberlin, "Letter," 501.
22 Stirling submitted an account of this loss on April 30, 1778 - *PCC*, Letters from General Washington, r168, i152, p17.
23 William S. Stryker, to General Edward Burd Grubb, April 6, 1893 transcribed in Wilson, *Book of the First Troop*, 11.
24 Tench Tilghman, Newtown, to James Tilghman, December 27, 1776, Tilghman, *Memoir of Lieut. Col. Tench Tilghman*, 149; Barth, Dorneman, Schwalm, "The Trenton Prisoner List".

25 Stryker, *Trenton and Princeton*, 172, 192, 392. Oliva says Rall died the evening of the battle, December 26. The exact location of his burial is unknown.
26 Stryker, *Trenton and Princeton*, 196; Barth, Dorneman, Schwalm, "The Trenton Prisoner List".
27 Tench Tilghman, Newtown, to James Tilghman, December 27, 1776, Tilghman, *Memoir of Lieut. Col. Tench Tilghman*, 149.
28 Trenton Historical Society, *History of Trenton*, 755; Shuman, *The Trenton Story*, 37; letter from Baltimore, December 31, 1776, Peter Force, *American Archives*, Series 5, III: 1509-1510; Notice in a number of New England papers including *Independent Chronicle* (Boston, MA), Thursday, January 23, 1777, 3.
29 Hall, *History of the First Presbyterian Church in Trenton*, 159-163. Citing damage assessment report of commissioners Joseph Phillips, Peter Gordon, and Sidney Barry acting in accordance with a 1781 New Jersey law. The accuracy of the inventory of damages was attested to by Alexander Chambers as a Trustee of the Church and sworn before Joseph Phillips September 7, 1782.
30 For example: *NJSA*, Legislature Series, Inventories of Damages by the British and Americans in New Jersey, 1776-1782, Damage Report Claims No. 311 Alexander Douglass Burlington County; No 313 Thomas Jenney Burlington; No 318 Jonathan Richmond Burlington.
31 *NJSA*, Legislature Series, Inventories of Damages by the British and Americans in New Jersey, 1776-1782, Damage Report Claim No. 10 William Plaskett.
32 White, "The Good Soldier White," 77. Knox did remember him and later offered him a commission, which he turned down.
33 Chamberlin, "Letter," 501.
34 How, *Diary of David How*, 41.
35 Wilson, *Book of the First Troop*, 11.
36 Chamberlin, "Letter," 501.
37 NARA M804, PF S34412 Hosea Husted; NARA M804, PF W465 Reuben Husted; Death notice of Hosea in *Washington Whig* (Bridgeton, NJ), June 7, 1823, 3; NARA M804, PF W2503 Cornelius Wells.
38 Avery, "The Battle of Trenton," 155. Avery also says the wounded officers were left on parole and the prisoners were marched to Yardley's Ferry, although he may have meant Johnson's.
39 McMichael, "Diary of Lieutenant James McMichael," 140.
40 Burgoyne, *Defeat, Disaster, and Dedication*, 20-21, 77-78.
41 Ryan, *Salute to Courage*, 58; Magee, "Major John Polhemus." 288-289.
42 Powell, "Elisha Bostwick's Memoirs," 102. He wrote this description after the battle when the prisoners were removed over the Delaware.
43 Collins, *A Brief Narrative*, 30-31.

**Chapter 10**

1 Curwen, *Journal of Samuel Curwen Loyalist*, 287. Curwen went to London in 1775 and returned to Salem after the war. Barrington's office was actually Secretary at War, rather than Secretary of War.
2 Gruber, *John Peebles' American War*, 74.
3 Mackenzie, *Diary of Frederick Mackenzie*, I:130.
4 Major General William Heath, Peekskill, to George Washington, December 26, 1776, *George Washington Papers*, Revolutionary War Series, VII: 445-446.
5 17th Regiment Order Book, *Early American Orderly Books, 1748-1817* [microform], r4, number 41.
6 Rodney, *Diary of Captain Thomas Rodney*, 47.
7 Nelson, *General James Grant*, 109-110 – citing Grant to Harvey, December 26, 1776, Letterbook, 1775-1777, *Ballindalloch Papers*, 2.
8 *AO13* bundle 25, 532-534.
9 Bamford, "Diary," 23.
10 Meunchhausen, *At General Howe's Side*, 1776-1778, 8-9.
11 Adlum, *Memoirs*, 100-104.
12 Robert Morris, Philadelphia, to George Washington, December 26, 1776, *George Washington Papers*, Revolutionary War Series, VII: 447-448.

13 Robert Morris to John Hancock, December 26, 1776, Smith, *Letters of Delegates to Congress*, V: 670, 673-675.
14 Elbridge Gerry, Baltimore, to Joseph Trumbull, December 26, 1776, Ibid., V: 671.
15 Samuel Adams, Baltimore, to Elizabeth Adams, December 26, 1776, Ibid., V: 669-670.
16 Francis Lewis, Baltimore, to Robert Morris, December 26, 1776, Ibid., V: 671-673; Elbridge Gerry, Baltimore, to Joseph Trumbull, December 26, 1776, Ibid., V: 670.
17 Marshall, *Passages from Diary*, I: 123.
18 Jackson, *Margaret Morris*, 58.
19 Rizzo and McShalkis, "The Widow who Saved a Revolution."
20 Ewald, *Diary of the American War*, 42-43.
21 Lundin, *Cockpit*, 199; Donop to Prince Frederick William of Prussia, January 7, 1777, quoted in: Huth, "Letters from a Hessian Mercenary," 496; Journal of the Fusilier Regiment von Knyphausen, 1776-83, *Hessian Documents of the American Revolution*, Morristown National Historic Park, section P, fiche 279, P.22; Journal of the Hessian Grenadier Battalion von Minnegerode, Ibid., section K, fiche 232, K.49; Account of Captain Henrich Bocking – senior captain of the Rall Regiment, in: Burgoyne and Mayer. "The Battle of Trenton, 26 December 1776: Reports from the von Jungkenn Papers," 26-27.
22 Lawrence had been helping with the giving out of protections and taking allegiance oaths in December.
23 *NJSA*, New Jersey Council of Safety Records, 1776-1778, Loose Records, Box 2, #18 – State of New Jersey against John Lawrence deposition of James Cox, Jr. April 1, 1777.
24 Ewald, *Diary of the American War*, 42-43.
25 Avery, *The Lord is to be Praised*, 24-25.
26 Lundin, *Cockpit*, 81; *NJSA*, New Jersey Council of Safety Records, 1776-1778, Loose Records, Box 2, #16 - "Evidence of Jno Pope concerning John Lawrence Junr." April 1, 1777; # 17 – Evidence of John Pope against Dr. Jonathan Odell, April 1, 1777; *New Jersey Gazette*, March 3, 1779, 3 for advertisement giving location and occupation of John Pope. For more on John Lawrence see *New Jersey Archives* (Documents Relating to the Colonial History of the State of New Jersey), X: 302n.
27 [Field], "A Recently Discovered Letter," 119.
28 Young, "Journal of Sergeant William Young," 258-9.
29 Reed, "General Joseph Reed's Narrative," 394.
30 Colonel John Cadwalader, Bristol, to George Washington, morning of December 26, 1776, *George Washington Papers*, Revolutionary War Series, VII: 442-443.
31 Colonel John Cadwalader, Bristol, to George Washington, December 26, 1776, 9 o'clock, Ibid., VII: 444-445.
32 Rodney, *Diary of Captain Thomas Rodney*, 23-24.
33 Reed, "General Joseph Reed's Narrative," 394-395; Reed, *Life and Correspondence*, I: 278; Rodney, *Diary of Captain Thomas Rodney*, 23-24.
34 Rau, "Sergeant John Smith's Diary of 1776," 268.

**Chapter 11**

1 Gill and Curtis, *A Man Apart*, 135; Cresswell, *Journal*, 178.
2 Gruber, *John Peebles' American War*, 74.
3 Mackenzie, *Diary of Frederick Mackenzie*, I:131.
4 Major William DeHart, Morristown, to George Washington, December 27, 1776, *Papers of George Washington*, Revolutionary War Series, VII: 453.
5 Robertson, *His Diaries and Sketches in America*, 117.
6 Bamford, "Diary," 23.
7 Nelson, *General James Grant*, 110-111 – citing Grant to Harvey, December 27, 1776, Letterbook, 1775-1777, *James Grant of Ballindalloch Papers*, 2
8 [Hall], *The History of the Civil War in America*, I: 251-252.
9 Kemble, "Kemble's Journal," 104. Actually, several hundred Hessians escaped from Trenton.
10 William Howe, New York, to James Grant December 27, 1776, *James Grant of Ballindalloch Papers*, r36.

11 Nelson, *General James Grant*, 110-111 – citing James Grant to von Donop, December 27, 1776, *Donop Papers*, Morristown NHP and Charles Cornwallis, New York, to James Grant, December 27, 1776 in *James Grant of Ballindollach Papers*, reel 36.
12 Howe's Order Book, General Orders, HQ New York, 27th December, *Early American Orderly Books, 1748-1817*, [microform], r4, number 40.
13 See: Fischer, *Washington's Crossing*, 279 and 524n7.
14 Prisoners of war were only released when the other side released, exchanged, a man of similar rank.
15 Adlum, *Memoirs*, 104-107.
16 17th Regiment Orderly Book, *Early American Orderly Books, 1748-1817* [microform], r4, number 41.
17 Sullivan, *From Redcoat to Rebel*, 96-97.
18 Ewald, *Diary of the American War*, 43-44; Journal of the Fusilier Regiment von Knyphausen, 1776-83, *Hessian Documents of the American Revolution*, Morristown National Historic Park, section P, fiche 279, P.22; Account of Captain Henrich Bocking – senior captain of the Rall Regiment, in: Burgoyne and Mayer. "The Battle of Trenton, 26 December 1776: Reports from the von Jungkenn Papers," 26-27.
19 Journal of the Hessian Corps… under Gen. von Heister, 1776-77, Letter AA (Part 1) – Fiche No. 3, Reports of von Donop, etc., AA 62 – 63 - letter of Surgeon Oliva, Trenton, January 13, 1777, *Hessian Documents of the American Revolution*, Morristown National Historical Park,
20 Barth, Dorneman, Schwalm, "The Trenton Prisoner List".
21 Stryker, *Trenton and Princeton*, 192. Oliva says Rall died the evening of the battle, December 26. The exact location of his grave is unknown.
22 Royster, *A Revolutionary People at War*, 111.
23 Executive Committee to Thomas Fleming (Colonel of 9th Virginia Regiment), December 27, 1776, Smith, *Letters of Delegates to Congress, 1774-1789*, V: 676.
24 Thomas Wharton, President of the Pennsylvania Council of Safety, to John Hancock, December 27, 1776, *PCC*, Pennsylvania State Papers, 1775-1791, I: 295, *PCC* [microform] r83. Also: Thomas Wharton to President of Congress, December 27, 1776, Wharton, "Thomas Wharton, Junr.," 435. This was one of several letters from Wharton this day. See n40 below. Wharton was essentially the governor of Pennsylvania although that title was not used.
25 Francis Lewis, Baltimore, to the New York Committee of Safety, December 27, 1776, Smith, *Letters of Delegates to Congress*, V: 678.
26 *JCC*, December 27, 1776, VII: 1042-1046; Burnett, *The Continental Congress*, 233.
27 Holt, "Continental Currency," 89-90.
28 Robert Morris, Philadelphia, to John Hancock, 11:00am December 27, 1776, Smith, *Letters of Delegates to Congress, 1774-1789*, V: 682.
29 Marshall, *Passages from Diary*, I:123-124.
30 David Griffith, Philadelphia, to Major Leven Powell, December 27, 1776 in Powell, *Biographical Sketch of Col. Leven Powell*, 72-74.
31 Avery, "Battle of Trenton," 155; How, *Diary of David How*, 41.
32 Colonel John Haslet, Trenton, to Caesar Rodney, January 1, 1777, Rodney, *Diary of Captain Thomas Rodney*, 52; *Delaware Archives: Revolutionary War in Three Volumes*, Wilmington: Chas. L. Story, 1919, III:1396. Several authors state his fall into the water happened on the crossing to Trenton, but in the letter he states, "On our victorious return from Trenton, I fell into the Delaware, at 3 o'clock, in the morning, …."
33 Dewey, *Life of George Dewey*, 280. "The Journal of John Dewey."
34 Smith, *Historical Collections*, Book 1, 89.
35 *George Washington Papers*, Revolutionary War Series, VII: 449 note 1. Davis, *History of Bucks County*, II: 125, 297. She was the widow of John Harris.
36 Burgoyne, *Defeat, Disaster, and Dedication*, 21; *Diary of Captain Wiederholdt*, 25-33. Translated by Dr. Ernst Kipping. Also stated in Davis, *History of Bucks County*, II: 125.
37 Bowen, *The Presbyterian Church Newtown.*
38 Dr. William Shippen, Sr. to his Brother, January 4, 1777, *PMH&B*, XXI (1897), 497-498.
39 Burgoyne, *Defeat, Disaster, and Dedication*, 77-79. 24 Learned and Grosse, *Diary of Captain Wiederholdt*, 25-33. Translated by Dr. Ernst Kipping.

40 Thomas Wharton, President of the Pennsylvania Council of Safety, to John Hancock, December 27, 1776, *PCC*, Pennsylvania State Papers, 1775-1791, I: 299, *PCC* [microform] r83. This was one of several letters from Wharton this day. See n24 above.

41 Stephen Moylan, Newtown, to Robert Morris, December 27, 1776 – carried by Colonel Baylor, *PCC*, Pennsylvania State Papers, 1775-91, r83, i69, p299.

42 George Johnston, McConkey's Ferry, to Leven Powell, December 29, 1776 in Powell, *Biographical Sketch of Col. Leven Powell*, 42-43.

43 NARA M804, PF W5944 Joseph Brearley– deposition of John Stevens.

44 Return of Prisoners taken at Trenton the 26th December 1776, *PCC*, Pennsylvania State Papers, 1775-91, r83, i69, p155; also *PCC*, Transcripts of letters from George Washington 1776, Unknown return of German mercenaries captured at Trenton – transcript, r186, i169, p433; Stryker, *Trenton and Princeton*, 201.

45 George Washington, Newtown, to President of Congress, December 27, 1776 in Fitzpatrick, *Writings of George Washington*, VI: 441-444.

46 George Washington, Newtown, to William Heath, December 27, 1776, in Ibid., VI: 444-445.

47 George Washington, Newtown, to Colonel John Cadwalader, December 27, 1776, in Ibid., VI: 445-447; *Papers of George Washington*, Revolutionary War Series, VII: 449-450.

48 Probably a colloquial spelling of fusil, a light flintlock musket.

49 Clyde, *Rosbrugh, A Tale of the Revolution*, 58-60.

50 Rodney, *Diary of Captain Thomas Rodney*, 24.

51 Peale, "Journal of Charles Willson Peale," *The Crayon*, III, 38.

52 Young, "Journal of Sergeant William Young," 259.

53 Reed, "General Joseph Reed's Narrative," 395-396.

54 Rau, "Sergeant John Smith's Diary of 1776," 268.

55 Reed, "General Joseph Reed's Narrative," 395-396; Reed, *Life and Correspondence*, I: 280-281. Also, Cadwalader, Burlington, to George Washington, December 27, 1776, 10:00pm, *GWPLOC*.

56 Rodney, *Captain Thomas Rodney's Diary*, 24.

57 Reed, *Life and Correspondence*, I: 278-281; Reed, "General Joseph Reed's Narrative," 396-397. Also, Cadwalader, Burlington, to George Washington, 10:00pm December 27, 1776, *GWPLOC*.

58 Thomas Nelson, Baltimore, to Thomas Jefferson, January 2, 1777, Boyd, *Papers of Thomas Jefferson*, II: 3-4.

59 NARA M804, PF S3620 Robert Wright; Reed, *Life and Correspondence*, I: 281-282.

60 Reed, *Life and Correspondence*, I: 280-281. Also, Cadwalader, Burlington, to George Washington, December 27, 1776, 10:00pm, *GWPLOC*; Rodney, *Diary of Captain Thomas Rodney*, 24.

61 Peale, "Journal of Charles Willson Peale," *The Crayon*, III, 38.

62 Rau, "Sergeant John Smith's Diary of 1776," 268.

63 Reed, *Life and Correspondence*, I: 280-281. Also, Cadwalader to George Washington, Burlington, 10:00pm December 27, 1776, *GWPLOC*.

64 Jackson, *Margaret Morris*, 58-59.

66 General Orders, Newton, December 27, 1776, in Powell, *Biographical Sketch of Col. Leven Powell*, 44-45; *Papers of George Washington*, Revolutionary War Series, VII: 448-449; Stryker, *Trenton and Princeton*, 353.

**Chapter 12**

1 Gruber, *John Peebles' American War*, 74-75

2 Mackenzie, *Diary of Frederick Mackenzie*, 131-132.

3 Robertson, *His Diaries and Sketches in America*, 117.

4 Howe's Order Book, HQ, New York, 28th December - *Early American Orderly Books, 1748-1817*, [microform], r4, number 40.

5 Bamford, "Diary," 23.

6 Marshall, *Passages from Diary*, I: 124.

7 Executive Committee (Robt Morris, Geo Walton, Geo Clymer), Philadelphia, to John Hancock, December 28, 1776, Smith, *Letters of Delegates to Congress, 1774-1789*, V: 683-4.

8 George Washington to Robert Morris, December 25, 1776; George Washington to Committee of Congress, January 1, 1777, Fitzpatrick, *Writings of George Washington*, VI: 436-437, 464.

9 Executive Committee, Philadelphia, to George Washington, December 28, 1776, Smith, *Letters of Delegates to Congress, 1774-1789*, V: 685-686. Washington agreed with them and wrote them on January 1, 1777 that by doing this, "I think they may be sent back in the spring so fraught with a love of liberty and property too, that they may create a disgust to the service among the remainder of the foreign troops, and widen that breach, which is already opened between them and the British." He also agreed with trying to get the New England men who would not extend their enlistments to go to Philadelphia and help get the frigates out to sea. George Washington to Committee of Congress, January 1, 777, *GWPLOC.*

10 Washington agreed and in his January 1, 1777 letter to Robert Morris, George Clymer and George Walton he reiterated the advantages to be gained. See: Fitzpatrick, *Writings of George Washington*, VI: 464.

11 William Hooper to Robert Morris, Baltimore, December 28, 1776, Smith, *Letters of Delegates to Congress, 1774-1789*, V: 689.

12 *Pennsylvania Evening Post*, December 28, 1776, 611-614.

13 Nelson, *General James Grant*, 110 –citing Grant to Donop, December 28 – Donop Papers, *Hessian Documents of the American Revolution*, Morristown National Historical Park.

14 Howe, New York, to Grant, December 28, 1776, *James Grant of Ballindalloch Papers*, r36.

15 17th Regiment Order Book, *Early American Orderly Books, 1748-1817* [microform], r4, number 41. At that time a pipe was approximately 100 imperial gallons or about 145 of our gallons today.

16 Ewald, *Diary of the American War*, 44; Journal of the Hessian Grenadier Battalion von Minnegerode, Hessian Documents of the American Revolution, Morristown National Historic Park, section K, fiche 232, K.49; Journal of the Regiment von Alt Lossberg, 1776-83, Ibid., section M, fiche 249, M.55, Journal of the Fusilier Regiment von Knyphausen, 1776-83, section P, fiche 279, P.23; Account of Captain Henrich Bocking – senior captain of the Rall Regiment, in: Burgoyne and Mayer. "The Battle of Trenton, 26 December 1776: Reports from the von Jungkenn Papers," 27-28.

17 Fischer, *Washington's Crossing*, Appendix K, 401.

18 Barth, Dorneman, Schwalm, "The Trenton Prisoner List."

19 Reed, "General Joseph Reed's Narrative," 397; Reed, *Life and Correspondence*, I: 281.

20 Peale, "The Artist-soldier," 38.

21 Rodney, *Diary of Captain Thomas Rodney*, 25-27.

22 Young, "Journal of Sergeant William Young," 259-260; Jackson, *Margaret Morris*, 59.

23 Rau, "Sergeant John Smith's Diary of 1776," 268-269.

24 Burgoyne, *Defeat, Disaster, and Dedication*, 21.

25 Lord Stirling, Newtown, to William Livingston, December 28, 1776, *Papers of William Livingston*, r3, frame 707.

26 George Washington, Headquarters, to Major General William Heath, December 28, 1776; George Washington, Newtown, to Brigadier General Alexander McDougall, December 28, 1776; George Washington, Head Quarters, to Brigadier General William Maxwell, December 28, 1776, Fitzpatrick, *Writings of George Washington*, VI: 447-450.

27 McCarty, "Revolutionary War Journal," 41.

28 How, *Diary of David How*, 41.

29 Dr. William Shippen, Sr. to his Brother, January 4, 1777, *PMH&B*, XXI (1897), 497-498.

**Chapter 13**

1 Mackenzie, *Mackenzie's Diary*, I: 132.

2 Gruber, *John Peebles' American War*, 75.

3 Cresswell, *A Man Apart*, 135; Cresswell, *Journal*, 178

4 General Howe, New York, to Lord George Germain, December 29, 1776, Stryker, *Documents relating to the Revolutionary History of the State of New Jersey*, I:369.

5 Kemble, *Kemble's Journal*, 104.

6 Bamford, "Diary," 23.

7 Howe's Orderly Book, *Early American Orderly Books, 1748-1817* [microform], r4, number 40, HQ New York, December 29.

8 General Howe, New York, to Grant, December 29, 1776, *James Grant of Ballindalloch Papers*, r36.
9 See: https://allthingsliberty.com/2016/07/was-richard-stockton-a-hero/ for a discussion of this.
10 Lt Col James Webster, 33rd Regt., Perth Amboy, to Col. Elisha Lawrence of the New Jersey Volunteers, December 29, 1776, McBurney, *Abductions*, 22.
11 Charles Lee to James Grant, December 29, 1776, *James Grant of Ballindalloch Papers*, r36.
12 Ewald, *Diary of the American War*, 44.
13 Adlum, *Memoirs*, 107.
14 George Johnston, McConkey's, to Leven Powell, December 29, 1776, Powell, *Biographical Sketch of Col. Leven Powell*, 41.
15 Robert Morris, Philadelphia, to Benjamin Harrison, December 29, 1776, Smith, *Letters of Delegates to Congress*, V: 693.
16 Ferling, *Ascent of George Washington*, 121.
17 George Washington, Newtown, to President of Congress, December 29, 1776, Fitzpatrick, *Writings of George Washington*, VI: 451-453.
18 Reed, *Life and Correspondence*, I: 281-282.
19 Davis, *History of Bucks County*, II: 125. The teapot was later made into spoons.
20 General Orders, December 29, 1776 in Fitzpatrick, *Writings of George Washington*, VI: 453-454.
21 George Washington, Newtown, to Pennsylvania Council of Safety, December 29, 1776, in Ibid., VI: 453.
22 Burgoyne, *Defeat, Disaster, and Dedication*, 21.
23 *Pennsylvania Evening Post* (Philadelphia, Pennsylvania), Tuesday, December 31, 1776, 617.
24 Executive Committee [Robert Morris, George Clymer, George Walton] to John Hancock, December 30, 1776, Smith, *Letters of Delegates to Congress*, V: 698-700.
25 Marshall, *Passages from Diary*, I: 124.
26 [Hall], *The History of the Civil War in America*, I: 255-256.
27 Learned and Grosse, *Diary of Captain Wiederholdt*, 25-33. Translated by Dr. Ernst Kipping.
28 Barth, Dorneman, Schwalm, "The Trenton Prisoner List."
29 George Washington, Newtown, to President of Congress, December 29, 1776, Fitzpatrick, *Writings of George Washington*, VI: 451-453.
30 Tench Tilghman (for Washington) to Thomas Mifflin, December 29, 1776, *Papers of George Washington*, Revolutionary War Series, VII: 474n.
31 George Washington, Bucks County, to Sir William Howe, December, 29, 1776; George Washington, Newtown, to Major General Charles Lee, December 29, 1776, in Fitzpatrick, *Writings of George Washington*, VI: 454-455.
32 George Washington, Newtown, to Charles Lee, December 29, 1776, Lee, *The Lee Papers*, II: 356-357.
33 Avery, "The Battle of Trenton," 155; McMichael, "Diary of Lieutenant James McMichael," 140; Wilkinson, *Memoirs*, I: 133.
34 How, *Diary of David How*, 41. Howell's Ferry was on the New Jersey side opposite Yardley's Ferry in Pennsylvania.
35 George Johnston, McConkey's Ferry, to Leven Powell, December 29, 1776, in Powell, *Biographical Sketch of Col. Leven Powell*, 43.
36 Rodney, *Diary of Captain Thomas Rodney*, 27; also mentioned by Peale, "The Artist-soldier," 38. NARA M804, PF S3620 Robert Wright.
37 *AO13*, bundle 19. Two other witnesses were Isaac Decou and Miss Sally Barnes, niece of Major John Barnes of the Loyalist forces. Also, Schuyler, *History of St. Michael's Church*, 79. During the British and Hessian occupation, her farm wagon and driver were impressed into service for 15 days and 12 "fat sheep" were confiscated. *NJSA*, Legislature Series, Inventories of Damages by the British and Americans in New Jersey, 1776-1782, Damage Report Claim No. 45 Elizabeth Pearson Burlington County.
38 [Field], "A Recently Discovered Letter," 119.
39 Sellers, "Charles Willson Peale, Artist-Soldier," 277-278.
40 Hagner, "Philip Hagner's Account."
41 Young, "Journal of Sergeant William Young," 260-261; Jackson, *Margaret Morris: Her Journal*, 60. Morris mentioned in her diary that they stopped to thank her.

42 Jackson, *Margaret Morris*, 60.
43 Rau, "Sergeant John Smith's Diary of 1776," 269.
44 Robert Morris, Philadelphia, to Richard Henry Lee, December 29, 1776, Smith, *Letters of Delegates to Congress*, V: 694.

**Chapter 14**

1 Luzader, *Saratoga*, 1-3.
2 Gruber, *John Peebles' American War*, 75.
3 Mackenzie, *Diary of Frederick Mackenzie*, I: 132.
4 Cresswell, *A Man Apart*, 135; Cresswell, *Journal*, 178.
5 *New-York Gazette, and Weekly Mercury* (New York, New York), Monday, December 30, 1776, 3.
6 Howe's Orderly Book, *Early American Orderly Books, 1748-1817* [microform], r4, number 40. HQ New York, December 30.
7 George Walton, Philadelphia, to Richard Henry Lee, 30 December, 1776 – evening, Smith, *Letters of Delegates to Congress*, V: 706.
8 Samuel Cleaveland, New York, to James Grant, December 20, 1776, *James Grant of Ballindalloch Papers*, r36.
9 Robert Abercromby to James Grant, December 30, 1776, Ibid., r36, frame 530.
10 Ewald, *Diary of the American War*, 44; Account of Captain Henrich Bocking – senior captain of the Rall Regiment, Burgoyne and Mayer. "The Battle of Trenton, 26 December 1776: Reports from the von Jungkenn Papers," 27.
11 Ewald, *Diary of the American War*, 44-45.
12 Hart. "Mary White," 159.
13 Committee of Secret Correspondence [Benjamin Harrison, John Witherspoon, Richard Henry Lee, Will Hooper], Baltimore, to the Commissioners at Paris, December 30, 1776, Smith, *Letters of Delegates to Congress*, V: 695-696.
14 John Hancock, Baltimore, to the States, December 30, 1776, Ibid., V: 703.
15 John Hancock to William Livingston "or the present executive power in New Jersey", December 30, 1776, *William Livingston Papers*, r3, item 719.
16 Charles Coxe to William Livingston, December 30, 1776, Ibid., r3, frame 716.
17 Executive Committee [Robert Morris, George Clymer, George Walton] to John Hancock, December 30, 1776, Smith, *Letters of Delegates to Congress*, V: 698-700.
18 Robert Morris, Philadelphia, to George Washington, December 30, 1776, Ibid., V: 704.
19 Parole signed by 20 officers, dated December 30, 1776, Newtown, Gates, *Horatio Gates Papers*, r4, frame 336. The next frame is the parole of Carle Fuhrer of the Knyphausen Regiment and signed at Trenton Falls on December 30, 1776.
20 Burgoyne, *Defeat, Disaster, and Dedication*, 21-22.
21 Jackson, *Margaret Morris*, 60.
22 Benjamin Rush, Crosswicks, to Richard Henry Lee, December 30, 1776, Smith, *Letters of Delegates to Congress*, V: 705-706; McBurney, *Abductions*, 22.
23 Williams, *Biography of Revolutionary Heroes*, 192.
24 Peale, "The Artist-soldier," 38. He also noted the bringing in of British prisoners from Princeton.
25 Young, "Journal of Sergeant William Young," 261.
26 Rau, "Sergeant John Smith's Diary of 1776," 269-270.
27 Rodney, *Diary of Captain Thomas Rodney*, 27-28.
28 Stryker, *Trenton and Princeton*, 246; Wilkinson, *Memoirs*, I: 133; McMichael, "Diary of Lieutenant James McMichael," 140; Dewey, *Life of George Dewey*, 280; George Washington to John Hancock, January 1, 1777, *GWPLOC*.
29 [Root], "The Battle of Princeton," 515-516. See statement about his correct identification in *BPMP*, Appendix I: item 111-112.
30 McCarty, "Revolutionary War Journal," 41.
31 Avery, "Battle of Trenton," 155.
32 How, *Diary of David How*, 41.
33 Wilkinson, *Memoirs*, I: 133.

34 General Orders, December 30, 1776, *Papers of George Washington*, Revolutionary War Series, VII: 484.
35 George Washington, Trenton, to the officer commanding at Morristown, December 30, 1776, in Fitzpatrick, *Writings of George Washington*, VI: 455-456.
36 George Washington, Trenton, to Robert Morris, December 30, 1776, in Ibid., VI: 457.
37 Nathanael Greene, Trenton, to Catharine Greene, December 30, 1776, Showman, *Nathanael Greene Papers*, I: 377.
38 Reed, *Life and Correspondence*, I: 282-283, Wilkinson, *Memoirs*, I: 133-134; Collins, *A Brief Narrative*, 30.
39 McMichael, "Diary of Lieutenant James McMichael," 140; NARA M804, PF W1092 John Stevens – his deposition and the supporting deposition of Israel Clark. 1st Hunterdon County Regiment militiaman Stevens says he went with Reed as a guide. There is no other documentary confirmation of this, but there was no reason for Stevens to lie and, even though Reed had some familiarity with the area, a guide was an appropriate and normal addition. Fischer, *Washington's Crossing*, 279-80; Reed, "General Joseph Reed's Narrative," 399-400; See also - Reed, *Life and Correspondence*, I: 283; Wilson, *Book of the First Troop*, 8; Wilkinson, *Memoirs*, I: 134-135; Peters, "A Scrap of 'Troop' History," 225-227.

**Chapter 15**

1 Lord North to the King from Bushy Park, December 31, 1776, Fortescue, *Correspondence of King George the Third*, III: 410.
2 Lord George Germain to William Knox, December 31, 1776 from Drayton, *Historical Manuscripts Commission*, 128. Also, *The Manuscripts of Captain Howard Vincente Knox* (From Volume VI of "Report on Manuscripts in Various Collections") prepared by The Historical Manuscripts Commission, Great Britain with a new Introduction and Preface by George Athan Billias, Boston: Gregg Press, 1972.
3 Memorial, December 31, 1776, Silas Deane. "The Deane Papers," I: 434-442.
4 Lieutenant Governor Marriot Arbuthnot, Halifax, to Germain, December 31, 1776, K.G. Davies, *Documents of the American Revolution*, XII: 278-279.
5 Gruber, *John Peebles' American War*, 75-76.
6 Mackenzie, *Diary of Frederick Mackenzie*, I: 132.
7 Bamford, "Diary," 23-24.
8 Kemble, *Kemble's Journal*, 105.
9 Robertson, *His Diaries and Sketches in America*, 117-118.
10 Cresswell, *A Man Apart*, 135; Cresswell, *Journal*, 178.
11 Leven Powell, Williamsburg, to Sally Harrison Powell, December 31, 1776, in Powell, *Biographical Sketch of Col. Leven Powell*, 21-23.
12 *Pennsylvania Evening Post* (Philadelphia, Pennsylvania), Tuesday, December 31, 1776, 617.
13 Marshall, *Passages from Diary*, I:124.
14 Burgoyne, *Defeat, Disaster, and Dedication*, 22, 79; Learned and Grosse, "Diary of Captain Wiederholdt," 25-33. Translated by Dr. Ernst Kipping.
15 James Smith, Baltimore, to [wife] Eleanor Smith, December 31, 1776, Smith, *Letters of Delegates to Congress*, V: 714.
16 William Whipple to Josiah Bartlett, Baltimore, December 31, 1776, Ibid., V: 715-716.
17 Colonel Cadwalader,Crosswicks, to George Washington, December 31, in *GWPLOC* and Reed, *Life and Correspondence*, I: 283-284; Journal of the Fusilier Regiment von Knyphausen, 1776-83, *Hessian Documents of the American Revolution*, Morristown National Historic Park, section P, fiche 279, P.23.
18 Joseph Hodgkins, Crosswicks, to wife, December 31, 1776, Wade, *This Glorious Cause*, 228-229.
19 Dwyer, *The Day is Ours!*, 379; NARA M804, PF S32864 Joseph Hodgkins.
20 Peale, "The Artist-soldier," 38.
21 Young, "Journal of Sergeant William Young," 261-262.
22 Stone, *Life and Recollections of John Howland*, 71.
23 NARA M804, PF S39,835 Philip Rodman.
24 Rau, "Sergeant John Smith's Diary of 1776," 270.

25 Brigade Orders, Bordentown, December 31, 1776, "Selections from Correspondence," *Proceedings of the New Jersey Historical Society*, I (1867-69), 38; Stryker, *Trenton and Princeton*, 431.
26 Jackson, *Margaret Morris*, 60.
27 Rodney, *Diary of Captain Thomas Rodney*, 28-30.
28 George Washington, Trenton, to Major General William Heath, December 31, 1776; George Washington, Trentown, to the friends of America in the State of New Jersey, December 31, 1776, Fitzpatrick, *Writings of George Washington*, VI: 458-460.
29 George Washington, Trenton, to the President of Congress, January 1, 1777 in Ibid., VI: 460-463.
30 Royster, *A Revolutionary People at War*, 118-119.
31 Fischer, *Washington's Crossing*, 281; Kidder, *A People Harassed and Exhausted*, 219.
32 George Washington, Trenton, to John Hancock, January 1, 1777, *GWPLOC*.
33 George Washington, Trenton, to Robert Morris, December 31, 1776, Fitzpatrick, *Writings of George Washington*, VI: 457-458.
34 Stryker, *Trenton and Princeton*, 254-255.
35 Avery, "Battle of Trenton," 156.
36 [Root], "The Battle of Princeton," 515-516.
37 Dewey, *Life of George Dewey*, 280.
38 Williams, *Biography of Revolutionary Heroes*, 185; NARA M804, PF S46399 Stephen Olney.
39 Powell, "Elisha Bostwick's Memoirs," 103. Washington wrote to Robert Morris on August 14, 1777 that, "In looking over my private acct with the Public, I find a credit to it of a blank number of silver dollars sent me by you whilst I lay at Trenton about the first of Jany – for want of the sum, I cannot babl the acct. and shall ask you for information on this head." Sol Feinstone Collection of the American Revolution, #2216.
40 NARA M804, PF S23925 Moses Smith.
41 NARA M804, PF S12558 Oliver Corey. He gives Captain Moody Dustin as commander of the life guard. Dustin was in a New Hampshire Regiment and Sullivan was from New Hampshire. Sargent's regiment was in Sullivan's Brigade at Trenton. The story is plausible. Corey was discharged at Morristown and returned home.
42 George Washington, Trenton, to Robert Morris, George Clymer, and George Walton, January 1, 1777, in Fitzpatrick, *Writings of George Washington*, VI: 463-464.
43 NARA M804, PF W459 Jacob Francis. This pension file application is quite extensive and gives much about his life after leaving the Continentals, including his service in the 3rd Hunterdon County Regiment of militia and his eventual marriage. He is often said to be a slave, but his pension file clearly states his indenture time was sold, not his person. For more on his life see: Larry Kidder, "The American Revolution of Private Jacob Francis," *Journal of the American Revolution*, March 6, 2018, online at: allthingsliberty.com.
44 NARA M804, PF W1964 Ebenezer White. Several other men from his regiment who left the service were Daniel Buck NARA M804, PF W14,432, who was also sick, and Isaac Lee NARA M804, PF W20463.
45 Johnston, *Yale in the Revolution*, 255.
46 Captain William Hull, Trenton, to Andrew Adams, January 1, 1777, Johnston, *Yale in the Revolution*, 278. Other officers who took new commissions in the new regiments included Thomas Grosvenor who advanced from captain in Col. Durkee's regiment to major of Col. Wyllys's regiment on January 1, 1777 and Col. John Paterson of the 15th Continental Regiment who was appointed colonel in a new Massachusetts regiment and then promoted to Brigadier General in February 1777. Ibid., 231, 243; Egleston, *Life of John Paterson*, 101-102..
47 Ibid., 248.
48 Fischer, *Washington's Crossing*, 281.
49 George Johnston, Philadelphia, to Leven Powell, January 5, 1777, Powell, *Biographical Sketch of Col. Leven Powell*, 46-47. F. Johnston [should be George Johnston, major in 5th Virginia Regiment in Adam Stephens' brigade], Philadelphia, to John Muir – merchant of Alexandria, January 5, 1777, *Powell Family Papers*, Hepburn Addition, Special Collections Research Center, Swem Library College of William and Mary.

**Chapter 16**

1 Robert Grant, London, to James Grant, January 1, 1777, *James Grant of Ballindalloch Papers*, r36.
2 Said during debate on the bill for restraining the trade of the New England colonies in 1775. Cobbett, Cobbett's *Parliamentary History*, XVIII: 446.
3 Hutson, *Adventures in British America.*
4 Grant to Richard Rigby, September 2, 1776, Nelson, *General James Grant*, 85.
5 George III to Lord North, January 1, 1777 8 min. pt. M. from Queen's House, Donne, *Correspondence of King George the Third with Lord North*, II: 51; Fortescue, *Correspondence of King George the Third*, 415.
6 Ambrose Serle, New York, to the Earl of Dartmouth, January 1, 1777, Stevens, *Facsimiles*, XXIV, item 2049.
7 Howe's Order Book, Head Quarters New York, January 1, 1777, *Early American Orderly Books, 1748-1817*, r4, item 40.
8 Howe to Grant, January 1, 1777, *James Grant of Ballindolloch Papers*, r37.
9 Muenschhausen, *Journal*, 9.
10 Burrows, *Forgotten Patriots*, 62-63; *Connecticut Gazette*, January 17, 1777, 2.
11 Gruber, *John Peebles' American War*, 76.
12 Cresswell, *A Man Apart*, 135; Cresswell, *Journal*, 178-79.
13 "Extracts from the Records of the Moravian Congregation at Hebron, Pennsylvania, 1775-1781," *PMH&B*, XVIII: 449-462, 450.
14 Jackson, *Margaret Morris*, 60-61.
15 Eddis, *Letters from America*, 175-179.
16 Annapolis, February 16, To the Printers. *New York Gazette, and Weekly Mercury*, February 27, 1775, 2.
17 Samuel Adams, Baltimore, to James Warren, January 1, 7777, Smith, *Letters of Delegates to Congress*, VI: 3.
18 William Hooper, Baltimore, to Joseph Hewes, January 1, 1777, Ibid., VI: 7-9.
19 Oliver Wolcott, Baltimore, to Laura Wolcott, January 1, 1777, Ibid., VI: 14.
20 Matthew Thornton, Baltimore, to Meshech Weare, January 1, 1777, Ibid., VI: 12-13.
21 William Hooper, Baltimore, to Joseph Hewes, January 1, 1777, Ibid., VI: 7-9.
22 Samuel Adams, Baltimore, to James Warren, January 1, 7777, Ibid., VI: 3.
23 Committee of Secret Correspondence, Baltimore, to Benjamin Franklin, January 1, 1777, Ibid., VI: 4.
24 Matthew Thornton, Baltimore, to Meshech Weare, January 1, 1777, Ibid., VI: 12-13.
25 Elbridge Gerry, Baltimore, to Joseph Hawley, January 1, 1777, Ibid., VI: 4-5.
26 William Hooper, Baltimore, to Joseph Hewes, January 1, 1777, Ibid., VI: 7-9.
27 Thomas Nelson, Baltimore, to Thomas Jefferson, January 2, 1777, Boyd, *Papers of Thomas Jefferson*, II: 3-4.
28 Marshall, *Passages from Diary*, I:125.
29 Burgoyne, *Defeat, Disaster, and Dedication*, 23.
30 Inman, "George Inman's Narrative of the American Revolution," 239-240.
31 Ewald, *Diary of the American War*, 48; Fischer, *Washington's Crossing*, 281, 525n14.
32 Collins, *A Brief Narrative*, 20-24.
33 Ewald, *Diary of the American War*, 48; Robertson, *Diaries and Sketches*, 118; Nelson, *General James Grant*, 111; A. Robertson, ADQM genl, Princetown, 1 o'clock, to General Grant, *James Grant of Ballindalloch Papers*, r36.
34 Robertson, *His Diaries and Sketches in America*, 118.
35 *James Grant of Ballindalloch Papers of Ballindalloch Castle, Scotland*; Microfilm, Library of Congress, r37, Correspondence, January, 1777. Von Donop to Grant, Cantonement Brunswick 6 January 1777 (translation of original in French then to English) *BPMP*, Appendix II; British sources, item 6.
36 [Root], "The Battle of Princeton," 54-57.
37 Nelson, General James Grant, 111; Robertson, *His Diaries and Sketches in America*, 118; O'Shaunessy, *Men who Lost America*, 252.
38 Fischer, *Washington's Crossing*, 291.
39 Collins, *A Brief Narrative*, 31.
40 Fischer, *Washington's Crossing*, Appendix K, 401.

41 Stryker, *Trenton and Princeton*, 256; George Washington, Trenton, to John Hancock, January 1, 1777, *GWPLOC.*
42 How, *Diary of David How*, 41-42. Both items remained in his family for many years. He later went out as a militiaman and served at the time of the Battle of Saratoga.
43 Robert Morris to George Washington, January 1, 1777, *GWPLOC.*
44 George Washington to Robert Morris, George Clymer, and George Walton, a Committee of Congress, January 1, 1777, *GWPLOC.*
45 *Pennsylvania Evening Post*, January 14, 1777, 20.
46 Joseph Reed to Council of Safety, January 1, 1777, Hazard, ed., *PA Archives*, Series 1, V: 151.
47 Young, "Journal of Sergeant William Young," 262.
48 Rodney, *Diary of Captain Thomas Rodney*, 30.
49 In his brigade orders, Mifflin misidentified Holland as a major. As a captain he also served as adjutant for the regiment. Holland was later killed at the Battle of Germantown. General Orders, Trenton, January 1, 1777, Fitzpatrick, *Writings of George Washington*, VI: 466.
50 Bordentown Brigade Orders, January 1, 1777, "Selections from Correspondence," *Proceedings of the New Jersey Historical Society*, I (1867-69), 39-40; Nathanael Greene, Trenton, to General John Cadwalader, January 1, 1777, Showman, *Nathanael Greene Papers*, II: 3.
51 McCarty, "Revolutionary War Journal," 41.
52 George Washington, Trenton, to John Hancock, January 1, 1777, *GWPLOC.*
53 George Washington to Robert Morris, George Clymer, and George Walton, a Committee of Congress, January 1, 1777, *GWPLOC.*
54 Private Lardner, Tacony, to Captain Smith, July 31, 1824 in Stryker, *Trenton and Princeton*, 442-443.
55 Wilkinson, *Memoirs*, I: 135; Stryker, *Trenton and Princeton*, 261-263.
56 George Washington to Robert Morris, George Clymer, and George Walton, a Committee of Congress, January 1, 1777, *GWPLOC.*
57 George Washington, Trenton, to John Hancock, January 1, 1777, *GWPLOC.*
58 Colonel John Haslet, Trenton, to Caesar Rodney, January 1, Rodney, *Diary of Captain Thomas Rodney*, 51-52.
59 Rush, *Autobiography*, 125 -126. See Royster, *A Revolutionary People at War*, 111 for discussion of people with Mercer's attitude.
60 Rush, *Autobiography*, 126-127.
61 *AO13* bundle 25, 532-534.

**Chapter 17**

1 Rush, *Autobiography*, 126-127.
2 Peale, "The Artist-soldier," 38; Sellers, "Charles Willson Peale, Artist-Soldier," 131.
3 Young, "Journal of Sergeant William Young," 262-263.
4 Stone, *Life and Recollections of John Howland*, 71-72. See also: Williams, *Biography of Revolutionary Heroes*, 193.
5 Manuscript of Samuel Massey, Captain 7th Co. Philade militia, 4th Battalion in 1777 - The Property of Louis C. Massey, great grandson, *John Reed Collection*, Record Group 10, Valley Forge NHP, transcribed in *BPMP*, Appendix 1, item 81.
6 Ewald, *Diary of the American War*, 48. Ewald gave the marching order as: "the vanguard under Colonel Donop consisted of the two Jäger companies, one hundred Hessian grenadiers, and two troops of light dragoons from the 16th Regiment. Then followed the light infantry and a number of 6-pounders, the English and Hessian grenadiers, the remnants of the decimated Hessian brigade, two English brigades, and the 16th Regiment of Dragoons."
7 Smith, *Battle of Princeton*, 19; Fischer, *Washington Crossing*, 327; Collins, *A Brief Narrative*, 19.
8 Robertson, *His Diaries and Sketches in America*, 118-119; Muenschhausen, *Journal*, 9, 58.
9 *James Grant of Ballindalloch Papers of Ballindalloch Castle, Scotland*; Microfilm, Library of Congress, r37, Correspondence, January, 1777. Von Donop to Grant, Cantonement Brunswick 6 January 1777 (translation of original in French then to English) *BPMP*, Appendix II; British sources, item 6.
10 Thomas Dowdeswell to Rockingham, January 16, 1777, Dowdeswell, "Operations in New Jersey," 135.

11 Fischer, *Washington's Crossing*, Appendix K, 401.
12 NARA M804, PF S2298 James Johnston.
13 Adams, *Diary and Autobiography*, II: 265.
14 Peale, "The Artist-soldier," 131.
15 Young, "Journal of Sergeant William Young," 262-263.
16 Clyde, *Rosbrugh, A Tale of the Revolution*, 55, 58-60.
17 Rush, *Autobiography*, 127.
18 Stone, *Life and Recollections of John Howland*, 71-72.
19 NARA M804, PF S5752 Thomas McGee.
20 McMichael, "Diary of Lieutenant James McMichael," 139.
21 Reed, *Life and Correspondence*, I: 286-287.
22 Dewey, *Life of George Dewey*, 280.
23 Stryker, *Trenton and Princeton*, 261-263.
24 Unidentified militiaman from unidentified source quoted by Dwyer, *The Day is Ours!*, 318.
25 F. Johnston [should be George Johnston, major in 5th Virginia Regiment in Adam Stephens' brigade], Philadelphia, to John Muir – merchant of Alexandria, January 5, 1777, *Powell Family Papers.*
26 Henry Knox, Trenton, to Lucy Knox, January 7, 1777, Knox, *Papers of Henry Knox* [microform], r3, i112.
27 Peale, "The Artist-soldier," 38; Sellers, "Charles Willson Peale, Artist-Soldier," 131.
28 Young, "Journal of Sergeant William Young," 262-263.
29 NARA M804, PF S2298 James Johnston.
30 NARA M804, PF S1061 William Morris. The *William Morris Tune Book, 1776-1777* is in the collection of the New York Historical Society and can be viewed on-line from the Society's website. Morris had served tours in both Captain John Mott's and Captain William Tucker's companies, as well as the five-month levies in the New York campaign, and had learned to drum at Elizabethtown from a British deserter who was a drum major.
31 Avery, "The Battle of Trenton," 155.
32 Hood, Account of the "Engagement at Trenton and Princeton .. the 2nd & 3d of Jany in 1777," #907 *Sol Feinstone Collection of the American Revolution*; [Hood], "Engagements at Trenton and Princeton, January 2 and 3, 1777," 263. Waln owned the stone grist mill at the stone bridge over the Assunpink Creek.
33 Rodney, *Diary of Captain Thomas Rodney*, 30.
34 *AO13* bundle 25, 532-534. He was kept at Newtown for three weeks and then escaped with several other prisoners who got safely to New Brunswick. He continued in Loyalist service on Staten Island and then South Carolina. He settled in East Florida after the war and then in Nova Scotia.
35 Henry Knox, Trenton, to Lucy Knox, January 2, 1777; January 7, 1777, Knox, *Papers of Henry Knox* [microform], r3, i109, i112.
36 Henry Knox, Trenton, to John Lamb, January 2, 1777, Leake, *Memoir of the Life and Times of General John Lamb*, 148-149.
37 Armes, *Nancy Shippen Her Journal Book*, 35-39. Nancy came from a very patriotic family and had two uncles who signed the Declaration of Independence.
38 NARA M804, PF S5310 Preserved Buffington.
39 McCarty, "Revolutionary War Journal," 41.
40 Williams, *Biography of Revolutionary Heroes*, 193; McMichael, "Diary of Lieutenant James McMichael," 140-141.
41 Hagner, Philip Hagner's Account, *Joseph Reed Papers* [microform].
42 *James Grant of Ballindalloch Papers of Ballindalloch Castle, Scotland*; Microfilm, Library of Congress, r37, Correspondence, January, 1777. Von Donop ltr to Grant, Cantonement Brunswick 6 January 1777 (translation of original in French then to English) *BPMP*, Appendix II; British sources, item 6.
43 Published accounts of this encounter are based on General James Wilkinson, *Memoirs*, I: 136, who quotes in a source note an "extract of a letter from a respectable inhabitant," dated Lawrenceville, August 22, 1816. Fischer, *Washington's Crossing*, 295; Stryker, *Trenton and Princeton*, 258 – Fischer describes Elias Hunt as a civilian and Stryker as "a farmer in that neighborhood." For Hunt's militia

connection see NARA M804, PF S1024 Israel Hunt; *NJSA*, RevWarMss 673, 689. NARA M804, PF W575 John Phillips. Maidenhead militiaman John Phillips probably took part in this ambush because he was with the "advance part of the army in the village" of Maidenhead and retreated "with the army to Trenton when the British Army advanced a second time on that place."
44 NARA M804, PF W391 James Barnett; NARA M804, PF S16981 William Montgomery.
45 NARA M804, PF S38202 Thomas Mc Gee.
46 Wilkinson, *Memoirs*, I: 136-138; Watts, "A Memoir of General Henry Miller," 426; Fischer, *Washington's Crossing*, 296-297.
47 Ewald, *Diary of the American War*, 49.
48 Robertson, *His Diaries and Sketches in America*, 119.
49 Wilkinson, *Memoirs*, I: 136-138.
50 Dewey, *Life of George Dewey*, 280.
51 Wilkinson, *Memoirs*, I: 136-138; Fischer, *Washington's Crossing*, 298.
52 Hagner, Philip Hagner's Account, *Joseph Reed Papers* [microform].
53 Henry Knox, Trenton, to Lucy Knox, January 7, 1777, Knox, *Papers of Henry Knox* [microform], r3, i112, 7; *Hessian Documents of the American Revolution*, Morristown National Historical Park, Von Donop to Heister, January 6 from Brunswick, AA 49 – 50.
54 Wilkinson, *Memoirs*, I: 138; Fischer, *Washington's Crossing*, 298.
55 Williams, *Biography of Revolutionary Heroes*, 193.
56 Henry Knox, Trenton, to Lucy Knox, January 7, 1777, Knox, *Papers of Henry Knox* [microform], r3, i112, 7; *Hessian Documents of the American Revolution*, Morristown National Historical Park, Von Donop to Heister, January 6 from Brunswick, AA 49 – 50.
57 Robertson, *His Diaries and Sketches in America*, 119-120.
58 Haven, *Thirty Days in New Jersey*, 44-47.
59 [Hood], Account of the "Engagement at Trenton and Princeton .. the 2nd & 3d of Jany in 1777," #907 *Sol Feinstone Collection of the American Revolution*; [Hood], "Engagements at Trenton and Princeton, January 2 and 3, 1777," 263-265.
60 Ewald, *Diary of the American War*, 49.
61 *James Grant of Ballindalloch Papers of Ballindalloch Castle, Scotland*; Microfilm, Library of Congress, r37, Correspondence, January, 1777. Von Donop ltr to Grant, Cantonement Brunswick 6 January 1777 (translation of original in French then to English) *BPMP*, Appendix II; British sources, item 6.
62 Howland, *Life and Recollections*, 74-75.
63 Ryan, *Salute to Courage*, 56. Ensign was the lowest commissioned rank and he normally carried the flag.
64 Journal of the Hessian Grenadier Battalion von Minnegerode, *Hessian Documents of the American Revolution*, Morristown National Historic Park, Fiche 232, K.49-50.
65 Henry Knox, Trenton, to Lucy Knox, January 7, 1777, Knox, *Papers of Henry Knox* [microform], r3, i112.
66 NARA M804, PF S12636 Isaiah Crandall.
67 *Pennsylvania Evening Post*, April 29, 1777, 237; Clyde, *Rosbrugh, A Tale of the Revolution*, 58-60.
68 Stone, *Life and Recollections of John Howland*, 72-74; Henry Knox Trenton, to Lucy Knox,, January 7, 1777, Knox, *Papers of Henry Knox* [microform], r3, i112.
69 For example, see *Dwyer, The Day is Ours!*, 318.
70 NARA M804, PF S2298 James Johnston; Stryker, *Trenton and Princeton*, 261-263.
71 Stryker, *Trenton and Princeton*, 263-264; Rodney, *Diary of Captain Thomas Rodney*, 30. See: Graydon, *Memoirs*, 247+ for info on Hausegger in New York as "prisoner".
72 NARA M804, PF W109 John Stevens; NARA M804, PF W10137 Titus Mershon.
73 George Johnston to Leven Powell, Philadelphia, January 5, 1777 in Powell, *Biographical Sketch of Col. Leven Powell*, 47. F. Johnston [should be George Johnston, major in 5th Virginia Regiment in Adam Stephens' brigade], Philadelphia, to John Muir – merchant of Alexandria, January 5, 1777, *Powell Family Papers.*
74 Peale, "The Artist-soldier," 38; Sellers, "Charles Willson Peale, Artist-Soldier," 131.
75 Haven, *Thirty Days in New Jersey*, 45.
76 NARA M804, PF W10367 Zebulon Applegate. He was originally from Middlesex County, New Jersey, but went to Philadelphia because of the British occupation of New Jersey.

77 "Abstracts of Pension Applications on File in the Division of Public Records, Pennsylvania State Library," *PA Archives*, Series 5, IV: 586-7.
78 Stone, *Life and Recollections of John Howland*, 72-74.
79 Benjamin Rush to editor of the *Pennsylvania Journal*, July 4, 1782, Butterfield, *Letters of Benjamin Rush*, 276. Letter signed Leonidas.
80 Benjamin Rush to Richard Henry Lee, January 6, 1777, Butterfield, *Letters of Benjamin Rush*, I: 124.
81 Rush, *Autobiography*, 127-128.
82 Rodney, *Diary of Captain Thomas Rodney*, 30.
83 Ryan, *Salute to Courage*, 56. Also: Custis, *Recollections and Private Memoirs of Washington*, 413. In this source Scott is quoted as saying, "To the last man, your excellency."
84 "Anecdotes of Old Gen. Scott," *Daily Constitutionalist* (Augusta, Georgia), July 17, 1835, 1. This unsigned article appeared in a number of newspapers across the country between 1835 and 1860. Just when it was written is unclear.
85 Powell, "Elisha Bostwick's Memoirs," 106. Troops firing too high was a common problem in 18th century warfare.
86 Parker, *Parker in America*, 251. Cites unknown issue of the *Virginia Historical Gazette*. Gives Parker as a captain, but he had been recently promoted to major. The same identical wording and citation is found in: *The American Mercury Magazine*, vol 14, Jan-June 1899, 443, and *The Virginia Magazine of History and Biography*, VI: 1898, 301.
87 Jones, *Life of Ashbel Green*, 173-175 – letter to his son dated September 20, 1842.
88 Wilkinson, *Memoirs*, I: 137-138.
89 Stone, *Life and Recollections of John Howland*, 72-74.
90 Henry Knox, Trenton, to Lucy Knox, January 7, 1777, Knox, *Papers of Henry Knox* [microform], r3, i112.
91 NARA M804, PF S11416 Daniel Smith.
92 Stryker, *Trenton and Princeton*, 264-267; White, "The Good Soldier White," 77-78; [Hood], "Engagements at Trenton and Princeton, January 2 and 3, 1777," 263-265. Also: *Sol Feinstone Collection* #907.
93 Henry Knox, Trenton, to Lucy Knox, January 7, 1777, Knox, *Papers of Henry Knox*, [microform], r3, i112.
94 Von Donop, Brunswick, to Heister, January 6, 1777, *Hessian Documents of the American Revolution*, Morristown National Historical Park, AA 49 – 50.
95 *NJSA*, Legislature Series, Inventories of Damages by the British and Americans in New Jersey, 1776-1782, Charles Axford, Jr.; *Caledonian* (St. Johnsbury, Vermont), July 4, 1843, 3. In another account, Richmond's tavern was severely damaged by British artillery during the battle. Mrs. Richmond had refused to leave town during the events that winter. The notice commented on the recent July 4 celebration and noted that the republicans of Trenton celebrated at her house, which she still lived in, and the federalists dined where the British artillery had been placed. *American Citizen* (New York City), July 16, 1803, 2.
96 For example, see: NARA M804, PF W4963 Enoch Gandy. Other men also described the battle as a "cannonade." See for example, NARA M804, PF S18587 Joseph Sayre. He was a Salem County, New Jersey militiaman who says he was "at the cannonade of Trenton very early in the year 1777." In other pension files men who had not been at the battle on December 26 simply refer to this day as the battle of or at Trenton.
97 Wilkinson, *Memoirs*, I: 138,
98 Inman, "George Inman's Narrative of the American Revolution," 239-240; Smith, *Battle of Princeton*, 19; Fischer, *Washington Crossing*, 327; Collins, *A Brief Narrative*, 19.
99 Gruber, *John Peebles' American War*, 76.
100 Holt, "Continental Currency," 106.
101 Brigade Orders, Bordentown, December 31, 1776, Stryker, *Trenton and Princeton*, 431; Adam Hubley, Jr., Bordentown, to an unknown person, January 4, 1777, Ryan, *Salute to Courage*, 60-61.
102 Thomas Nelson, Baltimore, to Thomas Jefferson, January 2, 1777, Boyd, *Papers of Thomas Jefferson*, II: 3-4.
103 Fischer, *Washington's Crossing*, 313.

**Chapter 18**

1 Muenschhausen, *Journal*, 58.

2 Von Donop, Brunswick, to Heister, January 6, 1777, *Hessian Documents of the American Revolution*, Morristown National Historical Park, AA 49 – 50.

3 McMichael, "Diary of Lieutenant James McMichael," 139-141.

4 Dewey, *Life of George Dewey*, 280.

5 NARA M804, PF W8367 George Blakey.

6 Rodney, *Diary of Captain Thomas Rodney*, 30; Muster Roll, Light Infantry Company of Dover, Delaware Public Archives Commission, *Delaware Archives: Revolutionary War in Three Volumes*, III: 1243. This was apparently made when the company left Morristown in mid-January, 1777 and contains information from December 14, 1776, including the desertion of Martinas Sipple. Rodney's published diary notes that Sipple later joined Col. David Hall's Delaware regiment and became a brave and faithful soldier.

7 White, "The Good Soldier White," 77-78.

8 Miller and Hart, *Peale Family Papers*, V: 51-52; Peale, "The Artist-soldier," 38; Sellers, "Charles Willson Peale, Artist-Soldier," 131.

9 Williams, *Biography of Revolutionary Heroes*, 194-195.

10 Peale, "The Artist-soldier," 38; Sellers, "Charles Willson Peale, Artist-Soldier," 131.

11 NARA M804, PF S23925 Moses Smith; Moses Smith death notice *National Aegis* (Worcester, Massachusetts), July 22, 1846, 3. Smith's accounts contain several inconsistencies, but the loss of his right hand at Trenton on January 2, 1777 seems accurate. He gives a detailed account in his pension application that fits with known facts. In his death notice that relates stories he told of his service he mistakenly says he lost his hand at the battle of Trenton rather than second Trenton, as related in his pension file. He also tells a completely different, but more heroic, story of his service after recovering. He also relates a colorful, but implausible, story about the battle of Trenton, which again was actually the battle of Assunpink. He tells a story in his pension file about capturing British horses at first Trenton that is plausible and is related in this work.

12 "Abstracts of Pension Applications on File in the Division of Public Records, Pennsylvania State Library," *PA Archives*, series 5, IV: 514.

13 Gibson, *Dr. Bodo Otto*, 179-180; Jordan, "Hospitals at Bethlehem and Lititz during the Revolution, 153. Gibson gives his name as Filson.

14 NARA M804, PF S960 Zadock Bowen.

15 Rush, Philadelphia, to Richard Henry Lee, January 14, 1777, Rush, *Letters*, 129; Rush, *Autobiography*, 127.

16 Runes, *Selected Writings of Benjamin Rush*, 327-329.

17 Wilkinson recalled that local school teacher Mary Dagworthy also lived at the house. Mary Dagworthy would later lead local efforts to help supply the Continental soldiers with needed items. For more on this see: Kidder, *Crossroads of the Revolution: Trenton, 1774-1783*, 278-279.

18 Stryker, *Trenton and Princeton*, 246. The Douglas house has been moved from its original location on Greene Street, the site of the German Lutheran Church. It is now at 165 East Front Street.

19 St. Clair, *A Narrative of the Manner in Which the Campaign Against the Indians, in the Year One Thousand Seven Hundred and Ninety-One, was conducted*, 242-243.

20 Private John Lardner, Tacony, to Captain John R.C. Smith, July 31, 1824, transcription in Stryker, *Trenton and Princeton*, 442-443.

21 [Hall], *The History of the Civil War in America*, I: 245-252, 245-246.

22 Lawrence H. Curry, ed., "Martin Hunter's Journal: America 1774-1778." *The Valley Forge Journal* IV No. 1 (June 1988), 1-34, 20. *BPMP*, Appendix II: British sources, item 14.

23 Avery, *The Lord is to be Praised*, 25.

24 Williams, *Biography of Revolutionary Heroes*, 193-194.

25 NARA M804, PF S18,305 Philemon Baldwin, says, "the surface of the earth was frozen & became hard as a pavement." Fischer, *Washington's Crossing*, Appendix K, 401. David M. Ludlum, "The Weather of Independence," *Weatherwise*, Nov/December 1998, vol 51, no 6, p43.

26 [Hall], *The History of the Civil War in America*, I: 257.

27 Stryker, *Trenton and Princeton*, 269-274; Wilkinson, *Memoirs*, I: 138-140. Benjamin Rush credits Joseph Reed for suggesting the maneuver. Butterfield, *Letters of Benjamin Rush*, 1094. For more on the three militia guides see: Kidder, *A People Harassed and Exhausted*, 226. A local tradition was recorded in John O. Raum's, *The History of New Jersey from its Earliest Settlement to the Present Time*, (Philadelphia: John E. Potter, 1877), II: 19, that a local woman, Mrs. Waglum, born Jinnie Jackson, offered her services at the Richmond Tavern to guide Washington and his troops to Princeton. Raum says, "Arrayed in a man's hat and coat, Jinnie rode at the head of the army, and guided them through the woods by Sandtown and Quaker Bridge, and they arrived safely in Princeton, the night before the engagement with the British troops." This is an intriguing story, but cannot be confirmed with contemporary authority, unlike the account of the militia guides. It is also suspect in saying that she offered her services at Richmond's instead of the Douglass house where the council was held and that she got them to Princeton the night before the battle there, when we know they arrived in the early morning shortly before sunrise.

28 NARA M804, PF S994 Alexander Douglass.

29 F. Johnston [should be George Johnston, major in 5th Virginia Regiment in Adam Stephens' brigade], Philadelphia, to John Muir – merchant of Alexandria, January 5, 1777, *Powell Family Papers*.

30 Dow, "The Life Guardsman," 277. Also in *Barre Gazette*, Barre Massachusetts, June 25, 1841, 1. The subject, Hugh Maxwell does not appear on roster of Life Guard, but it is not complete. Use of the term "life guard" does indicate he served in early part of war – which he describes – as Washington forbid use of this term later. Nothing stands out as terribly wrong in the account – minor mistake in number of artillery captured at Trenton (9 vs 6). However, may be somewhat romanticized.

31 Williams, *Biography of Revolutionary Heroes*, 196-197.

32 White, "The Good Soldier White," 77-78.

33 NARA M804, PF R11925 George Yard.

34 Stryker, *Trenton and Princeton*, 274-275.

35 NARA M804, PF W2503 Cornelius Wells; Death notice *Southern Patriot* (Charleston, SC), August 9, 1844, 2; Ibid., PF S9006 Cary McClelland.

36 [Hall], *The History of the Civil War in America*, I: 257-258.

37 Robertson, *His Diaries and Sketches in America*, 119-120.

38 Fischer, *Washington's Crossing*, 317.

39 Joseph Reed to Israel Putnam, January 2, 1777, *Joseph Reed Papers* [microform].

40 Young, "Journal of Sergeant William Young," 265-266.

41 NARA M804, PF S5310 Preserved Buffington.

42 McCarty, "Revolutionary War Journal," 41

43 Peale, "The Artist-soldier," 38.

44 NARA M804, PF S9124 Christopher Burlingame.

45 Ibid., PF S2298 James Johnston.

46 Ibid., PF S5570 William Hutchison.

47 Reed, *Life and Correspondence*, I: 288. For Reed to say that Mercer led with the flying camp was not correct. Mercer had commanded the Flying-Camp until early December when it was disbanded. Reed must have been referring to troops that had once been part of the Flying-Camp under Mercer.

48 Rodney, *Diary of Captain Thomas Rodney*, 32.

49 "An Account of the Battle of Princeton." *The Pennsylvania Evening Post*, 16 January 1777. The identification of John Cadwalader as the author is made in Smith, *The Battle of Princeton*, 38, and reiterated in the *BPMP*.

50 Howland, *Life and Recollections*, 75.

51 Rush, *Autobiography*, 127; Miller and Hart, *Selected Papers of Charles Willson Peale*, V: 52..

52 NARA M804, PF W1092 John Stevens.

53 Ibid., PF S1061 William Morris.

54 Ibid., PF W7560 William R. Green – supporting statement of James B. Green – his son.

55 *Pennsylvania Evening Post*, January 14, 1777, 20; Hunter Research, Fish and Ships, 15.

56 *Pennsylvania Evening Post*, January 21, 1777, 31.

57 Caesar Rodney to George Read, January 23, 1777, Rodney, *Letters to and from Caesar Rodney*, 170 – Rodney heard this story from Tucker while he commanded at Trenton in January and February 1777.

**Chapter 19**

1 Collins, *A Brief Narrative*, 32. This road, today's route 206, was called by various names. Post Road was common because it was the main road between New York and Philadelphia and, therefore, the road taken by postal couriers. It was also called the Upper Road and because it was a major colonial road it might be called the King's Highway, although there were several other main roads that carried that designation, and this name would not be used after independence was declared. It is best to think of road names as descriptive rather than official names. In Princeton, this road might be called the Maidenhead or Trenton road because that is where it went to, and in Trenton, for the same reason, it might be called the Maidenhead or Princeton road.

2 Smith, *Battle of Princeton*, 19. For more information on this group see "Notes on the composition of the Crown Forces transfers and recruits on 3 January 1777" in *BPMP*, Appendix III and: "Operations of the Army under Lt. G. Clinton (beginning on 12 February 1776)." David Library of the American Revolution, *Sol Feinstone Collection No. 132* (Card No. 409); [Hall], *The History of the Civil War in America*, I: 245-252; Inman, "George Inman's Narrative of the American Revolution," 237-248; Hale, "Letters written during the American War of Independence," 16.

3 Wilkinson, *Memoirs*, I: 141; Smith, *Battle of Princeton*, 19-20.

4 *BPMP*, 45; Hood, "Engagements at Trenton and Princeton, January 2 and 3, 1777," 263-265.

5 Rodney, *Diary of Captain Thomas Rodney*, 33; NARA M804, PF R6665 William McCracken.

6 Rodney, *Diary of Captain Thomas Rodney*, 33; *BPMP*, 42-48, Appendix IV. Tilton was afterwards a lieutenant colonel. Different sources give somewhat different compositions for the divisions, but the objectives of each are consistent.

7 White, "The Good Soldier White," 78. "A little before we got in sight of the enemy, our whole army halted. The captain sent me a sergeant with a bucket full of powder and rum, every man must drink a half gill. He came to me to know if I had drank any, I told him no: drink some, said he, I have, so I took a little."

8 Apollos Morris, aide-de-camp to Washington, *BPMP*, 50. Lieutenant John Armstrong: "As the day broke upon us, we discovered troops apparently on the march on the road from Princeton to Trenton. ... the Brigade [Sullivan's] was accordingly halted until Gen. Washington joined it." Undated "Memorandum of Gen. H. Mercer's ... services and character" by Lieutenant John Armstrong, enclosed in a letter to William B. Reed of Philadelphia dated 13 September 1839, in response to an inquiry of 8 July 1839 concerning the death of Mercer at Princeton, *BPMP*, Appendix 1: item 7. Wilkinson, *Memoirs*, I: 142. "We discerned the enemy, by the reflection of their arms against the rising sun ascending the hill in the wood near Cochran's."

9 [Root], "The Battle of Princeton," 516-518; NARA M804, PF S18574 Nathaniel Root.

10 [Hall], *The History of the Civil War in America*, I: 245-252; *BPMP*, 54. Cochran's Hill was also known as Millett's Hill.

11 Henry Knox, Morristown, to Lucy Knox, January 7, 1777, Drake, *Life and Correspondence of Henry Knox*, 39

12 [Hall], *The History of the Civil War in America*, I: 245-252.

13 "Major [Apollos] Morris's Account of the Affair at Trenton, 1776." MS Sparks 53 (Miscellaneous papers relating to the Revolution, 1752-1779, item 4, Harvard University Library, 11-19, *BPMP*, Appendix I: item 90. A "Mr. Richmond", an officer of Hitchcock's Brigade, later said that "Gen. Mercer with the Philada[lphia] Militia desired & were permitted the honor to begin the attack." Dexter, *Literary Diary of Ezra Stiles*, II: 118-120.

14 *BPMP*, 56; Undated "Memorandum of Gen. H. Mercer's ... services and character" by Lieutenant John Armstrong, enclosed in a letter to William B. Reed (1806-1876) of Philadelphia dated 13 September 1839, in response to an inquiry of 8 July 1839 concerning the death of Mercer at Princeton, *BPMP*, Appendix 1: item 7.

15 1778 Court Martial proceedings of Cornet Evatt, Great Britain, Public Record Office, War Office, Class 71, Volume 87, 343-361, *BPMP*, Appendix II: item 8.; [Root], "The Battle of Princeton,"; *BPMP*, 54, 61.

16 Fischer, *Washington's Crossing*, 330.
17 Ibid., 329; They went straight across what is today known as the D'Ambrisi Property. Bradley, Catts, and Selig. "Cheer Up My Boys the Day is Ours…", 22-24. Mawhood's troops attacking Mercer had the dismounted 16th Light Dragoons on the right flank, three companies of the 17th Regiment in the center, and the mounted 16th Light Dragoons on the left flank.
18 Collins, *A Brief Narrative*, 32-33.
19 Fischer, *Washington Crossing*, 330.
20 Collins, *A Brief Narrative*, 36-37.
21 [Hood], "Engagements at Trenton and Princeton, January 2 and 3, 1777," 265.
22 Morris, "Major Morris's Account of the Affair at Trenton, 1776." MS Sparks 53 (Miscellaneous papers relating to the Revolution, 1752-1779. Item 4, pp. 11-19. Harvard University Library, Cambridge, *BPMP*, Appendix 1, item 90; *BPMP*, 62; Rodney, *Diary of Captain Thomas Rodney*, 34.
23 Armstrong, John: Undated "Memorandum of Gen. H. Mercer's ... services and character" by Lieutenant John Armstrong, to Hugh Mercer Jr. in Fredericksburg, Virginia. Enclosed in a letter to William B. Reed of Philadelphia dated 13 September 1839, Collections of Princeton Battlefield State Park, Clarke House. *BPMP*, Appendix I: Primary Sources: Continental Army, item 7.
24 Root, "The Battle of Princeton," 515-516.
25 McMichael, "Diary of Lieutenant James McMichael," *PA Archives*, Second Series, XV: 203.
26 NARA M804, PF S 5501 Jacob Hefflebower.
27 Root, "The Battle of Princeton," 515-516.
28 John Belsches to the Earl of Leven, May 21, 1777, Hale, "Letters Written During the American War of Independence."
29 Lawrence H. Curry, ed., "Martin Hunter's Journal: America 1774-1778." *The Valley Forge Journal*, IV No. 1 (June 1988), 1-34, p. 20. *BPMP*, Appendix II: British sources, item 14.
30 Gilchrist, "The Tragedy of Captain William Leslie & Dr. Benjamin Rush," 25-30. The article gives further source notes and explains the deep relationship between Benjamin Rush and the Leslie family. Several days after the death, Rush came across the body and saw to it that it was interred with full military honors, with the approval of Washington.
31 "Lt. Armstrong's Account of the Engagement of the 3rd January" GD 26/9/513/5, National Archives of Scotland. *BPMP*, Appendix II, Primary sources, British, Item 3.
32 Rodney, *Diary of Captain Thomas Rodney*, 34.
33 NARA M804, PF S9006 Cary McClelland.
34 Skeen, *John Armstrong, Jr., 1758-1843: A Biography*, 3. After the battle he accompanied Mercer's troops to Morristown. He had lost his job as aide-de-camp with Mercer's death, but soon became aide to General Gates in the northern army.
35 *Diary of John Chilton, 3rd VA Regiment*, Virginia Historical Society Mss10: no. 106. Diary, 1777 January 3-September 8. Also published as "The old Virginia Line in the Middle States during the American Revolution. The Diary of Captain John Chilton, 3d Virginia Regt," *Tyler's Quarterly Magazine*, XII, (1931), 283-289, 283. See: Stryker, *Trenton and Princeton*, 455; Lee, *Memoir of Richard Henry Lee*, II, 165; Lieutenant Yates' affidavit on his case, January 14, 1777, *PCC*, vol 53, p47. Describes how he was wounded and then abused by British, shot, bayonetted, and finally died. See transcription in Collins, *A Brief Narrative*, 43-44.
36 Hale, "Letters Written During the American War of Independence."
37 NARA M804, PF S42758 Jonathan Grant.
38 NARA M804, PF S5501 Jacob Hefflebower. "He was carried to a hospital, in the neighborhood of Trenton, where he remained till the spring – when he went to Philadelphia. The wound which deponent received at the said battle, is still visible in his forehead."
39 [Root], "The Battle of Princeton," 515-516.
40 Caesar Rodney to George Read, January 23, 1777, Rodney, *Letters to and from Caesar Rodney*, 170 – Rodney heard this story from Tucker while he commanded at Trenton in January and February 1777. Robertson, *His Diaries and Sketches in America*, 120: "Untill about 8 o'clock a very Brisk fire of Small Arms and Smart Cannonading was heard in our Rear towards Prince Town." Jackson, *Margaret Morris*, 61. "3d -- This Morning between 8 & 9 oClock we heard very distinc[t]ly, a heavy fireing of Cannon".

41 [Hall], *The History of the Civil War in America*, I: 258.

42 *James Grant of Ballindalloch Papers of Ballindalloch Castle, Scotland*; Microfilm, Library of Congress, r37, Correspondence, January, 1777. Von Donop to Grant, Cantonement Brunswick 6 January 1777 (translation of original in French then to English) *BPMP*, Appendix II; British sources, item 6.

43 [Hall], *The History of the Civil War in America*, I: 251-252; Journal of the Hessian Grenadier Battalion von Minnegerode, *Hessian Documents of the American Revolution*, Morristown National Historic Park, section K, fiche 232, K.50-51.

44 Ewald, *Diary of the American War*, 49; "Ensign Glyn's Journal on the American Service with the Detachment of 1,000 Men of the Guards commanded by Brigadier General Mathew in 1776." *Varnum Lansing Collins, Revolutionary War Papers, 1913-1932*, Manuscript Department, Princeton University Library, Princeton, NJ. Transcript in *BPMP*, Appendix II, British sources, item 10.

45 The story of Rosbrugh is told by Hall, *History of the First Presbyterian Church in Trenton*, 163-64; Clyde, *Rosbrugh, A Tale of the Revolution*, 55; Sprague, *Annals of the American Pulpit*, 254-255. Benjamin Rush to Richard Henry Lee, January 14, 1777, Rush, *Letters*, 128. His widow Jean Rosbrugh received a pension from Pennsylvania. He left five minor children. "Abstracts of Pension Applications on File in the Division of Public Records, Pennsylvania State Library," *PA Archives*, series 5, V: 547-8.

46 *Pennsylvania Evening Post*, April 29, 1777, 237.

47 Dowdeswell, "Operations in New Jersey," 135.

48 Henry Knox, Morristown, to Lucy Knox, January 7, 1777, Drake, *Life and Correspondence of Henry Knox*, 38.

49 Hale, "Letters Written during the American War of Independence."

50 Rodney, *Diary of Captain Thomas Rodney*, 32: "Capt. Henry with the other three companies of Philadelphia light Infantry brought up the rear."

51 Lieutenant Peale serving with Cadwalader's militia wrote: "The sun had risen just before we saw Princeton. We proceeded as fast as possible, and were within a mile of the town, when we were informed that all was quiet. A short time after, the battalion just ahead of us, began an exceedingly quick platoon firing, and some cannon. We marched on quickly and met some of the troops retreating in confusion. We continued our march towards the hill where the firing was, though now rather irregularly. I carried my platoon to the top of the hill, and fired, though unwillingly, for I thought the enemy too far off, and then retreated, loading. We returned to the charge, and fired a second time, and retreated as before. Coming up the third time, the enemy retreated." Sellers, "Charles Willson Peale, Artist-soldier," 280.

52 NARA M804, PF W10367 Zebulon Applegate.

53 Haven, *Thirty Days in New Jersey*, 44-47.

54 Gratz. "Thomas Rodney," 8-9.

55 Sellers, *Charles Willson Peale, Artist-Soldier*, 280.

56 Collins, *A Brief Narrative*, 16.

57 Beale, Robert: "An Account of the services of Major Robert Beale of Westmoreland in the War of the Revolution, as written by himself." Mss 5:1 B3657:1 Virginia Historical Society, Richmond. *BPMP*, Appendix I: item 9.

58 Williams, *Biography of Revolutionary Heroes*, 198-199.

59 Wilkinson, *Memoirs*, I: 143.

60 Williams, *Biography of Revolutionary Heroes*, 198-199.

61 "Major Morris's Account of the Affair at Trenton, 1776." MS Sparks 53 (Miscellaneous papers relating to the Revolution, 1752-1779. Item 4, pp. 11-19. Harvard University Library, Cambridge, *BPMP*, Appendix 1: item 90.

62 "An Account of the Battle of Princeton." *The Pennsylvania Evening Post*, 16 January 1777. Also in Stryker, *Trenton and Princeton*, 446-448. Letter from an officer of distinction in General Washington's Army, dated Pluckemin, Jan. 5, 1777. Cadwalader identified as writer in Smith, *Battle of Princeton*, 38.

63 [Root], "The Battle of Princeton," 515-516.

64 James Read of Philadelphia to his wife from Morristown. *PMH&B*, XVI, 465-466. He was granted leave from the naval service to join a company of Philadelphia Associators as a junior officer.

65 "Descendants of Joran Kyn—Isaac Keen," *PMH&B*, IV: 350.

66 "An Account of the Battle of Princeton." *The Pennsylvania Evening Post*, 16 January 1777. Also in Stryker, *Trenton and Princeton*, 446-448. Letter from an officer of distinction in General Washington's Army, dated Pluckemin, Jan. 5, 1777. Cadwalader identified as writer in Smith, Battle of Princeton, 38.

67 Rodney, *Diary of Captain Thomas Rodney*, 136.

68 [Hall], *The History of the Civil War in America*, I: 251.

69 John Belsches to the Earl of Leven, Edinburgh, May 21, 1777, *National Archives of Scotland*, General Deposit 26/9/513/8, transcription online at https://www.17th.com/the-241st-anniversary-of-the-battle-of-princeton-surgeon-wardrops-account/. Transcribed by Dr. Will Tatum. McPherson recovered over several months during his captivity and was eventually exchanged and sailed home to Edinburgh. He was promoted to full captain on January 4 and retired in 1778 just a few years before his death.

70 Inman, "George Inman's Narrative of the American Revolution," 240.

71 *BPMP*, Appendix IV. This is a detailed analysis of the controversy surrounding this incident. NARA M804, PF S40389 Jacob Saylor – see deposition of Henry Harberger. See also: Bradley, Catts, and Selig, "Cheer Up My Boys the Day is Ours…", 36-40.

72 "Major Morris's Account of the Affair at Trenton, 1776." MS Sparks 53 (Miscellaneous papers relating to the Revolution, 1752-1779. Item 4, pp. 11-19. Harvard University Library, Cambridge, *BPMP*, Appendix I: item 90.

73 Beale, Robert: "An Account of the services of Major Robert Beale of Westmoreland in the War of the Revolution, as written by himself." Mss 5:1 B3657:1 Virginia Historical Society, Richmond. *BPMP*, Appendix I: item 9.

74 Collins, *A Brief Narrative*, 33.

75 Sullivan, "The Battle of Princeton," 55: "The 40th. Regiment formed in the College Yard".

76 Wilkinson, *Memoirs*, I: 144. This is at least claimed in Smith, *The St. Clair Papers*, I: 36-42, who prefaces this section with "In his own brief narrative, St. Clair says: ... ". It is unknown which "narrative Smith refers to, but this description is not in St. Clair, *A Narrative of the Manner in which the Campaign against the Indians, in the Year One Thousand Seven Hundred and Ninety-One, was Conducted*, 242-243. "Major Morris's Account of the Affair at Trenton, 1776." MS Sparks 53 (Miscellaneous papers relating to the Revolution, 1752-1779. Item 4, pp. 11-19. Harvard University Library, Cambridge, *BPMP*, Appendix I: item 90.

77 "We have a number of officers prisoners. I am just called on to command the infantry at the funeral of Capt. Leslie a British-officer, killed at Princeton. We bury him with military honors. On the field I saw lying another Captain of the name of Mostyn said to be the next heir to an estate of twenty-five thousand pounds per annum in England." Extract of a letter from a gentleman in the army to his friend in this city, dated Pluckemin, Jan. 5, 1777, *The Pennsylvania Evening Post*, 7 January 1777. On the identity of the prisoners see the letter by Donop to Sir William Howe, 6 January 1777 in *BPMP*, Appendix II: Item 6.

78 Haven, *Thirty Days in New Jersey*, 44-47.

79 [Root], "The Battle of Princeton," 518. Wertenbaker, *Princeton, 1746-1896*, 60. Citing Trustee Minutes, I, 236. – Minutes for September 24, 1783 (Accessed online May 3, 2017, at Princeton University Digital Library - http://pudl.princeton.edu/objects/7w62f826z) – The Trustees resolved to request Washington to sit for a portrait by Charles Willson Peale – "And ordered that his portrait, when finished be placed in the hall of the college in the room of the picture of the late King of Great Britain which was torn away by a ball from the American artillery in the battle of Princeton." Some sources suggest Alexander Hamilton was involved in the cannon fire on Nassau Hall. Thre is a common tradition that the cannon ball decapitated King George II in the portrait, but that cannot be verified.

80 Hageman, *History of Princeton and its Institutions*, I: 138.

81 Sellers, "Charles Willson Peale, Artist-Soldier." 272; Lord Stirling wrote from Newtown on 4 January: "Gen'l Washington's army passed thro' Prince Town about nine o'clock A.M. and the Enemy's army arrived there about 2 o'clock P.M. from Trenton," Hazard, *PA Archives*, V: 157; "Memorandum of Occurences attending the Armies of the United States ...," Manuscript of Samuel Massey, Captain 7th Co. Philade militia, 4th Battalion in 1777 - The Property of Louis

C. Massey, great grandson. John Reed Collection, Record Group 10, Valley Forge NHP, *BPMP*, Appendix I, item 81 - "about Sun rise an Attack began at Princeton which lasted about 2 Hours."

**Chapter 20**

1 Collins, *A Brief Narrative*, 36-39, 42-43; NARA M804, PF S 13,381 Ensign John Hendy, Northhampton County Militia. His company was "attached to a Battalion under the Command of Major Benjamin Van Campen which Battalion was annexed to the Brigade under the Command of Gen. Mifflin." See also: NARA M804, PF S 22,134 John Borrows, Philadelphia Militia. "The Philadelphia Militia were in front & broke and gave way, but were rallied & formed again by the exertions of Genls Cadwalader and Mifflin." The British "retreated towards the College, but were intercepted by the Massachusetts flying camp." There seems to have been a lot of confusion about the Flying-Camp that had been disbanded December 1.

2 White, "The Good Soldier White." 78.

3 Collins, *A Brief Narrative*, 34.

4 [Root], "The Battle of Princeton," 517-518.

5 John Potts to Owen Biddle, field of Action, near Princeton, Sunday Evening, Jan'y 5th, "Death of Major Anthony Morris, Jr., Described in a letter written on the battle-field, near Princeton, by Jonathan Potts, M.D." *PMH&B* (1877) I: 175-180. Also in: Ryan, *Salute to Courage*, 62.

6 Rogers and Lane, "Pennsylvania Pensioners of the Revolution," 263-271 passim; Shippen obituary - *Pennsylvania Evening Post*, January 18, 1777, 27; Wilson and Fiske, eds. *Appletons' Cyclopaedia of American Biography*, New York: D. Appleton and Co, 1888, V: 513; Bradley, Catts, Selig, "Cheer up Boys the Day is Ours", 28.

7 Young, "Journal of Sergeant William Young," 265-266. They were probably British mistaken for Hessians.

8 *Pennsylvania Packet*, Wednesday, Jan 22, 1777, 2.

9 Smith, *Battle of Princeton*, 28 – citing Apollos Morris and Thomas Rodney, 36-37.

10 Davis, *History of Bucks County*, II: 125-126).

11 Muster Roll, Light Infantry Company of Dover, Delaware Public Archives Commission, *Delaware Archives: Revolutionary War in Three Volumes*, Wilmington: Chas. L. Story Company Press, 1919, III: 1243. This was apparently made when the company left Morristown in mid-January, 1777 and contains information from December 14, 1776.

12 NARA M804, PF R6665 William McCracken; Sergeant Thomas Sullivan of the 49th Regiment of Foot wrote that, "When we came to the river that is near Princetown, a party of the Rebels were formed on one side of the bridge, and another party cutting it down. The 5th. Batallion, which marched in front of the Brigade with two 6-pounders, engaged them from the opposite side; and in a few minutes drove them from the bridge, which they had cut down, and retreated into the woods." Sullivan, "The Battle of Princeton," 57.

13 Williams, *Biography of Revolutionary Heroes*, 199. Rodney wrote that, "As soon as the enemy's main army heard our cannon at Princeton (and not 'til then) they discovered our manoeuvre and pushed after us with all speed and we had not been above an hour in possession of the town before the enemy's light horse and advanced parties attacked our party at the bridge but our people by a very heavy fire kept the pass until our whole army left the town." Rodney, *Diary of Captain Thomas Rodney*, 36.

14 NARA M804, PF S23621 George Espy; Egle, "The Constitutional Convention of 1776," 445.

15 Sullivan, "The Battle of Princeton," 56. See also George Washington to Congress, January 5, 1777, *George Washington Papers*, Revolutionary War Series, VII, 519-523: "The rear of the Enemy's army laying at Maidenhead (not more than five or Six Miles from Princeton) were up with us before our pursuit was over, but as I had the precaution to destroy the Bridge over Stony Brooke (about half a Mile from the Field of Action) they were so long retarded there, as to give us time to move off in good order for this place." Watching from his farmstead along the road, Robert Lawrence recorded that: "as soon as the battle was over [Washington] Ordered some of his men to be placed near the Bridge over Stoney brook on the Main Road to hinder the Regulars passing over and to pull up the bridge which was Scarcely done when the Regulars Apeared Which caused a Second fireing about three quarters of an hour appart from the first". Collins, *A brief Narrative*, 35-36.

16 Williams, *Biography of Revolutionary Heroes*, 199-200.

17 Collins, *A Brief Narrative*, 35; "Ensign Glyn's Journal on the American Service with the Detachment of 1,000 Men of the Guards commanded by Brigadier General Mathew in 1776." *Varnum Lansing Collins, Revolutionary War Papers, 1913-1932*, Manuscript Department, Princeton University Library, Princeton, New Jersey, *BPMP*, Appendix II: item 10.

18 Extract of a letter from Col. Jesse Root, in the Provincial service, dated Jan. 8, 1777, *The North British Intelligencer; or, Constitutional Miscellany*, Volume V, Edinburgh: Churnside and Wilson, 1777, 52.

19 Rodney, *Diary of Captain Thomas Rodney*, 37.

20 Magee, "Major John Polhemus, 289. Also, Ryan, *Salute to Courage*, 38-39; NARA M804, PF S40271 John Polhemus – he does not mention Trenton or Princeton.

21 NARA M804, PF W906 John Cheston.

22 Collins, *A Brief Narrative*, 33.

23 NARA M804, PF W10367 Zebulon Applegate – see both his main statement and supplemental statement; Haven, *Thirty Days in New Jersey*, 44-47. "Moulder's guns were saved and taken into camp at Morristown, when Moulder was called before a Court for disobedience of orders in risking the loss of his men. On receipt of the order to appear before Court, the Company formed and marched in silence to headquarters, where after a formal reprimand Moulder received his sword, and the boys after three hearty cheers, struck up 'Yankee Doodle,' and returned to their quarters in high glee."

24 Young, "Journal of Sergeant William Young," 265-266.

25 Robertson, *His Diaries and Sketches in America*, 120; Ewald, *Diary of the American War*, 49-50; Sellers, "Charles Willson Peale," 281.

26 Collins, *A Brief Narrative*, 16-17, 37.

27 Lee, *Memoir of the Life of Richard Henry Lee*, II: 164.

28 Ensign Thomas Glyn, entry for January 3rd, "Ensign Glyn's Journal on the American Service with the Detachment of 1,000 Men of the Guards commanded by Brigadier General Mathew in 1776." *Varnum Lansing Collins, Revolutionary War Papers, 1913-1932*, Manuscript Department, Princeton University Library, Princeton, NJ. *BPMP*, Appendix II: item 10.

29 J. E. Tyler, "The Operations in New Jersey. An English Officer describes the Events of December, 1776." *Proceedings of the New Jersey Historical Society* (April 1952), pp. 133-136; the description of the Battle of Princeton is on p. 135.

30 Inman, "George Inman's Narrative of the American Revolution," 240.

31 "Ensign Glyn's Journal on the American Service with the Detachment of 1,000 Men of the Guards commanded by Brigadier General Mathew in 1776." *Varnum Lansing Collins, Revolutionary War Papers, 1913-1932*, Manuscript Department, Princeton University Library, Princeton, NJ. Transcript in *BPMP*, Appendix II, British sources, item 10.

32 Rodney, *Diary of Captain Thomas Rodney*, 37.

33 Ewald, *Diary of the American War*, 49-50.

34 Lawrence H. Curry, ed., "Martin Hunter's Journal: America 1774-1778," *The Valley Forge Journal*, IV No. 1 (June 1988), 1-34, p. 20. *BPMP*, Appendix II: British sources, item 14; Account of Captain Henrich Bocking – senior captain of the Rall Regiment, in: Burgoyne and Mayer. "The Battle of Trenton, 26 December 1776: Reports from the von Jungkenn Papers," 27.

35 Lee, *Memoir of the Life of Richard Henry Lee*, II:164.

36 Thomas Dowdeswell to Rockingham, January 16, 1777, Dowdeswell, "Operations in New Jersey," 136. He was about 22 or 23 years old. He suffered from eye problems caused by exposure to the cold and damp and eventually lost his sight. He left America in April 1777 and retired from the army in June 1778. (133)

37 Collins, *A Brief Narrative*, 50-51.

38 Thomas Nelson, Baltimore, to Thomas Jefferson, January 2, 1777, Boyd, *Papers of Thomas Jefferson*, II: 3-4.

39 Thomas Rodney, Trenton, to Caesar Rodney, January 23, 1777, Gratz, "Thomas Rodney," 8.

40 Rush, *Autobiography*, 127.

41 NARA M804, PF W3991 James Giberson.

42 Gerlach, *New Jersey in the American Revolution*, 332-336. He transcribes portions of The Campaign Journal of a Militiaman, 1776-1777. Gerlach believes the writer of the journal was William Churchill Houston and it appeared in the *Princeton Standard*, May 1, 8, and 15, 1863.

# Notes for pages 332-337

43 Magee, "Major John Polhemus," 289. Also, Ryan, *Salute to Courage*, 38-39; NARA M804, PF S40271 John Polhemus – he does not mention Trenton or Princeton.

44 St. Clair, *A Narrative of the Manner in Which the Campaign Against the Indians, in the Year One Thousand Seven Hundred and Ninety-One, was conducted*, 242-243.

45 [Hood], "Engagements at Trenton and Princeton, January 2 and 3, 1777," 265.

46 Sellers, *Charles Willson Peale*, 282.

47 Howe to Grant, N. York Jan: 9th [1777] 11 o'clock A.M., *James Grant of Ballindalloch Papers of Ballindalloch Castle, Scotland*, r37.

48 Thomas Dowdeswell to Rockingham, January 16, 1777, Dowdeswell, *Operations in New Jersey*, 133, 136. He left America in April 1777 and retired from the army in June 1778.

49 Adlum, *Memoirs*, 107-108.

50 Gruber, *John Peebles' American War*, 77.

51 Col. John Chester, Wethersfield, to Col. Samuel Blachley Webb, January 17, 1777 from original in Webb MSS, Johnston, *Yale in the Revolution*, 61-62.

52 Avery, *The Lord is to be Praised*, 24.

53 Royster, *A Revolutionary People at War*, 119.

54 Ewald, *Diary of the American War*, 49-50.

55 Robertson, *His Diaries and Sketches in America*, 120.

56 Stryker, *Trenton and Princeton*, 458-459; Kemble, *Kemble's Journal*, 434-435.

57 Ferling, *Ascent of George Washington*, 121-122.

58 Shaw, *The Journals of Major Samuel Shaw*, 29. Also in Stryker, *Trenton and Princeton*, 480-481.

59 For a discussion of this see: Royster, *A Revolutionary People at War*, 119-120.

60 Almon, *Parliamentary Register*, XII: 392.

# Bibliography

## Manuscripts (original, digital, and microform)

*Early American Orderly Books, 1748-1817* [microform]. New Haven: Research Publications, 1977.

Embury, Susan Pindar. *A Grandmother's (Martha Reed, wife of John Shannon) Recollections of the Old Revolutionary Days.* 1875. Typescript in Trentoniana Room at the Trenton Free Public Library, Trenton, New Jersey. Another copy of this memoir is: Embury, Susan Pindor; 1875; General Manuscripts Miscellaneous Collection, Box 15; Manuscripts Division, Department of Rare Books and Special Collections, Princeton University Library.

Gates, Horatio. *The Horatio Gates Papers, 1726-1828.* Sanford, NC: Microfilminng Corp. of America, 1978. [microform]

Grant, James, *James Grant of Ballindalloch Papers, 1740-1819 (bulk 1760-1780).* Microfilm produced from originals in the National Archives of Scotland. Edinburgh, Scotland: National Archives of Scotland, 2003.

Great Britain, Audit Office. *American Loyalist Claims. Series 2, 1780-1835, AO 13* [microform] Exchequer and Audit Department.

Great Britain, Exchequer and Audit Department. *American Loyalist Claims. Series 1, 1776-1831, AO 12* [microform] Exchequer and Audit Department.

Hagner, Philip, Philip Hagner's account of the movements of the Am Army in & a[bout] 1776-1777 [apparently dated 1826] *Papers of Joseph Reed: 1757-1795, 1824-1842* [microform] filmed from material held by the New York Historical Society.

*Hessian Documents of the American Revolution,* Morristown National Historic Park [microform], Boston: G.K. Hall, 1989.

Hutson, James, A*dventures in British America, Papers Found in Scottish Castle Shed Light on Revolutionary War Era,* https://www.loc.gov/loc/lcib/0304/papers.html.

Knox, Henry, *The Papers of Henry Knox, 1719-1825* [microform]: Owned by the New England Historic Genealogical Society and deposited in the Massachusetts Historical Society., Boston : [The Society?], 1960.

Livingston, William. *The Papers of William Livingston* [microform]. Ann Arbor, MI: University Microfilms, [1986].

NARA M804. Revolutionary War Pension and Bounty-Land Warrant Application Files.

*Powell Family Papers,* Hepburn Addition, Special Collections Research Center, Swem Library College of William and Mary

Reed, Joseph. *Papers of Joseph Reed: 1757-1795, 1824-1842* [microform] Filmed from material held by the New York Historical Society.

Smith, Josiah B., *Historical Collections of Persons, Land, Business and Events in Newtown,* The Bucks County Historical Society, Doylestown, PA, 1942 (typescript).

*Sol Feinstone Collection of the American Revolution,* David Library of the American Revolution.

*Tudor Family Papers,* Massachusetts Historical Society collections online at http://www.masshist.org/database/519.

Washington, George, George Washington Papers at the Library of Congress (GWPLOC)

## Newspapers

*Dunlap's Maryland Gazette or The Baltimore General Advertiser*

*Freeman's Journal or New Hampshire Gazette* (Portsmouth, NH)

*Philadelphia Evening Post*

*Pennsylvania Evening Post*

*New York Gazette, and Evening Mercury*

*New York Mercury*

## Manuscript Collections – Published

Bonney, Catharina V.R., compiler. *A Legacy of Historical Gleanings.* Vol 1, Albany: J. Munsell, 1875.

Delaware Public Archives Commission. *Delaware Archives: Revolutionary War in Three Volumes.* Wilmington: Chas. L. Story Company Press, 1919.

"Extracts from the Records of the Moravian Congregation at Hebron, Pennsylvania, 1775-1781." *Pennsylvania Magazine of History & Biography*, XVIII: 449-462.

Force, Peter, ed. *American Archives: consisting of a collection of authentick records, state papers, debates, and letters and other notices of publick affairs, the whole forming a documentary history of the origin and progress of the North American colonies; of the causes and accomplishment of the American Revolution; and of the Constitution of government for the United States, to the final ratification thereof.* In 6 series.

*Journals of the Continental Congress, 1774-1789.* Washington: U.S. Government Printing Office, 1904-37.

Stryker, William S., *Documents Relating to the Revolutionary History of the State of New Jersey.* Archives of the State of New Jersey. Second Series. Trenton, N.J. : John L, Murphy Publishing Co., 1901-1917.

*Votes and Proceedings of the General Assembly of the State of New Jersey.* Various dates beginning 1776, organized and paginated by sessions.

### Diaries, Correspondence, Journals and Memoirs – published

_____. "Journal of a Pennsylvania Soldier: July-December, 1776." *New York Public Library Bulletin.* 1904, VIII, 547-549.

Abbatt, William, ed., *Memoirs of Major-General William Heath by Himself*, New York: 1901.

Adams, John. *Diary and Autobiography of John Adams.* L.H. Butterfield, ed. Cambridge: Belknap Press of Harvard University Press, 1962.

Adlum, John. *Memoirs of the Life of John Adlum in the Revolutionary War*, Howard H. Peckham, ed. Chicago: The Caston Club, 1968.

Aitken, James. *The Life of James Aitken, commonly called John the Painter, an Incendiary who was tried at the Castle of Winchester, on Thursday the 7th Day of March, 1777.* Second Edition. Winton: J. Wilkes, 1777.

Almon, John, *The Parliamentary Register; or, History of the Proceedings and Debates of the [House of Lords and House of Commons], containing an account of the most interesting speeches and motions; accurate copies of all the protests, and of the most remarkable letters and papers; together with the most material evidence, petitions, &c. laid before and offered to [either] House.* Volume I.

Armes, Ethel, ed. *Nancy Shippen Her Journal Book.* Philadelphia: J.B. Lippincott, 1935.

Avery, Rev. David. "Battle of Princeton – From the Diary of the Rev. David Avery." *The American Monthly Magazine*, XIX (July-December 1901) Washington, D.C.: National Society, D.A.R., 1901, 260-262.

_____. "Battle of Trenton – From the Diary of the Rev. David Avery." *The American Monthly Magazine*, XIX (July-December 1901) Washington, D.C.: National Society, D.A.R., 1901, 151-156.

_____. *The Lord is to be praised for the Triumphs of his Power: A Sermon, Preached at Greenwich, in Connecticut, on the 18th of December 1777. Being a General Thanksgiving through the United American States.* Norwich: Green & Spooner, 1778.

Bamford, Captain William. "Bamford's Diary: The Revolutionary Diary of a British Officer." *Maryland Historical Magazine* XXVIII (1933): 9-26.

Barber, John W. and Henry Howe. *Historical Collections of the State of New Jersey.* Newark: B. Olds, for Justus H. Bradley; New Haven: J.W. Barber, 1852.

Barth, Richard C., William E. Dornemann, and Mark A. Schwalm. "The Trenton Prisoner List." *The Hessians: Journal of the Johannes Schwalm Historical Association* XVI (2013), 75-90.

Baurmeister, Carl Leopold. *Revolution in America; Confidential Letters and Journals 1776-1784 of Adjutant General Major Baurmeister of the Hessian Forces.* Bernhard A. Uhlendorf, trans. New Brunswick: Rutgers University press, 1957.

Boyd, Julian P., ed. *The Papers of Thomas Jefferson.* Princeton: Princeton University Press, 1950-.

Breck, Samuel. *Recollections of Samuel Breck with Passages from his Note-Books (1771-1862).* H.E. Scudder, ed. Philadelphia: Porter & Coates, 1877.

Burgoyne, Bruce E., trans. *Defeat, Disaster and Dedication: the Diaries of the Hessian Officers Jakob Piel and Andreas Wiederhold.* Bowie, MD: Heritage Books, 1997.

____, comp. & ed. *Enemy Views: The American Revolutionary War as Recorded by Hessian Participants.* Bowie, MD: Heritage Books, 1996.

____, ed. "Diary of the Hessian Lieutenant [Jacob] Piel, 1776 to 1783," *Journal of the Johannes Schwalm Historical Association,* IV (1989).

____. and Hans Mayer, trans. "The Battle of Trenton, 26 December 1776 Reports from the Von Jungkenn Papers." *Journal of the Johannes Schwalm Historical Association,* V no. 4 (1996), 21-28.

____, trans. *The Diary of Lieutenant von Bardeleben and Other von Donop Regiment Documents.* Bowie, MD: Heritage Books, 1998.

Carleton, Sir Guy. *British Headquarters (Sir Guy Carleton) Papers, 1777-1783*, [microform] Washington, Microfilming Service, Recordak Corp., 1957.

Clinton, Sir Henry. *The American Rebellion: Sir Henry Clinton's Narrative of his Campaigns, 1775-1782.* William B. Willcox, ed. New Haven: Yale University Pres, 1954.

Chamberlin, William. "Autobiographical Letter of William Chamberlin." *Proceedings of the Massachusetts Historical Society*, Second Series, X, 1895-1896, Boston: Massachusetts Historical Society, 1896, 491-502.

Collin, Nicholas. *The Journal and Biography of Nicholas Collin, 1746-1831.* Amandus Johnson, trans. Philadelphia: New Jersey Society of Pennsylvania, 1936, 236-237.

Collins, Varnum Lansing, ed. *A brief Narrative of the Ravages of the British and Hessians at Princeton in 1776-77. A Contemporary Account of the Battles of Trenton and Princeton.* Princeton, 1906.

Cresswell, Nicholas. *A Man Apart: The Journal of Nicholas Cresswell, 1774-1781.* Harold B. Gill, Jr. and George M. Curtis, III, eds. Lanham, MD: Lexington Books, 2009.

_____. *The Journal of Nicholas Cresswell, 1774-1777.* Port Washington, NY: Kennikat Press, 1968. (reprint of 1924 edition)

Curwen, Samuel. *The Journal of Samuel Curwen Loyalist.* Oliver, Andrew, ed. Cambridge: Harvard University Press, 1972.

Davies, K.G., ed. *Documents of the American Revolution: 1770-1783 (Colonial Office Series)*, XII: Transcripts 1776. Dublin: Irish University Press, 1976.

Deane, Silas. "The Deane Papers." *Collections of the New York Historical Society.* XIX (1887).

Decatur, Stephen, Jr. *Private Affairs of George Washington: From the Records and Accounts of Tobias Lear, Esquire, his Secretary*. Boston: 1933.

Dewey, Adelbert M. *Life of George Dewey, Rear Admiral, USN, and Dewey Family History*. Westfield, Mass: Dewey Publishing Company, 189.

Donne, W. Bodham, ed. *The Correspondence of King George the Third with Lord North from 1768 to 1783.* London: John Murray, 1867.

Dow, Jesse E. "The Life Guardsman," *Graham's Lady's and Gentleman's Magazine*. XVIII, Philadelphia: George R. Graham, 1841.

Dowdeswell, Thomas. "The Operations in New Jersey: An English Officer Describes the Events of December 1776." J. E. Tyler, ed. *Proceedings of the New Jersey Historical Society*, vol 70, (1952), 133-136.

Eddis, William. *Letters from America.* Aubrey C. Land, ed. Cambridge: Belknap Press of Harvard University Press, 1969.

Ewald, Johann. *Diary of the American War: A Hessian Journal.* Joseph P. Tustin, trans and ed. New Haven: Yale University Press, c1979.

Eyre, Colonel Jehu. "Memorials of Col. Jehu Eyre." Peter D. Keyser, ed. *Pennsylvania Magazine of History and Biography* III (1879): 296-307, 412-425.

[Field, Mary] "A Recently Discovered Letter of the American Revolution," *Princeton University Library Chronicle* IV no 4 (June 1943), 111-122.

Fortescue, Sir John, ed. *The Correspondence of King George the Third from 1760 to December 1783.* Vol III: July 1773-December 1777. London: Macmillan and Co., 1928.

Graydon, Alexander. *Memoirs of His Own Times: With Reminiscences of the Men and Events of the Revolution.* John Stockton Littell, ed. Philadelphia: Lindsay & Blakiston, 1846.

Greene, Nathanael. *The Papers of General Nathanael Greene.* Showman, Richard K., ed. Chapel Hill: The University of North Carolina Press, 1976.

Greenwood, John. *The Wartime Services of John Greenwood: A Patriot in the American Revolution 1775-1783.* Westvaco, 1981.

Hale, Capt. W., "Letters Written during the American War of Independence. By the late Capt. W. Hale, 45th Regt." *1913 Regimental Annual.* The Sherwood Foresters. Nottinghamshire and Derbyshire Regiment. Col. H. C. Wylly, ed. (London, 1913), 9-59.

Hazard, Samuel, ed., *Pennsylvania Archives*, Series 1, Philadelphia: Joseph Severns, 1853.

Heath, William. *Heath's Memoirs of the American War. Reprinted from the original edition of 1798*; Rufus Rockwell Wilson intro and notes. New York: A. Wessels Company, 1904.

[Hood]. "Engagements at Trenton and Princeton, January 2 and 3, 1777." *The Pennsylvania Magazine of History and Biography* X, No. 3 (Oct., 1886), 263.

How, David, *Diary of David How, a Private in Colonel Paul Dudley Sargent's Regiment of the Massachusetts Line, in the Army of the American Revolution.* Morrisania, NY: 1865.

Howe, William. *The Narrative of Lieut. Gen. Sir William Howe, in a Committee of the House of Commons, on the 29th of April, 1779, Relative to His Conduct, During His Late Command of the King's Troops in North America.* Third Edition. London: H. Baldwin, 1781.

Huth, Hans, "Letters from a Hessian Mercenary," *Pennsylvania Magazine of History and Biography*, vol 62, issue 4, October, 1938, 488-501.

Inman, George, "George Inman's Narrative of the American Revolution," *The Pennsylvania Magazine of History and Biography* (1883) VII: 237-248.

Jackson, John W. *Margaret Morris: Her Journal with Biographical Sketch and Notes.* Philadelphia: G.S. MacManus, 1949.

Jones, Joseph H., ed. *The Life of Ashbel Green, V.D.M.* New York: 1849.

"Journal of a Pennsylvania Soldier: July-December, 1776," in *New York Public Library Bulletin* 1904, VIII, 547-549.

Kemble, Stephen. "Kemble's Journal", *Collections of the New York Historical Society for the Year 1883.* New York: New York Historical Society, 1884.

Lee, Charles. *The Lee papers: 1754-[1811].* New York: New York Historical Society, 1872-.

Lee, Richard Henry, *Memoir of the Life of Richard Henry Lee, and His Correspondence with the Most Distinguished Men in America and Europe.* Philadelphia: H.C. Carey and I. Lea, 1825.

Mackenzie, Frederick. *Diary of Frederick Mackenzie: Giving a Daily Narrative of his Military Service as an officer of the Regiment of Royal Welch Fusiliers during the Years 1775-1781 in Massachusetts, Rhode Island.* New York: New York Times and Arno Press, [1968].

Marshall, Christopher. *Passages from the Diary of Christopher Marshall, Kept in Philadelphia and Lancaster during the American Revolution.* Duane, William, ed. Philadelphia: Hazard & Mitchell, 1839-1849.

McCarty, Thomas. "The Revolutionary War Journal of Sergeant Thomas McCarty," edited by Jared C. Lobdell, *Proceedings of The New Jersey Historical Society*, Vol. 82, No. 1, January, 1964, 29-46.

McMichael, James. "Diary of Lieutenant James McMichael, Of The Pennsylvania Line, 1776 – 1778." *Pennsylvania Magazine of History and Biography* 16, (1892), pp. 129 – 159, and in *Pennsylvania Archives*, Second Series, vol. 15, 195 – 218.

Watts, Henry Miller. "A Memoir of General Henry Miller," *Pennsylvania Magazine of History and Biography* (1888) XII, 425-431.

Miller, Lillian B. and Sidney Hart, eds., *The Selected Papers of Charles Willson Peale and his Family, Volume 5, The Autobiography of Charles Willson Peale*, New Haven: Yale University Press, 2000.

Monroe, James. *Autobiography of James Monroe*, Stuart Gerry Brown, ed. Syracuse: Syracuse University Press, 1959.

Muenchhausen, Friedrich Ernst von. *At General Howe's Side, 1776-1778: The Diary of General William Howe's Aide de Camp, Captain Friedrich von Muenchhausen.* Ernst Kipping, trans. Monmouth Beach, NJ: Philip Freneau Press, 1974.

Muhlenberg, Henry Melchior, *The Journals of Henry Melchior Muhlenberg*, translated by Theodore G. Tappert and John W. Doberstein. Camden, ME: Picton Press, 1945.

Paine, Robert Treat. *The Papers of Robert Treat Paine.* Volume III: 1774-1777. Boston: Massachusetts Historical Society, 2006.

Peale, Charles Willson. "The Artist-soldier: A Chapter of the Revolution – Journal by Charles Wilson Peale." Rembrandt Peale, ed. *The Crayon* III (1856): 37-40.

Peebles, John. *John Peebles' American War: The Diary of a Scottish Grenadier, 1776-1782.* Ira D. Gruber, ed. Mechanicsburg, PA: Stackpole Books, c1998.

Peters, Thomas. "A Scrap of 'Troop' History," *Pennsylvania Magazine of History and Biography*, XV (1891), 225-227. Transcription of notes hand-written by Peters in an 1815 edition of the By-Laws of the First Troop Philadelphia City Cavalry and dated "near Baltimore 1818."

Powell, Robert C., ed. *A Biographical Sketch of Col. Leven Powell, including his Correspondence during the Revolutionary War.* Alexandria, VA: G. H. Ramey & Son, 1877.

Powell, William S. "A Connecticut Soldier Under Washington: Elisha Bostwick's Memoirs of the First Years of the Revolution." *The William and Mary Quarterly*, Third Series, VI (1949), 94-107.

Rau, Louise, ed. "Sergeant John Smith's Diary of 1776." *The Mississippi Valley Historical Review*, XX No 2 (Sept. 1933), 247-270. Original pages are digitized online at http://www.americanantiquarian.org/.

Reed, Joseph. "General Joseph Reed's Narrative of the Movements of the American Army in the Neighborhood of Trenton in the Winter of 1776-77." *The Pennsylvania Magazine of History and Biography* VIII (1884), 391-402.

Reed, William B. *Life and Correspondence of Joseph Reed.* Philadelphia: Lindsay and Blakiston, 1847.

Retzer, Henry J. "The New York-New Jersey Campaign, 1776-1777: Letters from the von Jungkenn Papers." *Journal of the Johannes Schwalm Historical Association*, V no. 4, 74-81.

Robertson, Archibald. *Archibald Robertson: His Diaries and Sketches in America: 1762-1780.* Lydenberg, Harry Miller, ed. New York: The New York Public Library, 1930.

Rodney, Thomas. *Diary of Captain Thomas Rodney, 1776-1777.* Caesar A. Rodney, intro. Wilmington: The Historical Society of Delaware, 1888.

Rodney, Caesar. *Letters to and From Caesar Rodney, 1756-1784.* George Herbert Ryden, ed. New York: DaCapo Press, 1970.

[Root, Nathaniel] Sergeant R---, "The Battle of Princeton," From *The Phenix* of March 24, 1832, published at Wellsborough, Pennsylvania. *Pennsylvania Magazine of History and Biography* XX (1896), 515-516.

Royal Commission on Historical Manuscripts. *Historical Manuscripts Commission, Seventeenth Report of the Royal Commission on Historical Manuscripts*, London: 1907.

Runes, Dagobert D., ed. *The Selected Writings of Benjamin Rush.* New York: Philosophical Library, 1947.

Rush, Benjamin. *The Autobiography of Benjamin Rush: His Travels through life together with his Commonplace Book for 1789-1813.* George W. Corner, ed. Westport, CN: Greenwood Press, 1970.

_____. *Letters of Benjamin Rush.* L.H. Butterfield, ed. Philadelphia: American Philosophical Society, 1951.

_____. *My Dearest Julia: The Love Letters of Dr. Benjamin Rush to Julia Stockton.* New York: N. Watson Academic Publications, 1979.

Ryan, Dennis P., ed. *A Salute to Courage: The American Revolution as Seen Through Wartime Writings of Officers of the Continental Army and Navy.* New York: Columbia University Press, 1979.

Sellers, Horace Wells. "Charles Willson Peale, Artist – Soldier." *The Pennsylvania Magazine of History and Biography* XXXVIII (1914): 257-286.

Serle, Ambrose. *The American Journal of Ambrose Serle.* Edward H. Tatum, Jr., ed. New York: New York Times, c1969.

Shaw, Samuel. *The Journals of Major Samuel Shaw, the First American Consul at Canton.* Josiah Quincy, ed. Boston, 1847.

Smith, Paul H., ed. *Letters of Delegates to Congress, 1774-1789.* Washington: Library of Congress, 1976-1985.

Smith, William Henry. *The St. Clair Papers. The Life and Public Services of Arthur St. Clair.* 2 vols. Cincinnati: 1882.

St. Clair, Arthur, *A Narrative of the manner in which the Campaign against the Indians, in the year one thousand seven hundred and ninety-one, was Conducted, under the Command of Major General St. Clair, together with his Observations on the Statements of the Secretary of War and the Quarter Master General, relative thereto, and the Reports of the Committees appointed to inquire into the Causes of the Failure thereof: taken from the Files of the House of Representatives in Congress.* Philadelphia: 1812.

Stevens, B.F. F*acsimiles of Manuscripts in European Archives Relating to America, 1773-1783*. 25 vols. Wilmington, DE: Millifont Press [distributed by Irish University Press, White Plains, NY], 1970.

Stiles, Ezra. *The Literary Diary of Ezra Stiles*. Franklin Bowditch Dexter, ed. Volume 2: March 14, 1776 - December 31, 1781. New York: 1901.

Stone, Edwin M. *The Life and Recollections of John Howland, Late President of the Rhode Island Historical Society*. Providence: George H. Whitney, 1857.

Sullivan, Thomas. *From Redcoat to Rebel: The Thomas Sullivan Journal*. Joseph Lee Boyle, ed. Bowie, MD: Heritage Books, 1997.

Sullivan, Sergeant Thomas. "The Battle of Princeton." *Pennsylvania Magazine of History and Biography*, 32 no. 1 (January 1908), 54-57.

Thacher, Dr. James. *A Military Journal During the American Revolutionary War, from 1775 to 1783*. Boston: Richardson and Lord, 1823.

Tilghman, Tench, *Memoir of Lieut. Col. Tench Tilghman, Secretary and Aid to Washington*. Albany: J. Munsell, 1876. Reprint Arno Press, 1971.

Washington, George. *The Papers of George Washington*. Revolutionary War Series. Philander D. Chase, ed. Charlottesville: University Press of Virginia, 1985-1997.

____. *The Writings of George Washington: From the original Manuscript Sources, 1745-1799*. John C. Fitzpatrick, ed. Washington: Government Printing Office, 1931-1944.

Watson, Elkanah. *Men and Times of the Revolution: or, Memoirs of Elkanah Watson*. Winslow C. Watson, ed. New York: Dana and Co., 1856.

Webb, Samuel Blachley. *Correspondence and journals of Samuel Blachley Webb*. Worthington Chauncey Ford, ed. New York: 1893 – reprinted by Arno Press, New York, 1969 in series Eyewitness Accounts of the American Revolution.

Wharton, Thomas. "Selections from the Letter-Books of Thomas Wharton, of Philadelphia, 1773-1783." *The Pennsylvania Magazine of History and Biography* XXXIV (1910): 41-61.

White, Joseph. "The Good Soldier White: A Revolutionary Veteran Speaks," *American Heritage* VII (1956); 74-79.

Wiederholt, Andreas "Diary of Captain Wiederholt of the von Knyphausen ." M.D. Learned and C. Grosse, ed., *Americana Germanica*, IV, 1, New York, London and Berlin, 1902, 25-33. Translated by Dr. Ernst Kipping.

Wiederholdt, Andreas. "Colonel Rall at Trenton," *Pennsylvania Magazine of History and Biography* XXIII (1899): 462-467.

Wilkinson, General James. *Memoirs of My Own Times*. Philadelphia: Abraham Small, 1816.

Young, William, "Journal of Sergeant William Young Written during the Jersey Campaign of the winter of 1776-77." *Pennsylvania Magazine of History and Biography*, VIII (1884), 255-278.

**Secondary Sources**

Anderson, Troyer Steele. *The Command of the Howe Brothers during the American Revolution*. New York: Octagon Books, 1972.

Arthur, Herman. *To Rule the Waves: How the British Navy Shaped the Modern World*. New York: Harper Collins, 2004.

Atwood, Rodney. *The Hessians: Mercenaries from Hessen-Kassel in the American Revolution*. Cambridge, Eng.; New York: Cambridge University Press, 1980.

Billias, George Athan. *General John Glover and his Marblehead Mariners*. New York: Henry Holt, 1960.

Bonk, David. *Trenton and Princeton 1776-77: Washington Crosses the Delaware.* New York: Osprey, 2009.

Bowler, R. Arthur. *Logistics and the Failure of the British Army in America: 1775-1783.* Princeton: Princeton University Press, 1975.

Bradley, Kevin, Wade P. Catts, and Robert Selig. *"Cheer Up My Boys the Day is Ours…": Field Survey, Preparation of Maps, and Preparation of Local and National Landmark/National Register Historic District Applications for the D'Ambrisi Property, Princeton, New Jersey.* (Draft) West Chester, PA: Commonwealth Heritage Group, May 2017.

Brewster, Charles W. *Rambles About Portsmouth: Sketches of Persons, Localities, and Incidents of Two Centuries: Principally from tradition and unpublished documents*, Portsmouth, NH: C.W. Brewster & Son, 1859.

Brown, Gerald Saxon. *The American Secretary: The Colonial Policy of Lord George Germain, 1775-1778.* Ann Arbor: University of Michigan Press, 1963.

Bowen, Diana R. *The Presbyterian Church Newtown, Pennsylvania 1734-1976.* Newtown, PA: Printique, 1976.

Burnett, Edmund C. *The Continental Congress.* New York: MacMillin, 1941.

Burrows, Edwin G. *Forgotten Patriots: The Untold Story of American Prisoners during the Revolutionary War.* New York: Basic Books, 2008.

John C. Clyde. *Rosbrugh, A Tale of the Revolution.* Easton: 1880.

Cobbett, William. *Cobbett's Parliamentary History of England: From the Norman Conquest, in 1066, to the Year, 1803.* Volume 18. London: Bagshaw, 1813.

Custis, George Washington Parke. *Recollections and Private Memoirs of Washington.* New York: Derby & Jackson, 1860.

Davis, Michael A. *The Trial of Abraham Hunt: An American Christmas Story.* Denver: Ghost Road Press, 2006.

Davis, W.W.H. *History of Bucks County, Pennsylvania.* New York: Lewis, 1905.

____. *Life of John Davis.* Doylestown, PA: 1886.

____. *Sketch of the Life and Character of John Lacy, Brigadier General in the Revolutionary Army.* Doylestown, PA: Privately Printed, 1868.

Drake, Francis S. *Life and Correspondence of Henry Knox, Major-General in the American Revolutionary Army.* Boston: Samuel G. Drake, 1873.

Dwyer, William M. *The Day is Ours! November 1776-January 1777: An Inside View of the Battles of Trenton and Princeton.* New York: Viking Press, 1983.

Eelking, Max von. *The German Allied Troops in the North American War of Independence, 1776-1783.* J.G. Rosengarten, trans. [Whitefish, MT]: Kessinger Publishing Company, n.d.

Egle, Wm. H. "The Constitutional Convention of 1776: Biographical Sketches of its members." *Pennsylvania Magazine of History and Biography* III: 438-446.

Egleston, Thomas. *The Life of John Paterson: Major General in the Revolutionary Army.* New York: The Knickerbocker Press, 1898.

Ferling, John. *Almost a Miracle: The American Victory in the War of Independence.* New York: Oxford University Press, 2007.

____. *The Ascent of George Washington: The Hidden Political Genius of an American Icon.* New York: Bloomsbury Press, 2009.

Fischer, David Hackett. *Washington's Crossing.* Oxford: Oxford University Press, 2004.

Gerlach, Larry R. *New Jersey in the American Revolution, 1763-1783: A Documentary History.* Trenton: New Jersey Historical Commission, 1975.

Gibson, James E. *Dr. Bodo Otto and the Medical Background of the American Revolution.* Springfield, IL: Charles C. Thomas, 1937.

Gilchrist, Marianne McLeod. "The Tragedy of Captain William Leslie & Dr. Benjamin Rush." *The Loyalist Gazette* XXXVII (1999): 25-30.

Gratz, Simon. "Thomas Rodney." *The Pennsylvania Magazine of History and Biography.* XLIII (1919) 1-23.

Gruber, Ira D. *The Howe Brothers and the American Revolution.* New York: Atheneum, c1972.

Guttmacher, Manfred S. *America's Last King: An Interpretation of the Madness of George III.* New York: Charles Scribner's Sons, 1941.

Hageman, John Frelinghuysen. *History of Princeton and its Institutions.* Philadelphia: Lippincott, 1879.

Hall, John. *History of the First Presbyterian Church in Trenton from the First Settlement of the Town.* Trenton: MacCrellish & Quigley, 1912.

[Hall, Captain William C.] An Officer of the Army. *The History of the Civil War in America.* vol. 1. London: 1780. The "Officer" was Capt. William C. Hall of the 28th Regt. of Foot.

Hamilton, Edward P. *Fort Ticonderoga: Key to a Continent.* Boston: Little, Brown, 1964.

Hart, Charles Henry. "Mary White – Mrs. Robert Morris." *The Pennsylvania Magazine of History and Biography* II (1878): 157-184.

Haven, Charles Chauncy. *Thirty Days in New Jersey Ninety Years ago, An Essay revealing new Facts in Connection with Washington and his Army in 1776 and 1777.* Trenton: 1867.

Holt, Byron W. "Continental Currency." *Sound Currency* V no 7, (April 1, 1898).

Huth, Hans, "Letters from a Hessian Mercenary," *Pennsylvania Magazine of History and Biography*, LVII, No 4, (October, 1938), 488-501.

Johnston, Henry P. *Yale and Her Honor-Roll in the American Revolution 1775-1783.* New York, 1888.

Jones, Kenneth S. and Donald Kloster. *Captain Oliver Pond's Hessian Fusiliercap: A Monograph.* Worcester, MA: Kenneth S. Jones, 1986.

Jordan, John W. "The Military Hospitals at Bethlehem and Lititz During the Revolution," *Pennsylvania Magazine of History and Biography* XX (1896): 137-157.

Ketchum, Richard M. *The Winter Soldiers: The Battles for Trenton and Princeton.* New York: Henry Holt, 1973.

Kidder, Larry. *A People Harassed and Exhausted: The Story of a New Jersey Militia Regiment in the American Revolution.* 2013.

Kidder, William L. *Crossroads of the Revolution: Trenton, 1774-1783.* Lawrence Township, NJ: The Knox Press, 2017.

Kipping, Ernst, *The Hessian View of America, 1776-1783.* Monmouth Beach, NJ: Philip Freneau Press, 1971.

Kwasny, Mark V. *Washington's Partisan War, 1775-1783.* Kent, OH: The Kent State University Press, 1996.

Lane, Wheaton J. *From Indian Trail to Iron Horse.* Princeton: Princeton University Press, 1939.

Leake, Isaac Q. *Memoir of the Life and Times of General John Lamb, an officer of the Revolution.* Albany: Joel Munsell, 1857.

Ludlum, David M., "The Weather of Independence," *Weatherwise*, Nov/Dec 1998; 51, 6: 38-44.

Lundin, Leonard. *Cockpit of the Revolution: The War for Independence in New Jersey.* New York: Octagon Books, 1972 [c1940].

Solomon Lutnick. *The American Revolution and the British Press, 1775-1783.* Columbia, MO: University of Missouri Press, 1967.

Luzader, John F. *Saratoga: A Military History of the Decisive Campaign of the American Revolution.* New York: Savas Beatie, 2010.

Mackesy, Piers. *The War for America: 1775-1783.* Cambridge: Harvard University Press, 1965.

Magee, Fannie S., "Major John Polhemus." *American Monthly Magazine*, IX, (Jul-Dec 1896) Washington, D.C.: National Society D.A.R., 1896.

McBurney, Christian. *Abductions in the American Revolution: Attempts to Kidnap George Washington, Benedict Arnold and Other Military and Civilian Leaders.* Jefferson, NC: McFarland & Company, 2016.

Nelson, Paul David. *General Horatio Gates: A Biography.* Baton Rouge: Louisiana State University Press, 1976.

Nelson, Paul David. *General James Grant: Scottish Soldier and Royal Governor of East Florida.* Gainesville, FL: University Press of Florida, 1993.

Osbourne, Peter. *Where Washington Once Led: A History of New Jersey's Washington Crossing State Park.* Yardley, PA: Yardley Press, 2012.

O'Shaunessy, Andrew Jackson. *The Men Who Lost America: British Leadership, the American Revolution, and the Fate of the Empire.* New Haven: Yale University Press, 2013.

Palmer, Dave R. *George Washington's Military Genius.* Washington, D.C.: Regnery Publishing, 2012.

Parker, Augustus C. *Parker in America, 1630-1910.* Buffalo, NY: 1910.

Paul, Joel Richard. *Unlikely Allies: How a Merchant, a Playwright, and a Spy Saved the American Revolution.* New York : Riverhead Books, 2009.

Ramsay, David. *The History of the American Revolution.* Philadelphia: Aitken, 1789.

Ritcheson, Charles R. *British Politics and the American Revolution.* Norman: University of Oklahoma Press, 1954.

Rizzo, Dennis and Alicia McShalkis. "The Widow who Saved a Revolution." *www.GardenStateLegacy.com December 2012.*

Roads, Samuel, Jr. *The History and Traditions of Marblehead.* Boston: Riverside Press, Cambridge, 1880.

Rogers, Mrs. Harry and Mrs. A.H. Lane. "Pennsylvania Pensioners of the Revolution." *Pennsylvania Magazine of History and Biography.* XLII, 259-277.

Royster, Charles. *A Revolutionary People at War: The Continental Army and American Character, 1775-1783.* Chapel Hill: The University of North Carolina Press, 1979.

Selig, Robert A., Matthew Harris, and Wade P. Catts. *Battle of Princeton Mapping Project: Report of Military Terrain Analysis and Battle Narrative, Princeton, New Jersey.* West Chester, PA: John Milner Associates, 2010.

Sellers, Horace Wells, "Charles Willson Peale, Artist-Soldier," *The Pennsylvania Magazine of History and Biography*, XXXVIII (1914), 257- 286,

Schuyler, Hamilton. *A History of St. Michael's Church Trenton: In the Diocese of New Jersey from its Foundation in the Year of Our Lord 1703 to 1926.* Princeton: Princeton University Press, 1926.

Shuman, Eleanore Nolan. *The Trenton Story.* Trenton: MacCrellish & Quigley, 1958.

Skeen, C. Edward. *John Armstrong, Jr., 1758-1843: A Biography.* Syracuse: Syracuse University Press, 1981.

Slagle, Robert Oakley. "The von Lossberg : A Chronicle of Hessian Participation in the American Revolution." PhD diss., The American University (1965).

Smith, Samuel Stelle. *The Battle of Trenton* (Reprint of 1965 edition): *The Battle of Princeton* (Reprint of 1967 edition) Yardley, PA: Westholme, 2009.

Smith, David M. *Whispers across the Atlantick : General William Howe and the American Revolution.* Oxford : Osprey Publishing, 2017.

Sprague, William Buel. *Annals of the American pulpit: or, Commemorative notices of distinguished American Clergymen of Various Denominations.* New York: Robert Carter & Brothers, 1859.

Stryker, William S. *The Battles of Trenton and Princeton.* Boston: Houghton, Mifflin and Company, 1898.

____. *The Continental Army at the Crossing of the Delaware River on Christmas Night of 1776.* Trenton: J.L. Murphy, 1896.

Thompson, Benjamin Franklin. *The History of Long Island: From its Discovery and settlement, to the present time.* Second Edition. New York: Gould, Banks & Col, 1843.

Trenton Historical Society. *A History of Trenton, 1679-1929; Two Hundred and Fifty Years of a Notable Town with Links to Four Centuries.* Princeton: Princeton University Press, 1929.

Tunis, Edwin. *The Tavern at the Ferry.* Baltimore: The Johns Hopkins University Press, 1973.

Wade, Herbert T. and Robert A. Lively. *This Glorious Cause: The Adventures of Two Company Officers in Washington's Army.* Princeton: Princeton University Press, 1958.

Ward, Harry M. *Major General Adam Stephen and the Cause of American Liberty.* Charlottesville: University Press of Virginia, 1989.

____. *Charles Scott and the "Spirit of '76".* Charlottesville: University Press of Virginia, 1988.

Weller, Jac. "Guns of Destiny: Field Artillery in the Trenton-Princeton Campaign 25 December 1776 to 3 January 1777." *Military Affairs* XX No 1 (Spring, 1956), 1-15.

Welsch, William M. "Christmas Night 1776: How Did They Cross?" in Todd Andrlik, Hugh T. Harrington, and Don N. Hagist, *Journal of the American Revolution allthingsliberty.com,* volume 1, Yellow Springs, OH: Ertel, 2013, 100-109.

Wertenbaker, Thomas Jefferson. *Princeton, 1746-1896.* Princeton: Princeton University Press, 1946.

Wharton, Anne H. "Thomas Wharton, Junr., First Governor of Pennsylvania under the constitution of '76." *Pennsylvania Magazine of History and Biography* V (1881): 426- 439

White, Rebecca, Nadine Sergejeff, William Liebeknecht and Richard Hunter. *A Historical Account and Archaeological Analysis of the Eagle Tavern, City of Trenton, Mercer County, New Jersey.* Trenton: Hunter Research, 2005.

Wickes, Stephen. *History of Medicine in New Jersey, and of its medical men, from the settlement of the province to A.D. 1800.* Newark, NJ: Martin R. Dennis & Co., 1879.

Wickwire, Franklin and Mary Wickwire. *Cornwallis: The American Adventure.* Boston: Houghton Mifflin, 1970.

Widmer, Kemble. *The Christmas Campaign: The Ten Days of Trenton and Princeton.* Trenton: New Jersey Historical Commission, 1975.

Wilkin, W.H. *Some British Soldiers in America: Primary Source Edition.* London: Hugh Rees, Ltd., 1914.

Williams, Catherine R. *Biography of Revolutionary Heroes: Containing the Life of Brigadier Gen. William Barton, and also, of Captain Stephen Olney.* Providence: Mrs. Williams, 1839.

Wilson, Joseph Lapsley. *Book of the First Troop, Philadelphia City Cavalry, 1774-1914.* Philadelphia: The First Troop Philadelphia City Cavalry, 1915.

**Index**

**A**

**F**



**G**

**H**

**M**

**N**



**O**

# Note on the Author

William L. Kidder, universally known as Larry, was born in California and raised in California, Indiana, New York, and New Jersey. He received his bachelor's and master's degrees from Allegheny College in Meadville, Pennsylvania.

Larry is a retired high school history teacher who taught for forty years in both public and private schools. He considers teaching to be both his vocation and avocation. During his 32 years of teaching at The Hun School of Princeton he enjoyed designing courses that gave his students the opportunity to develop the thinking, research, and writing skills that result from "doing history" and not just learning facts for a test.

Larry served four years of active duty in the US Navy and was assigned to the US Navy Research and Development Unit, Vietnam and then the destroyer USS Brownson (DD868) homeported in Newport, Rhode Island. In the 1980s he was the lead researcher and writer for the creation of the Admiral Arleigh Burke National Destroyermen's Museum aboard the destroyer museum ship USS Joseph P. Kennedy, Jr. (DD850) at Battleship Cove in Fall River, Massachusetts.

For over thirty years, Larry has been a volunteer at the Howell Living History Farm, part of the Mercer County Park System, in Hopewell, New Jersey. For varying lengths of time he has volunteered as an historian, interpreter, webmaster, and draft horse teamster This interest led to the writing of his first book that tells the story of the local schoolhouse that is now part of the Howell Living History Farm and is also a case study of a rural school in central New Jersey from the early 19th to the mid-20th century.

Active in historical societies in Ewing, Hopewell, and Lawrence townships, Larry has given a number of talks on local history to a variety of civic groups. He is also a volunteer for the Crossroads of the American Revolution National Heritage Area, coordinating its Meet Your Revolutionary Neighbors project. Recently he has become a member of the board of the Princeton Battlefield Society and has developed tours of the Princeton Battlefield for both adults and children. He is a member of the board of TheTenCrucialDays.org, an organization dedicated to promoting the historic sites associated with the Ten Crucial Days and educating the public about them. He is an avid member of the Association for Living History, Farm, and Agricultural Museums (ALHFAM), the Washington's Crossing Roundtable of the American Revolution, and the New Jersey Living History Advisory Council.

He can be contacted by email at larrykidder@gmail.com.

## *Relive the "Ten Crucial Days" of the American Revolution*

**Visit these historic sites:**

**Washington Crossing Historic Park**
This Pennsylvania state park and National Historic Landmark is where General George Washington's army began its epic crossing of the Delaware River the night of December 25-26, 1776, which may have saved our nation's quest for independence when the American Revolution appeared all but lost. This was the beginning of the Ten Crucial Days. The park offers a visitor center and more than 500 acres of American history, natural beauty, and family fun.

Located less than a mile from the park is **The David Library of the American Revolution**. It is a specialized research library, open free of charge to the public, dedicated to the study of American History between 1750 and 1800. This non-profit educational institution is a valuable and welcoming resource for anyone seeking information about virtually anything related to America's war for independence. It also offers lectures and events of interest to the historical community.

**Washington Crossing State Park**
This New Jersey state park lies opposite its Pennsylvania sister and is part of the same National Historic Landmark. It is the site where Washington's army landed after crossing the Delaware River to attack the Hessian brigade occupying Trenton. In addition to its historical significance, the 3,500-acre park is well known for its trails and wildlife habitat.

**Old Barracks Museum**
This museum in Trenton has a unique history dating back to 1758, when it was built to house British soldiers during the French and Indian War. It is a remnant of Trenton that helps visitors understand both the Battle of Trenton on December 26, 1776 and the Second Battle of Trenton on January 2, 1777. From military quarters to widow's home, from brothel to museum, the building offers visitors a fascinating look at the history of the area.

**Princeton Battlefield**

This New Jersey state park is where the Battle of Princeton was fought on January 3, 1777 - the capstone event of the "Ten Crucial Days" campaign that altered the course of the war. It is the site of what is considered to be the fiercest fight of its size during the long conflict. The 1772 Clarke House witnessed the battle and served as sanctuary for the wounded General Hugh Mercer, who died there nine days later; it contains period furniture and Revolutionary War exhibits.

**Learn more about these historic sites at:**

**www.tencrucialdays.org**

TenCrucialDays.org
December 25, 1776 - January 3, 1777